# Aftermath

# CRITICAL AMERICA

**General Editors: Richard Delgado and Jean Stefancic**

*From the Ground Up: Environmental Racism and the Rise of the
Environmental Justice Movement*
Luke Cole and Sheila Foster

*Nothing but the Truth: Why Trial Lawyers Don't, Can't, and
Shouldn't Have to Tell the Whole Truth*
Steven Lubet

*Critical Race Theory: A Primer*
Richard Delgado and Jean Stefancic

*Playing It Safe: How the Supreme Court Sidesteps Hard Cases and
Stunts the Development of Law*
Lisa A. Kloppenberg

*Why Lawsuits Are Good for America: Disciplined Democracy,
Big Business, and the Common Law*
Carl T. Bogus

*How the Left Can Win Arguments and Influence People:
A Tactical Manual for Pragmatic Progressives*
John K. Wilson

*Aftermath: The Clinton Impeachment and the Presidency in the
Age of Political Spectacle*
Edited by Leonard V. Kaplan and Beverly I. Moran

# Aftermath

## The Clinton Impeachment and the Presidency in the Age of Political Spectacle

EDITED BY

*Leonard V. Kaplan and
Beverly I. Moran*

*New York University Press*

NEW YORK AND LONDON

NEW YORK UNIVERSITY PRESS
New York and London

Library of Congress Cataloging-in-Publication Data
Aftermath : the Clinton impeachment and the presidency in the age of
political spectacle / edited by Leonard V. Kaplan and Beverly I. Moran.
p.   cm. — (Critical America)
Based on a conference held at the University of Wisconsin Law School in
Feb. 2000.
Includes bibliographical references.
ISBN 0-8147-4742-6 (acid-free paper) —
ISBN 0-8147-4743-4 (pbk. : acid-free paper)
1. Clinton, Bill, 1946– —Impeachment—Congresses.  2. Clinton, Bill,
1946– —Public opinion—Congresses.  3. Political culture—United
States—History—20th century—Congresses.  4. Presidents—United
States—Public opinion—Congresses.  5. United States—Politics and
government—1993–2001—Congresses.  6. Trials (Impeachment)—
United States—Congresses.  7. Public opinion—United States—
Congresses.   I. Kaplan, Leonard V.  II. Moran, Beverly I.  III. Series.
E886.2 .A44  2001
973.929—dc21            2001001549

New York University Press books are printed on acid-free paper,
and their binding materials are chosen for strength and durability.

Manufactured in the United States of America
10  9  8  7  6  5  4  3  2  1

*This book is dedicated to Jackie Macaulay, a true friend and a wonderful woman who spent her life taking care of her children while fighting bullies and fools.*

BEVERLY I. MORAN

*This book is dedicated to my family, Martha, Sarah, and Jonathan Kaplan.*

LEONARD V. KAPLAN

# Contents

       *David Novak*

PART  V   The Political Is Personal

21   The Spectacle and the Libertine                          279
       *David Kennedy*

22   The Political Is Personal                                297
       *Beverly I. Moran*

23   Dropped Drawers: A Viewpoint                             312
       *Drucilla Cornell*

       Conclusion: The Penultimate: The Meaning of
       Impeachment and Liberal Governance                    321
       *Leonard V. Kaplan*

       *Contributors*                                        *353*
       *Index*                                               *359*

# Acknowledgments

This collection is meant to start a conversation across political, moral, and religious divides on the problems of trust in public life. That interchange required that authors receive each others' manuscripts so as to comment on each others' work. For managing the essays as they came in and went out, my thanks go to Lynda Hicks, Keith Landers, Debi McNutt-Grassman, and David Ward. They put in long hours at no additional pay and often at times of personal crisis. Their competence, professionalism, and integrity demonstrates that a degree means nothing in the face of hard work done honestly and well.

Special thanks to Richard Delgado and Jean Stefancic for bringing this book to the NYU Press. Thanks also to Steve Maikowski, Cecilia Feilla, and Emily Park of NYU Press, for their hard work and support.

For their helpful comments to authors, I thank David Trubek, Louise Trubek, and Bill Whitford, all of the University of Wisconsin-Madison Law School. For their contribution to this project's intellectual and moral base, I thank Idit Dobbs-Weinstein of Vanderbilt University, Dr. Fran Erlich Price, Fred Harris of the University of Illinois Law School, Dirk Hartog of Princeton University, Leon Trakman of the Dalhousie Law School, and Stephanie Wildman of the University of California at Berkeley, Boalt Hall.

Finally, I thank the people who provided the intellectual stewardship for this text: David Canon and Ken Mayer, Drucilla Cornell, John Milton Cooper, Jr., Jean Bethke Elshtain, Robert Gordon, Lawrence Joseph, David Kennedy, Richard Neuhaus, David Novak, Linda Oakley, Elizabeth Rapaport, Lawrence Rosen, Eric Rothstein, Aviam Soifer, Lawrence Solan, Cass Sunstein, Stephen Toulmin, Leon Trakman, Frank Tuerkheimer, Mark Tushnet, and Robin West.

BEVERLY I. MORAN

Although the editors receive credit on the cover, it takes the combined effort of many other competent people to produce a coherent volume of essays. I would like to thank my coeditor, Beverly Moran, and join her in honoring the memory of Jackie Macauley, and the contributing authors for producing such thoughtful, insightful, and timely essays. It was a pleasure to work with Niko Pfund, Eric Zinner, and Despina Papazoglou Gimbel of New York University Press.

The process of putting this book together started with a conversation amongst various scholars, most of whom have contributed to this volume. Some of these contributors were able to attend a conference entitled, "Aftermath: Conversations on the Clinton Scandal, the Future of the Presidency, and the Liberal State," which was held at the University of Wisconsin Law School in February 2000.

The conference was supported both intellectually and economically by a number of individuals and organizations on campus. Special thanks to welcoming speakers Peter Carstensen and Judith Kornblatt; to panel chairs Charles Cohen, Mary Layoun, and Ann Althouse, and to commentators Heinz Klug and Carin Clauss. Thanks also to Walter Dickey for stimulating discussion with his presentation at the conference, and to Laura McClure who prepared a statement that linked Aristophanes to the Clinton scandal, but unfortunately could not join us. Thanks also to Theresa Dougherty for assistance in pulling it all together, and to Keith Landers, Dave Ward, and Michael Morgalla, whose help on many of my projects is always necessary and too frequently unmentioned. Pam Hollenhorst made sure, despite more than the general vicissitudes of putting on a conference, that everything went smoothly. I thank her for her tact and competency.

I would also like to thank the following conference sponsors and decision makers, including the Institute for Legal Studies, the University of Wisconsin College of Letters and Science Humanistic Fund, and the UW Law School; Kenneth B. Davis, Jr., Dean of UW Law School; Philip R. Certain, Dean of the College of Letters and Science; Peter Carstensen, Associate Dean for Research and Faculty Development; and Howard Erlanger, Director of the Institute for Legal Studies. Other university entities that provided support include the Department of Political Science, the Religious Studies Program, the Women's Studies Program, the Department of English, the Department of History, and the Remington Center.

I have already mentioned that the conference and the book represent a conversation amongst people of very different intellectual and disciplinary viewpoints. This conversation must be ongoing. The purpose of this book is to contribute to this ongoing conversation. I must thank several friends and colleagues for contributing to my ideas and providing emotional support with respect to my contribution to this conversation. I have already acknowledged my family—my wife Martha, my daughter Sarah, and my son Jon. I must also thank two friends from Canada, David Weisstub of the University of Montreal, and Phillip Anisman, one of the leading securities lawyers in Canada, the Old Commonwealth, for their intellectual and emotional support. More locally, Andrew Weiner, who is my coeditor for *Graven Images* and codirector of the Project for Law and Humanities, and Sonja Weiner, provided significant encouragement. I particularly want to express my appreciation to my colleagues—Ann Althouse, Charles Cohen, John Kidwell, Neil Komesar, Carl Rasmussen, Vincent Rinella, Robert Skloot, and Alan Weisbard—for their willingness to contribute to my mental health, and to provide intellectual feedback as well.

Finally, this book, from my perspective, would not have reached the light of day without the tireless, amused, and discreet support of Pam Hollenhorst, who has become the invaluable Assistant Director of the Institute for Legal Studies. If I were the managing partner of a law firm, I would certainly want Pam to be a partner.

LEONARD V. KAPLAN

# Introduction

## *Beverly I. Moran*

At the time, it seemed that 1998 would never end. On January 21, when most of us were still keeping our New Year's resolutions, Independent Counsel Kenneth Starr announced an investigation of President Clinton for perjury and obstruction of justice. The Counsel's suspicions stemmed from a pending action by Paula Jones, a former State of Arkansas employee, charging the then Governor of Arkansas with sexual harassment. In December 1997, as part of that suit, Jones's lawyers issued a subpoena to Monica Lewinsky, a former White House intern and sometime FOB (Friend of Bill). That subpoena was based on knowledge obtained from Linda Tripp, another government worker, that Lewinsky and Clinton had conducted an affair in the White House and that Lewinsky had implored Tripp to deny that affair under oath. Both Lewinsky and Clinton denied any sexual relationship, he in a deposition and she in an affidavit. They also denied engaging in obstruction of justice despite the President's attempts to find Miss Lewinsky a job and her own discussions with Linda Tripp. Thus, we spent a full year on the definition of sexual relations and the meaning of truth.

Even now it is hard to remember how these events and those that followed galvanized the American people. Either we tried to hide in disgust or we stayed riveted awaiting further installments. Each day brought new revelations both of facts and strategies. Until August 1998, the President offered complete denials combined with a series of legal maneuvers meant to derail the investigation. But when DNA evidence forced his hand, the President made a sort of public confession after first testifying before a grand jury on his definition of "is."

For eight months, political pundits opined that a proven affair combined with false testimony meant political death. Even the First Lady agreed that, if true, this was a serious matter. Yet the President did not fall on his sword. The confession merely threw us into a new stage of controversy.

Now the question became what to do, and how to think, about those eight months. Did the President lie or was it plausible that, having engaged in ten acts of fellatio with Lewinsky, he had truthfully testified to the lack of a sexual relationship? Was the job search for Monica just help for a friend or a sinister means of obtaining silence? Even if all the charges were true, did impeachment follow or was censure enough? The most gifted soap opera writer could not have kept the story line alive for so long. Yet we did. Through that summer, fall, and winter into the next year we played out this drama until the President was impeached but not convicted in February 1999.

While it may not be fashionable, I admit to a complete addiction to the Clinton scandal. For me it was the train wreck that kept me staring when I should have averted my eyes. It is from this interest, shared by many of the authors, that this volume was born.

When I first imagined a gathering of authors representing a wide range of political and religious views all writing about the Clinton scandal, I reserved an entire section for sex. Was I ever mistaken! Only two of these essays are about sex. One, by David Kennedy, offers amusing insights into one libertine's view of the Clinton scandal. He makes us reconsider what part our feelings played in our own response to underlying events. The second essay, by Linda Oakley, lets us in on the dirty secret— it was about sex and we just couldn't handle it. Using this insight as a starting point, Oakley explains why the elites were so out of touch with the masses on the question of what to make of the President.

So much for the thought that impeachment left some room to play. Even a year after the dust had cleared, we all took it terribly seriously.

## Politics

The volume starts with politics because that was where most of the essays fell, an unexpected result for a law series. It told us that, although most of our authors are law professors, we recognize that law was but a single element in a much larger drama.

Cass Sunstein echoes Oakley's concerns when he charts how opinion groups lost touch with each other when they banded together around internal conceptions that closed off outsiders. The American cult of individuality makes it hard to see how often our views reflect group values. Sunstein uses the Clinton scandal in order to illustrate that larger point.

One of the most painful essays in this section belongs to Elizabeth Rapaport who tries to explain how feminists dealt with a president who, on the one hand, gave them a place in the Democratic Party, and on the other, was accused of several types of sexual abuse.

Jean Bethke Elshtain returns to Rapaport's theme when she questions why women in general, and feminists in particular, were able to support the President and why Hillary Clinton's role as the wronged wife caused her star to rise. Starting with the slogan "the personal is political," Elshtain takes on the notion of public versus private to show how this concept, along with the gender divisions in emotional labor, shifts and changes with circumstance. The contrast between Clarence Thomas and Bill Clinton is one theme that comes up several times in this volume.

David Canon and Kenneth Mayer show us the importance of empirical research when they take on one of the most quoted comments about the scandal, that is, that it undermined President Clinton's legislative agenda. Rather than slow the Clinton program, Canon and Mayer demonstrate that legislation flowed as if there were no impeachment. This telling point makes us reconsider what we thought we knew about this impeachment and politics.

Finally, Leon Trakman offers us a mirror into American culture by contrasting the American impeachment odyssey with the political life of Pierre Trudeau. Often national events lend themselves to abstractions, for example, about the nature of law. By shifting to a Canadian focus, Trakman forces us to ask what this scandal says about us as Americans, a distinct group of people in a particular time.

## Law

Taking that more particular perspective, one set of essays in the law section tries to discern what the process revealed about our justice system. Frank Tuerkheimer begins by showing that the Starr prosecution was not very different either from other independent counsel investigations or from the average criminal prosecution. This is important information because, if the American people found Starr's procedures distasteful, perhaps they should care for their neighbors as they care for the President.

Robert Gordon expands on the contrast between what was done to the President and what occurs every day by exposing our tendency to moralize law. By making moral crimes of such behaviors as drug use, we justify long sentences and social excommunication for large segments of society. While we declare that our liberal state separates law from morality, our citizens are increasingly prosecuted for their moral failings. That it happened to the President illustrates a larger societal shift.

Aviam Soifer's meditations on Richard Posner's *An Affair of State* and Arthur Miller's *Crucible* make him question whether law—the American gold standard—paves a path away from justice.

Robin West dissects sexual harassment law, beginning with the conflation of consent and desire. This mistake in our thinking about sexual harassment makes us equate what we want with what is good, an equation that undermines our ability to govern sexual behavior. This emphasis on consent, often in form rather than in substance, is one reason why even rape can escape prosecution in seemingly normal circumstances.

The last two essays in this section address impeachment as a constitutional, legal, and political process. John Cooper compares America's three impeachments in order to chart how our most recent experience strengthened law as our civil religion. By arguing in favor of President Johnson's impeachment, not because he violated a particular law but because, by dismantling Reconstruction, Johnson became a threat to national security, Cooper makes a fascinating case for impeachment as a political process.

Mark Tushnet continues this theme by pointing out that a legalized impeachment process was not constitutionally mandated. By recalling the real politics of the moment, Tushnet traces the political steps that led to this legalization and questions whether we can ever return to a political impeachment process.

## Shaping Public Opinion

In contrast to earlier scandals when politics were less driven by public opinion, this was a very public spectacle. Thus it is no surprise that another large section is devoted to shaping public opinion. We begin with Andrew Weiner, who uses Shakespeare's *Twelfth Night* to guide us in understanding the confusions, multiple identities, and contorted positions the Clinton scandal reflects.

Linda Oakley appears next for her insights into how the healthcare crisis shaped public opinion in the President's favor.

Lawrence Solan uses linguistic analysis to explain how the American people evaluated truth in the Clinton matter. For Solan, the saddest aftermath of the impeachment is the increasing belief that lawyers wield tremendous power in abusive ways.

For Eric Rothstein, we miss the point if we fail to appreciate the spectacle. The symbolically attempted regicide makes Rothstein hope that, if nothing else, Bill Clinton has cured us of our need to turn presidents into heroes.

Lawrence Joseph ends this section with his impressions of the spectacle as it evolved and changed with each new twist and turn.

## *Religion*

For a volume filled with so many theologians, religion is one topic that got less attention than I had originally anticipated. Despite the religious implications of so much that drove the crisis, we have only four entries in this section.

The section begins with Stephen Toulmin and his analysis of the proper Christian response to another's sins. Using the medieval Church and the Reformation as reference points, Toulmin explains how far the modern-day Christian right has moved from the principles of privacy and forgiveness.

Building on the idea that America is a Protestant, perhaps even Evangelical, culture, Lawrence Rosen looks at our shared understanding of abuse of power, hypocrisy, and sin to demonstrate that President Clinton's struggle with temptation spoke to the public in ways that his opponents did not understand or appreciate. This is a particularly interesting point of view to contrast with Father Neuhaus who writes as a religious and a conservative about how the scandal caused the right to lose faith in its base. Before Bill Clinton, right-wing spokesmen were confident that they represented the Moral Majority. But as the scandal grew bigger and bigger and the sins multiplied like loaves and fishes, the Moral Majority was nowhere to be found, or at least nowhere in the polls.

David Novak maps out how social conservatives felt sold out by economic libertarians when the political response to the scandal failed to uphold moral standards. As we go to press, political pundits are making this very point about George W. Bush, whose election they see as the final rejection of the Reagan coalition.

## The Political as Personal

One striking aspect of the Clinton scandal was how human it was, ranging from the question of the proper relationship between husband and wife to the idea of honesty and its place in politics. Consider how often we were forced to look to our own hearts when judging the pageant and its players. This led me to consider that the political is personal, that is, that our experience as male or female, black or white, insider or outsider shaped much of our views of these matters.

These essays try to assess what the scandal meant to the author in his or her life. David Kennedy's essay on one libertine's view of the Clinton scandal finds many positive aspects to our shared experience, not the least of which is a more honest understanding of sexuality.

In my own essay, I explore how my life as a woman, a black, a child of the lower working class, and a law professor informed my impressions of the stakes and outcomes of this national display.

Drucilla Cornell completes the section with a return to the issues of private versus public. Cornell asserts that, in order to gain safety in the public sphere, women need zones of privacy. These zones are what allow women to occupy public space unmolested. Thus our understanding of both the public and the private requires special attention.

## Final Thoughts

What can we learn from taking these pieces together? In an event so driven by the troubled relationships between men and women, only one male, David Kennedy, considered a female perspective in penning his essay. True, no one can fully address a constitutional crisis, especially not in five thousand words. Nevertheless, taken as a whole, the lack of female concerns in male authors' pieces might make one wonder. After all, although our authors occupy different political territories, they share many common socioeconomic characteristics. Further, many work in sexually integrated communities. In a democratic society, mass support and understanding often make the difference between success and failure. When people so similar in so many ways fail to reflect on the effect of this crisis on the person next door, are we any closer to that understanding than we were after the Clarence Thomas confirmation hearings? This insight made me return to Sunstein's explanation of how we isolate ourselves into interest groups and thereby limit our ability to see each others' point of view.

Sex is another noteworthy absence. This scandal was born out of sex, some accused and some proved, so why did most authors shy away from the topic? In addition to Linda Oakley's hypothesis that we overidentified, Drucilla Cornell, Jean Bethke Elshtain, and Robin West show how our politics, law, and culture make it hard to create space for safe sex in the broadest meaning of that word.

Only two white authors, Lawrence Joseph and John Neuhaus, spent time on black peoples' role in these matters. When the second most memorable phrase from this period—after the infamous "it depends on what the meaning of 'is' is"— comes from Toni Morrison's declaration that Clinton is the first black president, and where the black masses and elites played a pivotal role, this absence is also noteworthy.

Finally, the almost complete absence of personal responses to what was, in many ways, a very personal series of events, made me recall Ntozake Shange's observation in *For the Girls Who Have Considered Suicide When the Rainbow is Enuf* that (some) people are so abstract that they abstract their own orgasms.

Nevertheless, the essays taken either as a whole or separately all express something unique about this important event. I originally conceived of this book as an extended conversation between people from many political and moral camps. That so many of the papers refer to one another, drawing on strengths and taking issue over differences, is a tribute to that conversation.

In the midst of the Clinton crisis, a conservative commentator cautioned people who wanted Bill Clinton removed that they needed to find another cause. It was simply not going to happen. While his point was political, this volume reflects the broader cultural point. In the end, this was not about one man or one affair. It was about what those acts revealed about the ways in which we handled law, religion, and politics at the end of the twentieth century. Whether we change our political process, move away from law or toward more enforced moral behavior, or revamp our understanding of sexual harassment or the private versus the public sphere, these essays add to the debate.

# Part I

# Politics

# Chapter 1

# A Case Study in Group Polarization (with Warnings for the Future)

## *Cass R. Sunstein*

Why did the overwhelming majority of Republicans, representatives and citizens alike, support the impeachment of President Clinton? Why did the overwhelming majority of Democrats, inside and outside Congress, oppose impeachment?

Consider some remarkable numbers. In the House of Representatives, 223 of 228 Republicans, or 98 percent, voted for impeachment on at least one count, whereas 5 of 206 Democrats, or 2 percent, voted for impeachment on at least one count. In the Senate, 51 of 55 Republicans, or 93 percent, voted to remove the President from office, whereas 0 of 45 Democrats, or 0 percent, voted to remove the President from office. Within the citizenry, there were also exceedingly sharp divisions, with the vast majority of Democrats believing that impeachment would be a mistake, and the vast majority of Republicans believing exactly the opposite. (Independents typically opposed impeachment, and helped produce the large anti-impeachment numbers among the public as a whole.) What accounts for this difference?

To get ahead of the story, I ask this question because I believe that the answer involves a general phenomenon, one with implications for a wide range of issues in a diverse democracy. The phenomenon, sometimes called group polarization, involves the tendency of like-minded individuals, engaged in discussion with one another, to fortify their prediscussion views, and indeed to move toward a more extreme point in the general direction in which they were already tending. If Republicans are talking with Republicans, if Democrats are talking with Democrats, if members of the religious right speak mostly to each other, and if the same is true for feminist organizations, there is a potential for a variety of different forms of extremism, and also for dismal failures in mutual understanding. This is a large part of the story of the Clinton impeachment, and it provides a range of insights, and also some serious warnings, for the future.

In the context of impeachment, it is far too simple to say that the large disparities in view were because one group was right and another wrong. (I do believe, incidentally, that this is true, because the impeachment was constitutionally unsupportable.) Whatever the appropriate stance on the impeachment question, it simply defies belief to suggest that the ultimate pattern of judgments is what one would expect if each person, whether ordinary citizen or legislator, had been consulting his own conscience; surely independent judgments would have led to far more defections from the party line. I think that this is particularly true on the Republican side (did so many Republicans really believe, in principle, that the President should be removed from office?), but it is plausibly true on the Democratic side as well. This amazing level of party solidarity, on a question of high principle, is not what one would expect if people were independently consulting their consciences.

With respect to legislators, as opposed to ordinary citizens, electoral self-interest undoubtedly played a role. For example, a vote by any particular Republican to defect from the party position might have played well with the general electorate, which was averse to impeachment; but it might also have increased vulnerability to a primary challenge within the party, and in any case have caused the defector a series of problems with the party leadership. For many Republicans, and for many Democrats, a defection might have seemed a lot more trouble than it was worth. But at least on a straightforward account of electoral self-interest, it is not plausible to attribute all these votes to perceived electoral pressures. Many Republicans and many Democrats would hardly have risked the political wrath of their voters if they had voted otherwise on impeachment. And even if we could explain the votes of these representatives in terms of electoral self-interest, it remains necessary to explain the sharply divergent positions of citizens, with the dramatic split between people who identify themselves with the two parties. Of course Democrats tend to like President Clinton much more than Republicans do. But on what ground would so many self-identified Republicans support impeachment, and so many self-identified Democrats oppose it?

I believe that much of the answer to the otherwise puzzling pattern of judgments lies in certain lawlike characteristics of collective deliberations—characteristics that tend to push groups in predictable directions. Above all, the pattern seems to have a great deal to do with group polarization. An understanding of this phenomenon helps explain some alarming behavior by individuals in social settings. It also sheds some new light on party-line voting, understood narrowly or broadly. At the same time, it raises a series of questions and doubts about processes of public deliberation, especially but not only in the context of highly visible controversies like impeachment.

There is a danger here for the future, about a political process in which like-minded people talk principally to one another. The warning is that this kind of talk can lead to unjustified extremism, through entirely predictable processes. And when various groups go in opposite extreme directions, confusion, confrontation, accusation, and sometimes even violence may be the ultimate result.

## Group Polarization

Although it has received little attention in law and political theory, group polarization is one of the robust findings of social psychology.[1] The central point here is that the outcome of a group deliberation tends to be a more extreme version of the tendency indicated by the initial predisposition of group members. Deliberating groups thus move not toward the middle, but toward within-group extremes. For example, a group of people who tend to oppose affirmative action is likely, after discussion, to oppose affirmative action with some vehemence. Those inclined to support gun control will, after discussion, do so with great enthusiasm. People who tend to think well of an ongoing military buildup will strongly favor a military buildup after discussing the problem with one another. Those who believe that President Clinton is likely a victim of a concerted right-wing attack are likely, after talking together, to think that this is undoubtedly the case. Those who fear that the President is a criminal and a liar who is protected by an indifferent public and an obsequious media are likely, after talking together, to believe that this is a very optimistic picture of the situation, one that is far too favorable to President Clinton.

There are two explanations for group polarization, involving two different mechanisms. Each of the mechanisms plays a role in producing group polarization and, as we shall see, each of them played a role in the impeachment debate. The first is based on persuasive arguments. The idea here is that people respond to the arguments made by others, and the "argument pool," in a group with some initial disposition A, will be strongly skewed in the direction of that disposition. Thus a group whose members tend to oppose affirmative action will hear a large number of arguments in favor of abolishing affirmative action, and a relatively small number of arguments for retaining it. If people are listening, they will have a stronger conviction in the same direction from which they began, as a result of their deliberation. If people who believe that President Clinton's impeachment was a constitutional atrocity speak to one another, they will be entrenched in this belief as a result of their conversation together, simply because they will hear a range of arguments to this effect (and few good arguments the other way). There is considerable empirical support for the view that the argument pool has this kind of effect on individual views.

The second mechanism has to do with social influence. The central idea here is that people have a certain conception of themselves and a corresponding sense of how they would like to be perceived by others. Most people like to think of themselves as not identical to but as different from others—but only in the right direction and to the right extent. If you think of yourself as the sort of person who favors gun control more than most people do (because, let's say, you think that you are unusually disposed to reject liberal homilies), you might shift your position once you find yourself in a group that is very strongly in favor of gun control. If you stay where you were, you may seem less favorably disposed toward gun control than most group members, and this may be disconcerting, thus producing a shift. Or if you believe that you have a relatively favorable attitude toward affirmative action, discussion with a group whose members are at least as favorable as you are might well push you in the direction of greater enthusiasm for it. Having heard group members, you might move your stated position, simply in order to maintain a certain self-conception and reputation, as one who likes affirmative action a bit more than most people do. If you want to seem to be unfavorably disposed to President Clinton, and so consider yourself, you may support impeachment in a group that does the same, not because you have a considered judgment in favor of impeachment but because you do not want to seem, in the eyes of the group, to be a defender of President Clinton. There is a great deal of evidence that social influence is an independent factor behind group polarization; consider in particular the fact that mere exposure to the views of others can have this effect, even without any discussion at all.

These points raise many questions about the value of deliberation and about the whole ideal of deliberative democracy, which lies at the heart of our constitutional order. Of course we cannot say, from the mere fact of polarization, that there has been a movement in the wrong direction; perhaps the more extreme tendency is better. But when group discussion tends to lead people to more strongly held versions of the same view with which they began, it may be nothing to celebrate. If social influences, rather than a full appreciation of relevant reasons, incline people in certain directions, the shifts that result may have very little to do with the merits of the case. Those who believe in deliberation are likely to be pleased to find that arguments and reasons have an impact. But if the impact is the product of a skewed argument pool, the resulting changes in judgment may be a product of happenstance and distortion rather than better thinking. I will return shortly to the relationship between the impeachment vote and group polarization.

## Cascades

The empirical findings on group polarization closely connect to theoretical work on social "cascades."[2] The question here is why social groups sometimes move quite rapidly in one direction or another—and why groups of like-minded people may move rapidly toward or against an extreme outcome such as impeachment.

### Information and Informational Cascades

A central point here is that when individuals lack a great deal of private information, they often rely on information provided by the statements or actions of others. If A is unaware whether abandoned toxic waste dumps are hazardous, he may be moved in the direction of fear if B seems to think that fear is justified. If A and B believe that fear is justified, C may end up thinking so too, at least if she lacks independent information to the contrary. If A, B, and C believe that abandoned hazardous waste dumps are dangerous, D will have to have a good deal of confidence to reject their shared conclusion. The result of this process can be to produce cascade effects, as large groups of people end up believing something—even something that is false—simply because other people seem to believe it too.

The same processes should be at work for political, legal, and moral questions; in fact we can easily imagine political, legal, and moral cascades, global warming cascades, racism cascades, religion cascades, even proimpeachment and anti-impeachment cascades. The same process may work for political candidates, as a fad develops in favor of one or another—a cascade "up" or "down," with victory-producing or ruinous consequences. Sometimes people are not entirely sure whether affirmative action is a good idea, whether capital punishment should be imposed, whether the Constitution protects the right to have an abortion, whether it is wrong to litter or to smoke, whether God exists, whether perjury counts as a high crime or misdemeanor. Many people, lacking firm convictions of their own, may end up believing what (relevant) others seem to believe. There is an obvious analogy here to the "persuasive arguments" account of group polarization—though for cascade effects, what is crucial is the very fact of the belief, not the grounds for that belief.

If the risk of social cascades is real, the White House was correct to be worried about any small shift in public opposition to impeachment. If (as I suspect) many ordinary citizens were not really sure whether the President should be removed from office, the large percentages who opposed removal were *fragile*. A small shift in the direction of proimpeachment sentiment—from 70 percent against to, say, 58 percent against, and falling—might have started a cascade effect, if what people thought was dependent on what (they thought) others thought.

### Reputation and Reputational Cascades

Thus far the discussion has involved informational pressures and informational cascades. When informational pressures are involved, people care about what other people think because they do not know what to think, and they rely on the opinions of others to show what it is correct to think. But there can be reputational pressures and reputational cascades as well.[3] Here people are influenced by what others say and do, not because they think that those others are likely to be correct (that would be an informational influence), but because they want to preserve their reputations. The basic idea is that people care about what others think of them, and they speak out or remain silent partly in order to cultivate the approval of others, even at the price of failing to say what they really think.

Suppose, for example, that A believes that hazardous waste dumps pose a serious environmental problem; suppose too that B is skeptical. B may keep quiet, or even agree with A, not because B thinks that A is right but simply in order to preserve A's good opinion. C may see that A believes that hazardous waste dumps pose a serious problem, and that B seems to agree with A; C may therefore voice agreement even though privately she is skeptical or ambivalent. It is easy to see how this kind of thing might happen with intense political debates. People who believe that President Clinton is a liar and a criminal might be entirely quiet in some contexts, or even agree wholeheartedly with people who speak out on President Clinton's behalf. People who believe that impeachment was a terrible idea might not say so, and may even endorse impeachment, simply to preserve their reputations in certain communities. Undoubtedly this happened among some of those who supported impeachment, including within the House of Representatives.

The consequence of all this can be cascade effects—large social movements in one direction or another—when a number of people appear to support a certain course of action simply because others (appear to) do so. Here, as with informational forces, what is true for publicly stated factual claims can be true as well for moral, legal, and political claims. This phenomenon is of course analogous to the "social influence" explanation of group polarization. The only difference is that the social influence explanation concerns presentation to self as well as presentation to others.

## The Dynamics of Impeachment

How does all this bear on the impeachment of President Clinton? And what are its general implications for scandals, problems, and other sources of sustained public conversation? At first glance the answer is straightforward, and what has been said thus far should supply the rudiments of a basic account.

### The Basic Account

Consider informational forces first. In both Congress and the nation, Republicans were talking mostly with Republicans; Democrats were talking mostly with Democrats. The result of these largely independent sets of deliberations was to deepen the Republicans' commitment to impeachment, to heighten the sense that the President had committed a high crime—indeed, to suggest that the President's arguments were weak and self-serving—and at the same time, to strengthen the sense, among Democrats, that Judge Starr was an unprincipled zealot, that the grounds for impeachment were implausible, and that this was not very far from a "coup d'etat" on the part of the far right.

To be sure, many diverse arguments were available to representatives and citizens alike; it was not as if the proimpeachment or anti-impeachment case was invisible to those who disagreed with it. But it does seem reasonable to think that many Republicans, perhaps especially among the citizenry, were affected by a distorted argument pool in which all or most of the articulated points had to do with the President's violation of his oath of office and failure to tell the truth under oath. In the relevant discussions, the best arguments on the President's behalf appeared infrequently, and when they appeared, they were likely to have been made half-heartedly. Many discussions among Democrats were affected by a similarly skewed pool of arguments in which the best claims on behalf of impeachment were not mentioned. No wonder that both groups would tend to polarize toward a more extreme version of views originally held.

Social influences and reputational forces were undoubtedly at work as well. A Republican who rejected impeachment—whether representative or citizen—would be signaling that he was a certain sort, one who was willing to defect from the general party-line view that serious misconduct by the President warranted removal from office. Any particular Republican could be sending out a large signal of tolerance for illegality and misconduct by high-level Republicans. Indeed, the signal could be far more dramatic and extreme than anything the defector might have intended. And for representatives in particular, the consequence could be severe reputational sanctions both within the House of Representatives and at the next election. If a range of Republicans could be persuaded to reject impeachment, the signal would of course be muffled, and perhaps a cascade of anti-impeachment votes would be expected. There is safety in numbers. But the collective action problem was quite serious; without concerted action by a nontrivial number of Republicans, any particular defector would be in potential trouble.

The same dynamic was at work for any Democrat who favored impeachment. The signal would be one of capitulation to a Republican witch-hunt—a signal that would be all the louder if very few Democrats were defecting. Once defections started, they could be hard to stop, because after a certain "tipping point" the loud signal would be muffled. Thus if a few Democrats had called for impeachment, a cascade might have happened here as well. This was the White House's worst nightmare; it explains why the White House believed it indispensable to keep as many Democrats as possible in line.

Here, then, is my basic account of the extraordinary party-line judgments among the citizenry at large, and also of the votes in both the House and the Senate. These were case studies in group polarization. Those who spoke with one another fortified their own preexisting views, and made them all the more extreme. In this light it is not surprising to find the change of heart among Republicans, such as Henry Hyde, who initially contended that impeachment should occur only if there were bipartisan support for it. Once the logic of group polarization had set in, his moderate view was bound to shift.

## Of Representatives and Constituents

Of course there are some differences between the legislative process and the contexts in which group polarization has been studied, above all because members of Congress are subject to external political sanctions. Even if members are persuaded that a certain course of action makes sense, they may vote otherwise simply because of what their constituents want. Hence a limited argument pool, for members of a particular party, may matter much less than a clear signal from the people back home. This point might explain some of the defections on both sides; certainly it explains why some members are able to resist party pressures and the logic of group polarization. Unambiguous electoral signals can be a powerful buffer against that logic (though for the reasons I have given, the signals themselves may be a function of group polarization within the electorate).

The same point bears on the relevance of social influence. Members of the Republican Party are likely to care a great deal what fellow Republicans think of them; but they probably care still more about what local voters think of them. To be sure, the two are not independent of one another. If a certain Republican seems like an outlier among Republicans generally—for example, if he seems less sympathetic to impeachment than his colleagues—his electoral prospects might be damaged simply by virtue of this signal. But analytically, the two are different. Here too the votes of constituents may matter more than group deliberations (taking members of the same party as the relevant group).

Because of the differences between representatives and constituents, it is even reasonable to think that polarization is likely to be more serious among the latter rather than the former. We can imagine a society—and it is not so far from our own—in which Republicans speak mostly with each other, at least about the issue of whether President Clinton should be impeached; we can imagine a society in which, on the same issue, Democrats speak mostly with one another too. If this is the situation, polarization should occur within political camps. Republicans will veer toward a proimpeachment position; Democrats will veer toward an anti-impeachment one. Of course there are multiple independent reasons why this may be so. Democrats tend to like President Clinton and Republicans tend not to like him. But part of electoral polarization, on the question of impeachment, is undoubtedly a result of the social mechanisms discussed here.

## Conclusion and a Warning

What lessons do these points have for social dynamics, especially in the context of highly visible public debates? Certainly they do not explain the whole picture. But they provide part of any account of why a vast majority of Republicans may think one thing and a vast majority of Democrats the opposite, when independent judgments by members would seem to make this pattern entirely inexplicable. For representatives, simple electoral calculations undoubtedly play a role; but a great deal depends on the limited information pool in the relevant communities and the particular signal given by defectors from the party. In the context of impeachment, I do believe that it helps explain an otherwise very puzzling set of judgments, perhaps above all the remarkable solidity of Republican proimpeachment judgments in circumstances in which the Constitution and large percentages of the public seemed to argue in the other direction.

If this explanation contains some truth, it helps account for party-line thinking more generally within legislatures and within the citizenry—and raises a host of questions and doubts about the value and consequences of group deliberation. Indeed we may regard the idea of "party-line thinking" very broadly. Often, for example, members of the Christian right, or of feminist organizations, will move in extreme directions, largely because their conversations tend to be internal, with like-minded people talking to one another. These are the right conditions for group polarization. Indeed, group polarization has generally been studied under laboratory conditions, with one-shot activities. In real life, what we may call "polarization games" are repeated, usually quite frequently. It is here that movement toward extreme positions, and misunderstanding of what opponents actually do and think, are especially likely.

Of course nothing I have said here demonstrates that group polarization moves people in bad directions. We can imagine many contexts in which it is entirely appropriate for people to end up with a stronger version of their initial position; perhaps discussion clarifies matters, and perhaps the argument pool, limited though it inevitably is, makes people see things in a clearer light. But nothing in the mechanisms that underlie polarization makes this inevitable. The most serious problems are likely to arise when deliberating groups, insulated from one another, polarize to more extreme positions partly because of their very insulation. In these circumstances, large groups—with initial tendencies that are different but not so very different—can shift in opposite extreme directions, with little understanding of how they have ended up in such different positions. It is in this setting that group polarization carries a risk of balkanization, confusion, and even violence.

The nation managed to avoid the worst of these problems in connection with impeachment, though in my view members of both parties—the Republicans far more than the Democrats—suffered a great deal from their failure to engage the arguments put forth by the other side. If there is a warning here, there is therefore a lesson as well—about the need for deliberating groups to avoid the forms of insulation and homogeneity that can lead them, by ironlike laws of social interaction, in unjustifiably extreme directions.

### NOTES

1. See Roger Brown, *Social Psychology: The Second Edition* (New York: Free Press, 1986); Cass R. Sunstein, "The Law of Group Polarization" (unpublished manuscript 3/2000), for general overviews, with citations to the relevant empirical literature.

2. See Sushil Bikhchandani, David Hirshleifer, and Ivo Welch, "Learning from the Behavior of Others: Conformity, Fads, and Informational Cascades," *Journal of Economic Perspectives* 12, no. 3 (Summer 1998): 151–70.

3. See Timur Kuran, *Private Truths, Public Lies: The Social Consequences of Preference Falsification* (Cambridge: Harvard University Press, 1995).

# Chapter 2

# Sex and Politics at the Close of the Twentieth Century

## *A Feminist Looks Back at the Clinton Impeachment and the Thomas Confirmation Hearings*

### *Elizabeth Rapaport*

When the Lewinsky scandal was fresh, when we were all still wondering how far the press would go, and whether this bimbo eruption would have political legs, the reaction of feminists to the President's Predicament was eagerly anticipated. In time it became clear that feminism had found its place in the Democratic Party, and would defend the party and the President. Not surprisingly, feminists were criticized for abandoning principle and putting the past and potential achievements of the movement at risk.

While the feminist defense of Clinton *is* tenable, the case on the record has weaknesses that render it susceptible to charges of opportunism. How *ought* a principled feminist movement respond to a consensual liaison between a powerful ally and a young subordinate? Of course no unique feminist response should be expected. Although feminists have found a home in the Democratic Party, feminists within and outside the party differed in their responses to the Clinton-Lewinsky affair, and in their judgments as to whether feminists should support impeachment and removal from office.

There was a bright optimism among the founding generation of feminists and others of the sixties generation, Clinton's generation, that profound and liberating changes in sexual life could be achieved by feminists and their male allies, that new truths and new ways of living were to be discovered. There was also a fierce rejection of these aspirations by social conservatives. The impeachment season gave us an opportunity to hear from both sides about what they had learned in the last thirty years.

*I*

In January 1998 reports that the Independent Counsel was investigating an alleged affair of President Clinton's with a White House intern appeared in the respectable news media. The President denied having "sexual relations with that woman, Miss Lewinsky."[1] Almost eight months later, in August, after Lewinsky had testified before a grand jury and turned over a semen-stained dress, Clinton was forced to acknowledge an intimate relationship with the then twenty-two-year-old intern. There followed a period of intense speculation about whether the President would resign. President Clinton was condemned for morally reprehensible and politically reckless behavior. His ability to withstand pressure to resign from political and media elites, including the leadership of his own party and members of his own administration, was dissected. A constant feature of the scandal was the mildness of public reaction; although the public was having fun, it couldn't be persuaded that the scandal was the stuff of national political crisis. As the story devolved, the President would not brook resignation, and his ardent detractors would not allow the scandal and the President's second term to run its course. In October, the House of Representatives voted for an impeachment investigation; in December, Clinton was impeached; in February 1999, the Senate trial ended in an acquittal.[2]

Mainstream and official feminists, by which I mean national feminist organizations associated with the Democratic Party and women Democratic Party officeholders, tended to be restrained in their comments before Clinton's admission; after his admission they responded with moral condemnation of the President's conduct. "It was wrong."[3] They then joined the effort to dissuade Congress from investigating and ultimately impeaching the President. But the lineaments of the position solidified in August and September, which mirrored that of the Democratic Party, had been on offer from some prominent feminists from much earlier days. In January Susan Estrich sketched the position: The President had shown "bad judgment" in engaging in sex with an intern, his conduct was "deeply troubling"; but a consensual relationship does not constitute sexual harassment, much less is it criminal, much less does it rise to the level of an impeachable offense.[4] In March Gloria Steinem contributed an op-ed piece to the *New York Times* in which she echoed this position. But while Estrich used the language of conventional moral rebuke, Steinem did not condemn the sex or the man. She absolved Clinton of any moral or political blame because the sex was consensual. Thirty years ago, she wrote, the women's movement had developed a "common sense guideline to sexual behavior . . . no means no, yes means yes." With women who have made accusations, like Paula Jones or Kathleen Willey, Clinton took "no" for an answer. He may have been guilty of indecorousness, some passes were "clumsy" or even "gross," but nothing more. Thus Steinem offered an explicitly feminist criterion for judgment of sexual relationships, including those between the powerful and the humble, which she also believed was shared by the American public and especially women.[5] After Clinton's admission in August, National Organization of Women president Patricia Ireland, and other feminist leaders, brought the issue of power imbalance into her reading of the Clinton-Lewinsky affair. She found Clinton's conduct to be an "abuse of power" but not one that would lead feminists to call for resignation or impeachment:

> Consensual sex with a White House intern is an abuse of power by the president, but consensual sex is not illegal harassment and it is not an impeachable offense . . . Nor is it in the best interests of our country for the president to resign.[6]

Little public attention was paid to another relevant and available model for critique of Clinton's affair with the intern, namely, antifraternization regulations imposed in hierarchical organizations like the armed forces, some civilian workplaces, and schools and universities. (Apparently the Clinton White House did not adopt such policies.) These regulations, which have goals similar to those of sexual harassment law, typically ban relationships between persons of disparate rank regardless of consent. Sexual harassment law distinguishes between unwelcome but consensual sex, which violates the law, and welcome contact, which does not.[7] Antifraternization policies ban both welcome and unwelcome sex. Invocation of the antifraternization model could have been the occasion for a public discussion of complex and wide-ranging questions involving competing claims to sexual freedom and the case for protection against exploitation in different kinds of workplaces and organizational settings. This might have constituted a feminist agenda for the Clinton scandal. Nothing like this happened.

Instead, feminists responded to the President's affair with the intern by concluding that (1) it was merely a breach of private morality, or (2) it was neither morally nor politically problematic for feminists (consensual sex), or (3) it was exploitation not barred by law, and lacking sufficient gravity inherently or when measured against the value of the President to his feminist allies (Which? Why?) to justify casting the President out of office.

Those who successfully sought to impeach the President and subsequently failed to remove him from office were obliged to proceed in the face of a broad American consensus that sex with the intern did not merit loss of the presidency. The congressional Republican right and Independent Counsel Starr found this a bitter lesson and could never quite believe that it was so. But because it was so, the impeachment could only go forward on the basis that what mattered was not the sex but the lies—to the public, his family, and members of his administration and staff—and the alleged perjury and obstruction of justice.[8] No doubt there were some Americans for whom perjury and obstruction issues were indeed the heart of the matter, but for the majority of Clinton's supporters and opponents the impeachment and trial were about sex.

## II

That feminists would be part of this consensus, though, requires some explanation. For thirty years feminists have insisted that the personal was also political. Feminists have striven to combat the hysterical blindness that had kept women as well as men from publicly naming wrongs suffered by women at home and on the job. Common but formerly unacknowledged expressions of male privilege came to be seen as incongruous and unacceptable in a genuinely democratic society.

Many feminists had certainly long condemned the kind of conduct the President sought to conceal, whether perjuriously or lawfully: President Clinton took advantage of a young woman, who, like so many before her, was intoxicated by the musk of power. He told her, she told her interrogators, that he had had hundreds of such "affairs."[9] The Lewinsky scandal came to light because another foray of the President's eventually gave rise to a sexual harassment lawsuit, undoubtedly politically motivated, in which Ms. Lewinsky became embroiled. Then-Governor Clinton encountered Paula Jones at a hotel while both were there on Arkansas State business; she was working at the registration desk for a conference sponsored by the state agency that employed her. Clinton had Jones escorted to his hotel room by a state trooper, his bodyguard and procurer. While the trooper guarded the door, the Governor allegedly dropped his pants and groped his dubiously voluntary guest, a stranger to him, who, unlike Lewinsky, had not sought his attentions.[10]

Since the blood of feminists, and many other Americans, is made to boil by the exploitation of the young and vulnerable (even the young of Beverly Hills), and since the Jones episode looks like nothing if not criminal assault, why do we defend this President?

A summary of the reasons we defended the President's tenure in office:

> The Constitutional Argument: The Starr investigation, the impeachment, and the trial were politically motivated, and not rooted in any threat to the integrity of national government.
>
> The Political Argument: In order to pursue justice and equality for women, feminists must ally with the Democratic Party. Realistically, feminists have nowhere else to go and will lose if the Republicans, and especially the Republican right, defeat President Clinton. ("He's a SOB, but he is our SOB.")
>
> The Hypocrisy Argument: Every member of the Republican right, and indeed the whole Congress, have condoned the exploitation of women and the lying about it on the part of other members of the club. That condonation makes liars of those who cry liar now. Moreover, these hypocrites have opposed every advance for women. They come to the bar of justice with unclean hands.
>
> The Liberal Argument: The President's lies, even if perjury, were about merely private conduct. Neither the conduct nor the lies implicate his ability to conduct the public's business.
>
> The *Kulturkampf* Argument: For Clinton-haters the President represents a detested value system—call it sixties culture, call it baby-boomer morality. The disgrace of Clinton and his rout from office is part of a campaign to restore patriarchal sexual and familial values. Those who identify as targets of that reaction—proponents of a secular, pluralist state, feminists included, are frightened and repelled by what they see underlying the impeachment drive: Sexual McCarthyism,[11] a "Savanarolan purity crusade,"[12] an American version of the Taliban.[13] To defend the President, then, is to defend the ultimate target of his committed detractors, ourselves. United front politics against a common enemy is clearly indicated. (A no-brainer.)[14]

It is the liberal argument which is problematic for feminists. While political expediency is sometimes justifiable, and feminists have as much right to compromise as any other constituency, feminists presumably do not want to abandon the insights that have driven the movement. Women have suffered precisely because the forms of exploitation to which we are subject have been dismissed as merely personal, and therefore both trivial and not susceptible to legal or political redress. Therefore, when mainstream and official feminists defend Clinton on the grounds that because his conduct is not reached by current law it should be consigned to the realm of private morality (it's between Bill and Hillary) their work is at best unfinished and at worst seriously flawed. Have feminists given up too much and compromised too far in defending the President?

The weakness in the feminist critique of Clinton's affair with Lewinsky was the unwillingness of those representing mainstream feminism forthrightly and unambiguously to apply feminist principle to Clinton's affair with Lewinsky. The issue of principle is not marital fidelity. Feminism is not dedicated to the defense of monogamy. Nor does it turn on whether Lewinsky consented to or initiated the affair. Consent could be relevant in a case involving a woman who can fend for herself, where some modicum of equality is evident. (We all have our guesses about Monica Lewinsky: I see a neurotic kid.) Feminism is not dedicated to the defense of chastity. The issue is exploitation of office. When the powerful persist in trolling for susceptible interns, fresh cohorts of young women are forced to fight the battle that feminists of my generation hoped to win for our daughters: the battle to be taken seriously rather than reduced to sexual assets or perks. Bill Clinton, in a pattern of conduct with women expressed with Lewinsky, hurt our cause.

The weakness then in the mainstream defense of Clinton was to dilute or muffle a feminist critique of his affair with Lewinsky, and to adopt instead the liberal dichotomy between private and politically significant action. Acknowledging Clinton's failures as an ally, however, does not create a bar of principle against support of the President's continued tenure in office. At the close of the century, feminists have a share of power and influence we lacked thirty years ago, and like any other constituency we make political accommodations. And, as with other constituencies, we can hurt as well as help ourselves by so doing. Politics does make strange bedfellows. To cite a striking but hardly unique example, the black voters of Alabama embraced George Wallace, contrite, and willing to work with them and for them, when he sought to reenter Alabama politics; this was despite his civil rights era history in Alabama and his racist bid for the Democratic Party nomination for the presidency in 1968. The Clinton Administration's and the Democratic Party's positions on such issues of critical importance to feminists as reproductive rights and the patriarchal yearnings of his socially conservative opponents need little rehearsal. In context, the question of this alliance is not a difficult one; costs to feminists of maintaining the alliance are lessened by forthright recognition that we support the President despite his exploitative record and not because we don't think sexual exploitation is the stuff of politics.

## III

Feminists have been taken to task for failure to render consistent responses to the Clinton scandal and the allegations of sexual harassment made against Justice Clarence Thomas by Anita Hill during his Senate confirmation hearings in 1991.[15] These are the two highest profile sex scandals of the contemporary feminist era.

Thomas and the Senate were passionately denounced by feminists during the confirmation hearings. Feminist outrage on the former occasion was above all directed at the denigration of Anita Hill by the Senate. The hearings were a watershed and Anita Hill a messenger of change. Anita Hill came onto the national stage at a time when powerful men believed it was possible to deny that they and their colleagues routinely exploit or condone the exploitation of subordinates, and to deny without political risk.

Republican Senators excoriated Hill as a liar and Democratic Senators thought that, as in the past, little attention should be paid to accusations like Hill's against a member of the club. Women knew perfectly well that what Republicans said was unimaginable conduct on the part of the nominee happens all the time, and what Democratic Senators dismissed as trivial was painfully important to working women in both human and economic terms.

Hill accused Thomas of sexual harassment while she was a young attorney and he was her supervisor. Thomas persisted in asking Hill out for dates despite her refusals; she told him she did not want to date her supervisor. He also subjected the religious, reserved Hill to lewd and explicit sex talk. This situation lasted for some months while Hill was working for Thomas at the Department of Education, where he was Assistant Secretary for Civil Rights. Then he stopped, but resumed when she went to work for him again after he assumed the chairmanship of the Equal Employment Opportunity Commission.[16]

There are two forms of sexual harassment recognized in federal law: quid pro quo—demanding sex under threat of job reprisal, and hostile work environment—imposing demeaning conditions on women on the job.[17] Hill made no allegations of the former kind. Thomas's alleged conduct may well have been sufficiently "severe or pervasive"[18]—the applicable legal standard—to constitute the latter under then existing or current federal sexual harassment law.[19] Regardless of legal sufficiency, Thomas took advantage of his position to humiliate a devout and proper subordinate, knowing that she could not send him packing without paying a high professional price. Long before the hearings brought her unwanted notoriety, her tenure at the EEOC brought on a hospitalization for job-related stress and ended with her abrupt abandonment of Washington to teach law in her native Oklahoma.[20]

The criticism that feminists are inconsistent in supporting Clinton but opposing the confirmation of Thomas has little purchase on those feminists who condone the sexually exploitative conduct of neither. Thomas's conservative political and legal views would have made him an exceedingly unpalatable nominee to the Supreme Court in a feminist calculus even if Hill's allegations had never come to light. The disquieting features of the politics of the Thomas confirmation hearings arise from other quarters. The prospect of the second black Supreme Court nominee in American history being rebuffed for conduct previously ignored by the Senate was unsettling. In the case of the Clinton impeachment, it was the President's opponents who were subject to charges of hypocrisy; had the Senate failed to confirm Justice Thomas in any part because of Hill's accusations, we would have been treated to the spectacle of a black man being turned away for behavior common and condoned among the Senators who discredited him.[21] But perhaps because the racial politics of the hearings were so absorbing, I did not give much thought in 1991 to another question to which the Thomas confirmation hearings gave rise: In examining Thomas's relationship with Hill, were we as a nation raising the bar for the conduct of powerful men with the women in their professional orbit, or opening the door to what has been called sexual McCarthyism? The answer to this question, when considered in light of the last near decade and the impeachment trial, is, I think, both.

## IV

President Clinton stands accused by social conservatives of amoralism or immorality in the conduct of his family and sexual life, and as representative of the moral failings of his generation of liberals. Further, conservatives regard these adulteries as disqualifying him for the presidency both because they reveal a lack of "personal virtue" that is a necessary if not a sufficient condition for political leadership and because of the failure to provide exemplary leadership as husband and father.[22] Social conservatives called for his resignation on these grounds; some thought the libertinage was sufficient grounds for impeachment and removal from office. While liberals congratulated the American public throughout the impeachment season for their good sense in rejecting calls to impeach because of merely private failings, conservatives lamented the degradation of American values.

Liberals predictably responded with alarm about the designs conservatives had upon privacy; the corruption of values that liberals saw was in the media and political culture of scandal. Feminists understood that the conservative defense of the family as the foundation of a healthy society is implicitly a call for the strengthening of patriarchy. It is female chastity that is critical to family virtue; it is the subordination of women to men that is necessary to the operation of the kind of family for which conservatives yearn.

Conservatives have fundamentally misread the sexual values of the sixties culture they see embodied in the President. David Frum's diagnosis is typical and revealing:

> [W]hat's at stake in the Lewinsky scandal is not the right to privacy, but the central dogma of the baby boomers: the belief that sex, so long as it is consensual, ought never to be subject to moral scrutiny at all.[23]

Frum is surely correct that sixties political liberals and radicals valued sexual expression and sexual experimentation. It was a hallmark of the era. But coupled with it was the value placed on sexual honesty. The idea of sexual liberation contained at its core the commitment to be honest about desire and honest with those with whom sexuality was shared. Adultery was part of the package of repression and deception of self and others that was rejected by sixties culture. The plan was to invent and institute sexual relationships in which all interested parties gave, as it were, informed consent, and were willing participants. Thus monogamy was a choice, not an obligation. Neither exclusivity nor heterosexuality were accepted as universal norms. There was ample basis for the moral criticism of practice in sixties sexual culture, which of course is not to say that insight or rectitude were more or less common than in other cultures.

While liberals and radicals of the sixties and younger persons influenced by that culture retain some allegiance to these values, there has in the main been a retreat toward convention. That culture, though, nurtured and took the imprint of the feminist and homosexual rights movements: Among the most enduring influences of the sixties culture, and from the conservative point of view among the most objectionable, are the notions of parity of legitimacy of female and male sexual interests, and straight and gay sexual interests. However, with these signal exceptions, sixties culture has not sustained its innovative momentum and has not developed enduring novel institutions to rival conventional marriage.

Few of Clinton's proponents defended the President on grounds that could be called sixties or sexual liberationist grounds. The dominant response, shared by many feminists, was an assignment of Clinton's affair to the realm of private morality, a matter which, apart from the impact of the scandal itself, did not implicate his ability to faithfully and competently discharge the obligations of his office. The sexual politics of the Clinton impeachment turned on the different meanings assigned to sexual privacy by liberals and conservatives. For conservatives it is a shield for decadence that screens conduct of great relevance to public welfare from moral and political accountability. For liberals it is the paradigm of a domain of life where consenting adults should not have to endure state oversight, where autonomous choice and pluralism should hold sway.

## V

Contemporary feminism has a complex relationship with liberal norms. Feminists have good reasons to endorse the liberal value of sexual privacy. Social conservatives in power would certainly have other targets as well but would be dedicated to the repression of women. But feminists have vital interests that have led us to press for reforms that redraw the boundaries between the sphere of private conduct and conduct subject to public scrutiny. The reform of rape law to allow the prosecution of dates, boyfriends, and husbands and the invention of sexual harassment law are critical examples. Each of these reform regimes has disquieted liberal concerns for privacy. Absent the framework provided by sexual harassment law, an event like the Hill-Thomas Senate confrontation could not have occurred. The law and the politics that produced it contributed along with other cultural changes to the climate in which Supreme Court nominees and presidents, like business executives and factory foremen, are obliged to answer for conduct that would have been politically and legally invisible three decades ago. There have been occasions, notably the campaign to curb pornography by creating civil liability for harm to victims of pornography,[24] when many feminists paid insufficient heed to concerns voiced by feminists and others about the dangers of repression when the state is invited to impose censorship.

In 1991 feminists responded viscerally and aggressively to the Hill-Thomas confrontation, forcing liberal allies and conservative opponents to reckon with the impact of sexual harassment on women. In 1998, official and mainstream feminists were on the defensive. They injected little in the way of a distinctive feminist voice or content into the public debate. Feminism was perceived as complicit with the trivialization of sexual exploitation and a defender of conventional marital morality. The issues ducked about sex and power are not easy ones, nor was the conjuncture auspicious—the hard Republican right in full cry, seemingly ready to take any political risk to discredit the President and the Democrats. During the next scandal, there will again be jeremiads about the decline of patriarchal civilization. Feminists will have other chances to focus intellectually and politically on the historical and natural objectives of the movement, which include both combating sexual exploitation and holding out the hope of a better sexual future.

### NOTES

1. "What's News World-Wide," *Wall Street Journal,* January 27, 1998, A1.

2. See Jeffrey Toobin, *A Vast Conspiracy: The Real Story of the Sex Scandal That Nearly Brought Down a President* (New York: Random House, 1999), the fullest account to date of the Clinton scandal and impeachment.

3. Barbara Vobejda, "Key Constituency Reverses Itself; Women's Groups Condemn Clinton Behavior, but Support Tenure," *Washington Post,* August 22, 1998, A08.

4. Susan Estrich, "Unimpeachable Evidence," *Denver Post,* January 27, 1998, B11. Susan Estrich was Michael Dukakis's campaign manager.

5. Gloria Steinem, "Feminists and the Clinton Question," *New York Times,* March 22, 1998, section 4, 1.

6. *Wall Street Journal,* "What's News Wold-Wide."

7. See *Meritor Savings Bank v. Vinson,* 447 U.S. 57 (1986).

8. See Richard A. Posner, *An Affair of State: The Investigation, Impeachment, and*

*Trial of President Clinton* (Cambridge: Harvard University Press, 1999) for a defense of the gravity of the legal case against Clinton; and Robert W. Gordon, "Legalizing Outrage," this volume, for a critical assessment of the case's substantiality.

9. *Referral from Independent Counsel Kenneth W. Starr to the House of Representatives,* 473–74 (September 11, 1998).

10. Clinton claims no recollection of such an encounter with Jones. While the two almost certainly spent time together in a hotel room, Jones's prim account of the meeting has been challenged by Toobin, *A Vast Conspiracy,* 154–59.

11. Alan M. Dershowitz, "Sexual McCarthyism," in *Sexual McCarthyism: Clinton, Starr and the Emerging Constitutional Crisis* (New York: Basic Books, 1998).

12. Gordon, "Legalizing Outrage," this volume.

13. Robin West, "Sex, Harm, and Impeachment," this volume.

14. See Posner, *An Affair of State,* 199–216, and works cited therein, for an enlightening account of the *Kulturkampf* waged during the Clinton impeachment.

15. See, for example, Cynthia Tucker, "Feminism: Clinging to Clinton Costs Women's Movement Its Credibility," *Atlanta Constitution,* September 30, 1998, 12A.

16. See Jane Mayer and Jill Abramson, *Strange Justice: The Selling of Clarence Thomas* (Boston: Houghton Mifflin, 1994).

17. See *Meritor Savings Bank v. Vinson.*

18. *Meritor Savings Bank v. Vinson,* 67, supplies this standard.

19. See *Harris v. Forklift Systems, Inc.,* 510 U.S. 17 (1993), in which the Court attempts to clarify the "severe or pervasive" standard.

20. Mayer and Abramson, *Strange Justice,* 112.

21. Senator Samuel Metzenbaum, the member of the Senate Judiciary Committee whose staff initiated contact with Hill, candidly told *Time* magazine reporter Hays Gorey soon after he learned of Hill's allegations, "If that's sexual harassment, half the senators on Capitol Hill could be accused." Mayer and Abramson, *Strange Justice,* 235.

22. See Posner's discussion in *An Affair of State.* Also see William J. Bennett, *The Death of Outrage: Bill Clinton and the Assault on American Ideals* (New York: Free Press, 1998); and David Novak, "The Clinton Scandal: Law and Morals," this volume. Novak discusses the relationship between political and "personal virtue."

23. David Frum, "A Generation on Trial," *Weekly Standard,* February 16, 1998 (1998 WL 17902054; page references not available). David Frum is a contributing editor to the *Weekly Standard.*

24. See Judith R. Walkowitz, "Male Vice and Female Virtue: Feminists and the Politics of Prostitution in Nineteenth Century Britain," in Ann Snitow, Christine Stansell, and Sharon Thompson, eds., *Powers of Desire: The Politics of Sexuality* (New York: Monthly Review Press, 1983), who argues on the basis of historical example that "social purity" alliances between conservatives and feminists to promote state regulation against vice and abuse of women have led to the harsh and repressive regulation of women.

# Chapter 3

# Public, Private, and the Gender Division of Emotional Labor

## *Jean Bethke Elshtain*

For a full year and more, the United States found itself in the throes of an often acrimonious round of debates concerning what is public and what is private in light of the nature of the impeachment charges brought against President Bill Clinton by the U.S. House of Representatives. Nothing was resolved definitively as a result of this crisis; indeed, a moment of decisive resolution of questions pertaining to public and private will never arrive. Why is that? Because public and private are terms of discourse that help to structure political life and thought and, as well, to create and to sustain categories of inclusion and exclusion. And these will always be contentious. I will bring in the American crisis of the presidency in the body of this paper. But to begin, it is necessary to ask ourselves about the categories of public and private themselves and what conceptual and political work they have been called upon to do historically. That will help to pave the way for treatment of the gender division of labor and how it maps onto the public and private—or does not, as the case may be.

A caveat before I begin. I realize that the locution—"gender division of labor"—conjures up some thoroughly stale neo-Marxist approach to the structure of work life long overtaken by fast-changing structures of work and the relationship of men and women to work. But I want to signal that although much has changed, there are some hoary emotional divisions and tropes that remain remarkably intact. These divisions surfaced intensely—or so I shall claim—in the Clinton scandal and in other public psychodramas of the recent past. First things first, however, so I shall turn to an exposition of why it is that the categories of public and private are necessary to liberal democratic politics.

Much of this ground may be familiar, but a bit of backdrop is necessary. As I argued in my book, *Public Man, Private Woman: Women in Social and Political Thought*,[1] images of public and private "are necessarily, if implicitly, tied to views of moral agency; evaluations of human capacities and activities, virtues, and excellence; assessments of the purposes and aims of alternative modes of social organization."[2] Although this essay is not explicitly about any male-female divide in thinking through the public and private, it is certainly the case that clusters of images concerning the excellences of men and women—what they share in general; how they might differ—are part of this longer story. Public and private are so tricky to deal with, at least in part because of their very ubiquity. Although public and private are terms of ordinary discourse, one finds widespread disagreement over their respective meaning and range of application within and between societies, as indeed is true of all open-textured terms of political discourse. Minimally, however, the public and the private are twin force fields that help to create a moral environment for individuals, singly and in groups; to dictate norms of appropriate or worthy action; to establish barriers to action, particularly in areas such as the taking of human life, the regulation of sexual relations, the promulgation of familial duties and obligations, and the arena of political responsibility.

Public and private are imbedded within a dense web of associational meanings and intimations and linked to other basic notions: nature and culture, male and female, as well as views of work, ideas about authority, community, death, and God. Public and private, although pertaining in some form in *all* societies beyond basic kinship structure modes of social organization, play a much bigger role in certain modes of social and political life than in others. In the West, public and private are fundamental, not incidental or tangential, ordering principles. And part of what has been thus ordered is a general view of what is political and what is not; what belongs under the purview of politics and what does not; what in principle should be included under the political label and what should be off limits; and what activities or relationships not now included under politics, or public life, can and should be thus incorporated. In other words, disagreements about what is public or private, political or personal, themselves enter into and help to constitute political life. There are massive bodies of thought—philosophical, political, theoretical, theological, sociological, legal, on and on—devoted to sorting this out, often in ways that are contentious from some other point of view.

Given that one cannot present the whole picture in a single paper, let me stay on the ground of general theoretical comments at this point. I will turn to concrete cases and examples as we proceed. Let us assume as backdrop Western history up to the emergence of what I'm going to call the "modern liberal synthesis" associated with John Locke and other liberal social contract thinkers generally. What is particularly interesting from a later vantage point is the fact that Locke's epistemology presumes a split between reason as formal rationality and passion, by contrast, as scarcely contained desire.[3] The public-private split also, at least in part, marked an epistemological divide. In public and political life, human beings reasoned in a way that pushed them to get their interests met. In private life, passions could be displayed so long as they remained undisruptive of the overall social order.

One irony of liberal contractarianism is the fact that family life, in this scheme of things, was put under a more thoroughgoing description of what was private in contrast to public than ever before. The further implication was that women's concerns and interests were hidden from political view. At least the older notion of patriarchy had recognized the centrality of the family to *public* life, however constrained that life was for many men and all women. Losing the notion of any public dimensions to family life was a huge loss in the victory of modern liberalism, and it took many generations of social activism (much of it in reaction to what social contractarian liberalism had wrought) to alter this privatization of the family.

And this wasn't the only loss: over time one also sees a privatization of religion, turning religion into a kind of private club where members go to find solace or justification or something equally self-directed. My claim, in sum, is that the effect of various public-private splits effected by the triumphant liberal consensus was to further privatize the private world and to reduce the concerns of women to whatever could be expressed in a language of often cloying sentiment, as that private world was cut off even further from public discourse. Women were key players within social bodies as churchgoers or union members, and in these and similar civic spaces powerful political and social concerns about the legitimacy of family commitments as a form not just of private but of public membership of a particular sort, could be sustained. Unions in countries with a strong tradition of Catholic social thought, for example, emphasized the idea of a "family wage," trying desperately to prevent the full marketization of the life of every single member of the family so that families could actually enjoy something called "family life." Slowly but surely the family wage or living wage idea disappeared, dissolved in the acids of market modernity.

Also, as Western societies became more "secularized," greater suspicion began to fall on what it meant to bring "religious arguments" to the public sphere; thus, women were struck another blow as their language of concern got stripped of much of the force of the Christian ethic of *caritas*, hence of its potential power to challenge power and to seek remedies to social ills. Women increasingly defined their entrance into the public world along the lines of censorious moralism (like the Temperance Campaign): *that* was permitted and even expected (if resented) because it branded women as politically unreliable and given to "emotional" and "moralistic" issues that would admit to no commonsensical interest-based political solution.

By the time we get to John Stuart Mill, the "deal" is pretty well set for the dominant liberal synthesis. A few of its central points as they bear on our subject are:

(1) A split between reason and passion;

(2) The denigration of all that is not reason, understood narrowly;

(3) Whatever is not Reason is Instinct (the worst part of human nature; something backward to be overcome);

(4) History and tradition can never be an argument in favor of something because Progress tells us that progress itself is a further wrenching of humanity away from its less rational past;

(5) If liberty is denied, power of the most petty and nasty sort is pursued (an explanation for why so many women are petty and nasty, presumably);

(6) Where there is least liberty, the urge for power is most forceful and least controllable; thus, women turn the domestic arena into a field of force in which they play unscrupulous private power games; and

(7) If women received public liberty (not power, interestingly enough), their quest for private power would cease.

That, really, is the sum total of Mill's case—that and his famous "harm principle" from the great essay, *On Liberty*. We see here many of the strengths and weaknesses inherent in the liberal position as it entered the twentieth century. The strengths include a preparedness to challenge received social forms on the basis of certain strong commitments to human liberty or equality, however flawed the understanding of these may be. The weaknesses have become ever more visible to us over time—a naive teleology of progress, the "sanitization" of liberty from power, a rigid separation of reason from other possible sources of human illumination and knowledge, including "the passions," a deepening of the public-private split, a subsumption of the most vital areas of human existence for most people—work, family, and religion—into the private, thus giving these areas no legitimate political role unless or until political issues emerged that might transform concerns that arise from these spheres into grist for the public mill. And no doubt first and foremost, as it underscores all else, an ever more radical set of presuppositions about human beings as self-sovereign, self-possessing, rights-owning entities. Lost along the way was any deeply social account of the self or understanding of the self-in-community. (And a social construal of rights differs importantly from a more individualistic construal—a topic unto itself I cannot explore here.)

Nevertheless, the insistence that public and private needed to be distinguished and some form of distinction honored became stunningly clear with the emergence of twentieth-century totalitarianism. Indeed, one problem with the American feminist slogan of the 1970s—"The personal *is* political"—is that it replicated a central presupposition of the "totalizing" regimes that have haunted the twentieth century. Now, don't get me wrong, I'm not arguing that feminists wanted such a politics. I'm insisting, instead, that they didn't pay sufficient attention to the implications of the claim that the personal is political *tout court*. It is within frameworks that have a totalizing drive, that *declare nothing off limits* as everything is defined politically—family life, friendship, every twitch of the mouth and nod of the head—that any distinction between public and private is impossible to sustain.

Those of us who were frustrated with the ways in which the public-private distinction was being played out in American society were drawn for understandable reasons to a slogan that declared everything "personal" to be "political." But this slogan was troubling from the beginning, because it seemed (at least to me) simply to reverse the order feminists descried, one in which a too rigid bifurcation between public and private pertained. In other words, by proclaiming the personal political, feminists collapsed the two categories, presuming an identity of, rather than a relationship between, public and private. Here are a few of the critical points I made at the time that yet pertain: If there are no distinctions between public and private, personal and political, it follows that no differentiated activity or set of institutions that are genuinely political, that are, in fact, the bases of order, purpose, liberty, and justice in a political community can be identified.[4] For, remember, the claim that "the personal is political" was not that personal and political are interrelated in important and fascinating ways previously hidden by certain modes of thinking and acting; nor that the personal and political may be analogous to one another along certain axes of power and privilege, but that the personal *is* political. What was asserted was an *identity*, a collapse of one into the other. By definition nothing "personal" was exempt from political definition, direction, and manipulation—neither sexual intimacy, nor love, nor parenting. This stood in contrast to a more nuanced approach to public and private that might enrich the public by bringing to it legitimate concerns that were too often hidden from view, having been labeled "private."

Now let's turn to one of the areas of contention in which women figure centrally, arenas in which women are absolutely key players, that of cultural representations of men and women that tap into what might be called the emotional and ethical center of gravity for women and men respectively.

What dimensions of personal life are appropriately political and what are not in American society at present, in light of our own versions of the public-private distinction? At present we confront an irony, namely, that groups of sexual protestors who specifically seek to politicize their sexual identities and claim group recognition based on those identities may insist, at the same time, that their intimate lives are "nobody's business." Can you consistently have it both ways? I submit that you cannot consistently do this, even as I understand that the logic I am criticizing speaks to real concerns and that feminists, along with everybody else, are forced to operate within the framework of the current liberal synthesis. Nevertheless, problems remain that cannot be explained away by the intrinsic difficulties inherent in these matters.

To unpack this, let's go to the case that perplexed all of us and perplexed others about us, namely, the matter of President Clinton, reflecting, as we go, on what this case tells us about the innate contestability and slipperiness of the categories of public and private. For some, what happened to President Clinton was entirely illegitimate because it concerned his personal life exclusively, or at least did so in the first instance. They also argue that subsequent troubles—charges of perjury under oath, witness tampering, trying to prevent a grievant from having her day in court, and so on—cannot be reckoned as serious breaches of the *public* trust because they flowed from personal behavior.

I shall not enter into the complexities of American jurisprudence, a field in which I am minimally competent in any case. But this much needs to be said: Americans at the beginning of the twenty-first century are dealing with a very different "public" square from the one that pertained a half-century ago. It is, in many salutary respects, far more inclusive and decent, especially where race and gender relations are concerned. One defining feature of the Clinton Administration was its boosting of nearly all aspects of the mainstream liberal feminist agenda: don't budge an inch on abortion; forge forth with the full panoply of punitive sanctions available in the sexual harassment arsenal; don't let men hide behind the notion of "private" behavior if that behavior shows clear reliance on a lopsided power disparity, and includes other features that suggest that the term "consent" should always be bracketed or treated with skepticism; make it permissible for the sexual histories of men accused of harassment to be brought into the courtroom as relevant to establish a possible pattern of behavior (legislation President Clinton supported and signed), and so on.

There is, perhaps, some historic irony we will be able to savor a few years from now in the fact that mainline liberal feminists rushed to the President's defense by saying, in effect: "But we didn't mean that male leaders who supported our agenda should ever fall into the zone of legal danger and culpability," as if the only men who would *ever* be guilty of anything damaging to particular women would automatically be political "reactionaries." As such, feminists would feel justified in attempting to undermine him politically by using gender bias or sexual harassment as a weapon. Here one calls to mind the Clarence Thomas case where risqué comments by Thomas, allegedly made a decade earlier, were brought up in an attempt to derail Thomas's nomination to the U.S. Supreme Court. In the Thomas case, then, we see "the personal is political" being interpreted enormously broadly to include a case in which no favors were sought or given; no punishment exacted; no threats made; no requirements to break the law proffered, and so on. That the target was an African American male is doubly troubling, as the feminist ardor in this matter conjured up a vast array of images of the oversexed, salacious black man—but, again, that is another topic. When we get to President Clinton, however, whose behavior toward women has apparently been dubious if not contemptuous his entire adult life, or has been on many well-documented occasions, "the personal is political" is forgotten and a concept of privacy as broad as the concept of sexual harassment played out in the Hill-Thomas case is proffered instead.

Let's parse this further. President Clinton's troubles emerged in a very public venue—a courtroom—where one Paula Jones presented a case that the President of the United States, as Governor of Arkansas, had sexually harassed her. Jones was a low-level, just-above-minimum-wage clerk in a state office. We can't get into all the particulars here, but suffice it to say that the charge was initially declared meritorious—how *serious* it was is another matter—and it was said that Jones deserved her day in court. It was in an attempt to deny Jones's lawyers access to his sexual history, the legitimacy of which endeavor President Clinton had himself signed into legislation as an appropriate line of inquiry in any sexual harassment matter, that his troubles began. Here enters Monica Lewinsky's false sworn affidavit and the President's false testimony, under oath, in a court of law. It all began to unravel.

President Clinton was not impeached because he exercised deplorable judgment in his "private" life. For this very basic reason—which feminism helped put into play and which I adjudge a good thing overall—what goes on in the Oval Office is not enveloped within a private *cordon sanitaire*. Those who hold to this view insist that anything to do with sexuality is by conceptual fiat in a "zone of privacy," so why shouldn't this pertain in the President's case? A plausible response would go like this: One of the things we have learned, *given conceptual struggles* over the meaning and scope of public and private, is that many serious matters can be papered over with the claim that it is "nobody's business" but that of the participants involved. Sometimes, indeed, this is the case. I would submit it is the case in the overwhelming majority of extramarital affairs which should *neither be nor become a political issue* unless or until these relationships interfere in a palpable and destructive way with the carrying out of public office. (That is why the destructive "outing" of public officials for adultery under the sponsorship of smut-peddler Larry Flynt, a pornographer who specializes in violent and especially degrading representations of women, was so vile and so utterly beside the point.) In a liberal democracy, not every sin is a crime. Indeed, even in medieval society, when the Christian synthesis pertained, not every sin was a crime, as St. Thomas makes clear.

But some sins may be so corrosive of public life that they cross over into a public concern. Other sins may involve crimes. Therefore they are public issues *prima facie*. Let's return to the case at hand and assume that the President and Ms. Lewinsky both "consented" to the relationship. Consent is no magic wand. Nagging questions remain, and serious problems are not automatically erased. Was this wise or reckless? Was it decent or degrading? Was it damaging to all concerned, consent or no consent? Now take matters one step further. The relationship, or provision of sexual services, in this case, involved employer and employee and took place in the employer's place of work, which also happens to be one of the sacred *civic* sites of the American people. One can hardly imagine a more public place in which to carry on intimate transactions. This, then, was no "discreet affair," especially when one considers that a small army of staffers was enlisted by the President to facilitate his sexual assignations and an even larger number to cover matters up once they turned sour. Surely this crossed the boundary into the public sphere on every scale— ethical, legal, and political.

Such a conclusion does not lead to any knockdown answer about what should have been done that wasn't done or what shouldn't have been done that was. But, minimally, the implication is clear: these are serious matters that should be discussed seriously in large part because they pertain so directly to the way public and private are defined and behavior in each sphere evaluated. What happened, in the American debate about this matter, was the display of an astonishing and unstable combination of views, namely, that the President of the United States is a person of low moral character (and low moral character here is construed as a "private" matter) but that he is doing a "good job" nonetheless (with "good job" being his presidential activity). It isn't so easy to unpack what these disparate evaluations on the part of the public meant at the time or will mean over the long haul, but I submit that the gender division of emotional labor had a good bit to do with these evaluations—a point I will turn to in a moment.

This much can be said with confidence: the disjuncture between the President's character and his "job" shows just how pervasive is one version of a public-private split in contemporary liberal America. Let me clarify matters in the following way: The standard on the sexual activity outside marriage of elected officials begins precisely with deciding whether this is a public matter or not. It is public from the beginning, or so I have claimed, depending upon when, where, and how intimate assignations occur. Or, alternatively or correlatively, matters become public when it is clear that there is a direct bleeding over of private behavior into public action. If one considers the corrosive effect of lying on a person's social relationships across the board—from family and friends to colleagues and fellow citizens—one has some intimation of what I mean.

The nuanced form of assessment here adumbrated is not the one that has triumphed in the Clinton debate. Instead, Americans were asked to "forgive" the President, he having sinned, his personal life *only* having been besmirched. The vast majority of Americans agreed with this. The implication here, of course, is that the vast majority of Americans may want the great bulk of legislation attempting to regulate male-female relations in the workplace to be jettisoned. That, it seems to me, is one possible long-term implication of the Clinton scandal.[5] And it is a sobering implication because it suggests that many American citizens feel more "at home" with a rigid public-private separation, with sex falling *entirely* under the private description, than with a more complex and nuanced approach to public and private: how they relate; how they bleed into one another; how, in particular instances, one may undermine the other and vice versa.

Now let's turn to how the presuppositions of a "gender division of emotional labor" played into this scandal. One item that perplexed many observers was the fact that women consistently "went easier" on the President, and found his behavior less troubling, than did men. Women, in fact, rallied in interesting and curious ways: they "forgave" Bill and they identified (it seems) with his wronged wife, as Hillary Clinton's approval ratings soared. Thus, the President's wife, who had entered the White House with the strongest feminist credentials of any woman who has served as First Lady, captured public approval at long last as one who had stood by her man. That she published a book (if one can call such productions books) about playing hostess at the White House and the various menus and dinnerware at state dinners is unsurprising. She determined to mine the deep vein of lady-lore that continues to persist and wronged-wife lore that is astonishingly powerful. The person women hated was Monica Lewinsky who got to be a temptress, even a stalker, a home-wrecker, a slut, and so on.

Men, interestingly, criticized Clinton for recklessness and for drawing a young woman about the same age as his daughter into a forlorn sexual adventure. He, father and leader, should have been protecting young women, not using them for sexual servicing. Again, an aspect of traditional male emotional labor kicks in. But men didn't dominate this emotional discourse: women did. Sexist stereotypes abounded, nearly all of them embodying highly negative images of men ("They all lie about sex," "He couldn't help it, he's a guy") and of the younger Ms. Lewinsky. But she was seen as the wicked temptress as Mrs. Clinton benefited from the classic image of noble, pure, self-sacrificing, wronged wife and Clinton drew sympathy as a guy who just couldn't help himself. Because a pop-therapeutic idiom triumphed in the popular discussion, an idiom that women, as emotional laborers, "feel comfortable" with (you should talk about your feelings, strive to reach closure, all that sort of thing), it was almost impossible to engage in a strenuous *civic and political debate* about a civic and political matter. Clinton was construed as a poor fellow with an addiction. He needed therapy, not censure. It followed that either one was a nice person who forgave and understood, or one was a cruel accuser who did not.

One could do a thought experiment here of the most basic, even crude, kind, namely, a reversal and try to imagine a female president engaging in Bill Clinton's behavior with a young man. Toward whose side would the female public rally in such an instance? It is easy enough to predict: they would circle the wagons of emotional support around the wronged "First Man" who had trusted his wife, the President, who had betrayed that trust. There would be no "gals will be gals" talk or "She just couldn't help herself and needs help." In this scenario, the President/woman would have been shamed out of office and public support for her would have plummeted. The young man in question would have been seen as a rather spineless wimp incapable of standing up to the powerful temptress or as someone with ambitions of his own who aimed to blackmail her. And men? This scenario would have drawn men together with women in one roaring chorus of condemnation: no gender gap would have emerged as it did in the Clinton case.

All this gestures to congealed and ready-to-hand images that appear to have lost little of their serviceability. Think here of the psychodrama of the Death of Princess Diana, a spectacle that raised many similar concerns and was dominated by the all-too-familiar tropes. Because Diana was the beautiful "Queen of Hearts," her husband could be portrayed as the unfeeling, emotionally frozen, perhaps even caddish husband, or former husband. A double standard on emotional labor was glaringly evident. Diana's own self-confessed and ill-chosen liaisons didn't tarnish her status as royal victim at all, whereas Charles's one long-term relationship, reactivated after his marriage had gone sour, branded him an unfeeling brute. The tabloidization, and with it a particular sort of pop-feminization along the lines of daytime talk shows and soap operas, with their overwhelming female audiences, appears to have triumphed.

Consider as well that Diana was contrasted not only to her emotionally frozen former husband but also to the icy unfashionable monarch. Queen Elizabeth and her family may have had what it took to steel their subjects to fight Hitler but they appeared helpless when confronted with media representations that cast them as emotionally removed, hence unwilling to weep on television by contrast to the emotionally febrile People's Princess. The important thing was that she—Diana—was one who could *feel* things. Diana's stories of "low self-esteem" and addictions to self-help regimens of all kinds, her bulimia, were all displayed for public consumption—a public now given over to the once private concerns of women. Or, perhaps better put, a public immunized against the integrity of a rich concept of privacy and a robust understanding of public life as a civic activity which seeks, instead, the privatization of public life as a melodramatic playing out of ancient tropes in postmodern guise. What was most troubling, perhaps, in the Death of Diana frenzy was the fact that it was no longer acceptable to afford private grief the time and space it requires. Instead, the currents of this emotionally fraught epoch seep into every cultural pore. Women may have come a long way. But archetypal representations and simplistic story lines are alive and well, alas.

To the extent my argument is compelling, it complicates the claim I made above that Americans continue to be devoted to a strong bifurcation of public and private—at least where "private affairs" and their possible public implications are concerned—but the meaning of public and private is altered in the playing out of a public psychodrama in privatized, or at least noncivic, language and imagery. That which we urgently insist is separate we then blur by conflating or collapsing public life into categories that fail to do justice to public life by definition. Along the way, intimate life too is denuded as it takes on board many of the stock and by-now banalized categories of the "confessional" pop-therapeutic culture, a culture that plays to women's concerns that were once women's strengths.

What do I have in mind here? To answer that question a full exploration of public and private through the prism of the gender division of emotional labor would be necessary. I hope that many other examples that either help to confirm or serve to challenge my basic claims and examples will emerge over time as Americans continue to ponder this sad, messy affair and its implications for our understanding of public and private.

NOTES

1. Jean Bethke Elshtain, *Public Man, Private Woman: Women in Social and Political Thought* (Princeton: Princeton University Press, 1981; second edition, 1992).

2. Elshtain, *Public Man, Private Woman,* 4.

3. Of course, Locke's position is more complex than these few words make clear. For a fuller discussion, see *Public Man, Private Woman.*

4. Here I draw upon *Public Man, Private Women,* as I have at various points throughout.

5. I would agree, and I have argued many, many times over the years, that much of the whole sexual harassment armamentariam got draconian, petty, and at times ludicrous, especially in university settings. Nevertheless, the notion of respect for the dignity of persons (with women included in the category) imbedded here is worth preserving.

# Chapter 4

# Everything You Thought You Knew about Impeachment Is Wrong

## *David T. Canon and Kenneth R. Mayer*

If we had to describe, in two or three sentences, the surpassing oddness of Clinton's impeachment, it would go something like this: A Democratic president, by any reasonable definition of the term, had "sex" with a twenty-two-year-old White House intern and repeatedly lied about it, both publicly and under oath. So of course it makes perfect sense that the main consequence was that two Republican Speakers of the House lost their jobs.

One of the most interesting features of the impeachment episode is that virtually all the predictions about what would happen or what impeachment would mean—from both elected leaders and the "punditocracy"—were wrong. Throughout 1998 and early 1999, there was nearly universal agreement that Clinton was fatally wounded by the scandal. Both his supporters and his opponents made their case for or against impeachment by arguing that the decision could have devastating constitutional consequences either way.

Yet one year later, the legacy of Clinton's impeachment is scarcely detectable. Clinton's popularity remains inexplicably high for a president at the end of his second term (significantly higher than Reagan's, and just shy of Eisenhower's low-sixties approval rating through 1960). Early claims that the thirteen House Managers would face electoral retribution for their efforts have proven overstated. Trust in government is *higher* now than in November 1998. About the only significant institutional consequence has been the demise of the Independent Counsel law. It may well be true that many Republicans and Democrats in Congress are barely on speaking terms, but partisan vitriol has more to do with long-standing ideological polarization

in Congress than with any fallout from impeachment. The one-time constitutional crisis has vanished with hardly a ripple. Why were these early
predictions and analyses so off the mark?

Our goal in this chapter is threefold. First, we intend to establish the
validity of our claim that the impeachment process was seen as a dangerous constitutional confrontation. Second, we intend to show that these
early predictions were incorrect and that the impeachment had no significant aftermath. And finally, we will offer some explanations for why
these initial impressions were so far off the mark and provide our own
interpretation of why both the public and political leaders have appeared
to move on.

### Early Impressions and Predictions: Dire and Wrong

The general contours of the impeachment timeline are well known: the
intersection of the Paula Jones sexual harassment lawsuit against the
President and the Independent Counsel's investigation of Whitewater;
Linda Tripp turning over recordings to the IC's office, on which Monica
Lewinsky discussed an affair with the President and efforts by Vernon
Jordan to get her a job; Clinton's deposition in the Paula Jones lawsuit, in
which he denied ever being alone with Lewinsky or having "sexual relations" with her; the Independent Counsel investigation; the infamous
stain on Lewinsky's blue dress; the DNA test; the impeachment and trial.

When the *Washington Post*, ABC News, and the *Los Angeles Times* reported on January 21, 1998 that Independent Counsel Kenneth Starr had
expanded his investigation to include allegations that President Clinton had
lied to cover up a sexual affair with a twenty-two-year-old White House intern, reactions typically ranged from shock and disbelief (among Clinton's
political allies) to outrage (among his foes). After Clinton appeared to
hedge, telling *NewsHour* host Jim Lehrer that "there *is* no improper relationship," pointedly using the present tense, even his defenders became concerned that there might be something to the story after all.[1] The following
week, when Clinton issued a more forceful denial (his famous finger-wag-
ging statement that "I want you to listen to me, I'm going to say this again,
I did not have sexual relations with that woman, Miss Lewinsky"), concern
arose about the consequences for Clinton if it turned out he was trying to
cover up the affair by lying about it.

A consensus quickly emerged that Clinton was finished, and that resignation or impeachment was inevitable. Consider the following remarks by guests and panelists on Sunday morning talk shows the first week after the story broke:

Wolf Blitzer, *CNN Sunday Morning*, January 25, 1998:

> Despite the president's repeated and carefully worded public denials, several of his closest friends and advisers both in and out of government, now tell CNN they believe he almost certainly did have a sexual relationship with former intern Monica Lewinsky. And they're talking among themselves about the possibility of a resignation.

George Stephanopoulos, *This Week*, January 25, 1998:

> I think it depends on the answer to only one other question. You know, we can sit here and talk for days, but there's one question. Is he telling the truth, the whole truth and nothing but the truth? If he is, he can survive. If he isn't, he can't.

Sam Donaldson, *This Week*, January 25, 1998:

> This isn't going to drag out. We're not going to be here three months from now talking about this. Mr. Clinton, if he's not telling the truth and the evidence shows that, will resign, perhaps this week.

> Secretary of Defense William Cohen was reported as having said in a private meeting that if the charges were true, "it's all over."[2]

These predictions of Clinton's demise seemed perfectly reasonable; less explosive allegations about extramarital affairs had derailed Gary Hart's 1988 presidential campaign, and had very nearly brought Clinton's 1992 campaign to an early end. It was hard to see how the President could survive.

The public seemed torn by the allegations, exhibiting support for Clinton while also expressing grave concern over the more serious allegations of perjury and obstruction of justice. Although Clinton's job approval rating rose after the initial set of revelations, several polls indicated an even split on impeachment if the obstruction or perjury charges proved true. A late January 1998 Gallup poll found that when individuals were asked if they would favor impeachment if they "were convinced that Bill Clinton lied under oath or participated in attempts to get the woman to lie under oath," 46 percent said yes, and 46 percent said no.[3]

Clinton continued to insist that he had done nothing wrong—that he had neither lied about having sex with Lewinsky nor encouraged her to lie about the affair—until he gave a videotaped deposition to the Independent

Counsel's office on August 17. In that deposition (which was made public in September), Clinton admitted to "inappropriate, intimate contact" with Lewinsky. Yet he persisted in the sorts of linguistic hairsplitting that drove many to distraction: sparring with the IC lawyers over the meaning of the words "is" and "alone," and insisting that *receiving* oral sex did not constitute sexual relations. After Clinton gave a nationally televised speech that night—conceding publicly for the first time that he had carried on a relationship with Lewinsky that was "not appropriate"—Republicans were quick to announce the end of his presidency, and GOP leaders looked forward to significant gains in the 1998 midterm elections. While some Democrats strongly defended Clinton, others were much more tepid in their support, warily keeping their options open until the direction of public opinion became clearer. Still others were blunt in their criticism: Senator Joseph Lieberman (D-Conn.), on the floor of the Senate, called Clinton's behavior "disgraceful" and said it compromised the President's ability to lead the country, and House Minority Leader Richard Gephardt (D-Mo.) refused to rule out impeachment.[4]

By October 1998, public weariness over the whole affair had tempered GOP rhetoric, and even House Speaker Newt Gingrich had started to portray the midterm elections as a contest of ideological agendas rather than as a referendum on presidential scandal.[5] Still, the Republicans had history on their side, as midterm elections had produced gains for the opposition party in the House in every case since 1934. Going into the election, the typical prediction was that the Republicans would achieve a small seat gain in the House, and perhaps even reach the filibuster-proof threshold of sixty seats in the Senate.[6] On election day, Newt Gingrich was bolder, predicting that Republicans would gain twenty seats in the House.[7]

The results of the midterm elections—in which the GOP lost five seats in the House and picked up nothing in the Senate—sent shockwaves through the party. Within three days, Gingrich had resigned rather than fight a revolt in his own party, and many observers saw the election as a sure sign that the Republicans had to end the impeachment process. That prediction too was wrong, as the GOP pushed ahead with impeachment hearings, ultimately voting largely along party lines to approve two articles of impeachment in December 1998.

By the time the House opened hearings on the question, the impeachment controversy was being cast as a Manichean struggle for the soul of representative democracy and constitutional self-government. Representative James Sensenbrenner (R-Wis.), who opened the House Managers' presentation in the Senate, told Senators that their vote on conviction would "set the standard of conduct of public officials in town halls and courtrooms everywhere and the Oval Office for generations."[8] Representative Stephen Buyer (R-Ind.), another House Manager, argued that Clinton's "persistent and calculated misconduct and illegal acts, has set a pernicious example of lawlessness, an example which, by its very nature, subverts respect for the law. His perverse example inevitably undermines the integrity of both the office of the President and the judicial process."[9]

Clinton's supporters were no less vigorous in arguing what impeachment and conviction would mean, depicting the case against the President as the work of vengeful right-wing fanatics willing to torch the Constitution and nullify two presidential elections. Sean Wilentz, professor of history at Princeton University, testified before the House Judiciary Committee that "it is no exaggeration to say that upon this impeachment inquiry, as upon all presidential impeachment inquiries, hinges the fate of our American political institutions. *It is that important.*"[10] Representative John Lewis (D-Ga.) argued on the House floor that Clinton's foes "have been too quick to pick up the hammer of impeachment and swing it with reckless abandon. So bent are they on the destruction of this President that they would knock down the very pillars which support our constitutional system."[11] Ronald Dworkin defined impeachment as "a constitutional nuclear weapon . . . [that] gives politicians the means to shatter the most fundamental principles of our constitutional structure."[12] Representative Eliot Engel (D-N.Y.) called the effort to impeach Clinton "a bloodless *coup d'etat.*"[13]

Even after the Senate limped to a conclusion in February 1999, acquitting Clinton on both Articles of Impeachment, it appeared that the legacy would be bitter. Although Clinton was conciliatory in public, in private he was said to have vowed an "all-out war" against congressional Republicans and the House Managers.[14] His detractors continued to raise allegations—Juanita Broaddrick went public the week after Clinton's acquittal with her charge that Clinton had sexually assaulted her in 1978—and in July 1999 Federal District Court Judge Susan Webber Wright, who was presiding over the Paula Jones case, cited Clinton for contempt and fined him $90,000 for giving false testimony in his January 1998 deposition.[15]

Of all the bits of conventional wisdom concerning Clinton's impeachment, the one that comes closest to being correct is the assessment that "the system worked." As John McCain (R-Ariz.) said, "the process went forward the way that the framers intended. That revalidates the Constitution and it means that whatever happens to the reputations of individual presidents, the Presidency remains strong."[16] Or, as William Safire stated, "That's why we can take heart at how The System Worked. We underestimated the House and it did itself proud. We trusted the Senate and it went by the Constitutional book. Thus can the nation say, with Vernon Jordan, 'Mission accomplished.'"[17]

While we basically agree with the conventional wisdom in this instance, we offer one important amendment to the argument that the constitutional system worked as planned. Our constitutional framework was premised on the framers' distrust of the unwashed masses. The Electoral College, the indirect election of Senators, and the system of separated powers are testament to that basic truth. The elaborate system of checks and balances gave rise to a limited central government that was intended to control the passions of the public.

However, with Clinton's impeachment, public opinion served as a moderating influence on the institutions rather than the other way around. Furthermore, the House of Representatives was supposed to be the institution that would be responsive to the wishes of the people while the Senate would be more removed from the public, by virtue of its six-year term and indirect election. However, the partisan Republicans in the House ignored the consistent public support for the President and opposition to impeachment. Frustrated House Managers said they were "baffled" by the strong public support for the President and could not believe that the public would not listen to their pleas to "uphold the rule of law." The Senate, despite all its rhetoric about not listening to the public and reaching an independent judgment, proved to be more responsive to public opinion (although the level of partisanship there was as high as in the House). Thus, the intended role for the two chambers was reversed.

## Evidence for the Absent Aftermath

Evidence for the absence of an aftermath is abundant. Most obviously, Clinton remained in office and finished his second term. His wife is now a Senator from New York. Clinton maintained a reasonably good relationship with the Speaker of the House, which helped produce an average level of success in getting his agenda passed, despite the predictions that his presidency would be mired in postimpeachment partisanship and rancor. Clinton's Vice President had the chance to succeed him in office, and his popularity remained at remarkably high levels. Finally, impeachment was a nonissue in the 2000 congressional or presidential elections, contrary to predictions made immediately after Clinton's acquittal in the Senate.[18]

Most of this evidence for the "no aftermath" argument is self-evident. However, two points require more extensive discussion—Clinton's interactions with Congress and the electoral fallout. Unlike the other issues that we have discussed to this point, the definitive answers on these topics will not be known until early 2001. Thus we are heading into the dangerous waters of political prognosis that have been so treacherous for the impeachment issue. We will also discuss one area in which the impeachment fallout may have some long-term consequences—the institution of the presidency.

### Governing after Impeachment

Congress was extremely partisan and acrimonious in the year leading up to impeachment and for several months after the Senate's acquittal. Republicans fumed as it became evident that Clinton would survive. Democratic supporters of the President wanted revenge for what they viewed as a partisan attempt to overturn the results of the 1996 and 1998 elections. The rhetoric was overheated, even by the standards of Washington politics. One of the most publicized incidents was when Representative Dan Burton (R-Ind.) called the President a "scumbag" (or, as the *New York Times* put it more delicately, "a vulgarity for a condom"),[19] and refused to apologize for the outburst. A few months later Representative J. D. Hayworth (R-Ariz.) called Clinton an "unprincipled, philandering president" who had presided over "the most corrupt administration in U.S. history."[20] The public maintained two positions throughout the process. As Ann Coulter, author of *High Crimes and Misdemeanors: The Case against Bill Clinton* and a regular columnist in *Human Events,* explained, "According to a recent *USA Today*/CNN/Gallup Poll, 81% call Clinton's presidency a success. Yet similarly whopping majorities view him as a lying pervert." (Coulter does not mince words when expressing her views about the President. In her book she called him a "horny hick.")[21]

The public continued to express confidence that Clinton could govern in the immediate aftermath of impeachment, with a February 11, 1999 Gallup poll showing that 77 percent of the public believed that Clinton could "govern effectively." But many commentators feared that the government would grind to a halt as partisan tensions remained high. Republicans were not in the mood to deal with Clinton and several key leaders, including House Majority Leader Dick Armey (R-Tex.), House Whip Tom DeLay (R-Tex.), and Senate Majority Leader Trent Lott (R-Miss.), did not trust the President. "If he lied to the American people, his closest advisors, and under oath in a court of law," they argued, "how do we know that he's not lying to us now?"

The evidence coming from Capitol Hill in the early months of 1999 seemed to validate the concerns over gridlock. The Senate dragged its feet on approving presidential appointments, especially for the judiciary. Major legislative initiatives, including Social Security reforms, were derailed. The acrimony even spilled over into the foreign policy realm, where Congress is typically more willing to defer to the President. In one key incident on April 29, 1999, the House failed to support a resolution endorsing the NATO bombing campaign in Kosovo (by a tie 213-213 vote). Tom DeLay actively worked to defeat the resolution and only thirty-one Republicans supported Clinton's position. Speaker Hastert voted in favor, but remained on the sidelines. An angry Richard Gephardt (D-Mo.) blamed "right-wing extremists" in the House for producing "a low moment in foreign policy and the history of the institution."[22] Six months later the Senate rejected a treaty to ban the testing of nuclear weapons that Clinton had negotiated (by a 48-51 vote). The rest of the year was not much better, as Clinton's success rate in Congress in 1999 hit the second-lowest level since the *Congressional Quarterly* started keeping records in 1953: 37.8 percent (the only lower mark was Clinton's 36.2 percent level in 1995). This compares to success rates of 50.6 percent, 53.6 percent, and 55.1 percent in the previous three years (1996–98).[23]

While 1999 was not an especially productive year, and 2000 probably will not be much better, Clinton's troubles with Congress cannot be attributed to the fallout from impeachment. The Senate's obstructionism on appointments was hardly new, having emerged in 1995. The legislative productivity of 1999–2000 does not appear to be much different than the last two years of the other two-term presidents since the Twenty-Second Amendment was ratified—Eisenhower and Reagan. According to David Mayhew's landmark study on lawmaking within a divided government, only five pieces of significant legislation were signed into law in Eisenhower's last two years (1959–60). Reagan was more productive, getting twelve pieces of major legislation passed in his last two years (which is exactly the average over a two-year period for all post–World War II presidents).[24] However, the relative activity of the 1987–88 Congress can be credited to the hyperactive Speaker Jim Wright (D-Tex.), more than the lame-duck leadership of President Reagan.

It is too early to know how many pieces of significant legislation will pass in Clinton's last two years, but it probably will be somewhere between Eisenhower and Reagan. Thus far, it appears unlikely that he will have success on entitlement reform, campaign finance reform, fast track authority on trade policy, major tax cuts, or healthcare. However, given improved relations between Clinton and Speaker Hastert and the confluence of electoral and historical incentives that we will outline below, Clinton and the Republican Congress are likely to have a fairly decent record in the last two years. Major legislation that passed in 1999 included banking overhaul, a missile defense program, and new rules on satellite television. So far the only major bill to pass in 2000 has been permanent normal trade relations for China. However, at least some of the following issues are likely to be acted upon before this Congress adjourns: an incremental step on campaign finance (having to do with disclosure of funding for issue advocacy ads), bankruptcy overhaul, electricity deregulation, an internet tax moratorium, managed care regulation, "marriage penalty" tax relief, product liability claims, and an increase in the minimum wage.

To the extent that Clinton and congressional Republicans are not successful on a broad range of issues, it will be more attributable to the 2000 elections than impeachment. With control of the House within their reach, congressional Democrats have little incentive to compromise with Republicans; Democrats hope to get some political mileage out of running against a "do-nothing Congress." However, congressional Republicans and Clinton have strong incentives to work together. The Republicans desperately want to pass enough important legislation to avoid the "do-nothing" tag and to increase their chances of maintaining control of the House.[25] Clinton wants to go out with some historical achievements to help remove the stigma of impeachment from his political legacy. In his 1999 State of the Union message, which was delivered shortly before the Senate acquitted him, the President presented an ambitious agenda that was "more characteristic of a first term than a political exit."[26] While Republicans are not interested in much of this agenda, there is some common ground. For example, a package deal of tax incentives for small business and a minimum wage increase would attract majority support in Congress and the President's signature.

A similar set of circumstances produced unexpected cooperation between congressional Republicans and Clinton in 1996. After the government shutdown and public battles between Clinton and Gingrich, few predicted that they would pass major legislation on welfare reform, crime, healthcare, and a minimum wage increase shortly before the fall elections. Whether overlapping incentives will produce a similar flurry of activity in the second half of 2000 remains to be seen. However, it seems clear that lingering bitterness over impeachment is not driving the legislative process at the end of Clinton's presidency.

### Elections 2000—"Does Anybody Care about Impeachment?"

In the month following the acquittal, many pundits argued that the impeachment would loom large in the 2000 elections. Congressional Republicans continued to believe that the public would finally turn against the President, and by implication Democrats who supported him, if they made "trust" and "character" central themes in the campaign. Democrats were equally convinced that there would be a public uprising against the House Republicans who led the witch-hunt. For example, Ronald Dworkin argued, "In the 2000 elections we should support congressional challengers who run against the impeachment managers, and who make the illegitimacy of the impeachment a campaign issue."[27] Backlash against the impeachment leaders got an unexpected boost early in the process from pornography mogul Larry Flynt, who started his own campaign to expose hypocritical politicians who criticized Clinton while carrying on their own extramarital affairs. Flynt took out full-page ads in the national newspapers offering one million dollars to anyone who would come forward with evidence of an affair with a member of Congress. Bob Barr (R-Ga.) and Henry Hyde (R-Ill.), two of the House Managers, both had their extramarital affairs exposed but did not suffer any serious political damage. The one prominent victim of Flynt's campaign, mentioned in the introduction to this chapter, was Speaker Robert Livingston (R-La.), who resigned his seat in Congress just as his own personal indiscretions were about to be exposed. Fueled by Clinton's claim that he would "wage a personal crusade" against his foes, Clinton's supporters established a web site early in 1999 that promised to raise millions of dollars toward that end. Trent Lott (R-Miss.) said it was "deeply troubling that the president views closure of this constitutional process as an opportunity for revenge."[28] However, little appears to have come from this effort.

The absence of a backlash against the House Managers has not translated into an electoral boost for Republicans. Impeachment is simply a nonissue in the 2000 elections. Both parties tested impeachment-related ads early in the election season, but they have largely disappeared. The Republican National Committee ran an ad in targeted congressional districts on the budget process. The ad opens with the word "Remember?" across the screen as the announcer says, "Remember the double-talk?" It then accuses the President of engaging in double-talk on budget negotiations. One Democratic challenger, Jay Inslee of Washington, ran an ad attacking Representative Rick White (R-Wash.) for supporting Clinton's impeachment. However, this strategy has not spread to other races and has not come up in the presidential race.

Perhaps the starkest evidence for the absence of an aftermath in the electoral arena is the stunning lack of success of the House Managers' PAC that was established in July 1999 to support Republican candidates who may have been politically damaged by their position on impeachment. The stated goal of the PAC was to "develop a base of at least 500,000 people who would provide contributions and volunteer support for Republican candidates."[29] Through the first three months of 2000, the Managers' PAC raised $75,082.97 and listed only two contributions to Republican candidates: $5,000 to James Rogan (R-Calif.) and $319 to Chris Cannon (R-Utah).[30]

Early in the election season it appeared that one identifiable consequence of impeachment would be that it helped a few targeted Republicans raise money from "Clinton-haters." Three of the top fifty fund-raisers through the end of 1999 were House Managers, and two of them were numbers one and six (James Rogan and Bob Barr, respectively). By the end of the March reporting period, Rogan had raised $3.8 million while his challenger, state Senator Adam Schiff, had raised $1.8 million. This could end up as the costliest House race in U.S. history. Rogan has used the impeachment issue in his fund-raising letters, saying that because Clinton is out to get him for revenge, he has to defend himself. However, the issue has not appeared in the campaign. Instead, one of the hottest issues in the campaign has been the slaughter of 1.5 million Armenians at the hands of the Turks from 1915 to 1923. The large Armenian population in Rogan's district wants the Administration to pressure Turkey to call the deaths a "genocide."[31] The campaign is also revolving around other local issues such as the Burbank airport and housing development in the Verdugo Mountains.[32] The race is seen as too close to call. In the only other close race involving a House Manager, Bill McCollum is running behind Democrat Bill Nelson in the Florida Senate contest. Again McCollum has used impeachment in fund-raising letters, but it has not been an issue in the campaign.

## Institutional Implications

Several possible institutional implications should be briefly noted. First, as we mentioned above, one consequence of the impeachment saga was the death of the Independent Counsel law on June 30, 1999. Under the new regulations the Attorney General will exert much more control over politically sensitive investigations.[33] Second, damage may have been done to the institution of the presidency in four areas: Secret Service protection, executive privilege, confidentiality of communication with advisors, and future "harassment" lawsuits. Several former presidents and the Clinton Administration argued that Secret Service agents should not have to testify about the conduct of the President. This could lead future presidents to excuse agents from the room, when they may be needed for protection. The topic of executive privilege is too vast to explore in detail here, but our sense is that future presidents' use of executive privilege has not been dramatically changed by the Clinton affair. After surveying the case law on presidential privilege, Robert Spitzer concluded that "these cases fortify presidential prerogative as much as, if not more than, they erode it, primarily because the affected presidential actions represent such a small portion of formal official duties, powers, and responsibilities."[34]

We see the last two institutional implications as potentially the most serious. Presidents need to be able to talk to their advisors without concern that they will be hauled before a court to testify about the conversation. Presidents need to be able to try out crazy ideas and talk about things in private that they would not want to say in public. It remains to be seen how future presidents will be affected by Kenneth Starr's investigation of Clinton, but damage may have been done to the advising networks in the White House. Finally, we have little doubt that future presidents will be subjected to harassing lawsuits because of the colossal error in judgment by the Supreme Court in *Jones v. Clinton*: "If the past is any indicator, it seems unlikely that a deluge of such litigation will ever engulf the Presidency. As for the case at hand, if properly managed by the District Court, it appears to us highly unlikely to occupy any substantial amount of petitioner's time." Have less prescient words ever been uttered by the Court?

Despite these possible institutional implications (and we stress *possible* because these consequences will not be known for at least a decade), the aftermath of the impeachment is far less significant than almost all political observers were predicting a year ago.

## Conclusion

How did Clinton manage to survive, in the face of compelling evidence that he *did* perjure himself in both the original Lewinsky deposition and in his grand jury testimony (and more than likely obstructed justice as well)? And why has the impeachment's legacy shrunk to nearly undetectable levels? In our view, these two questions are almost identical, for the answer to one tells us much that we need to know about the other.

The received wisdom attributes Clinton's survival to (1) the public's willingness to distinguish between official misconduct and even the most prurient private misdeeds; (2) confidence in Clinton's official performance as President, as typified by the health of the economy; (3) strategic blunders by Republicans, who were too often viewed as more interested in settling old scores than in running the country; (4) perceptions that Starr was running an inquisition rather than a legitimate law enforcement investigation; and (5) public revulsion at the hypocritical moral stances taken by political leaders whose own peccadilloes often could match the President indiscretion for indiscretion.[35] A less sympathetic view is that Clinton got through with his long-standing pattern of trashing his opponents and relying on endless stonewalling to blunt the impact of his own misbehavior.[36]

All these explanations are true to some degree. But with the benefit of hindsight, we find it telling that public support for impeaching Clinton has actually *risen* in the past year. In December 1998, 35 percent of the public approved of the House decision to impeach Clinton. In December 1999, 50 percent approved. In February 1999, 64 percent of the public approved of the Senate vote to acquit; in December 1999, approval had dropped to 57 percent.[37] One reasonable interpretation of these numbers

is that in the teeth of a process that could have resulted in Clinton's removal, much of the public recoiled. One year later, when the question of
removal was hypothetical, people were more likely to voice their disapproval of Clinton. Whether this has anything to do with Starr or GOP
tactics, we cannot say (although we suspect there is something there). But
it does suggest that there is a built-in public presumption against using
the ultimate constitutional tool without "smoking gun" evidence of presidential malfeasance. And unlike constitutional scholars such as Akhil
Amar, who has voiced concern that the Clinton impeachment scandal has
weakened the presidency as an institution, we are more sanguine about
the prospects of the presidency making a full recovery.[38] The presidency
has shown a remarkable ability to adapt to changing political and legal
contexts (Ronald Reagan was elected only six and a half years after Nixon
resigned), and, as Robert Spitzer has noted, "one may not simply assume
that a weak or failed presidency . . . automatically injures the institution
or that the injury lingers long after the term of that particular 'failed'
president."[39] The President, even under adverse conditions, retains an
often-decisive ability to shape agendas and create new policy structures,
and these advantages are driven by the inherent character of the office
rather than by the political skill of any one Chief Executive.[40]

## NOTES

1. "Clinton: There Is No Improper Relationship," Federal News Service Transcript, *Washington Post*, January 22, 1998, A13; John F. Harris, "Clinton Denies
Affair," *Washington Post*, January 22, 1998, A1.

2. Richard Berke, "White House Acts to Contain Furor as Concern Grows,"
*New York Times*, January 26, 1998, A1.

3. www.gallup.com/poll/releases/pr980123.asp. A January 1999 Gallup poll,
conducted just before the Senate trial, found that a majority was, in fact, convinced that Clinton had lied under oath (79 percent) and had obstructed justice
(53 percent). www.gallup.com/poll/releases/pr990116.asp.

4. Dan Balz, "Leading Senate Democrat Blasts Clinton's Behavior," *Washington Post*, September 4, 1998; Ceci Connolly, "Gephardt Says Clinton Could Be
Impeached," *Washington Post*, August 26, 1998.

5. Dan Balz, "On Defensive, Hill GOP Weighs Strategy for Clinton Inquiry,"
*Washington Post*, September 29, 1998.

6. Karen Forestel, "Elections Expected to Produce Modest Gains for Republicans," *Congressional Quarterly*, October 24, 1998; Karen Forestel, "Senate: GOP

on the March," *Congressional Quarterly*, October 24, 1998. William Kristol had predicted in October that Republicans would gain forty seats; Janny Scott, "The Speaker Steps Down: The Pundits; Talking Heads' Post Mortem: 'All Wrong, All the Time,'" *New York Times*, November 8, 1998.

7. Ceci Connolly, "Three Years of Missteps, One Sudden Fall," *Washington Post*, November 8, 1998.

8. *Congressional Record*, January 14, 1999, S59-02.

9. *Congressional Record*, February 8, 1999, S1344.

10. Statement of Sean Wilentz before the House Judiciary Committee, December 8, 1998, 2. Available at <http://www.house.gov/judiciary/101325.pdf>.

11. *Congressional Record*, December 17, 1998, H11782.

12. Ronald Dworkin, "A Kind of Coup," *New York Review of Books*, January 14, 1999, 61.

13. *Congressional Record*, December 18, 1998, H11918.

14. Richard L. Berke and James Bennet, "The President's Trial: The House Race," *New York Times*, February 11, 1999.

15. Roberto Suro, "Clinton Is Sanctioned in Jones Lawsuit," *Washington Post*, July 30, 1999.

16. Quoted in R. W. Apple, "The President's Acquittal: News Analysis," *New York Times*, February 13, 1999, A1.

17. William Safire, "Let the Perp Walk," *New York Times*, February 11, 1999, A33.

18. It is possible to argue that one item on this list, Hillary's Senate campaign, may actually be seen as a consequence of impeachment: without the public sympathy that Hillary Clinton received as the victim of her husband's philandering, her Senate campaign may not have been as credible.

19. Don Van Natta, "Panel Chief Refuses to Apologize to Clinton," *New York Times*, April 23, 1998, A20.

20. Michael Murphy, "'Kinder' Hayworth Mails Vitriolic Fund Letter," *Arizona Republic*, July 15, 1998, A1.

21. Ann Coulter, "Polls Don't Say What Pollsters Say They Say," *Human Events* 55:6 (February 12, 1999): 6.

22. Karen Hosler, "House Leaders Trade Recriminations: Tie Vote on Airstrikes Shows Political Fissure," *Baltimore Sun*, April 30, 1999, 1A.

23. *Congressional Quarterly Weekly*, 57:48 (December 11, 1999): 2987.

24. David R. Mayhew, *Divided We Govern: Party Control, Lawmaking, and Investigations, 1946–1990* (New Haven: Yale University Press, 1991), 52–73.

25. Lizette Alvarez, "House Republicans Fret About 'Do Nothing' Tag," *New York Times*, February 12, 1999, A1.

26. Sue Kirchhoff, "Activist President Presses on in Hope of Tempering History's Judgement," *CQ Weekly* 57:5 (January 30, 1999): 238.

27. Ronald Dworkin, "The Wounded Constitution," *New York Review of Books*, March 18, 1999.

28. Alison Mitchell, "The President's Trial: The Overview," *New York Times*, February 12, 1999, A1.

29. Tom Squitieri, "Impeachment Managers Go Online," *USA Today*, July 7, 1999, 1.

30. Federal Election Commission web site (www.fec.gov).

31. William Booth, "The Battle for the House; Ignoring Impeachment; in California's 27th, Rogan and Rival Woo Armenians with Issues beyond Clinton's Trial," *Washington Post*, May 10, 2000, A6.

32. Jean Merl, "Elections/27th Congressional District; Local Issues Key to High-Profile Race; Rogan's Role in Clinton Impeachment Puts Contest in Spotlight, but the Campaign Stresses Voters' Other Concerns," *Los Angeles Times*, April 18, 2000, B1.

33. Roberto Suro, "As Special Counsel Law Expires, Power Will Shift to Reno," *Washington Post*, June 30, 1999, A6.

34. Robert Spitzer, "Clinton's Impeachment Will Have Few Consequences for the Presidency," *PS: Political Science and Politics* 32 (September 1999): 543.

35. See, for example, John Zaller, "Monica Lewinsky's Contribution to Political Science," *PS: Political Science and Politics* 31 (June 1998): 182–87.

36. Charles Paul Freund, "Secrets of the Clinton Spectacle," *Reason* 31 (April 2000): 22–28.

37. Data are from the Gallup Poll, www.gallup.com/poll/releases/pr991221.asp.

38. Akhil Amar, "The Unimperial Presidency," *New Republic*, March 8, 1999.

39. Spitzer, "Clinton's Impeachment Will Have Few Consequences for the Presidency," 541.

40. Kenneth R. Mayer, *With the Stroke of a Pen: Executive Orders and Presidential Power* (Princeton: Princeton University Press, forthcoming 2001).

# Chapter 5

# Pierre Elliot Trudeau
## *A Canadian Scandal?*

## *Leon E. Trakman*

The attack on the personal morality of Pierre Elliot Trudeau, one-time flamboyant Prime Minister of Canada, is comparable only in some respects to the scandal surrounding Bill Clinton.[1] Trudeau's "crimes" were grounded in his politics and only secondarily in his lifestyle. His perceived public harm lay in his federalist loyalties and his distributive agenda. His "crimes" were an unqualified hostility toward Canadian separatists and his left-leaning economic and social agenda. The excuse for undressing him publicly was provided by moral outrage at his audacious personality and grandiloquent lifestyle.

What Bill Clinton and Canadian Prime Minister Pierre Elliot Trudeau had most in common, however, was the public reconstruction of their personae. An arrogant intellectual with a political mission, Trudeau was recast by the media as a moral degenerate, a fun-seeking fop who danced while Canada burned. A reluctant confessor to infidelity, Clinton was cast as a political ogre who carelessly dismantled the political and religious fabric of American society. In truth neither man was truly cast or fairly judged. Both Emperors were dressed—and undressed—as much by attributes ascribed to them as by norms possessed by them. Their clothes of degeneracy were provided, in some measure, by a libertarian right aided by media sensationalism.

The moral "sins" of these two men, however, were also depicted differently. Pierre Elliot Trudeau's personality invited caricature. Talk about his womanizing popularized more than it harmed him. Rumors about his alleged bisexuality remained just that. Trudeau's critics concentrated on his political agenda, his vision of Canada, his social and economic reform agenda, and his authoritarian style of leadership. Unlike Bill Clinton, no sexual slur or lie threatened to unseat him. Trudeau was depicted in Quebec as a traitor who surrendered his native land to English Canada. In much of English Canada, by contrast, he was seen as a social reformer who forfeited capitalism to socialism and prosperity to national debt. Behind disaffection with Pierre Elliot Trudeau was *patent* affront at his political ideology, fervent nationalism, socialist leanings, and dictatorial means of fulfilling his agenda. Although his sexual morality provided some ammunition for those who attacked him, it was seldom the center of their attacks. Unlike Clinton, Trudeau was more frequently criticized for his candor than his lack of it. Like Nixon, Trudeau resorted to contentious means to satisfy his ends. Unlike both, he paid a smaller price for his excesses.

Behind disaffection with Bill Clinton was the depiction of him as a degenerate who had surrendered decency itself. He was condemned for his sexual transgressions and for lying about them. Attacks on Trudeau, in contrast, centered on his politics. He was eventually disempowered because of his political agenda, not his sexual proclivities.

This essay is primarily about the orchestrated undressing of Pierre Elliot Trudeau, the politician. The undressing of Bill Clinton, the man, is left to other essays in this volume. Comparisons are odious; but they *are* interesting.

## Focal Points

Several questions linger about Pierre Elliot Trudeau the man. To what political values did he ascribe? How did he manifest or promote those values? How similar were his values to those of Bill Clinton? These and other questions are considered in relation to two of Trudeau's political values. First, Trudeau displayed a vehement antipathy toward separatists in Quebec who sought sovereignty-association with the rest of Canada. Second, Trudeau sought to extend the social net in Canada. In seeking to further both these values, Trudeau's assailing wit and aggressive argument contrast starkly with Clinton's conciliatory style. Where Clinton perfected the art of compromise as a means of political survival, Trudeau used confrontation to accomplish his idealized ends.

No analysis of Trudeau would be complete without considering the relationship between his personal style and politics. Was this Quebec aris-

tocrat with socialist leanings fiscally irresponsible and the primary author of Canada's huge national debt? Was he prone to political contradiction? Was he an arrogant Nixon without a Watergate, or a sexual predator
without a Monica?

Discourse about Trudeau focuses on his political agenda, his fervent
nationalism, and his passionate war of words with separatist leaders in
his native Quebec. Let us start there.

## *Trudeau's Political Agenda*

Pierre Elliot Trudeau is alleged to have asserted that the state has no place
in the bedrooms of the nation. He included *his* bedroom. But Trudeau's
assertion was part of his political ideology. He subscribed to the separation between the public and private life of a prime minister. At the same
time, Trudeau knew that, however much Canadians scoffed at his private
life, he would not be impeached on account of it. His real sin was his political agenda and the way he went about implementing his distributive
goals. His early private jet-setting life that gave rise to unbridled Tru-
deaumania *did* fuel personal attacks on his moral character. Onslaughts
on his character in turn *did* serve as pretexts for attacks on his political
ideology. But it was his political ends themselves that were most flamma-
ble. His personal lifestyle merely helped to light the fuse. But let us start
at the beginning, if there is one.

Trudeau's elite political background is readily apparent. His resumé reflects his intellect, his commitment to political and constitutional reform,
and his relentless pursuit of federalist and egalitarian goals. Born on October 18, 1919 in Montreal, Quebec, he was the bilingual son of a francophone father and a Scottish mother. Unlike Clinton, Trudeau grew up
with wealth and social standing. He was an intellectual. A law graduate of
the University of Montreal, he earned an M.A. in Political Economy at
Harvard University in 1945. He attended the *Ecole des sciences politiques*;
and capped off his formal education in 1947 with a stint at the London
School of Economics. Called to the Quebec Bar in 1943, Trudeau combined law with politics and teaching. In 1949, he became an advisor to
the Privy Council. In 1950, he cofounded and codirected the *Cité Libre*,
an academic journal of social policy. In 1961 he became Associate Professor of Law at the University of Montreal and a researcher at the *Institut
de recherches en droit public*. Lawyer, professor, politician, and scholar,

Trudeau was ready for serious politics. He became increasingly active in the Liberal Party of Canada and became a member of Parliament. He was rewarded in 1967 with the coveted portfolio of Minister of Justice. In 1968 Pierre Elliot Trudeau became acting President of the Privy Council, leader of the Liberal Party, and Prime Minister of Canada.

Trudeau's political accomplishments were marked by both diversity and single-mindedness. Committed to law and order in unstable political times, he implemented the War Measures Act in 1970 in response to the violent "October Crisis" in Quebec.[2] Dedicated to official bilingualism in Canada, Trudeau instigated the Official Languages Act in 1969. A proponent of economic reform in inflationary times, he introduced the controversial Wage and Price Controls Act in 1975 that likely contributed more than any other single act to his political downfall.

Pierre Elliot Trudeau's most single-minded endeavors, however, lay in his federalism and his left-leaning agenda for social and economic reform. Trudeau earnestly desired to wrench Canada from its colonial roots. Even more vehement was his opposition to Quebec separatism. Trudeau played a historic role in the victory of the "no" forces in the Quebec Referendum on Sovereignty-Association in 1980. In 1982 he oversaw the repatriation of the Canadian Charter of Rights and Freedoms from the United Kingdom. That same year, he presided over the enactment of the Constitution Act of Canada.

By 1982, Trudeau had accomplished what no other Prime Minister had done. He had "invented" a distinctly Canadian constitution. He had also brought it home to Canada. Only partially committed to an American-style Bill of Rights, "his" Charter of Rights and Freedoms was dedicated to equality rights almost as much as to individual rights. He entrenched bilingual language rights in the Constitution and more marginally, multicultural rights. He also oversaw the redistribution of federal resources along both regional and socioeconomic lines.

Several of Trudeau's victories, however, also proved to be his Achilles' heel. His first weakness derived from his open hostility toward Quebec separatists who threatened his image of a unified Canada. A further source of vulnerability lay in his commitment to the redistribution of wealth along egalitarian lines. Each of these weaknesses gave rise to its particular detractors. Each is a saga in itself.

For much of his political career, Trudeau was placed in a contradictory yet typecast box. His critics in Quebec depicted him as an instrument of English Canada. In their view, he was a traitor to his native Quebec and his francophone roots. His critics in English Canada, notably those in the West, condemned him for imposing a contemptible "Quebec-style" socialism upon Canada as a whole. Trudeau's box was formidable indeed. The left side was constructed by passionate separatists in Quebec. The right side was devised by single-minded libertarians in Western Canada. Each side blamed him for perpetuating the ills of the other.

In some respects, Trudeau found the box convenient. The critique of the Quebec separatists helped as much as it hindered him. His loss of support in Quebec, after all, contributed to the growth of his support in English Canada, particularly at a time when Quebec separatism seemed to threaten the very dissolution of Canada. The critique of Trudeau's social and economic agenda from the libertarian right, however, was a far greater threat to his political life than his resistence to Quebec separatism. Not unlike right-wing critiques of Bill Clinton, Trudeau's conservative detractors feared that he might erode their libertarian values. They argued that he would relentlessly increase taxation and introduce an ever-widening array of costly social programs at the expense of individual rights. These fears were grounded in fact. A self-assured yet moderate egalitarian, Trudeau practiced what he preached. He enunciated an agenda for the redistribution of wealth that he implemented in the Canadian Parliament through his Liberal government.

Despite his political empowerment, however, Trudeau faltered. His allies within the largely English-speaking electorate ultimately deserted him. He did not face a Clinton-like impeachment, only to continue to enjoy high popular approval ratings. Eventually he lost his base of popular support in English Canada as he had done earlier among moderate separatists in Quebec. Despite his federalist leanings, he was ultimately discredited because he was a Quebecer. He was chastised for repressing the capitalist spirit of Canada. He was defeated because his protection of Canada from the threat of separatism was less valued in English Canada than the egalitarian agenda they imputed to him.

## Trudeau, the Man

The romance with Trudeau, the man, began in the late 1960s. Not unlike the decade-old image of Bill Clinton as a debonaire and charming man, Trudeau's youthful charm gave rise to his popular appeal. More flamboyant than Bill Clinton, Trudeau was a youthful, swaggering Prime Minister. He dressed with flash and lived in kind. But in 1971, Trudeau married. Still armed with dashing flash, he supposedly swept a twenty-two-year-old, beautiful, wealthy English Canadian, Margaret Sinclair, off her feet. They had three sons and a torrid marriage. Unlike the Clintons to date, they had a public divorce in 1984.

Canadians shared in the bitter quarrels of the Trudeau family and took sides as well. The indiscretion of the Trudeaus lay in the public nature of their marriage and divorce. Their popular appeal lay in their glamour. Their shame derived from a media that painted them in the color and temper of the day. Trudeau was variously depicted as the victim of an emotional, unstable, and demanding wife and as a cold and indifferent husband.

Their marriage ended as it had begun, with extravagant overstatement, now characterized by blame and bitterness. The public was tired of, but still fascinated by, this enticing couple. It too had gone through the divorce of its Prime Minister and his beautiful wife.

In her postdivorce life, Margaret Trudeau entered another world of glitz, globe-trotting with the likes of the Rolling Stones. Pierre dated the rich and famous, including Barbra Streisand and others of her ilk. Margaret Trudeau faded from public view. Pierre Trudeau resurfaced as a partisan Federalist in the mid-1990s, contemptuously challenging Quebec's separatist government at carefully chosen times. He resurfaced again as the out-of-wedlock father of a child born to a prominent young liberal woman. Canadians, for the most part, did not cry foul. No "Monica scandal" erupted. Some thought that the older Trudeau still had what it took; he was no longer Prime Minister and was free to engage in a consensual relationship; there was no violated wife. The conservative mainstream press did little to fuel public sentiment against him. There were a few low punches emanating primarily from Quebec. Most newspapers, however, kept silent.

Margaret and Pierre Trudeau again emerged, as a couple, several years later. This time they quietly endured the pain of tragic death, as their youngest son died in a skiing accident. Whatever their failings, the Trudeaus seemed to be caring parents, not unlike Bill and Hilary Clinton. Some Canadians mourned with them. Others complained that a greater effort had been made to find the missing Trudeau than would have been made for an "ordinary" Canadian. Many simply read the news.

Trudeau, the man, had a complex personality. He was, among other things, a man of conviction and force, steadfast in political resolve, uncompromising on matters of principle, and also bound by conscience. These personal characteristics are unlikely to be first-choice descriptions for Bill Clinton. At the same time, both men likely *are* complex personalities. Any comparison between them should also take into account the differences between them in time, place, and space. I will return to this later.

Two narratives describe some of Trudeau's personal attributes. The one presents Trudeau standing his ground on a matter of conscience, possibly at the expense of his then-fledgling career. The other features him as an older man, aggressively challenging Quebec separatists long after he had completed his term as Prime Minister of Canada. Let us take a brief look at each narrative.

Some time before Trudeau became Prime Minister, he was asked to lead a human rights delegation to the United Nations. Disagreeing with the Canadian government's position on moral grounds, Trudeau is reputed to have removed himself from the delegation and the Canadian government was forced to replace him. Politically ambitious though he was, Pierre Elliot Trudeau appeared to be unwilling to lend his voice to a cause that offended his conscience. It would be harsh to suggest that Clinton lacks conscience. It would be reasonable to suppose, however, that few politicians would stand steadfast on moral grounds at the expense of their political ambitions. Al Gore's somewhat disingenuous position on the refugee status of Elian Gonzalez well illustrates this point.

The second narrative depicts an aging Trudeau engaging in a war of words with the separatist government of Quebec. Responding to criticism by the separatist premier of Quebec, Lucien Bouchard, of his constitutional reforms of years before, Trudeau bluntly retorted:

> I accuse Lucien Bouchard [the Premier of Quebec] of having betrayed the population of Quebec during last October's referendum campaign [on sovereignty-association with Canada]. By distorting the political history of his province and of his country, by spreading discord among its citizens with his demagogic rhetoric and by preaching contempt for those Canadians who did not share his view, Lucien Bouchard went beyond the limits of honest and democratic debate. Truth must be restored in order to rehabilitate democracy in Quebec.[3]

Yet there was another side to the complex Trudeau. This side was affirmative, imaginative, and creative. Trudeau also invited his political foes to collaborate with him in accomplishing a shared dream. He engaged in a gentle rhetoric. He disarmed with an appearance of diplomacy and Clinton-like charm. In his second article in the *Montreal Gazette* on February 17, 1996, for example, Trudeau expressed his "dream" of Quebecers actively working to unite Canada. He skillfully attributed that dream to his detractors:

> I do not doubt for one instant that they [Quebecers, including their separatist government] would be capable of making Quebec an independent country. But I have always believed that they have the stature to face a more difficult and nobler challenge—that of participating in the construction of a Canadian nation founded on democratic pluralism, institutional bilingualism and the sense of sharing.

How could Trudeau be both accuser and conciliator? How could he heap accusations of deception and betrayal upon a succession of separatist premiers in Quebec—René Lévesque, Jacques Pariseau, and Lucien Bouchard—and then disarm his detractors with dreams of strength in unity? How did he shift with the political tides of change? How could he be so different from Bill Clinton and yet be compared to him?

## Trudeau, the Nationalist

In the early 1980s Trudeau was in his last term of office. It was the greatest contest of his leadership. He wanted national unity. The Parti Québécois, the official government of Quebec, wanted to separate from Canada. The Charter of Rights and Freedoms was Trudeau's rallying call for unity. To implement it and repatriate the Constitution from the Parliament of the United Kingdom, Trudeau needed the support of the ten Canadian provinces. Eighteen months of contentious federal-provincial negotiations ensued. Political and personal differences were the order of the day. Party loyalties were stretched and divided. Government ministers dissented on constitutional issues, notably in Quebec.

The courts were called upon to provide definitive decisions on the authority of the federal and provincial governments to engage in such pervasive constitutional lawmaking. The Supreme Court of Canada and various provincial courts were required to determine the constitutional future of Canada. Could Trudeau repatriate the Constitution? What was the constitutional justification for doing so? Could Canada repatriate the constitution without the support of Quebec? What were the limits on such action? The Supreme Court ruled, in significant measure, in favor of the proposed constitutional reforms.

In 1982, nine of the ten provinces of Canada consented to the repatriation of the Canadian Constitution. Quebec Premier René Lévesque, leader of the ruling party in Quebec, dissented. Canada's new Constitution Act was signed on April 17, 1982, but without the signature of Quebec. Pierre Elliot Trudeau had won; but he had also lost. He had won his brand of Canadian unity, securing manageable compromises from nine of the ten provinces. But he had not won the political support of Quebec. However bound Quebec was by Canada's new Constitution Act, the disdain of Quebec was intractable. Trudeau never regained Quebec's support for the Constitution, and no Canadian Prime Minister has done so since.

There is likely no overpowering parallel in Clinton's presidency to date. Clinton has proposed no new constitution. He has engaged in no comparable battle over the polity. He has enunciated no commensurate national dream. But the comparison is unfair. The constitutional future of Canada was waiting for a Trudeau. The same was not so in the United States. Nor is it fair to argue that, since Bill Clinton has not had to defend the United States from separatists, he is not a committed nationalist.

## Trudeau's Political Legacy

What is the political legacy of Pierre Elliot Trudeau, the man? In a 1999 article entitled "Trudeau's Legacy Endures," Stanley Oziewicz sums up the contribution of the then eighty-year-old Trudeau. "It is 15 years since Mr Trudeau retired from politics but, love him or loathe him, his achievements still fascinate."[4] What makes Trudeau so fascinating? To ask the question is to invite debate about the man, his values, beliefs, and practices. Not unlike Bill Clinton, Trudeau was criticized as a sexist and also for sexual excesses attributed to him in his "private" life. But in his public life, Trudeau pioneered gender-based reform. His political triumphs included, among others, the 1972 appointment of Muriel McQueen Fergusson as the first woman Speaker of the Senate, and in 1980, the appointment of Jeanne Sauve as the first woman Speaker of the House of Commons. His supporters lauded these appointments as trailblazing. His detractors saw them as nothing less than political opportunism. The truth likely lies somewhere in between. Some would argue that a comparable tension between gender affirmation and sexual excess applies to Bill Clinton.

If Trudeau was, indeed, a trailblazer, what trails did he blaze and how did he go about blazing them? Take, for example, Trudeau's vision of bilingualism and multiculturalism in Canada. In September 1965, long before he spearheaded the adoption of a new Canadian constitution, Trudeau declared that a constitution can permit the coexistence of different cultures and ethnic groups within a single state. He retained these beliefs throughout his career as Prime Minister despite strong opposition, and enshrined them in a Charter of Rights and Freedoms. He argued for a Canada that promoted, not merely tolerated, cultural difference. His federal state was multicultural, and it consisted of more than the sum of its discrete cultural parts.

The triumph of these beliefs constituted Trudeau's greatest victory. He promoted the constitutionality of his federalist vision. But therein also lay his greatest failure: the disquiet of Quebec, and over time the political estrangement of Western Canada. He fostered beliefs that were visionary yet short-lived, empowering but also disempowering. He enriched the Canadian state but he also sowed disharmony within it.

There are few fair comparisons between Trudeau and Clinton in this regard. Trudeau ascended to the prime ministership in a young country that prided itself on its "cultural mosaic." Clinton ascended to the presidency in an America in which rugged individualism transcended multiculturalism. Canada was prepared for the constitution which Trudeau introduced. America had no corresponding expectation of Bill Clinton.

Trudeau's successes and failures are best understood in light of debate over the political constancy of his vision, the manifestation of that vision in practice, and the legacy it left behind. Reflections on Bill Clinton will be added on occasion.

## Political Inconsistency?

Pierre Elliot Trudeau has been accused of being politically inconsistent. One inconsistency imputed to him is that he recognized cultural differences *in* Canada, including Quebec, while denying the distinctiveness *of* Quebec. Furthermore, he is said to have favored the constitutional entrenchment of individual liberty while simultaneously adhering to a social reform agenda that repressed individual liberty. However, I would argue that neither inconsistency imputed to him was evidence of inconstancy.

Trudeau readily acknowledged cultural differences in Canada. These acknowledgments are evident in his constitutional endorsement of bilingual education, multiculturalism, denominational schools, and Native rights within the Charter of Rights and Freedoms. But Trudeau fervently denied that Quebec was sufficiently "distinctive" culturally to warrant according it legally "distinct" status. His refusal to treat Quebec distinctively in law is not inconsistent with his acceptance of cultural difference in Canada, including in Quebec. After all, Trudeau adhered to a vision of Canada as a pluralistic state. He sought unity in cultural diversity, not political division. He envisaged Canada as more than the sum of its provincial parts and Quebec as an integral part of the whole of Canada. According to this view, there was every reason to resist separatists who sought to dissociate Quebec from the rest of Canada. There was no justification for according political sovereignty to Quebec.

Trudeau is also accused of having fluctuated between adherence to liberal individualism and to the welfare state. In truth, Trudeau was a pragmatist who was both a liberal and a social democrat. Despite his reservations about the rugged individualism adopted by Canada's neighbor to the south, Trudeau subscribed to significant elements of that liberal dream. Section 7 of "his" Charter of Rights and Freedoms enunciated the sanctity of "life, liberty and security of the person." Section 2 entrenched individual rights like the freedom of expression and association. At the same time, Trudeau conceived of the Canadian state as a social democracy that justified constraining individual liberty. Section 1 of the Charter justified limiting individual rights in the interests of a "free and democratic society." Section 15 protected equality rights from the exercise of individual rights on enumerated and analogous grounds. Section 25 preserved the treaty and related rights of aboriginal people from the exercise of both individual rights and state powers. In so balancing individual, group, and state rights and powers, Trudeau was being politically pragmatic. If the whole of Canada was to be greater than the sum of its parts, Trudeau reasoned, the Charter ought to protect both individual and group rights. If Canada was to be whole, there was no virtue in justifying either individual rights at the expense of group identity, or the converse.

None of this is to suggest that Trudeau's career was without ambivalence. Trudeau, for example, fluctuated between modest admiration for a rights-conscious United States in his early years as Prime Minister to disdain in his latter years for the manner in which it exercised its power globally. He criticized American foreign policy on the grounds, *inter alia*, that it was intolerant of other nations. Yet he agreed to allow the United

States to conduct cruise missile testing over Canadian airspace, despite strong opposition in Canada.

Nor was Trudeau's ambivalence wholly unprincipled. Pierre Elliot Trudeau appreciated the realities of global power. But he also feared its abuse. In expressing these realities and fears, he can hardly be accused of self-doubt. Nor can he be fairly challenged for lacking the courage of his convictions.

How does Bill Clinton compare to Trudeau, if at all, in matters of inconstancy? Ambivalence can certainly be attributed to Bill Clinton. So can pragmatism. Bill Clinton, one can argue, is a capitalist who is ambivalent about the reach of capitalism and is sometimes simply pragmatic. One can argue further that he is ambivalent about guilt and confession and pragmatic in responding to the aftershock of discovery. A less kind word would be "guileless," but pragmatism takes many forms. Trudeau dressed his guile in the garb of sophistry, just as Clinton dressed his in engaging charm.

## Trudeau's Downfall

What caused Trudeau's political downfall? Trudeau's demise can be attributed primarily to his economic and social reform agenda, not to his position with regard to Quebec. Concerned about inflation, Trudeau dedicated himself in the 1970s and early 1980s to controlling spending. Focusing on wage and price control legislation, he alienated the right wing of the Liberal Party. Committed to a controversial federal National Energy Program, he antagonized the oil-rich west of Canada. Defeated for a short time in the late 1970s, Trudeau's Liberal government was resurrected in 1980 and finally defeated in 1984. Trudeau stepped down as party leader that same year. In so doing, he ended a career as the longest serving prime minister in the Western world. This, again, distinguishes Trudeau from two-term Bill Clinton. If Rome was to be built or burned, Trudeau had longer to do it in than Clinton.

What was Trudeau's political legacy? Many of his critics condemned him for precisely those values that they shared. Pierre Elliot Trudeau, who had so vehemently defended Canadian federalism against Quebec separatists in his beloved Province of Quebec, was denigrated by economic conservatives from English Canada as a suspect francophone reformist from Quebec. Others pointed to an apparent conflict between his francophone roots in Quebec and his commitment to a nationalism beyond Quebec. Yet others attacked his moral integrity, masking their dislike of his social and economic reforms in moral arguments.

Perhaps his strongest critics were those who waged war on his economic reforms. Well-known Canadian author and columnist Peter Newman was quite direct in his criticisms in his book *The Canadian Heritage*. Trudeau's government, he maintained, had carelessly overspent, leaving Canada with a deep legacy of debt. Illustrating his thesis, Newman charged that the Trudeau government had produced a $38.5 billion deficit over a sixteen-year period. To this, Newman said, Trudeau had added 1,200 percent to the national debt. Newman illustrated his critique by stating that what had been a $17 billion debt when Trudeau came to power had grown to over $200 billion when Trudeau was finally defeated. Newman concluded that conservative Prime Minister Brian Mulroney who succeeded Trudeau's Liberal government was left with less than 15 percent of discretionary spending power over the annual budget. Newman's inference was apparent. Trudeau's overspending had robbed the unfortunate Conservative government of the flexibility to govern Canada efficiently.

Others were even less charitable to Trudeau the person. Pierre Elliot Trudeau, they maintained, had been a self-indulgent prime minister. A coddled child of Quebec wealth with dubious morals, he had overlived and overspent at Canada's expense. He had embarked on a social reform agenda that echoed the indulgence of privilege. Being irresponsible in the extreme, he had surrendered Canada to poverty, just as he had abandoned Quebec to Canada. The analogy between Trudeau and Scott Fitzgerald's Gatsby was all too apparent. Just as Gatsby's high-born friends carelessly squandered the well-being of their hapless victims, Trudeau had carelessly squandered Canada's wealth, leaving Mulroney to bear the blame.

The truth is many-sided. Some of the criticism leveled against Trudeau was accurate. The product of wealth, he was self-indulgent. He was sometimes arrogant and contemptuous and often intolerant. But he was also a formidable Canadian and a distinguished Quebecer whose achievements contributed to his downfall. He was willing to follow his own social and economic vision. He had the courage to implement and act upon his vision. He not only said: he also did.

How does Bill Clinton's economic agenda compare to that of Trudeau? Clinton clearly stands to the right of Trudeau. His economic and social reforms are less ambitious than those championed by Trudeau. But Clinton has also contributed less to the national debt than Trudeau did. The Clinton era has been marked by comparative economic stability, low inflation, high employment, and a respectable balance of trade. Economic historians may be kinder to Bill Clinton than they were to Pierre Elliot Trudeau in this respect. But it all depends on their point of view.

### Further Parallels to Clinton

Are there further parallels between Bill Clinton and Pierre Elliot Trudeau? Some parallels can be drawn between their liberal and communitarian agendas and their conceptions of "democratic pluralism." There are limited parallels as well in their personal style, charm, and popular appeal. Both encountered their nemesis in the political right. Both were subject to challenge on moral and political grounds. Trudeau's conservative foes gathered force in Western Canada. Clinton's political detractors gathered strength in middle America and the West. Both leaders were weakened by political challenges disguised as moral condemnation.

Trudeau and Clinton also shared some personal attributes and experiences. Both were vilified as well as liked. Both were victims of political condemnation disguised as moral righteousness. Both were survivors. They also shared some political attributes. Pierre Elliot Trudeau was committed to a vision of a unified Canada along socially democratic lines. Clinton likely shared that vision in part in relation to the United States, but lacked the opportunity, political will, or both, to realize it. Both endured scandals and were condemned on sexual grounds, among others.

There are, however, real differences in the contexts surrounding these two men. Much of what Trudeau was able to do politically in Canada, Clinton could not have accomplished in the United States. Canada is a middle power. The United States is a superpower. Canada adheres to a parliamentary system of government. The United States adheres to a presidential model. Trudeau could not have prevailed over a hostile Congress as he did over a Liberal-dominated Parliament. Trudeau could not have survived the political onslaught of contemptuous Republican Senators as he dominated the Canadian Parliament. Trudeau did not face the risk of impeachment. Nor did a conservative Canadian press enclose him in a glass cage, as the American press did with Bill Clinton.

Some of the key issues faced by Trudeau were also quite different from those faced by Clinton. Trudeau's attempts to promote bilingualism in

Canada, for example, do not compare readily with Clinton's less success-ful attempts to promote biculturalism between Anglo and Mexican Americans. The United States is simply not separated by a geographical and cultural divide of the magnitude or kind that divides Quebec from English Canada.

Trudeau's era was also singularly different from that of Clinton. The paramount scandal in Trudeau's heyday lay in the undemocratic excesses of Richard Nixon. The tone of leadership, personal lifestyle, and political values of Trudeau's day were also set by Richard Nixon. Like Nixon, Trudeau was depicted as arrogant. Like Nixon, he was accused of usurp-ing the democratic process, notably in adopting the War Measures Act in his struggle against Quebec extremists. Democratic rights, powers, and privileges were the order of the day. Outrage at the sexual morality of world leaders was not in vogue then. Nor was a conservative Canadian press during Trudeau's era likely to openly debate his national leadership on account of his sexual indiscretion. The publicized debate on the sexual promiscuity of national leaders was left to the 1990s and to the leadership of Bill Clinton.

## Conclusion

What is the likely legacy of Pierre Elliot Trudeau compared to that of Bill Clinton? Trudeau likely will go down in Canadian history as a formidable leader who changed the constitutional and political landscape of Canada. He will also be remembered for his fiscal excesses. Clinton, by contrast, will more likely be remembered for the "Monica affair" than for his many economic and political successes both domestic and international. In de-fense of Clinton, his term as former President has just begun. His life after the presidency could well parallel Richard Nixon's resurrection after a humiliating abdication.

Nor do I conclude that Pierre Elliot Trudeau was a decisive leader who stood his political ground, while Clinton lost his political will when faced with frontal attacks on his moral fiber. Trudeau clearly was a strong leader. But his resilient political will was significantly bolstered by the parliamentary system in which he functioned. Trudeau had the support of the Liberal Party, and the Liberal Party constituted the government of his day. He could maintain an uncompromising stance with opposition parties in fulfilling his agenda. He could also survive politically except in the event of a no-confidence vote by Parliament in his government. Bill Clinton lacked some of these luxuries. He had to face off against a Republican-dominated Senate or Congress. He could be—and was—impeached. He had a far more significant institution to protect, namely, the presidency of the United States of America.

Had Pierre Elliot Trudeau been President of the United States, could he have implemented his social and economic vision? The answer is probably not. Trudeau held office with a majority liberal government for a significant period of his leadership. As prime minister in a constitutional democracy, he was less constrained than an American president. Contemptuous and intolerant toward his critics, he was unlikely to have secured the approval of an estranged Congress and Senate, or win the praise of a critical American press.

Given these political realities in the United States, Bill Clinton's alleged tendency to move to the right to appease his critics is understandable. His willingness to deny welfare benefits to poor Americans and reduce the capital gains tax on the wealthy is intelligible. However committed Trudeau might have been to egalitarian reform in the Canada of his day, this position is far less tenable in Bill Clinton's United States today.[5]

## Postscript

Pierre Elliot Trudeau passed away on September 28, 2000 at the age of eighty, several months after this essay was written. His death was unlike any other this country has known. He was more than a long-standing Canadian Prime Minister. He was part of almost every Canadian family, friend and foe alike. When Trudeau chastised a political challenger, Canadians debated the point at home. When he refused to leave the podium as other dignitaries ran for cover from bottle-throwing Quebec separatists, Canadians debated his tenacity. When he was acclaimed for his televised address on world peace to the U.S. Congress, Canadians were proud of his erudition, intellect, and international profile.

Pierre Elliot Trudeau stood apart from other world leaders. He was distinguished for an unparalleled passion for his country. He is remembered for an uncanny ability to combine the motley jester with the serious statesman in the same performance. Historians will depict him as having the talent of the matador and the strength of the bull. Like the matador, he knew how to goad others on. Like the bull, he had strength for the charge. Trudeau was a paradox. He was respectfully disrespectful toward his opponents. He was rationally impassioned in articulating his ideas.

Trudeau's flaws—and they were many—were quite human. Prone to youthful tomfoolery, he informed fellow Canadians that he would not kiss their babies but would gladly kiss their mothers. Intolerant of dissension in his own ranks and confrontational toward his opponents, he seldom gave leeway. But he seldom sought leeway for himself.

Clinton is a young man. He will, one hopes, share Trudeau's long and largely healthy life. He will undoubtedly leave behind a public legacy. He will, one prays, not lose a child or have that loss hasten his death, as Trudeau's death was hastened by the loss of his youngest child. But Clinton is unlikely to be remembered for having the passion of his convictions. Unlike Trudeau, his political life has been marred by an all-consuming defense of his person, not by an offensive directed at those who challenged his worldly dreams. Unlike Trudeau too, Clinton's personal flaws have diminished his considerable political acumen. Trudeau's flaws, in contrast, somehow helped to produce a greater whole.

But I cannot be objective at this time. Like other Canadians, I too am in mourning.

### NOTES

1. My thanks to the editors, Beverly Moran and Len Kaplan, for their astute observations in the preparation of this essay. Any errors, however, are attributable to me alone. This essay was written with the support of the Social Sciences and Humanities Research Council of Canada.

2. This "crisis" was precipitated by the kidnapping of a British diplomat, James Cross, and Quebec Cabinet minister, Pierre LaPorte, by the Quebec separatist movement, the Front de Libération du Québec, commonly called the AFLQ. At the apparent request of the Liberal premier of Quebec, Trudeau invoked the War Measures Act which provided for extraordinary powers of arrest, detention, and censorship. Despite this measure, LaPorte was killed by his abductors. Some critics argue that in invoking this Act, Trudeau abused his power, undermining Canada as a liberal democracy and exacerbating tension and violence in Quebec. His supporters contend that his action was appropriate. This debate still persists today.

3. Pierre Trudeau, "Pierre Trudeau's Essay on the Referendum," *Montreal Gazette*, February 3, 1996, B3.

4. Stanley Oziewicz, "Trudeau's Legacy Endures: Admired Leader Who Made

Canada Appear Interesting and Trendy Turns 80," *South China Morning Post*, October 18, 1999, at 1999 WL 28995023; page references are not available.

5. For a select bibliography of books about Pierre Elliot Trudeau, see Christina McCall-Newman, *Grits: An Intimate Portrait of the Liberal Party* (Toronto: Macmillan of Canada, 1983); Kenneth McDonald, *His Pride, Our Fall: Recovering from the Trudeau Revolution* (Toronto: Key Porter Books, 1995); Peter C. Newman, *The Canadian Revolution, 1985–1995: From Deference to Defiance* (Toronto: Penguin Books Canada, 1995); Peter C. Newman, *Nation Divided: Canada and the Coming of Pierre Trudeau* (New York: Knopf, 1969); Richard Gwyn, *The Northern Magus: Pierre Trudeau and Canadians*, ed. Sandra Gwyn (Toronto: McClelland and Stewart, 1980); George Radwanski, *Trudeau* (Toronto: McClelland and Stewart, 1978); Guy Laforest et al., *Trudeau and the End of a Canadian Dream* (Toronto: McGill Queens University Press, 1995); Ivan L. Head and Pierre Elliott Trudeau, *The Canadian Way: Shaping Canada's Foreign Policy, 1968–1984* (Toronto: McClelland and Stewart, 1995); Pierre Elliott Trudeau, *The Essential Trudeau*, ed. Ron Graham (Toronto: McClelland and Stewart, 1999).

For books by Pierre Elliot Trudeau, see *Federalism and the French Canadians* (New York: St. Martin's Press, 1968); *Lifting the Shadow of War*, ed. C. David Crenna (Edmonton, Alberta: Hurtig, 1987); *Against the Current: Selected Writings 1939–1996*, ed. Gerard Pelletier (Toronto: McClelland and Stewart, 1996); *Towards a Just Society: The Trudeau Years*, ed. Thomas X. Axworthy (Markham, Ontario: Viking, 1990); *Memoirs* (Toronto: McClelland and Stewart, 1993).

# Part II

# Law

# Chapter 6

# Comparing the Independent Counsel to Other Prosecutors
## Privilege and Other Issues

## *Frank Tuerkheimer*

The turnover of tape recordings was pivotal in the crisis that led to the resignation of President Nixon. Litigation over questions of privilege concerning tapes subpoenaed by the grand jury led to the October 20, 1973 Saturday Night Massacre, *the* event that put impeachment of the President on the national agenda. Litigation leading to the turnover of tapes to the petit jury resulted in the divulgence of the "smoking gun" tape: the June 23, 1972 tape recording proving irrefutably that the President had assented to using the CIA as a false pretext to halt an FBI investigation getting too close to facts linking the Committee to Re-Elect the President to the Watergate burglars. Immediately after disclosure of the tape, President Nixon resigned. In both cases the President claimed the sought-after tapes were privileged; in both cases he lost. In one of the historical ironies of the period, the seminal authority on the turnover of the tapes was *Branzburg v. Hayes*, 408 U.S. 665 (1972), a case initiated by the Nixon Justice Department just a few years earlier in which it attempted to have a reporter for the *New York Times* divulge his sources which contained information on the Black Panthers.

In *Branzburg*, Caldwell asserted a journalist's privilege and the Department of Justice countered there was no such privilege. The Supreme Court agreed. The centerpost of its reasoning was the premise that the "grand jury is entitled to every man's evidence" except where protected by a constitutional, common law, or statutory privilege. There being none, the claim of privilege was rejected. The logic of *Branzburg* drove the decision in *United States v. Nixon*, 418 U.S. 683 (1974), in which the Supreme

Court held that a valid claim of executive privilege with respect to tapes could be overcome by showing that such tapes were essential to the resolution of criminal charges involving conduct in the White House.

The many court battles between Independent Counsel Kenneth Starr and the Clinton White House went over much the same ground, and the same underlying principle applied. With the exception of one matter having nothing to do with the ultimate impeachment and removal issues, claims of privilege were overridden and the Independent Counsel prevailed, as the Special Watergate Prosecutor had done a generation earlier. In only one of these cases was the Independent Counsel's position in the litigation contrary to what most prosecutors would have done. In one other possible privilege issue, not reaching the litigation level, the Independent Counsel ventured into an area most prosecutors would have stayed away from.

This essay will review these privilege controversies. While many have expressed the concern that Mr. Starr's investigations went too far and were out of control, his approach to privilege in his effort at getting at the facts only partly supports this concern. After reviewing these privilege controversies, the essay will comment on the two instances where the Independent Counsel clearly deviated from what an ordinary prosecutor might do. In both instances of such deviation, the results were unfortunate for the Independent Counsel.

## Parent-Child Privilege

One of the more searing memories of the Independent Counsel's investigation into possible perjury by President Clinton in the Paula Jones deposition relates to the grand jury appearance of Monica Lewinsky's mother, Marcia Lewis. Videotapes shown on the evening news and photographs in the newspapers contrasted a composed, almost elegant Mrs. Lewis entering the courthouse prior to her grand jury appearance with a drawn, harried, and broken-down woman leaving. The change in her image was understandable: Mrs. Lewis was questioned about conversations with her daughter in which her daughter confided in her about a very troubling sexual dalliance with a married man who happened to be President of the United States. The state, through compulsory grand jury process, was inquiring about such conversations, conversations that obviously took place because a very troubled daughter had needed advice and had turned to her mother for help and guidance. Was this a *legally* permissible intrusion into matters that the law says should be private and beyond the power of the state to inquire into?

The answer is a resounding yes. Although there are district court cases to the contrary—*In re Agosto*, 553 F. Supp. 1298 (D. Nev. 1983) and *In re Grand Jury Proceedings (Greenberg)*, 11 Fed. R. Evid. Serv. 579 (D. Conn. 1982)—the general federal rule is that no protection is afforded communications between parents and children. See *United States v. Erato*, 2 F.3d 11 (2d Cir. 1993) in which the Second Circuit cited seven other Federal Court of Appeals Circuits holding there is no such privilege at 2 F.3d at 16. Mr. Starr therefore was well within his legal prerogatives in questioning Mrs. Lewis in the grand jury about conversations with her daughter. Was it a wise thing to do? It was not.

The image of a shattered Marcia Lewis leaving the courthouse after her grand jury appearance could not have enhanced Mr. Starr's image with the public. While prosecutors will generally refrain from attempting to pierce parent-child confidentiality in instances where the relationship is harmonious, failure to respect a larger, nonlegal notion, created by a public sensitivity not grounded in law but in something perhaps deeper, can be fatal. The case of Justice Hortense Gabel and her daughter Suhkreet is illustrative. In 1988 Justice Gabel, a New York Supreme Court Justice (the trial part, in the New York State judicial structure), Bess Myerson Grant, a former Consumer Affairs Commissioner, and Andy Capasso, a friend of Ms. Grant, were indicted on conspiracy and bribery charges relating to Ms. Grant's hiring of Justice Gabel's daughter while a messy financial tangle related to a divorce between Andy Capasso and his wife, Nancy Capasso, was pending before Justice Gabel. Once Justice Gabel's daughter, who had not been able to secure employment, was hired by Ms. Grant, Justice Gabel's rulings suddenly took a turn adverse to Nancy Capasso. (See *Washington Post*, July 23, 1987, C1.) The jury acquitted all defendants. (*Los Angeles Times*, December 23, 1988, 5, col. 1.) Despite the strength of the circumstantial evidence based on rulings suddenly and unusually favorable to Andy Capasso once Suhkreet was hired by Ms. Grant, the specter of a daughter testifying against her mother did not enhance the prosecution's case and possibly was its major weakness.

While a federal prosecutor is not an elected official, it would be naive to assume that there is an impenetrable wall between public opinion and the conduct of a prosecutor. Marcia Lewis's testimony did not enhance Mr. Starr's image. Since Miss Lewinsky had discussed her affair with the

President on the Tripp tapes, clearly admissible under federal law, and since she had discussed it with several friends, Mrs. Lewis's testimony was hardly necessary to convince Miss Lewinsky that there was ample proof of her sexual relationship with the President and the falsity of her denial. The purpose of calling her mother was, therefore, not so much to attain additional evidence as to manifest a show of force. Miss Lewinsky, however, did not knuckle under, but the image of a heartless prosecutor was conveyed to the nation. Far from weakening Miss Lewinsky, it weakened the Independent Counsel. Given the overwhelming evidence that Miss Lewinsky's denials were false, most prosecutors would not have called the mother: it was too much of a "little gain, much to lose" proposition. Mr. Starr, to his misfortune, did not see it that way.

### *The Hillary Clinton Attorney-Client Litigation:* In re Grand Jury Subpoena Duces Tacem, *112 F.3d 910 (8th Cir),* cert. denied, *521 U.S. 11-5 (1997)*

As part of the Whitewater investigation, a federal grand jury in Arkansas issued a subpoena to the White House requiring production of all documents created during meetings of White House counsel and Hillary Clinton. Mrs. Clinton, her private counsel, and White House counsel attended these meetings. The district court quashed the subpoena on the grounds that Mrs. Clinton had a reasonable but mistaken belief that attorney privilege applied and that the work product privilege prevented disclosure of the notes to the grand jury. (Presidential claims of executive privilege were abandoned during the litigation.) The Independent Counsel appealed to the Eighth Circuit, which reversed the lower court.

After briefly discussing a jurisdictional issue, the Eighth Circuit, relying on the broad language of the *Branzburg* decision, held that an entity of the federal government could not use the attorney-client privilege (where the attorney was a government attorney) in the context of a grand jury subpoena. The court noted that government attorneys represent a public, not a private interest, and that they were under a statutory duty to report criminal misconduct to the Attorney General. A person who wished to speak with an attorney and wished to have the full protection of the attorney-client privilege, the court stated, should speak to a private, not a public attorney.

The second issue related to the applicability of a basic concept under attorney-client privilege law: where parties with similar interests meet, along with their attorneys, vis-à-vis the outside world conversations taking place in such meetings are privileged. Mrs. Clinton tried to avail herself of this doctrine. The court found it inapplicable, principally because there was no concurrence of interests. Mrs. Clinton, the court noted, had the clear interest of avoiding allegations of crime. White House counsel, on the other hand, as attorneys in the Executive Branch, had no such interest. While larger political interests might have overlapped, the narrow legal interest did not; hence the concept providing the umbrella of attorney-client privilege to meetings among parties (and their lawyers) of similar interest did not apply here.

Finally, the court addressed Mrs. Clinton's claim that she reasonably believed her conversations with her attorneys and White House attorneys were privileged; hence they were privileged in fact. This argument was based on numerous cases holding that where a person reasonably believes he or she is talking with an attorney, the privilege will apply even if that person is not an attorney. The court rejected this argument by invoking the distinction between mistakes of fact and mistakes of law. Mrs. Clinton's mistake was not a factual one: she did not believe that White House counsel represented her personally; rather, she believed in the legal conclusion that what she told White House counsel was privileged. The court expressed its unawareness of any authority, and Mrs. Clinton had brought none to its attention, holding that a client's beliefs on the law of privilege, however well grounded in good faith, could take an otherwise unprivileged conversation and make it privileged.

I have worked as a government prosecutor three times: in the Southern District of New York as an Assistant U.S. Attorney, in the District of Columbia as an Associate Special Watergate Prosecutor, and in the Western District of Wisconsin as United States Attorney. In each position, I have had numerous meetings with persons and their attorneys. Some of these persons were defendants or potential defendants, others were disinterested witnesses, still others were complainants. My responsibility in all cases was the same: to enforce federal law. The attorney for the person present also had a responsibility: to look out for the client. It would never have occurred to me or to the other participants in such a meeting that they could validly assert their attorney-client privilege with respect to my notes. How is Mrs. Clinton's situation *legally* different from this one, occurring daily? It is only different in the *political* context of the investigations, of the shared enmity between the White House and Mrs. Clinton for the Independent Counsel. But such a political linkage, strong as it might be, does not change the underlying legal reality that the attorneys have different clients and different responsibilities. The rulings were correct, and Mr. Starr did the right thing in pursuing the evidence.

### *Attorney-Client, Executive Privilege Litigation in the Context of White House Personnel:* In re Grand Jury Proceedings, 5 F. Supp. 2d 21 (D.D.C.), cert. denied, *524 U.S. 912 (1998)*

Bruce Lindsey was one of President Clinton's attorneys; Sidney Blumenthal, like Lindsey, was a "senior" presidential advisor. Both were subpoenaed to the grand jury by the Independent Counsel; Lindsey and Blumenthal claimed executive privilege with respect to their conversations with the President and Mrs. Clinton on the President's deposition in the Paula Jones case. Lindsey also asserted a presidential attorney-client privilege. This case differed from the Eighth Circuit litigation in that no private parties were involved: Lindsey and Blumenthal were on the White House staff, and it was their job to advise the President.

The Independent Counsel, relying on the Eighth Circuit decision, urged the court to find that there was no attorney-client privilege. The White House urged that the law in the District of Columbia was otherwise, and such a privilege did exist, and it was absolute. The Attorney General filed an *amicus* brief. The role of the Attorney General is interesting: she is an appointee of the President and the nominal superior of the Independent Counsel, thus related by lines of authority to both parties to the litigation. Perhaps reflecting the chain-of-command middle ground, the Attorney General took the middle ground position that there was an attorney-client privilege, but it was a qualified one and could be overcome if a showing comparable to the showing that defeated executive privilege in the *Nixon* case could be made.

The district court held that there was an attorney-client privilege for government attorneys in their official capacity, but it was qualified.[1] The court concluded that the Independent Counsel had met the burden of overcoming the claim of privilege. But because elucidation of that conclusion would have required divulgence of what was then secret grand jury information, the court did not elaborate on its conclusion. The district court also found that, under *Nixon,* executive privilege presumptively applied but could be—and in fact was—overcome by the showing of need and the nature of the sought-after evidence.

In concluding that the attorney-client privilege was qualified, the court made many of the same observations made in the Eighth Circuit litigation: government attorneys, representing the United States and not any one individual, are required to report misconduct to the Attorney General, and if President Clinton wanted advice on the Paula Jones lawsuit, he had his private attorneys. While those arguments were sound in the context of Hillary Clinton's claim of attorney-client privilege, they pose problems in the context of the presidential claim of attorney-client privilege.

As we know, the Independent Counsel subsequently, pursuant to Title 28, U.S. Code, Section 495(c), gave the results of the grand jury investigation into the President's deposition in the Paula Jones case to the House of Representatives for it to consider under its constitutional mandate to impeach or not to impeach the President. There seemed a general consensus that White House counsel could legitimately serve the President on the impeachment question, and indeed, White House counsel played a major role both in the impeachment proceedings in the House of Representatives and in the removal trial in the Senate. If the privilege were overridden, as the district court held, could not the House or the Senate have subpoenaed the President's lawyers as part of either of those proceedings and, under the district court's test, compelled the divulgence of information imparted by the President to the very lawyers representing him in those proceedings? It might be argued that impeachment and removal proceedings are not criminal proceedings, but that distinction appears to cut the other way. In terms of national interest, impeachment and removal are of far graver public concern than a criminal case. If the privilege can be overcome in a grand jury investigation because the search for truth compels overriding the privilege, surely the privilege would not prevail in the latter cases.

In light of the close nexus between the grand jury investigation and the impeachment process, how can one define the beginning of the impeachment process? If the President's White House lawyers have an unchallenged right to defend him in the impeachment and removal process, surely they cannot be subject to subpoena and be required to divulge what their client has told them. Any lawyer, to say nothing of the caliber of attorneys representing the President, would be aware that the entire process is on a continuum, and conversations relating to a grand jury investigation focusing on the Paula Jones deposition could easily be the initial stages of an impeachment process with the same focus, as indeed it was. If the legitimacy of an absolute attorney-client privilege is recognized vis-à-vis the impeachment and removal process, that absolute privilege must also exist during the grand jury investigation that can lead to possible impeachment and removal.

It does seem, therefore, that seeking such evidence was overly aggressive. Doing so gave the Independent Counsel the satisfaction of requiring White House lawyers to be the ones to raise the specter of impeachment as a defense to the subpoena. Perhaps because White House lawyers expected such hardball, there was little evidence provided once privilege was overruled. The controversy did not spawn much public flak but it revealed the pit-bull nature of the Independent Counsel's office. As a matter of historical perspective, it never occurred to anyone during the Watergate investigation to issue a grand jury subpoena to Fred Buzhardt, Len Garment, James St. Clair, or any other of the White House counsel occupying a position similar to Lindsey's. Perhaps those were gentler days.

### Is There a Secret Service Privilege? In re Sealed Case, *148 F.3d 1073 (D.C. Cir.)*, petition for stay pending application for certiorari denied, *524 U.S. 1301 (1998) (Rehnquist, C.J.)*

When the Independent Counsel subpoenaed Secret Service agents to the grand jury, to testify about presidential conduct—specifically to determine whether, according to the agents, the President and Ms. Lewinsky were alone for any significant period of time—a Secret Service privilege was raised by the Secretary of the Treasury through the Attorney General. White House counsel had written to the Independent Counsel that the privilege was not the President's to assert or waive. The district court refused to recognize a privilege and granted the Independent Counsel's motion to compel Secret Service agents to testify. The Court of Appeals, in a unanimous per curiam decision, affirmed the district court's decision.

The court's decision was a blend of the notion from *Nixon* that "new privileges are not lightly created nor expansively construed" (148 F.3d at 1075, quoting *Nixon* at 710) with the hobbled nature of privilege claim asserted. The claim was hobbled for three reasons.

First, it was not asserted by the President, but rather by the Secretary of the Treasury. Presumably, the purpose of the privilege was to give the President the assurance that there was no need to duck or avoid Secret Service protection for fear that the President's protectors would testify against him. The Court of Appeals correctly noted that if it were up to the Secretary of the Treasury to assert the privilege, the Secretary could waive it. How then could the President derive any measure of security from a privilege it was not the President's to assert or waive?

Second, the privilege advanced was not an absolute one. It was agreed that if Secret Service agents actually witnessed criminality, they could legitimately divulge it. Only if their observations, in hindsight, were not evidentiary of criminality would a privilege apply. Since the purpose of the privilege was to keep the President from avoiding his protectors, the court reasoned, the President would have no knowledge as to whether the privilege applied or didn't; hence the calculus of whether to elude his protection became far too complicated to warrant the exclusion of otherwise admissible evidence.

Finally, the court noted, the likelihood that the President would be inclined to avoid his protectors would be greatest when the conduct was in private—a time of minimal danger to the President. The value of a privilege, therefore, would be minimal. In light of its inevitable impediment to the search for truth, for all these reasons the privilege was found not to exist.

## Does the Attorney-Client Privilege Survive the Client?
### Swidler v. Berlin, *524 U.S. 399 (1998)*

In each of the three privilege litigations so far mentioned, the Independent Counsel prevailed. None of these reached the Supreme Court. The only privilege litigation arising out of the Independent Counsel's investigations to reach the Supreme Court was also the only loss the Independent Counsel suffered in these cases. The Supreme Court, by a six to three vote, reversed a divided Court of Appeals, holding that the attorney-client privilege survived the client's death.

Shortly before his death, Vince Foster, a White House lawyer and close friend of President and Mrs. Clinton, spoke to a private attorney in connection with his role in the dismissal of employees in the White House Travel office. Congressional and possibly other investigations into these firings loomed. Foster's attorneys took three pages of handwritten notes during the two-hour meeting. Nine days later Foster committed suicide. The Independent Counsel, through a grand jury subpoena, sought the three pages of notes. Foster's former attorneys moved to quash the subpoena; the district court granted the motion. On appeal, a divided Court of Appeals reversed. The majority found that in the context of a grand jury investigation conducted after the client's death, important information would be lost and little if any deterrence to full disclosure to any attorney would be inhibited. Justice Rehnquist, speaking for the majority of six, reversed the Court of Appeals. Justices O'Connor, Scalia, and Thomas dissented.

The Court noted that judicial authority and commentators were virtually unanimous that the privilege survived death. The many cases where the privilege was held not to apply—in testamentary cases involving disputes between persons claiming that privilege under the deceased client—analysis always proceeded on the theory that the nonapplicability of the privilege to those instances was an exception to a general rule of applicability. The majority found that the search for truth was not significantly frustrated by applying the privilege posthumously on the empirical predicate that if the rule were otherwise, clients would not reveal as much to their attorneys. It distinguished the *Nixon* case on the ground that *Nixon* involved the scope of a privilege never before asserted (the confidentiality of presidential conversations) while the attorney-client privilege was as old as privilege law itself.

The dissent urged that what little interest there was in affording a deceased client's reputational interest protection was outweighed by the possible exculpatory nature of the evidence to a defendant on trial.[2] Justice O'Connor noted that authority for the proposition that the privilege survived the client's death was not monolithic, that there were instances where the privilege did not apply and that the criminal justice system's "twofold aim . . . that guilt shall not escape or innocence suffer" was thwarted by the majority decision.

Clearly the weight of precedent is on the side of the majority. The concern that communications of a deceased client will constitute admissible exculpatory evidence seems far-fetched. How will a defense attorney know to subpoena the attorney for a deceased client? Should it be done as a matter of course? Is the attorney for the deceased client duty-bound to alert the defense attorney to the need to subpoena the attorney if the defense attorney is understandably unaware of the supposedly dynamite exculpatory evidence the attorney possesses?

## Summary

We have, then, five instances in which questions of privilege were triggered by the actions of the Independent Counsel: asking Marcia Lewis about conversations with her daughter, seeking notes of Hillary Clinton's meeting with White House lawyers and her own lawyer, asking White House counsel about conversations with the President about his deposition in the Paula Jones case, trying to learn what Secret Service agents saw in connection with Monica Lewinsky's visits to the White House, and obtaining notes of conversations with Vince Foster taken shortly before his death. In all but the latter case, the Independent Counsel prevailed (or no issue was raised in the Marcia Lewis case) and in the one instance where the Independent Counsel did not prevail in the courts, the Supreme Court split six to three against him and the Court of Appeals went in favor of his position by a divided panel.

Most prosecutors would not have questioned Mrs. Lewis and the historical track record suggests the questioning of Lindsey was out of line. Thus, from an overall point of view, the Independent Counsel's interface with privilege issues cost him something, but not much. In two other areas of deviation from what most prosecutors do, however, the cost was high.

## The Unkept Immunity Agreement

In a November 15, 1999 article in the *New Yorker* entitled "The Secret War in Starr's Office: How the Prosecutors Wrecked the Best Case against the President," Jeffrey Toobin describes events in the Independent Counsel's office in the two-week period following notice to the Independent Counsel that the President had carried on a sexual affair with a White House intern and had lied about it in a deposition in the Paula Jones lawsuit. Two weeks of frantic negotiations between two attorneys in the office of Independent Counsel and William Ginsburg, then Miss Lewinsky's lawyer, led to an oral understanding that in exchange for her testimony she would receive immunity from prosecution. Prior to that understanding Miss Lewinsky had prepared a written statement of her relationship with the President in which she acknowledged (1) that she and the President had a relationship of physical intimacy that included oral sex but not intercourse; and (2) that the President had told her to deny the relationship if asked about it. Independent Counsel attorneys drafted an agreement embodying immunity for Miss Lewinsky in exchange for truthful testimony about her dealings with the President which they forwarded to attorney Ginsburg which Miss Lewinsky, Mr. Ginsburg, and a legal associate then signed. When it was returned to the Independent Counsel, it was not signed.

The prosecutors who had negotiated with Mr. Ginsburg urged it to be signed; other prosecutors on the team opposed signing it because no one had actually interviewed Miss Lewinsky—they were relying on her written statement and proffer made through the attorneys. Mr. Starr acceded to the view that there was no agreement. Failure to sign an agreement reached between prosecutors and attorneys for a witness, an agreement reduced to writing by the prosecutors and given to the witness's attorneys for signature, was out of step with what most prosecutors would do under like circumstances. This misstep resulted in a delay that turned out to be a major and perhaps presidency-salvaging bonanza to the President.

Many months later, with new attorneys, Miss Lewinsky agreed to be interviewed. On that later occasion she adhered to her written statement of the January–February 1998 period. As a result, the delay yielded nothing. It cost a great deal. In the early 1998 period the President's position denied anything even hinting of a sexual relationship with Monica Lewinsky. It was during this period that the President made the now infamous statement that he had not had sexual relations with "that woman, Miss Lewinsky." Had he made such an outright denial under oath in a proceeding that was part of a grand jury investigation or before the grand jury itself, it is doubtful that his presidency could have survived the later proof of the falsity of his statement. The occasion did not arise, however, because no immunity understanding with Miss Lewinsky was in place. By the time it was, the world had heard about the dress containing physical evidence conclusively supporting Miss Lewinsky's version of her sexual dalliance with the President. By then, the President had changed his position from outright and emphatic denial to an admission of an "improper" course of conduct with Miss Lewinsky, a concession permitting the preservation of his presidency. This preservation is directly attributable to the delay incident to the Independent Counsel's failure to do what other prosecutors routinely do—live up to their spoken agreements.

## Assisting in the Removal Process

As we know, the President was impeached by the House of Representatives and tried before the United States Senate. During the removal trial, the House Managers sought to take the deposition of Monica Lewinsky. They obtained the assistance of the Independent Counsel who invoked the immunity agreement with her which required her cooperation. This involvement of the Independent Counsel in the removal process enraged a number of Senators. Whether that rage caused votes to switch or solidify will probably never be known. It is clear, however, that this involvement was out of line and not the kind of step an ordinary prosecutor would take.

Perhaps the closest analogy is the use of the grand jury after indictment. The grand jury is an investigative institution whose responsibility it is to determine whether criminal charges should be brought. Once an indictment has been returned, the grand jury may not be used as a pretrial discovery device. The prosecutor, as the defense attorney, is limited to the discovery provisions of the Federal Rules of Criminal Procedure. An effort to use the grand jury for discovery purposes will at the least result in the suppression of evidence and possibly in the dismissal of the indictment. How is the conduct of the Independent Counsel related to such an abuse?

Title 28, United States Code, Section 595(c) delineates the responsibilities of the Independent Counsel in connection with the impeachment process. It provides that "an independent counsel shall advise the House of Representatives of any substantial and credible information which such independent counsel receives in carrying out the independent counsel's responsibilities under this chapter, that may constitute grounds for an impeachment." Once the President is impeached, the statutory role of the Independent Counsel in the process is terminated, much as the role of the grand jury is over once an indictment is returned. Nothing in the mandating section gives the Independent Counsel a role in the removal proceeding, just as the grand jury has no role in the pretrial process. Assisting the House of Representatives after impeachment was beyond the Independent Counsel's mandate.[3] Prosecutors do not, as a rule, exceed their authorized powers in such a manner.

NOTES

1. Generally, when a qualified privilege is urged, the logical response is that the confidentiality the privilege is designed to insure cannot be attained since the person speaking in a qualifiedly privileged context cannot know whether the privilege will be overridden in a subsequent proceeding. The court responded by observing that in the quarter-century since *Nixon* had created a qualified executive privilege, presidential advisors had not been inhibited.

2. A deceased's acknowledgment that he or she committed the crime someone

else is charged with could be admitted over a hearsay objection under the declaration against interest exception. Rule 804(b)(3). The rules, however, require that corroborating circumstances indicate the trustworthiness of the statement. Justice O'-Connor does not discuss the evidentiary subtleties involved in utilization of a confession to an attorney to exonerate an accused.

3. The ethics advisor to Mr. Starr, Georgetown Law Professor Sam Dash, resigned for related reasons. See Editorial, *Washington Post*, November 22, 1998, C6.

# Chapter 7

# Legalizing Outrage

## *Robert W. Gordon*

In the Clinton-Lewinsky scandal's early stages the makers of public opinion analyzed the affair in moral terms. They disagreed on exactly what was wrong with Clinton's conduct. Some condemned him for adultery, some for betraying the implicit compact with his wife and the people that had once elected him President that he would avoid new sexual entanglements. Others thought Clinton's sex life was nobody's business but his own and Hillary's; but were troubled by a powerful man's exploitation of a vulnerable younger woman in his workplace, or by his disregard for the dignity of his office. Clinton supplied fresh reasons for denunciation when he denied on television any sexual involvement with "that woman" and kept denying it until it became unmistakably clear that the denials were false: now he was a liar as well as an adulterer, defiler of his office, and (possibly) sexual harasser.

For Clinton's fiercest critics, his affair and lies about it were just more evidence confirming his gross unfitness for his office, to be added to his history of draft evasion, "Whitewater" financial misdeeds, and "bimbo eruptions" in Arkansas, the selling of access to the White House to Asian influence-peddlers, the firing of the White House travel staff, and the collection of FBI files on political enemies. Out of this critical constituency developed a well-financed fringe of extremists with access to radio stations, religious pulpits, right-wing publishers, TV talk shows, and Internet sites, who relayed to audiences of millions their theories that Bill and Hillary Clinton routinely arranged to silence with threats, or even murder, associates such as Vincent Foster who might expose their crimes and vices. To cultural conservatives, whether or not they believed the paranoid conspiracy theories, Clinton's character defects symbolized the defective mentality and habits of an entire era, "the sixties," with its contempt for discipline and the military virtues, its slovenly permissiveness in raising children and indulging criminals and welfare dependents, its hostility to religion, its sexual laxity, and its postmodern, multicultural relativistic approaches to objective truth and absolute morals.

For such critics nothing less would serve to cure the social disease than to cut away its source at the top, to purge the presidency of the polluting presence of Clinton and his sixties values and manners. He must be forced to resign in disgrace, and if he would not do so, he must be impeached.

Their problem was that they could not bring the great majority of their fellow citizens—consistently about 60 to 65 percent of people surveyed in opinion polls from the time the scandal first broke to Clinton's acquittal in the Senate—to agree that Clinton's wrongdoing justified his removal from office. Faced with this persistent refusal, conservative critics denounced the people themselves as having been fatally infected with the sixties' diseases of permissiveness and relativism.

Yet if anyone had tried to count all the moral denunciations of Clinton's affair in 1998, he would surely have found it the most reviled adulterous affair in history. Hardly anyone except Nelson Mandela and Vaclav Havel passed up the chance to condemn it. On the affair's impropriety there was as close to a universal moral consensus as one is ever likely to find in a contentious pluralistic society.

The issue that divided the country was not whether Clinton's conduct was wrong but what to do about it. Most people viewed the attempt to remove him from office as inappropriate, out of proportion to the scale and type of Clinton's wrongdoing. Yes, Clinton had trouble controlling his sexual appetites: this was regrettable in a president, but not exactly news about this incumbent, and not uncommon among recent presidents, including the generally admired John F. Kennedy. Yes, it was troubling that his paramour was a young employee; but she had apparently initiated the affair, it was clearly consensual, and she was not complaining of harassment. Yes, Clinton had lied about the affair; but most people will lie to conceal an extramarital affair; and lying to the people, sometimes about matters of much greater moment, was also not uncommon among recent presidents, including the generally admired Ronald Reagan. The notion that extramarital sex and lying about it should automatically expel a person from political office set a standard that many officeholders, including some of Clinton's most vocal critics, could not satisfy; so that their attacks seemed either overly puritanical or else hypocritical and opportunistic.

To be sure, many of the same people seemed to think that Clinton's offense was not wholly private, because the President is a public figure who should set a moral example and uphold the dignity of his office. This judgment pointed to some measure of official condemnation. The most obvious response was a congressional joint resolution of censure, which would have drawn wide bipartisan support.

This consensus solution was never sought because the fiercer wing of Clinton's critics thought it too feeble an expression of their outrage. If Clinton were shameless, literally without shame, he would be sure to view censure alone as meaningless. The critics wanted a big, public repudiation of Clinton's false values and affirmation of their own values, a national ceremony of confession, purgation, and penitence—not just to reprove Clinton, but to humiliate him and expel him from public life. The fiercer critics were represented well out of proportion to their numbers in the House of Representatives, where the Gingrich Revolution of 1994 had entrenched right-wing radicals in the party leadership and on the Judiciary Committee, almost all of whom enjoyed security of tenure in districts gerrymandered to guarantee them safe seats. The radicals managed to thwart the popular and congressional majority's desires and to block the censure option. Yet they were still left with the problem of finding a suitable public channel for their outrage. The channel they eventually stumbled into was the criminal law.

A series of chance events had opened this channel up: Paula Jones's sexual harassment lawsuit; the Supreme Court's incautious ruling refusing to postpone the lawsuit until Clinton left office; a right-wing foundation's supply of money and lawyers to Jones to keep her suit going long after an ordinary plaintiff would have settled; the trial judge's decision to allow Jones's lawyers to inquire broadly in discovery into Clinton's relationships with other women; Linda Tripp's disclosure of the Clinton-Lewinsky affair to the Jones lawyers and Kenneth Starr's Office of Independent Counsel (OIC) just before the President gave his deposition in the case. In the deposition, Jones's lawyers, briefed by Tripp, asked Clinton whether he had had a sexual affair with Lewinsky. Clinton denied it; and so opened the door to criminal investigation of his conduct by an OIC with an unlimited budget and investigative staff, no real supervision by any other authority, and strong motives to pin something on President Clinton—all the stronger because the OIC's other investigations, into Whitewater, Foster, "Travelgate," and "Filegate" had failed to turn up any hard evidence of his wrongdoing.

Clinton's critics now had a legal case. From this point forward, the anti-Clinton forces denied they were puritanical moralists trying to drive Clinton out of office for sex, or lying about sex. His real vice was that he had committed serious felonies, the crimes of "perjury" and "obstruction of justice."

Chance played such a large part in enabling the Starr investigation and impeachment proceedings that one could easily conclude that the Clinton crisis had no implications beyond its singular facts. But the way the crisis developed illustrates a more general and pervasive tendency in American public culture, a drive to legalize outrage, to channel moral rage through the framework and processes of the law. The crisis also illustrates the ironic consequences of this strategy, as legalization often denatures and delegitimates moral judgment, and the party of outrage then attempts to overcome the strategy's self-undoing by remoralizing the law, trying to convert legal judgment back into moral judgment.

This argument may seem surprising at first. We are used to thinking that modern liberal societies separate law from morals, only deploy criminal law to control behavior that causes concrete harms to persons and property as opposed to merely offending them, and leave judgments of morality to religious communities and individual conscience. Most states since the 1970s have repealed legislation criminalizing fornication, adultery, sodomy, abortion, and the sale and use of alcohol, contraceptives, and obscene literature, or have backed off from trying to enforce them. We are used to thinking that modern penal regimes replace premodern impulses to punish—to condemn deviance as sin and to give voice to the wronged community's cries for vengeance—with Enlightenment reasons to administer only as much punishment as will deter the offender and others tempted to offend likewise.

But this story of liberalized criminal law is partly an illusion. In large areas the law has been remoralized—not simply to condemn, deter, and punish conduct of which the majority disapproves, which is always an aim of the criminal law, but also to express outrage at the offenders and their conduct, to label and shame them as transgressors outside the pale of respectable society, and to give voice to the victims' and the general community's cries for revenge. The most visible symbol of remoralized law is the revival of the death penalty after its near extinction in the 1970s and its abolition almost everywhere else in the world. States are not only executing many more prisoners, but are attaching death as the penalty to many more crimes. Death penalty advocates rarely argue any more that it deters crime more effectively than life imprisonment does; they urge instead its expressive virtues as a punishment that articulates the victims' and the community's rage at the offender and his offense and their demand for retribution, a life for a life.

The movement for the expression of outrage finds another channel in the vogue for incarceration, for longer sentences (longer by far than those in other advanced societies), for building a vast new archipelago of prisons to hold those sentenced, and for the suppression of reforms and prisoners' suits to make prison conditions less savage. The mania for incarceration has been driven by a moral panic that demonizes types of criminals, especially African Americans, as moral monsters, "superpredators" beyond hope of rehabilitation or redemption. Like most moral panics this one is very selective in its targets. The crackdown has been especially severe on drug offenders, manifested in "zero tolerance" for even low-level offenses such as simple use and possession; on repeat offenders, manifested in "three strikes" laws requiring long prison sentences for third offenses, even trivial ones; and on juvenile offenders, who are increasingly sent to adult jails.

The use of the law to express moral outrage, however, inevitably runs into limits that cool and deflect its passion. Some of these stem from law's formality and proceduralism, which critics call "technicalities," but liberals cherish as the essence of legality itself. Police and prosecutors have to run some procedural hurdles before putting people away, to show they have acted with regularity in arrests, searches, interrogations, and the handling of evidence; and have assembled enough evidence to be able to withstand cross-examination and counterproof and to prove every element of the crimes charged beyond a reasonable doubt. "Due process" means that the more severe the sanction, the more burdensome these formal requirements must be. Due process thus delivers strategic resources to the defense, so that defendants who can afford good lawyers may bargain with prosecutors for reduced penalties or avoid them altogether. The result is an alchemy that converts much of the actual discourse of criminal law from moral denunciation into technical arguments over procedure and proof and the haggling of the plea-bargaining bazaar.

The pure white flame of outrage is also necessarily tempered by the fact that systems make mistakes. Some innocent and many relatively innocuous suspects, especially those who get (as most of them do) only cursory defenses, are sentenced to long prison terms; while some monstrous criminals, especially if rich and well-represented, may escape altogether or with light sentences.

The parties who want the criminal law to express their outrage have responded to such demoralizing features of the justice system by trying to suppress or conceal them. New state and federal legislation drastically reduces criminal defendants' abilities to challenge convictions on appeal, and moves challenges onto a "fast track" that gives the convicted no real chance to prepare a case. Many states deny competent legal aid to the mass of defendants who can't afford their own lawyer by paying public defenders a pittance ($500 to defend a capital case) or assigning the dregs of the bar to defend them. Primarily, the new punitive moralism diagnoses the main problem with criminal justice as excessive discretion to be lenient, and tries to reduce that discretion by means of absolute categorical rules. This movement has given us mandatory minimum sentences for (even first-time, small-time) drug offenders, "three strikes" legislation mandating huge sentences for repeat offenders, however trivial their prior offenses; the Federal Sentencing Guidelines depriving judges of discretion to tailor sentences to what they perceive as relevant characteristics of the offender; and the abolition of parole.

These experiments have led to predictable disasters. Discretion in the application of rules is as necessary a component of the rule of law as is formality, indispensable as a matter of fairness and unavoidable as a matter of fact. No system can operate fairly or rationally if its rules are applied literally and mechanically without taking into account significant variations in particular cases. Either the application will produce obvious gross injustices, or the operators of the system will find a way to work around them. For example, by eliminating the sentencing discretion of federal judges, the Federal Sentencing Guidelines have effectively transferred it to twenty-seven-year-old assistant U.S. attorneys to exercise in their charging and plea-bargaining decisions.

Things are much worse if discretion is not transferred. Two years after California passed its "three strikes" law it was found that many more defendants were given long prison terms for drug possession (not sale) under the law than for all violent offenses combined. Prosecutors under political pressure to keep their conviction numbers up tend to go after "easy kills," the minor offenders such as simple possessors of drugs and the "mules" who carry them for dealers. In the name of promoting moral values, the culture of law enforcement has impaired the enforcers' elementary capacity for moral judgment: the ability to distinguish between the gravity of offenses and the culpability of offenders. Even law-and-order conservatives are beginning to express concern about a system that is imprisoning minor offenders at record rates and enormous cost to taxpayers, turning them into hardened and unemployable convicts while yielding few or no marginal gains in public safety.

What does any of this have to do with the pursuit of President Clinton? Quite a lot, as it turns out. The anti-Clinton forces' drive to channel their moral outrage through legal forms and proceedings entangled them in the thicket of formality that deflects such passions. Their response was to try to bypass the legalisms that were frustrating their designs and to re-moralize his case. The ultimate result—because the object of their rage was not some obscure black defendant caught smoking pot but a president popular for his policies if not his character—was to discredit their crusade by making them appear to be partisan fanatics.

When Clinton's affair with Lewinsky fell into the hands of Kenneth Starr's OIC, the legal channel that chance had opened up was very narrow. The case against him had to be that by denying sex with Lewinsky in his deposition in the *Jones* case and by tacitly permitting Lewinsky—or actively encouraging her by asking his friend Vernon Jordan to help find her a job—to file a false affidavit in the case denying any sexual involvement with him, Clinton had committed "perjury" and "obstruction of justice," serious felonies in the statute book carrying heavy maximum penalties.

Factually and legally, the case was unpromising. The questions Clinton answered in the deposition were diffusely and confusingly worded; and he later claimed, implausibly but not irrefutably, that he had intended only to give evasive answers, not directly false ones. Perjury statutes require that false statements be "material," meaning that they be "capable of affecting the outcome" of the proceeding in which they are given. Arguably nothing Clinton said about his affair with Lewinsky, a consensual affair that happened five years after he supposedly made a pass at Paula Jones in Arkansas, and in a different workplace, had any bearing whatever on Jones's claim that Clinton had sexually harassed her. The "obstruction" charge required evidence that Clinton had asked Jordan to get a job for Lewinsky in return for her false testimony. But the job search had started well before anyone thought Lewinsky might be a witness in *Jones*, and was plainly motivated chiefly by Clinton's wishes to do a favor for a former lover and assuage his guilt over the affair, to keep her away from the White House, and to encourage her to keep the affair secret—not just from the *Jones* court but from everyone, especially his wife and the press. These defects in the case alone, suitably magnified by a defense lawyer, would make it easy for a sympathetic jury to acquit.

The bigger problem with the case was that even if it could be proved, Clinton's attempt to prevent the *Jones* court from learning about his affair with Lewinsky was basically trivial, because it could have had little or no effect on justice for Jones. The *Jones* case was dismissed and then settled, but even if it had gone to trial there was almost no chance the Lewinsky evidence would have been admitted at that trial. Clinton's and Lewinsky's lies about their affair could not plausibly have caused anyone any actual harm. Prosecutors have to consider such things before deciding to prosecute. Some crimes—including perjury, obstruction of justice, bribery, fraud, and extortion—are very broadly defined, and thus cover a lot of low-level as well as serious misconduct. Overstating deductions on your tax return, or understating the value of goods you brought back from Italy in your suitcase, are technically crimes; but if the amounts are small, no sensible official would have you arrested or tried for a felony; at most you will have to pay a fine or penalty.

Similarly, evasion and distortion of the truth by witnesses in legal proceedings are everyday occurrences. When freedom or large amounts of money are at stake, people lie. When she brought her lawsuit against Clinton, Paula Jones claimed that after she rejected his sexual advances her career had suffered. This was untrue: she had in fact received merit pay increases and promotions on schedule. The legal system expects lies like this, and routinely deals with them through the ordinary resources of the adversary process—cross-examination and contradicting proof, or sanctions for discovery abuse.[1] If parties to a civil case are caught lying about an important fact in the case, they pay the price by losing the case. Prosecutions for perjury, as a means of punishing the lying witness or deterring other witnesses, are rare; for perjury in civil cases rarer still, and only likely when a witness has lied about a central fact at issue in the case; for perjury in civil discovery prosecutions are almost unheard-of; and for perjury in discovery on issues unimportant to the underlying case (as the Lewinsky affair was in *Jones*) they are virtually nonexistent. The reasons are obvious. It is a silly waste of prosecutorial resources to deploy them against people who have done little or no harm, and where other sanctions are available to police their misconduct. And it's an injustice to use a big penalty to crush a small offender.

The anti-Clinton forces responded that such defenses were wearisome "technicalities," that the bad conduct was not to be viewed through the lens of a nitpicking "legalism" but was gross misconduct unbecoming of the President. As William Bennett put it in *The Death of Outrage,*

"[L]egalism and the rule of law are two different things. In the hands of skillful and deceitful men, the former can easily be manipulated to dodge or even subvert the latter, and thus further poison the wells of public life."

To bypass legalism, the anti-Clinton forces proceeded to remoralize the case against him. First they condemned Clinton as a status offender, more culpable than the ordinary defendant because he was President. Second, they focused on his person rather than his offense, demonizing him as a man of exceptional depravity. Finally they relied on absolute categorical judgments that refused to consider any differences of degree of culpability.

Suspecting that many people would be reluctant to condemn Clinton for trying to hide his affair with another woman, unrelated to the actual case, in a lawsuit brought to embarrass him and financed by his political enemies, the OIC called the President to testify before the grand jury to ask him whether he had lied in his deposition. The aim was to put him in the position of having to confess to possible perjury, or to commit a fresh perjury by denying he had lied. The tactic ingeniously created a more formal and imposing setting than a discovery deposition in a defunct civil case, one in which the President's denials of wrongdoing would seem more grave and culpable. Ordinary defendants sidestep traps like the one the OIC set for Clinton by invoking their Fifth Amendment privilege not to incriminate themselves: but for political reasons, as the OIC knew, the President could not "take the Fifth."

The stubborn fact remained that Clinton's lies in the *Jones* deposition, or lies before the grand jury about lies in the deposition, only mattered to the legal system if they could have interfered with justice for Jones. But the point of calling Clinton to the grand jury was not to investigate an ordinary crime: it was to set the stage for a status offense, to produce a public spectacle of a president defying the rule of law by testifying falsely under oath. Starr argued that conduct that might be overlooked in an ordinary citizen was unforgivable in a president. A public display by the chief magistrate of his contempt for law by lying under oath does exceptional damage to the rule of law. It sends a message that lawbreaking is all right if you can get away with it and encourages others to lie. Though perjury is common, routinely tolerated, and not prosecuted, nonetheless when a conspicuous lie comes to public attention, the system has to respond symbolically to affirm the importance of truth telling and to deter others. Especially well-known violators have to be treated more severely than anyone else.

The argument for exemplary punishment was probably the anti-Clinton forces' strongest card. But it was a moral and political argument, not a legal one. And it was only convincing if you thought there was no way to separate private from public character, the man from the President. Yet Clinton's lies concerned his sex life, private if anything was. The lawsuit that got him into so much trouble had been filed against him as a private person. The Supreme Court had allowed the suit to go forward on that basis. As the defendant in *Jones*, Clinton was not charged with the President's duty to execute the laws, only with the ordinary citizen's duty to obey them. Treating him so much more severely than any ordinary litigant seemed arbitrary and vindictive.

Starr's most spectacular attempt to pour moral outrage back into the cramped categories of the law came in his "Referral" to the House. Starr denied that his office was concerned with Clinton's sex life. Yet his Referral spells out every single physical detail as obsessively as a French New Realist novel. Starr's excuse was that all this detail was required to pin down a legal offense, Clinton's denial of having had "sex" with Lewinsky, when "sex" had been defined as among other things touching breasts and genitals. For this purpose, a dry summary of Lewinsky's contradicting evidence would have sufficed. But Starr and his staff really went to town in their "Narrative" of the affair, adding such gratuitous details as Clinton's being on the phone while receiving oral sex, Hillary's being away during one of their meetings, the couple's exchanges of suggestive banter, and many more. The obvious real purpose of this detail was to inspire public disgust with Clinton by painting his affair in the tawdriest possible colors. Outrage, through the channels of the law, had returned to its real object of horrified fascination, sex.

However, Starr's narrative unexpectedly humanized the participants. Clinton came across not as a cunning seducer and monster of predation but as an awkward and guilt-stricken overgrown adolescent, Lewinsky as a sexually aggressive and experienced but also a touchingly insecure young woman. Starr meanwhile came across as a Puritan pornographer, obsessed with sex and the destruction of the President. Most readers were horrified at the brutal invasion of the lovers' privacy, and the dumping of the details into the public domain. Their horror grew as it became apparent how the OIC had gathered its evidence. The OIC had subpoenaed family members to inform on and put pressure on their children, reporters to inform on their sources, bookstores to inform on their customers' reading habits; the Clintons' lawyers, closest aides, and even their

Secret Service guards to reveal the most intimate aspects of their personal lives; Lewinsky's family, closest friends, and former lovers to reveal what she had told them, and her psychiatric records and personal computer files. They squeezed and squeezed Lewinsky herself to drain her of every last humiliating detail of her personal and sexual life.

And all for what? Not to catch a master terrorist, a drug boss, or a Mafia chieftain, but a hapless schmo with a sexual secret. Starr's staff did not help their case by protesting that all their wretched excesses were the standard tactics of professional prosecutors. The tactics, alas, were standard indeed. Their use to discover exactly which of Bill's body parts had touched exactly which of Monica's—a fact of no conceivable moment even to Paula Jones while her case was pending, and to nobody whatsoever once the case was settled—seemed literally insane.

The attacks on Clinton as a bad moral example failed because the public viewed his sins more as private failings than as abuses of his office. The attempts to paint him as a moral monster failed because their narrative detail made him look simply weak in an ordinary human way and his pursuers fanatic partisans obsessed with sex.

What remained for the anti-Clinton forces was the main strategy of legalized outrage, categorical moralism. Clinton had committed (or, well, sort of maybe almost committed) offenses that fit the statute book's definitions of serious felonies, and by so doing had (in a frequently repeated formula) "attempted to destroy the rights of the plaintiff in a federal civil rights action against him."

Categorical arguments by their nature demand that their audience ignore all particulars of context. This one required an exceptionally thick veil of ignorance. To accept it we had to pretend that *Jones v. Clinton* was a regular, legitimate sexual harassment case. We had to forget that Paula Jones's original grievance was that an *American Spectator* story had reported that someone called "Paula" had sought out an affair with Governor Clinton and voluntarily gone to his hotel room, and that it was only after her family got interested in a big money settlement and book contract that they switched their target to Clinton himself; that Jones sued to recover huge damages because of a single encounter in which, if one believed her, Clinton exposed himself to her in a hotel room; that her claim that her job prospects had suffered when she rejected him was provably false; that after her first lawyers quit because she would not settle, her case was taken over by ideological Clinton-haters who saw the case as a vehicle for gathering, under the authority of federal court subpoenas, an enormous trash heap of gossip associating Clinton with various women and then dumping it all onto the public record. We had to set aside the ordinary intuition that people have a moral privilege to conceal the secrets of their intimate personal lives from adversaries with no legitimate interest in, and only malicious motives for, exposing them. We had to accept the premise that the *Jones* lawyers' manipulation of the civil rights laws and civil litigation for partisan and vindictive ends represented "the rule of law"; and that Clinton's attempt to foil and evade them put the "rule of law" in mortal danger.

Starr and the impeachment leaders were willing to draw as thick a veil as needed over the actual background that led up to Clinton's lies. Starr's Referral explored the context of the Clinton-Lewinsky sexual affair and the job search that followed it in excruciating detail; but gave no context for the questions asked Clinton in the *Jones* case beyond a bare outline of the formal proceedings. Indeed Starr sternly maintained that context was irrelevant. "There is no excuse for perjury. Never, never, never," he told Diane Sawyer in an interview. In his congressional testimony he elaborated:

> [N]o one is entitled to lie under oath simply because he or she does not like the questions or because he believes the case is frivolous, or that it is financially motivated or politically motivated. . . . [P]erjury is extraordinarily serious business. It is insidious. The courthouse cannot operate if perjury is allowed either to be excused or to be minimized. . . . And it does not matter whether the issue has to do with sexual harassment, or bankruptcy, or the criminal law. It is all dreadfully serious. . . . Witnesses tell the truth. It doesn't matter what the underlying subject matter is. Once you are in court under oath, you tell the truth.[2]

Starr's is a classic categorical, absolutist, "zero-tolerance" position on lying in official proceedings. It's a remarkably and frighteningly statist position. For the categorical moralist the importance of yielding up complete and accurate truth telling before the official tribunal, or the official inquisitor, always trumps every other imaginable competing moral value. It doesn't matter how great or trivial the public interest is in knowing the truth, how precious are the values or relations sought to be protected by concealing it, how legitimate or illegitimate the motives of the questioner are for trying to expose it.

And that's not all. Since all lies pollute and defile the legal system, it follows that the state must deploy its full resources to investigate and prosecute such lies, and the maximum penalties to punish them, against even the most minor offenders. There *are* no minor offenders: "It is all dreadfully serious." Actions are either right or wrong; if wrong, they are wrong all the way down. That was, as it had to be, the justification for the $10 million, seven-month OIC investigation; and the second impeachment in history of a president.

As I've said, categorical moralism pervades our remoralized criminal justice system, especially in the treatment of black, drug, youth, and sex offenders, where it provides savage penalties for minor offenders in the belief that society must proclaim its absolute intolerance of deviance and cast the deviants into the outer darkness. Such offenders have few champions among the respectable. But categorical moralism proved a fiasco when turned against a defendant with whom respectable folks could easily identify, a popular president and middle-class white guy. For at bottom categorical moralism is dangerous and loony, and when ordinary people can imagine it directed against themselves they have no trouble recognizing that.

The public was already aware of the dangers of categorical moralism in the doings of Independent Counsels with unlimited budgets and no accountability.[3] In Clinton's case, most people had no trouble seeing the problem with the Starr-House position. The modern state governs and regulates and taxes its citizens by getting them to respond to inquiries—job and loan application forms, tax returns, reports to regulatory agencies, affidavits, and answers to questions in legal proceedings, customs declarations, and the like—under the penalty of perjury. Predictably many people who fill out the forms and answer the questions slant them so as to exaggerate the facts that help their positions and minimize or conceal the facts that don't. Usually their deviations from strict truth are minor, as when a taxpayer slightly overstates deductions, or a job applicant who, when asked if he has ever been arrested replies "no," when in fact he was once arrested by mistake and his arrest record torn up in recognition of the mistake.

Sometimes lies are really important, like the lies of a witness who is deliberately framing a suspect for a crime, or manufacturing a case to collect civil damages. Yet on occasion the legal system overlooks even serious lies. Police perjury ("testilying") about the circumstances of arrests and searches in order to satisfy procedural formalities is depressingly common in many of our criminal courts. In highly adversary proceedings such as custody disputes after divorce, nobody seriously expects that the stories the parties tell about their former spouse's conduct are going to be the exact and literal truth. And if people are questioned in any context about hitherto secret extramarital affairs, no reasonably worldly person can expect complete candor in their replies.

So you didn't have to be a moral philosopher, just a person of average experience, to figure out what was wrong with the categorical position in Clinton's case. It suggested that if anyone fudged the truth in any of the multifarious official settings of our heavily legalized society, the government would not only be permitted but required to send its great armored battalions of FBI agents, prosecutors with subpoenas, and grand juries crashing into the most intimate corners of his life to get at the truth; to interrogate families, friends, and neighbors; to dig up dirt on witnesses and use it to extract cooperative testimony against him; and to exert its utmost to send him to prison. This might be Kenneth Starr's or Henry Hyde's picture of "the rule of law," but to most Americans, libertarian by instinct, it sounded more like Stalin's. The notion that every legal infraction must be met with the maximum sanctions, that every lawbreaker is an enemy of society, that there are no gradations of wrongdoing, no distinctions that matter between serious and trivial offenses, no occasions for discretion, would if carried out in practice be totalitarian and morally blind. Those who start crusades to purge the social body of every impurity of thought and deed invariably end up devouring their own children.

Some observers of the investigation and impeachment of President Clinton, putting it together with other Independent Counsel investigations that have wreaked havoc on the careers, finances, and family lives of political figures and their associates to nail them for trivial violations of law, have blamed the whole mess on the—now fortunately defunct—Independent Counsel law. True, the law was very badly designed: it appointed each Counsel with a designated target in view, gave him unlimited funds to pin something on that target, and exercised no control on, or supervision of, his conduct. Some counsels naturally enough saw their mandate as some investigative reporters do, to bring down a high official; and Starr's OIC was one of them. But several of the counsels appointed under the law went about their business soberly and discreetly, and if they found only minor offenses, declined to prosecute and closed down their offices in short order and at minimal expense.

Other observers see the impeachment mess as an aspect of a more general tendency to legalize politics, to recruit the legal system and especially the criminal law to take over tasks that would be better left to political conflict and resolved by the court of public opinion in the media and through elections. The tendency began in the aftermath of the Watergate scandal: its fruits were the Independent Counsel Act, the Democrat-inspired prosecutions of Reagan Administration officials in the Iran-Contra affair, and the Republican payback for Watergate and Iran-Contra in the many investigations and prosecutions of Clinton Administration officials, including Clinton himself.

In an alternative, more sophisticated history, the legalization of political conflict began in the civil rights movement, when blacks who were shut out of normal political channels turned to the courts. Their successes were then widely imitated by other liberal social movements that used the law as an instrument with which to further their political aims. In recent years conservatives have turned the tables, established legal-political action groups of their own like the Rutherford Institute, and used them to pursue their own agenda in courts newly staffed by conservative judges.

But I think more was going on in this scandal than the legalization of political conflict, and that was the legalization of moral and social outrage. The crusade against Clinton had the flavor of the purity and temperance crusades of the early twentieth century, when (as Joseph Gusfeld has argued in *Symbolic Crusade*) the small-town Protestant reformers who sought the legal prohibition of alcohol sales were as concerned with getting the state to declare their values as the right and true ones, and their opponents as immoral and wrong, as they were with reducing alcohol consumption. In recent years we have seen a renewed interest in using the legal system and especially the criminal law as a mouthpiece for outrage. The anti-Clinton crusaders were able to get as far as they did in part because they worked through prosecutors accustomed to the climate of remoralized criminal law, with its tendency to demonize even minor lawbreakers, to believe that in the Manichean battle with evil any tactic is justified to bring them down, and its categorical refusal to distinguish between gradations of offenses.

Happily, in this case, the public saw the obsessive pursuit of a man with real but relatively minor and understandable moral failings for what it was, a vast overreaction. They also saw the criminal justice process up close, and recoiled at much of what they saw, especially when the prosecutors defended practices such as pressuring a daughter to talk by threatening to jail her mother as the workaday tactics of their trade. Is it too much to hope that the public will become as sensitive to the system's current excesses directed against less prominent and popular victims than the Clintons? That they will see that the problem with the system is not that it expresses moral judgment, but that its mindless categorical moralism drives out discriminating moral judgment? Probably that is too much to hope for; but the steady good sense of the majority through the moral panic of 1998, its refusal to be whipped into a lynch mob mentality by the political and media frenzy, may give legitimacy and encouragement to those who would restore to administration of the law the discretion to be fair.

NOTES

1. In the *Jones* case, for instance, the trial judge penalized Clinton for what she believed were his false statements about Lewinsky in discovery by imposing a large fine for contempt accompanied by a stinging rebuke.

2. See *Impeachment Inquiry Pursuant to H. Res. 581: Appearance of Independent Counsel: Hearing before the House Comm. on the Judiciary*, 105th Cong. 182 (1998), reprinted in *Impeachment of President William Jefferson Clinton, The Evidentiary Record Pursuant to S. Res. 16*, Volume IX, Transcript of November 19, 1998 Presentation by Independent Counsel Kenneth Starr, Hearing Ser. No. 66, S. Doc. No. 106–3, at 18, 32, 113 (1999).

3. IC David M. Barrett spent four years and $10 million to indict former Secretary Henry Cisneros for making false statements to the FBI about the amounts he had paid a former mistress in 1989 while he was mayor of San Antonio. IC Donald Smaltz took four years and $17 million to prosecute former Secretary of Agriculture Mike Espy on thirty counts for receiving gifts and favors such as sports tickets totaling at most $35,000.

# Chapter 8

# The Gold Standard and Guilt-Edged Insecurities
## *The Impeachment Crucible as Tragic Farce*

### *Aviam Soifer*

> There is nothing either good or bad, but thinking makes
> it so.                                                     —Hamlet

### *Prelude: Shining Moments?*

At least one prize glittered. Moments after the formal acquittal of William Jefferson Clinton ended his impeachment trial, the Senate leaders of both parties presented Chief Justice William H. Rehnquist with a plaque featuring a golden gavel. Usually, majority leader Senator Trent Lott of Mississippi explained, with minority leader Senator Tom Daschle of South Dakota smiling at his side, one must preside over the Senate for a hundred hours to be awarded the golden gavel. But the Chief Justice's duty in presiding over the impeachment trial apparently was close enough for government work. Rehnquist, wearing his now-famous gold-striped robe, took the plaque and then quickly left the Senate chamber to a standing ovation from all the Senators and many of those in the public galleries.[1]

We are left wondering many things about that moment and about the meaning of the Chief Justice's role in presiding, particularly during the Senate's closed sessions. The Chief Justice's very presence suggested that the Senate's secret proceedings might constitute a familiar kind of trial. But we are also left in the dark about how much gold covers that plaque, for example, and who paid for it. And now we might want to know if the

Chief Justice declared the gift on his annual income reporting forms. Certainly he has since failed to recuse himself even in cases in which the Senate has been directly involved. Yet one does not need the *Antiques Roadshow* to grasp that the plaque the Chief Justice received is surely worth much more than its weight in gold as a collector's item. Are we soon therefore to face another impeachment for possible judicial "high crimes and misdemeanors"?

Probably not.

After all, how could the Vice President preside, as the Constitution provides, and how many stripes is Al Gore likely to demand? Notwithstanding the (almost) priceless gold gavel the Chief Justice recently received, we can be sure that he will avoid legal difficulties entirely. We can count on prosecutorial discretion—and the commonsense wishes of the American people—can't we? And if the Chief Justice were to be impeached and tried, could anyone else fill Rehnquist's shoes in reprising the role of the Lord Chancellor in Gilbert and Sullivan's *Iolanthe*, the self-proclaimed inspiration for the Chief Justice's unprecedented decision to appear gold-striped a few years ago? After all, it is the Chancellor who sings, "The law is the true embodiment / Of everything that's excellent, / It has no kind of fault or flaw, / And I, my Lords, embody the law."[2]

The Clinton impeachment imbroglio helped to underscore how deeply, publicly problematic it has become to determine who or what embodies the Rule of Law today. Notwithstanding all the experts gleefully exploiting the leisure of the theory class, the impeachment debacle demonstrated how controversial the reification of the law has become. The Rule of Law begins to seem like an indefinable shibboleth, an incantation that allows everything and anyone who can afford it to pass. The abstract Law seems to have no true embodiment, no clear benchmark, no place where anyone can go look it up definitively. This is a sad truth. So many people—including Supreme Court justices who should and probably do know better—seek someone, anyone authoritative, to say it ain't so. But did anyone who really thought about it ever think that the law is now, or ever was, as good as gold?

## The Gold Standard

It turns out that even if the Chief Justice's souvenir for presiding over the impeachment were worth only its weight in gold, we still could not be sure what even that cliché means. On the one hand, no less weighty an expert than Alan Greenspan recently proclaimed that gold remains the "ultimate form of payment."[3] On the other hand, the price of gold has been plummeting for years. And today there actually is no legal gold standard. Yet as with many other matters for which standards now seem elusive—thereby causing people to yearn for a Golden Age that never was—upon closer examination there may never have been much of a firm gold standard either. As President Franklin Delano Roosevelt told the press early in his presidency, for example: "As long as nobody asks me whether we are off the gold standard or gold basis, that is all right, because nobody knows what the gold basis or gold standard really is."[4] Roosevelt made this crack a few days after he took abrupt action prohibiting banks from paying out or exporting gold coin or bullion. This was a key part of the Bank Holiday, Roosevelt's first major presidential action to deal with the Depression.

Congress almost immediately backed Roosevelt's constitutionally shaky action with a Joint Resolution. Even a Supreme Court notoriously suspicious of Roosevelt then held, as a constitutional matter, that an explicit reference to a gold standard in a private contract—or in a government obligation—in practical effect included the paper legal tender equivalent, or perhaps some measurement of purchasing power.[5] Surprisingly, sources ranging from conservative economists to Chief Justice Hughes, the author of the five to four majority opinions for the Supreme Court in the *Gold Clause Cases* (1935), generally have agreed with Roosevelt that the very concept of a gold standard is malleable at best.[6] Yet Justice McReynolds led four bitter dissenters in the *Gold Clause Cases* in decrying the Court's "monstrous" decision to allow the federal action suspending gold payments—which was certain to produce "unending humiliation" and "legal and moral chaos."[7] Soon, however, Secretary of the Treasury Henry Morgenthau, Jr., joined a few others in setting the price of gold each morning in random fashion (to foil speculators) as the President finished his breakfast in bed.[8] So what *does* it mean, then, to be as good as gold? Even if, ultimately, a gold standard is mainly a matter of what the market will bear, are gold and law both commodities for which the world's governments constantly remake the market?

### Judge Posner and the Hard Rule of Law

The jury is still out about what to do in situations in which the ability to pay clearly influences most legal outcomes. But Judge Richard A. Posner is undoubtedly our leading expert about the relationship of law and the economic aspects of life symbolized by gold. Moreover, he has recently written yet another book, *An Affair of State* (1999). This time he offers a learned, often careful, always entertaining account of the Clinton impeachment. By considering a few key elements of Posner's provocative account, we will discern important missing elements. These are matters that implicate the Golden Rule in ways that Posner seems to miss entirely in his thrust toward clear standards and expertise. Posner can thus serve as an exemplar of a crucial, recurring error at the intersection of law and politics.

In *An Affair of State*, Posner frequently displays a keen appreciation of paradox. Several times, for example, he recounts blunders that turned out to aid the blunderer, false dawns, and a recurrent theme of "strength in weakness" (e.g., 180, 264). Though he is customarily a lover of binary choices, Posner states that matters such as politics, lying under oath, personal characteristics, and even public opinion all exist on a spectrum (147, 151–52, 162–63, 165). Indeed, he is willing to concede that the American public "is prepared to allow that a President may be a little above the law" (230), and even that some principles of the Rule of Law "are better left in aspirational than in implemented form" (194). Throughout most of the book, however, Posner reverts to his characteristic *Weltanschauung* of either/or choices concerning how to divide a fixed pie. Posner can thus appear charmingly shocked—shocked I tell you—to discover that the impeachment saga produced "two diametrically opposed narratives to choose between" (91–92). Moreover, he sounds amazed by the further news: "The problem is that both narratives are correct" (1992: 92).

The book is most intriguing and rewarding when Posner struggles with such uncertainty. He is also often quite funny, particularly at Rehnquist's expense. But Posner generally reverts to handy dichotomies—apparently the better to appear balanced or certain, my dear. He cannot resist, for example, when it is "tempting to conclude (though overgeneralization is a danger here) that the left intelligentsia lacks a moral core, while the right intelligentsia has a morbidly exaggerated fear of moral laxity" (240). Notwithstanding his proclaimed awareness of the dangers of overgeneralization, Posner's next sentence reports that the academy's response to the Clinton crisis provides "evidence that academic law, moral and political theory, and the study of history are soft fields despite the intelligence and toughmindedness of many of their practitioners" (ibid.). Contrasting "hard fields," Posner explains, entail "agreement on the methods for resolving disagreement [which] enables consensus to be forged despite the differing political agendas of the practitioners" (ibid.).

This Manichean view of academia is interesting in itself, but it takes on added significance as Posner repeatedly treats law as if it were a hard field. In the entire, sorry impeachment saga, Posner often seems to seek to embody the law almost, if not entirely, alone. Posner can discern from a distance—while also keeping his day job and pouring out often first-rate scholarship—that, for example, O. J. Simpson was "clearly guilty" (174). He then compares what he considers a clear miscarriage of justice by the Simpson jury—and its not entirely happy consequences for Simpson—with Clinton's acquittal and with Clinton's likely happier postacquittal fate. Through his innovative long-distance learning project, Posner also knows, after all, that: "The evidence of [Clinton's] guilt was overwhelming, and barely contested even by his lawyers" (241). You don't have to be there to decide, for "what a witness's demeanor reveals is not whether the witness is lying, but whether he's a good actor" (125).

## Law as Applied and the Jury

Because the law is hard and clear to Posner, as a general rule he hardly worries about its application to the facts. It therefore follows, for example, that prosecutorial abuses matter little. As Posner accurately notes, even gross abuses by a prosecutor would, under current law, neither bother most grand juries (Posner does not consider how different grand juries can be in the District of Columbia) nor serve to invalidate a conviction on appeal. If abuse of the grand jury process almost never produces reversible error, such abuses are simply of little concern to Judge Posner. The Independent Counsel statute was a bad idea, Posner tells us quite convincingly, and Kenneth Starr may have overreached as well as blundered. But that doesn't really matter—indeed, it hardly computes at all in Posner's final "Balance Sheet" chapter. In his binary Rule of Law calculus, there is little weighing of equities and scant attention to what others may think of the complex context of reality.

Posner thus conducts a bench trial—and from a very high bench at that. Law is for the authorities, and Posner undoubtedly is an authority. This may help explain why, in his otherwise careful dissection of the impeachment process through comparison with "regular" law, Posner perceives no analogy for the basic role that our law generally assigns to the

American jury. That the public's input is left out of a proper impeachment scheme entirely, as Posner describes it, troubles him not one bit. The jurors' application of common sense—their thoughts about mercy as well as outrage, equity as well as rigorous enforcement of the law—usually arises through an unpredictable conversation that includes diverse experiences as well as different viewpoints. All this mushiness in the application of the law to the facts is too soft to fit Posner's legal equations. This appellate judge may favor pragmatism, but it is the ersatz pragmatism of a lofty perch from which standards can be readily identified and cleanly maintained. It is hardly the pragmatism of the grass roots or the streets. Indeed, this form of legal justice must be vigilant in fending off popular justice everywhere.

Posner is correct, of course, in viewing the House of Representatives as analogous to a grand jury in the context of impeachment. He is also right that the Senators offered only a travesty of legal judgment regarding the Clinton affair. With their enthusiastic *ex parte* contacts and loud reveling in their own prejudgment judgments, they hardly resembled judges we would accept in a "real" legal case. (However, this phenomenon almost surely has less to do with the popular election of Senators than Posner's critical clucking would have us think, particularly if one takes a more balanced and more critical view of the wisdom of the Senate's acquittal of President Andrew Johnson than does Posner.) Nonetheless, the judgment of the American people throughout the Clinton fiasco ought to remind us, at least by analogy, of the complex and crucial roles that juries still play as they balance, mitigate, and at times even change the formal rigor of the law. Posner notes that "judges like other professionals grow moral calluses" (147). To many people, that is part of the problem, not the solution.

*Petit* jurors do not figure in Posner's account.[9] Indeed, the normal functioning of the popular will, as expressed through our jurors (and even the large shadow that juries cast over many more cases than they actually decide because of their potential role in judging) complicates the either/or choice between popular and legal justice that Posner posits throughout the book (see, e.g., 92, 146, 185, 198, 230, 237). Posner defines "legal justice" as "the justice meted out by judges and other authorized officials"; moreover, he insists that the confusion of popular and legal justice is "illegitimate" (92). But the temporary community of any jury room renders this dichotomy of popular versus legal justice much less clean and crisp than Judge Posner bemoans and fears.

Recognition of popular input in ascertaining what the law is and ought to be hardly means, *pace* Posner, that popular justice should be dismissed as lacking in standards. Ask most American juries about World War II, for example, and the jurors might well not share Judge Posner's knowledge that "American participation in World War II and the Cold War was motivated (primarily anyway) by national interest rather than by considerations of morality. Nor is morality central to our politics and attitudes. Freedom and wealth are."[10] They would probably want to consider the evidence and argue about it together before agreeing with the majestic sweep of Posner's assertion. A cross section of citizens might not be quite as facile about boiling things down to their essences, elevating wealth over morality, and distilling a hard gold standard from the murky, even at times disgusting, dross of mixed motives and fallible human beings.

## *Poetry and Alchemy*

Richard Posner is justly famous as an innovator, primarily but not exclusively for his focus on the intersection of law and the pursuit of wealth. Yet brief consideration of just a few examples drawn from the soft humanities reveals why people have gone for the gold with such fervor for so long. The bottom line will suggest how problematic any standard bottom line may be.

John Donne's poetry offers an excellent place to start. Gold served as a "master-image" for Donne, "which he could never stop thinking about for long."[11] Donne said of gold, for example:

> And as no fire, nor rust can spend or waste
> One dram of gold, but what was first shall last,
> Though it be forced in water, earth, salt, air,
> Expressed in infinite, none will impair.[12]

Throughout Donne's work, as well as in many contemporaneous writings, gold is portrayed as the best thing nature could produce, the purest and least changeable element imaginable. Moreover, gold was thought to be capable of purifying other entities. It served as "the highest and most potent" elixir.[13] Thus, for example, Donne proclaimed Christ to be:

> all gold when he lay down, but rose
> All tincture, and doth not alone dispose
> Leaden and iron wills to good, but is
> Of power to make even sinful flesh like his.[14]

In fact, it was widely believed that gold was the quintessence of life—and that the legendary Philosopher's Stone "is nothing other than gold digested to the highest degree."[15] But where did this wonderful gold come from?

Alchemists, from whom Donne borrowed heavily, believed that the sun was the source of gold. And many of the key laws of the elaborate pseudoscience of alchemy entailed the production, care, and nurturing of gold.[16] Skillful use of a crucible was among the most fundamental elements of success in the pursuit of pure, hard gold. And yet, "When it came to shape-changing, nothing was as good as gold."[17]

### On Wielding the Crucible: "All That Glitters . . ."

The talented alchemist, like the talented poet or playwright, had to be able to separate the gold from the dross. Alchemy was considered a hard science—hard to understand and difficult to perform. The best technique required skillful use of a crucible or melting pot. Through a process called calcining, a technique of heating material to a very high temperature without fusing the metals involved, it became possible to get rid of more volatile matter and thereby to extract the desired gold. A crucible— defined as synonymous with a melting pot—functioned not to merge separate elements, but rather to do precisely the opposite. Our core image of the American melting pot thus entirely misapprehends how a melting pot actually functions.[18]

However, to go through a crucible can also have a related but different meaning. In this second sense, a crucible affords a severe test. To be in a crucible therefore is to face the kind of hot fire that "melts down all concealment."[19] But ridding ourselves of all concealment may not always be a good thing. A messy, indeterminate kind of moral balancing test may be necessary to determine when to probe further and when to leave human frailty alone. Struggling with this kind of decision is a far cry from the hot and quick results that a crucible can provide. Yet like computers, crucibles are dependent on the quality of the material put in and the skill of the people who manipulate that material. Ultimately, people other than the operators will and ought to determine how successful a crucible or an impeachment proceeding might have been.

Critics of Independent Prosecutor Starr and of the House Judiciary Committee often claimed that a new witch-hunt was under way. Few noticed, however, how closely the entire Clinton impeachment affair was related to the best literary response to our own historical accusations of witchcraft, Arthur Miller's *The Crucible*. Bill Clinton is certainly no John Kennedy—nor is he a John Proctor. (Proctor cared little about public opinion, no matter what the views of the focus groups, and he fought an uphill battle for principle rather than to save his skin.) Yet before both the public sagas of Clinton and Proctor even began, both men had been unfaithful to their wives. It was the subsequent statements of the two young women, who apparently remained jealously smitten, that set both dramas in motion.[20] A complex intermingling of private motivations and the demands of service to public principles characterized the two prosecutions that followed. In both cases, secret illicit sex offstage triggered a massive tangle of accusations, shadings of truth, and untrustworthy confessions in full view of the audience.

The congruence between fact and fiction goes further. For example, John Proctor decided upon his final action—to tear up the false confession that would have saved his life and instead to die to protect his name—primarily on the basis of spin control. *The Crucible*'s denouement thus revolves around Proctor's concern about how his confession is likely to play in Salem village. And in both cases, as Posner points out, one can sometimes lose by winning, and vice versa.

There is no question that Miller wrote *The Crucible* in part as a critical commentary on the Red Scare of the early 1950s. As Miller drove off to do his initial historical research in Salem, for example, he stopped to visit his friend Elia Kazan, whom he said he "loved like a brother" and who had directed Miller's previous Broadway successes.[21] Kazan had just returned from testifying willingly and naming names before the House Un-American Activities Committee (HUAC), and their close friendship abruptly ended.

After *The Crucible* opened in January 1953, the American Bar Association joined right-wing activists in picketing the play, purportedly because of its unsympathetic depiction of Puritan judges. On the other hand, the cast and the audience joined in a moment of silence when they learned that the Rosenbergs had been executed. Within five years, not only had Miller been divorced and then married to the Golden Girl, Marilyn Monroe, but the State Department had denied him a passport to attend the play's premiere in Belgium. Miller was called before HUAC; and subsequently convicted of contempt of Congress when he refused to testify.[22]

The playwright refused to name names, though he publicly and insistently decried true believers on all sides. To Miller, the great problem was that if people might no longer mention God's beard and Devil's horns, "the world is still gripped between two diametrically opposed absolutes" (*The Crucible*, 33). In apparent contrast to Judge Posner's sense of the satisfactions of hard science, however, Miller maintained that "[t]he concept of unity, in which positive and negative are attributes of the same force, in which good and evil are relative, ever-changing, and always joined to the same phenomenon . . . is reserved to the physical sciences and to the few who have grasped the history of ideas" (ibid.).

From the perspective of our recent impeachment drama, what seems most interesting about *The Crucible*, however, is how complex and relative the play turns out to be in its treatment of its central theme of loyalty and deception. The pivotal moment in *The Crucible* occurs when Elizabeth Proctor, forced into a corner under the harsh questioning of Deputy Governor Danforth, lies about John Proctor's lechery to save his name. We are clearly meant to admire Elizabeth's uncharacteristic and tragic falsehood. "[I]t is a natural lie to tell" (114), as Reverend Hale proclaims, but Elizabeth is trapped and her lie leads directly to the conviction of both the Proctors. Elizabeth is heroic when she lies, but certainly not earlier when she is so rigidly principled that she entirely refuses to forgive her husband for his earlier trespasses. Although John Proctor was not always loyal to Elizabeth— and he was mightily offended by his minister's devotion to golden candlesticks—clearly he is meant to be seen as a much better person than the girls, who are completely loyal to Abigail and faithful to the story she has concocted. And Reverend Hale, who during the course of the play moves far from his reliance on book learning and holy law in the quest for witches to total denunciation of the court and its processes, grows to embrace the idea that no principle can be worth the sacrifice of a life (132).

Yet *The Crucible* ends with John Proctor's decision to die. He does so partially out of loyalty to his friends and their memories, but primarily and, we are to believe, nobly because of his concern for his own reputation. Notwithstanding the context of McCarthyism, Miller thus seems to embrace neither loyalty nor the truth as trump. Rather, what people will believe—what one's reputation will be, what spin will be put on one's actions—seems to become the ultimate standard for judgment. This seems a strangely unprincipled benchmark. Yet this reading of *The Crucible* underscores the play's relevance to the Clinton impeachment and to the problem of shame within a culture in which whether something is shameful and what is shameful has become deeply controversial, to the particular horror of the group Posner describes as "moralistic conservatives" (*An Affair of State*, 200).

## Lifetime Achievement, Law, and the Role of the Audience

By now our society's answer to Attorney Joseph Welsh's legendary challenge to Senator Joseph McCarthy—"Have you no sense of decency, sir, at long last? Have you left no sense of decency?"[23]—may be a clear "Yes." Less than two months after President Clinton received his acquittal and the Chief Justice had gathered up his new gold gavel, in March 1999 the Academy of Motion Picture Arts and Sciences bestowed its annual Lifetime Achievement award on Elia Kazan. (Was the Senate gavel presentation inspired by the Oscars or, more likely, by some Rotary Club Roast?) To be sure, considerable controversy surrounded the decision to hand Kazan this special Oscar because some remembered Kazan's willingness to cooperate with HUAC in the early 1950s. The Academy Awards broadcast turned out to be quite anticlimactic, however. The frail, eighty-nine-year-old director and writer stumbled through a few uninspired words, to the applause of many and the silence of some. Yet to award the famous golden statue to Kazan—who had not only cooperated with HUAC, but had also taken out a full-page advertisement in the *New York Times*, delivered a lecture at Harvard, and written a story for *Reader's Digest* explaining why he was proud to name names[24]—smacked of both tragedy and farce. Unlike some who had been close to Kazan and who loudly proclaimed that they could never forgive him, Arthur Miller supported the award. Parsed carefully, however, it is hard to know how forgiving of his old friend Miller actually is. He wrote, "Perhaps all one can hope for is to find in one's heart praise for what a man has done well and censure for where he has tragically failed."[25]

Ultimately such judgments belong to history's jury. They ought to involve a blend of heads and hearts—and of people with different perspectives who strive to follow the Golden Rule. It is difficult if not impossible to love one's neighbor as oneself. And it is sadly true that even those who clearly do evil generally have good reasons justifying their behavior. This is why the confusion of ends and means is so familiar, but also so troublesome. When John Proctor counterattacks, for example, he uses low tactics much like those used by his attackers. When Judge Posner insists on the Rule of Law as an end in itself, he echoes Deputy Governor Danforth. A sense of skepticism even about one's own most firmly held values goes a long way toward understanding, and perhaps tolerating, even the blatant faults that are so obvious in others. Moreover, even the legal justice system needs such play in the joints.

At the end of the *The Just and the Unjust*, an old judge who has had a stroke explains a vital point to his lawyer-son, the character through whom readers have shared an insider's view of the workings of a district attorney's office and the unpredictability of juries. The judge notes:

> The ancient conflict between liberty and authority. The jury protects the Court. . . . There's no focal point with a jury; the jury is the public itself. That's why a jury can say when a judge couldn't, "I don't care what the law is, that isn't right and I won't do it." It's the greatest prerogative of free men. They have to have a way of saying that and making it stand. They may be wrong, they may refuse to do things they ought to do; but freedom just to be wise and good isn't freedom. We pay a price for lay participation in the law; but it's a necessary expense.[26]

As Horace Walpole once observed, "[T]he world is a comedy to those that think, a tragedy to those that feel."[27] By now, we ought to understand that the world is both—and that if history does repeat itself, it is probably as tragic farce. We certainly should be worried about the very short attention span of the public today. Moreover, Court TV and Judge Judy serve to legitimize glib judgments by those not present. Many share Judge Posner's disdain for witness demeanor evaluation, and the belief that they can judge adequately at a great distance from the courthouse.

There is still something to being there in person, however, and to attending to the way in which live performances really are different, and do create communality. In a successful production of *The Crucible*, for example, members of the audience look up together at the end of Act III to see whether the great yellow (gold?) bird is there, as Abigail and her minions scream and point.[28]

Even if we know that neither the devil nor a judge with a definitive answer is sitting up there, we have gained something—soft and elusive though it may be—by temporarily suspending disbelief together. To be sure, the communal search for morality lacks clarity and consistency. Notwithstanding true belief in legal answers that can be scientifically discovered and applied, however, it is also the case that no one really has a hard, clear, glittering legal standard.[29]

In the quest for justice, we surely are wiser when we trust and rely on others as well as ourselves. Indeed, we particularly need one another to reinforce the imperative to continue to question authority and to be able to laugh together. Many people yearn for the certainty of crisp legal rules.[30] Such a legal gold standard, however, tends to undermine the pursuit of justice. And zealous crusading for the gold produces folly or tragedy, or both. Children know that even a muffled Midas touch suffocates the best of human instincts.

NOTES

1. Richard W. Stevenson, "The President's Acquittal: The Chief Justice Rehnquist Goes with the Senate Flow, 'Wiser, but Not a Sadder Man,'" *New York Times*, February 13, 1999, A12.

2. Before becoming a Supreme Court Justice, Rehnquist had no experience as a judge. As a rising star in the Nixon White House, however, he may have been consulted about the short-lived new costumes for the presidential guard.

3. Jonathan Fuerbringer, "An Icon's Fading Glory: Now, the Gold Rush Is to the Exits," *New York Times*, June 15, 1999, C1. The gold standard is still considered the gold standard in other realms as well. See, e.g., Jonathan Wilson, "Bloom's Day," review of Saul Bellow's *Ravelstein*, *New York Times* Book Review, April 23, 2000, 6 ("Now here [Bellow] comes, at the age of 84, writing in his gold-standard prose as an antidote to mindlessness, in a lovely, haunting novel.") There are even "goldbug" investors still, albeit the poorer for their faith in recent years. See James Collins, "Gold People," *New Yorker*, July 17, 2000, 32.

4. Quoted in Kenneth W. Dam, "From the Gold Clause Cases to the Gold Commission: A Half Century of American Monetary Law," 50 *U. Chi. L. Rev.* 504, 510 (1983). Dam points out that at most the United States can be said to have been on the gold standard only from 1879 to 1933; the international gold standard lasted at most only from 1879 until its collapse near the start of World War I, to be briefly revived from the mid-1920s until 1931 when Britain left it again. Dam, "From the Gold Clause Cases," 506.

5. Two wonderfully concise explanations of, and illuminating commentary about, the Gold Clause Cases tangle were published soon after this event by young academics John P. Dawson, "The Gold Clause Decisions," 33 *Mich. L. Rev.* 647 (1935) and Henry M. Hart, Jr., "The Gold Clause in United States Bonds," 48 *Harv. L. Rev.* 1057 (1935). As Dawson summarized it, "Monetary history has provided no basis for the widespread faith in gold as a stable index of value." Dawson, "The Gold Clause Decisions," 676.

6. Milton Friedman, "Real and Pseudo Gold Standards," 4 *J. L. & Econ.* 66 (1961). See also Henry G. Manne and Roger LeRoy Miller, eds., *Gold, Money and the Law* (Chicago: Aldine Publishing, 1975). On the Gold Clause Cases (*Norman v. Baltimore and O. R.R.*, 294 U.S. 240 [1935]) and companion cases involving both private and public obligations payable in gold, see generally J. Willard Hurst, *A Legal History of Money in the United States, 1774–1970* (Lincoln: University of Nebraska Press, 1973).

7.  294 U.S. 317, 379, 381.

8.  Arthur M. Schlesinger, Jr., *The Coming of the New Deal* (Boston: Houghton Mifflin, 1959), 241.

9.  The book's comprehensive index does not mention juries or jurors, and I found only a single passing reference when Posner explains that a federal judge can require a civil jury to answer specific questions of fact under Fed. R. Civ. P. 49. Richard A. Posner, *An Affair of State: The Investigation, Impeachment, and Trial of President Clinton* (Cambridge: Harvard University Press, 1999), 197.

10.  Posner, *An Affair of State*, 155. In the next sentence, Posner elevates "the rule-of-law values that Clinton has flouted" to the level of "important ingredients in America's success," apparently primarily because "they are essential to the freedom and wealth that distinguish the United States from most other nations."

11.  John Carey, *John Donne: Life, Mind and Art* (New York: Oxford University Press, 1981), 10.

12.  "To the Lady Bedford," in *John Donne: The Complete English Poems*, ed. A. J. Smith (London: Penguin, 1971), 231–32.

13.  Edgar H. Duncan, "Donne's Alchemical Figures," reprinted in *Discussions of John Donne*, ed. Frank Kermode (Boston: D. C. Heath, 1962), 73, 82, quoting Paracelsus, *Book Concerning Long Life*.

14.  "Resurrection, Imperfect," in *John Donne: The Complete English Poems*, 327, 328. Of course, Donne used a similar metaphor involving the transformative perfection of gold in praise of women.

15.  Duncan, "Donne's Alchemical Figures," 85, quoting Michael Sendivogius, *The New Chemical Light*.

16.  My favorite example, which echoes but inverts Robert Gordon's discussion of the impeachment process, involves the idea that the weight of gold would increase if the gold were buried in the earth and fertilized constantly with human urine and pigeon dung. See Carey, *John Donne*, 160, quoting Paracelsus. The connection between gold and human excrement is also a staple in some branches of psychoanalysis. Even George Washington in 1785 described the "knowing farmer" who transformed everything he touched into manure, the first step to reaching gold. Patricia A. Martin, "Bioethics and the Whole: Pluralism, Consensus, and the Transmutation of Bioethical Methods into Gold," 27 *J. of Law, Medicine and Ethics* 316 (1999).

17.  Carey, *John Donne*, 185. Carey observes that gold was fascinating and "immensely important" to Donne as an image source because it "united the maximum of constancy with the maximum of inconstancy." Mircea Eliade noted that "the alchemist takes up and perfects the work of Nature, while at the same time working to 'make' himself"; and added that in many cultures gold was "the symbol of sovereignty and autonomy." Mircea Eliade, *The Forge and the Crucible: The Origins and Structures of Alchemy*, trans. Stephen Corrin, 2d ed. (Chicago: University of Chicago Press, 1978), 47, 52. Eliade also notes, "The history of science

recognizes no absolute break between alchemy and chemistry." *The Forge and the Crucible*, 9. Ironically, recent troubling revelations about Eliade's own past underscore his concern for how one can "make" oneself anew. See Umberto Eco, "Murder in Chicago," *New York Review of Books*, April 10, 1997.

18. Louis Marshall, a very successful lawyer and a key leader within the Jewish community, made this point in a speech criticizing the widespread enthusiasm that surrounded Israel Zangwill's famous play, *The Melting Pot* (1908). Marshall proclaimed, "It was clear that Zangwill is not a metallurgist or else he would know that in the art of metallurgy the great effort made is that the various elements composing the melting pot shall be separated into their constituent parts, so that the copper shall be fused with the copper, the silver with the silver, and the gold with the gold." Charles Reznikoff, ed., *Louis Marshall, Champion of Liberty: Selected Papers and Addresses* (Philadelphia: Jewish Publication Society, 1957), 809. But Zangwill's happy assimilationist message, rather than the facts carefully marshaled, carried the day. For a keen discussion of this and of pluralism generally, see Carol Weisbrod, *Emblems of Federalism* (forthcoming).

19. Deputy Governor Danforth, the lead judge, in Arthur Miller, *The Crucible* (New York: Viking, 1964), 89 (citations are to this edition).

20. Miller acknowledged that the play "is not history in the sense in which the word is used by the academic historians" (*The Crucible*, 2), and that he took the liberty of fusing some characters and changing Abigail from an eleven-year-old to a seventeen-year-old who is "a strikingly beautiful girl with an endless capacity for dissembling" (8–9). (Miller does not mention that he reduced Proctor's age, changing him from a man in his sixties to one in his mid-thirties.) Though many have commented on the accuracy of Miller's history, Edmund S. Morgan does the best job of both crediting and critiquing what Miller wrought in "Arthur Miller's *The Crucible* and the Salem Witch Trials: A Historian's View," in *The Golden and Brazen World: Papers in Literature and History, 1650–1800*, ed. John M. Wallace (Berkeley: University of California Press, 1985), 171.

21. Arthur Miller, *Timebends: A Life* (New York: Grove Press, 1987), 332. A few years earlier, Kazan even commissioned a screenplay from Miller set on the New York docks. Later, the New York docks became the setting for *On the Waterfront* (1954), Kazan's famous Academy Award–winning drama about loyalty and independence. See Thomas H. Pauly, *An American Odyssey: Elia Kazan and American Culture* (Philadelphia: Temple University Press, 1983), 182–85.

22. Miller's conviction, which occurred in 1957 and was thus several years after the Senate censured Senator Joseph McCarthy late in 1954, was reversed by an *en banc* panel of the D.C. Circuit in 1958, on the grounds that the Committee chair had not pressed his question with sufficient precision. *Miller v. United States*, 259 F. 2d 187 (D.C. Cir., 1958) (*en banc*).

23. Quoted and discussed in Ellen Schrecker, *Many Are the Crimes: McCarthyism in America* (Boston: Little, Brown, 1998), 264.

24. Pauly, *An American Odyssey*, 156–160.

25. Bill Hewitt, "Question of Honor," *People*, March 29, 1999, 95. Rod Steiger, for example, whose role in *On the Waterfront* significantly boosted his acting career, told the press, "I don't think that time excuses the crime. Nobody was supposed to destroy someone else for their own ambition"; while Karl Malden, who also had a juicy role in that film, proclaimed, "There's no place for politics in any art form. If that's the way he chose to get out of a problem who are we to judge?" (Hewitt, "Question of Honor," 95). For a particularly entertaining essay probing *On the Waterfront* within the context of Kazan's testimony, see Stephen Hunter, "Elia Kazan's Defense of Informers; He Named Names. 'Waterfront' Tells Why," *Washington Post*, Sunday Arts, March 28, 1999, G01.

26. James Gould Cozzens, *The Just and the Unjust* (New York: Harcourt, Brace, 1942), 427–28. The entire novel can be read as a sardonic undercutting of a quotation from Lord Hardwicke that appears on the first page of the book: "Certainty is the Mother of Repose; therefore the Law aims at Certainty."

27. Quoted in Otto Reinert, ed., *Classic through Modern Drama* (Boston: Little, Brown, 1970), xxviii.

28. Posner is confident in generalizing, for example: "Liberals rather like treating adults as children; that is what paternalism means, and liberal policies tend to be paternalistic" (*An Affair of State*, 204). But it can also be a mistake to treat children as adults, a point underscored in *The Crucible* and missed entirely by Judge Posner in *DeShaney v. Winnebago County Dep't of Social Servs.*, 812 F. 2d 298, 301 (7th Cir. 1987), *aff'd*, 489 U.S. 189 (1989). In an opinion that Chief Justice Rehnquist tracked closely as the Supreme Court affirmed, Posner insisted that "*The state does not have a duty* enforceable by the federal courts to maintain a police force or a fire department, or *to protect children from their parents*. The men who framed the original Constitution and the Fourteenth Amendment were worried about government's oppressing the citizenry rather than about its failing to provide adequate social services" (emphasis added).

29. A fine example of such false certainty may be found in Justice Field's statement for the Court upholding contractual gold clauses after the Civil War. Field proclaimed "the fact, accepted by all men throughout the world, that value is inherent in the precious metals; that gold and silver are in themselves values, and being such, and being in other respects best adapted to the purpose, are the only proper measures of value." *Bronson v. Rhodes*, 74 U.S. (7 Wall.) 229, 249 (1869).

30. For an intriguing essay about Italian and American legal formalism, that analogizes formalism to the gold standard that was in effect during "the greatest inflations and depressions in the world's history," see Guido Calabresi, "Two Functions of Formalism: In Memory of Guido Tedeschi," 67 *U. Chi. L. Rev.* 479, 483 (2000).

Chapter 9

# Sex, Harm, and Impeachment

## Robin West

Conservative and liberal legal commentators on the Clinton impeachment agreed on very little, but they agreed emphatically on the characterization of the various sexual behaviors which triggered the scandal. They all agreed that the President's sexual relationship with Monica Lewinsky, although indecorous, indiscreet, disloyal, ill-advised, kinky, revolting, juvenile, thoughtless, immoral, and reckless, was nevertheless consensual, and therefore not criminal, and that it was welcome, and therefore not sexual harassment. They all concluded, then, and reiterated mantra-style that although it might have been a breach of private morality, this noncriminal and nontortious and non–civil rights-violating private sex should not be the basis for the impeachment of the President.[1] They also agreed over the characterization of the "sex" at the heart of the charge of sexual harassment brought by Paula Jones. Conservative and liberal commentators agreed that, if true, this alleged encounter in a hotel room constituted a boorish and obnoxious although seemingly pathetic instance of indecent exposure. But at most it presented a weak case for "sexual harassment," involving as it did a solitary incident and only trivial, or at any rate nonactionable, damage. So here as well, they agreed that this appalling but nevertheless nontortious sexual conduct should not be the basis for the impeachment of the President.[2] Rather, it was the perjurious lying about the Lewinsky affair that in turn corrupted the legal process to which the noninjured Jones was entitled—even assuming the fatal flaws in her underlying claim—that legitimately was at the heart of the drive to impeach.[3] And finally, liberal and conservative lawyers seemingly agreed, after the impeachment process had wound down, that the claim of forcible, violent rape made by Juanita Broaddrick, which came to light only after the Senate failed to convict the President of a single offense, was "too little, too late": that although quite serious if true, it very possibly was not true, was at any rate unprovable, whether or not it was provable it was ancient history, and in any event, it was not a case which could ever have been prosecuted. For all these reasons it too was irrelevant to questions of fitness for office, and should not be the subject matter of impeachment proceedings.[4]

We were left, then, with a Greek-style chorus: the President's persecutors and prosecutors, his defenders, and eventually Clinton himself, were singing slightly different melodies, but nonetheless doing so in harmony: it wasn't the sex—immoral, kinky, pathetic, nondecorous, ill-advised, exploitative, and perverse but nevertheless not tortious, not provably criminal, and not a violation of anyone's civil rights—that was or should have been at the heart of the inquiry, but the lying about it under oath.[5] It was not his sex life that was under investigation, it was his contempt for the Rule of Law. It was not Clinton's insulting, injurious, or demeaning behavior toward women—although that behavior and its endless media dissection were certainly enough to entertain, circus style, the voting and nonvoting public—but rather his insulting behavior *toward the judiciary*, and toward the special prosecutors appointed by the judiciary, and toward the House prosecutors, and generally toward the Rule of Law and toward the legal process, that was legitimately at the heart of a constitutional and political crisis.

This conventional, choral wisdom among lawyers regarding the irrelevancy of the President's sexual behavior, as was often remarked, was joined not just by the President's prosecutors and defenders, but more strikingly by many (though certainly not all) feminist lawyers who took a position on the President's impeachment over the course of the year.[6] This struck many as puzzling and possibly hypocritical. Why would feminists, of all people, seek to trivialize sexual violence, sexual harassment, and sexual exploitation, after a two decades-long effort to heighten public concern, even public alarm, about the seriousness and frequency of the occurrence of these very offenses? Could it really be simply of no moment—virtually unworthy of comment—that the so-called leader of the free world admittedly exploited, most likely harassed, and quite possibly raped women, apparently as a matter of course and apparently with notable frequency, and, until the disastrous impeachment, seemingly with no consequences?

In these comments, I want to make two separate observations regarding the legal consensus. First, I want to briefly note some of the reasons for the legal consensus, particularly among feminists. In the second and longer part of these comments I want to argue that the consensus position—that it was the lying, not the sex, that was at the heart of the impeachment process—although correct, nevertheless rested in part on, and then unfortunately perpetuated, deeply confused understandings about the role of consent in our legal and moral understanding of sexual relationships.

## The Legal Consensus

Why, then, the legal consensus, and why feminist-legal support for it? The reason ascribed to feminists by conventional wisdom likely has some truth to it: unlike his predecessor, Clinton had been supportive of both reproductive rights and parental leave policies and had appointed significant numbers of women to high-ranking positions in the executive and judicial branches. Feminism is a political as well as legal movement, and as such is rightly interested in preserving those political gains. But there were other reasons as well. First, feminist lawyers are lawyers as well as feminists, and the legal consensus, as a legal matter, was right. The Lewinsky affair *was* clearly consensual, and therefore it was noncriminal, and it was also welcome, and therefore it was not sexual harassment.[7] This is not a close question.

Paula Jones did fail to allege significant employment-related injury, and some such injury is a necessary part of a claim for sexual harassment, and therefore there was no violation of her civil rights.[8] This, though, is not such a close question, and here there were a few discordant tones, from some feminist lawyers as well as others.[9] Common sense, for one, rebels: surely, one might think, if *that's* not on-the-job sexual harassment, then perhaps something is wrong with sexual harassment law.

Finally, Broaddrick's allegedly violent sexual encounter with the President *was* a long time ago, and very likely could not have been successfully prosecuted had it been brought—although here the chorus goes minor and atonal in a humorless, postmodern kind of way. If believed, after all, Broaddrick suffered a violent rape. Nevertheless, it is clear that Clinton's sexual behavior was neither tortious, provably criminal, nor demonstrably violative of anyone's civil rights. It could not have been and should not have been the basis for an impeachment inquiry. On the doctrine alone, feminist lawyers were right to join the legal consensus.

There were, however, nondoctrinal reasons as well for the remarkably widespread endorsement, among feminist lawyers, of the conventional legal wisdom—that sex is and should be irrelevant to the questions surrounding the President's impeachment. Most importantly, many people across the political spectrum, including many lawyers and feminists, justifiably feared a *Kulturkampf*.[10] The fear, often stated by the President's defenders, including his lawyers, was that the conventional choral mantra notwithstanding, the President *was* in fact being persecuted for his cultural rather than his legal transgressions: his lack of a respectable, blueblood genetic pedigree; his manifest antiracism;[11] his willingness and apparent desire to empower women both nationally and globally in the productive rather than reproductive realms of life; his obvious distaste for traditional militaristic markers of aristocratic masculinity; his participation in the countercultural movements during the sixties; his striking ease among sexual outsiders, such as out gays and lesbians; his evident enjoyment of nonreproductive, extramarital, nontraditional, and nonmissionary-style sexual practices—practices still illegal, even between married couples, in a number of states—and as a part of all this, his apparent contempt for the constraints of traditional marriage.[12] By virtue of training, education, professional identity, professional ethics, and gut instinct, many lawyers, certainly including liberal and feminist lawyers, have a well-honed reaction to such a danger. For, to whatever degree that suspicion was well grounded—to whatever degree the drive for impeachment *was* premised on President Clinton's cultural rather than legal transgressions—the impeachment drive *itself* was a profoundly illegal act of considerably greater importance than the President's perjurious deposition. Impeachment of a president for being a cultural outsider would obviously wreak far greater harm on core liberal and Rule of Law values—such as a restrained, whether or not minimal, state, due regard for individualism and privacy, and perhaps most important, a prosecutorial system activated by genuine criminality or civil wrong rather than by pique at the cultural markers of particular individuals—than the contempt shown by the President for the sexual harassment action that had been filed against him.

From the perspective of the lawyer-spectator, the impeachment drive during much of the year seemed close to collapsing into just such an overtly frightening spectacle. Only on the very thin surface was it about perjury. Underneath, it was about sex all the way down—and never more so than in its three climactic moments: the delivery of the Starr Report to

Congress and their delivery of that report to the nation, the President's televised "grand jury" testimony, and Monica Lewinsky's testimony to the House. All three episodes, as conveyed to the consuming public, were sex-drenched, while ritualistically couched in the mantralike denial that the sex mattered. As suspicion grew, particularly among lawyers, that the impeachment drive was in fact so motivated—that that was what was really going on—it became all the more important to the President's attackers to emphasize that the President's sexual behavior was *not* at the heart of the drive to impeach him; to insist all the more compulsively that the President's perjury, and "not the sex," was at the heart of the President's troubles. And it became important to a wide swath of liberal and legal and liberal-legal opinion—including, overwhelmingly, liberal feminist lawyers—to insist that the President *ought* not to be persecuted for these cultural transgressions, even while expressing suspicion that he was in fact being persecuted for precisely that. As bad as sexual harassment, sexual exploitation, or underenforced rape laws may be, even for women, a Western-style fundamentalist version of the Taliban would be worse: No feminist lawyer wants to witness a fundamentalist religious coup, much less give reckless aid to one. To even suggest that the President's sexual behavior was something to worry over tempts those fates. As macabre and mediocre as the impeachment episode was, so long as it stuck with incidents of perjury, it wasn't terrifying. A sexual inquisition, by contrast, might have been.

Relatedly, the conventional legal wisdom—that it was only the President's perjury, not his underlying sex life, that could or should possibly sustain his impeachment—was a healthy response from a feminist perspective, particularly considering the position against which it was routinely pitted. The (nonlegal) cultural moralists who from the outset *did* explicitly focus upon the moral depravity of the President's sexual behavior—whether or not they found it impeachable—did so, for the most part, out of a commitment to the institutions of marriage and family, not out of a concern about harassment in the workplace, or sexual violence against women, or even the sexual exploitation of young women.[13] Their condemnation of the President's sex life, in other words, was at heart a condemnation of his promiscuity and his contempt for his marriage vows, rather than worry over the harm his actions caused women. Further, their support of traditional marriage in turn was seemingly premised not on its life-enhancing nurturant qualities, but on its institutional and patriarchal power: the family and marriage are bedrock societal institutions not only because they entrench hierarchy, tradition, and gender roles, keeping men up and women down, but also because they keep everyone relatively passive. Against this backdrop of strange bedfellows, to argue that the President's sexual conduct, and not just his lying about it in a deposition, might be a real cause for worry, was to risk being misheard as condemning eros. That's a major risk indeed in a culture still as committed to a punitive and regimented conception of marriage and family, a regular, productive, wealth-maximizing, and spirit-killing consumerism and commercialism, and an obsessive, itchlike, sadistic, masochistic, public econosexual compulsion—the unpleasurable sex of *Melrose Place*—on the other. We need more, not less, eros, pleasure, eroticism, caresses, love, tenderness, care, and mutual affection in our lives. We need more, not less, disruption of the drumbeat call for material production, wealth, and accumulation of consumer goods coming from both the private and public spheres. We need more, not less, spontaneity and joy.

## The Discourse

Let me turn now to the costs, which I think were substantial, of the legal consensus—that the sex was private, and therefore although perhaps immoral, was legally inconsequential, while the perjury was so serious as to have been impeachable. Again, let me restate, in my view the consensus view was entirely correct: the President's alleged sexual transgressions could not have been and should not have been the basis of impeachment, for both doctrinal and cultural-legal reasons. But nevertheless, a correct legal and cultural and political conclusion can rest on erroneous or simply confused arguments, and that confusion itself can have costs. Here, there are two.

First, the consensus view, and the powerful distinction it both drew and relied on between the private wrong against "morality"—within which women are enveloped—and the public crime against the legal system—within which women as women are typically erased—cleanly echoes centuries of dismissive disregard for sexual harms sustained by young, weak, or otherwise vulnerable women, inflicted by alpha men, in private, particularly when those men hold positions of great power and responsibility. The President's behavior itself—a little harassment here, a little exploitation there, compulsive flirtation everywhere, a possible rape a long time ago—might be, for the most part, relatively harmless, sometimes comical, sometimes pathetic, examples of a mind-set toward women and sex. Nevertheless, it is just that mind-set that has at its core a disregard of women's subjective well-being that is centuries old, global in scope, and in many times and places mind-numbing in its reckless cruelty. That the legal consensus formed so quickly around the irrelevancy of the sex and the triviality of any harms that might have been done to the women in its course was disturbing, if not surprising, for that reason alone.

But second, and less obviously, the legal "bottom line"—that we should all focus on the lying, not the sex—had another rhetorical cost: it furthered rather than corrected the conceptual confusion regarding a range of sexual offenses from violent rape, to sexual harassment, to the nontortious but nevertheless sometimes harmful sexual exploitation of subordinates in hierarchic environments, such as schools, work, and the military. More specifically, the confused discussion surrounding all three cases—Lewinsky, Jones, and Broaddrick—both reflected and further entrenched ways of thinking about the role of *consent* in or to sexual behavior that are both widespread and dysfunctional. In each case, the claimed relation of consent to the underlying sexual conduct and its value was confused at best, and it was a confusion that was worsened rather than alleviated by the conventional chorus—that it was the perjury, not the sex—regarding the Clinton impeachment scandals. I'm not sure it could have been otherwise. But nevertheless, these are additional harms occasioned by the entire scandal, and we ought to accord them their due. Unlike the harms visited by the scandal that were noted, harms on our constitutional form of government, on our daily dwindling trust in elected officials, on prosecutorial conduct, on popular understandings of and respect for the Rule of Law, these harms—harms that go to the quality of our discourse, and hence indirectly to the quality of our sexual relations—might even be remediable.

## Lewinsky: Desire, Sex, and Value

Let me start with the discourse surrounding the Lewinsky affair. Again, and as noted, virtually all commentators agreed that the Lewinsky affair, because it was both consensual and welcome, constituted neither rape nor sexual harassment. But nevertheless, there was plenty of public discourse regarding the moral valence of the legal underlying conduct, and in that nonlegal discourse a few basic arguments were staked out, and then vigorously defended, early on. First of all, moral conservatives, of course, saw clear reasons to condemn the President's affair as morally wrongful—rather than simply sleazy—and they did so, for the most part, on the basis of the harm done the institution of marriage. Much of the public likely endorsed this conventionally conservative view, although presumably a sizable silent minority (or majority) did not: at least if we judge by conduct, there must be huge numbers of people who find extramarital workplace affairs neither wrongful nor sleazy. Perhaps for reasons too obvious to belabor, the basis of disagreement between the much publicized conservative condemnation of the President's affair with Monica Lewinsky, and the libertine or libertarian's more permissive stance rarely received a public airing.

That implicit debate (made explicit, and nicely so, in David Kennedy's contribution to this volume) however, is not what I want to focus on here. While social conservatives shadowboxed with libertarian defenders, a somewhat more explicit debate was joined between liberals and feminists over how that affair ought to be characterized. It is that debate that I want to focus on here.[14] On one side, Clinton's supporters, invoking long-standing norms of liberal argument, emphasized not only the consensuality, but also the mutual welcomeness of the affair: because it was obviously desired on both sides, it was neither criminal, tortious, *nor harmful*—at least, not harmful to Lewinsky. It was, admittedly, a private misstep—a serious affront to his marriage and family—but certainly not wrong in any way *to Monica*. Lewinsky, after all, not only consented to the affair, but welcomed it.[15] She *wanted* it; it couldn't possibly have hurt her. On the other hand, to some of Clinton's feminist critics, the affair constituted the example *par excellence* of sexual exploitation.[16] The relationship was wrong and harmful, and furthermore harmful *to her*, not because of the damage done to either the institution of marriage or the institution of the presidency, but because the affair itself was the product of a truly absurd imbalance of power. Sexual relationships between individuals with such grotesquely unequal amounts of social, political, or economic power—as between, say, presidents and interns, or CEOs and secretaries, or professors and undergraduates, or colonels and privates—like economic relationships between corporate employers and unskilled laborers—are only apparently and superficially "welcome." Underneath the appearances, they are, by virtue of the power imbalance, deeply coercive—so coercive as to render the desire for them inauthentic. They are not sexual harassment, but this is only because sexual harassment law requires that the sex be "unwelcome" as well as unequal.[17] The inequality of these relationships, however, makes them coercive and therefore wrong-ful, and they are unequal, and hence wrong, regardless of whether or not they are inauthentically "desired."

Both sides of this feminist-liberal debate, I want to suggest, are pre-mised on a non sequitur. First, it doesn't follow from the inequality of power in a relationship, sexual or otherwise, that the relationship is therefore coercive, harmful, or wrong, much less that it wasn't truly de-sired. We welcome relationships, sexual and otherwise, of unequal power all the time; the rarity is an equal relationship. Clinton's relationship with Monica Lewinsky surely wasn't either coercive or undesired simply be-cause it involved parties with unequal amounts of political power.

More importantly, though, it doesn't follow from either the welcome-ness of a relationship, or a contract, or a change in the world, that it is therefore a good relationship, contract, or change, or that it is in any way good for the parties who welcome it. It doesn't follow from my desire for something that it would be good for me, or that it won't harm me. I might want something that will nevertheless do me considerably more harm than good. To insist otherwise is to definitionally collapse "that which is desired" with "the good," and for no reason: vast amounts of human experience counsel to the contrary. Even as adults, what we want is often not good for us. The liberal insistence that the President's affair with Lewinsky was relatively harmless because desired explicitly rests on this conflation of that which is desired with that which is good.

The feminist rejoinder—that because the affair was unequal it couldn't possibly be *truly* desired—conflates the two implicitly: if something is wrong, or harmful, or unequal, it just couldn't possibly also be desired. Whatever is harmful, then, must in some perhaps nonobvious way be sub-tly coercive even if seemingly desired. An affair between an intern and a president quite dramatically fits the bill.

I have written elsewhere on why we seem currently driven, in sexual and nonsexual contexts both, to make this obvious logical mistake, and I won't repeat those arguments here.[18] It is worth noting, however, that what we lose *in this context* by collapsing the concepts of "that which we desire" with "that which is good for us" is a clear understanding of the harms sometimes occasioned by precisely these sorts of fully desired, wel-come relationships. Women who enter into relationships with powerful mentors, teachers, or political figures might come out of the relationship just fine, or even strengthened, or might make that relationship the basis of an adult life. But often—often enough to worry—they don't, and when they don't it is, in turn, in part because they have internalized a conception of themselves as of value *because of* their sexual attractiveness. The effect of such an internalized understanding of oneself can indeed be harmful, and it can be harmful because it is, quite precisely, objectifying—one's self-worth becomes attached in a literal way to one's value as an object of someone else's sexual desire. The consequence is a severe diminution of one's appreciation or even awareness of one's own abilities, one's own capacity for independence, of the subtleties and interest and even importance of one's own emotions or feelings, of the potential contribution of one's intellect, or political savvy, or artistic sensibility—in short, of one's subjective life and objective impact in the world. Eventually the diminution in appreciation of these attributes becomes a diminution of the abilities, the subtlety, the contributions, capacity for independence, and emotional subtlety themselves. That is a real loss in terms of human capital, human well-being, flourishing lives, and individual self-esteem. It is a loss which is flatly denied by the obfuscatory liberal claim that because the relationship is desired, it is therefore good. And it is a harm that is only obscured, not clarified, by the counterfactual feminist assertion that because the relationship is unequal, it is therefore coercive and not truly desired at all.

Finally, it is a harm that is badly obscured—and perhaps even denied—by the recurrent suggestion, now being argued by a number of feminist commentators, that the harm suffered by women in consensual and welcome unequal sexual relationships on the job simply is *the same harm* as that targeted by sexual harassment law, and for that reason, the current "welcomeness" requirement in sexual harassment law ought to be abandoned.[19] The harm occasioned by sexually exploitative relationships which are desired as well as consented to by both participants is simply not the target of sexual harassment law. Sexual harassment is defined as sexual advances or sexual behavior in an employment context that is *unwelcome*, not unequal. To conflate the two badly trivializes and confuses understanding of sexual harassment law, as well as the unwelcome sex that is its target, as I will discuss below. But second, it confuses and even in effect erases understanding of the harms sometimes occasioned by welcome, desired sex as well. There is a difference, not just of severity, but of kind, between the harm brought on by unwelcome sex—the harm of sexual harassment—and the harms sometimes brought on by welcome sex between persons of vastly disparate status, wealth, prestige, or position. We need to develop better ways of thinking about and talking about the unwelcome sex that is illegal because it constitutes sexual harassment. However, we also need to develop better ways of thinking about and talking about the harms—sometimes quite severe—that may be occasioned by welcome and hotly desired sex that is neither illegal nor violative of anyone's civil rights. That we haven't done so—and that we rarely even feel it as a lack—evidences not only the degree to which we have habitually collapsed our understanding of the good with the satisfaction of desire, but also the degree to which we have collapsed the legal with the morally unproblematic.

## Paula Jones: Consent, Sex, and Desire

Second, the Paula Jones case. Paula Jones sued Bill Clinton for sexual harassment, and the gravamen of a sexual harassment case—the harm at its core—is *unwelcome* sex or sexual behavior, imposed at work or school and leading to injury. Yet commentators repeatedly—even routinely—characterized the nature not only of her case, but of sexual harassment law generally—as being about "nonconsensual" workplace sex, rather than unwelcome sex or sexual advances.[20] In the *Jones* case itself, this mischaracterization leads to absurdity—the sexual behavior she was complaining of was indeed unwelcome, but it was surely neither consensual nor nonconsensual: she wasn't complaining about sexual advances that happened after she turned him down, because there weren't any, she was complaining about the initial sexual advance itself, to which she obviously had no time to either consent or not consent. But more generally, the claim that sexual harassment law is about nonconsensual sexual behavior is a mistaken characterization of the law. Sexual harassment law targets *unwelcome* sex,[21] not "nonconsensual sex," and the categories do not perfectly overlap: "quid pro quo" sex on the job, for example, may well be both unwelcome and consensual. If we can't understand and distinguish unwelcome sex—or undesired sex—from nonconsensual sex, then we have failed to understand what even the "quid pro quo" branch of this law is all about. Furthermore, it is a misunderstanding that is seemingly ubiquitous—or at least enough so as to invite the question why.

One reason we might confuse the "unwelcome sex" that is the target of sexual harassment law with "nonconsensual sex" may be that we now tend, as a culture, to ideologically conflate not only whatever we desire, or want, or welcome, with the good, or with value, as discussed above, but also, and quite distinctly, whatever we consent to with what we want, welcome, or desire. We tend to think that whatever we consent to must be something we desire. Given the conflation of the "consensual" with the "desired," the concept of "consensual-but-unwelcome" does indeed seem ideologically oxymoronic. Inferentially, then, as a culture we are ill-equipped to see not only the harms, but also simply the unwelcomeness, caused by anything other than coercion: if it's bad, it must be the case that it wasn't desired, but furthermore, if it's not desired, it must be the case that it was coerced as well. If we put together these two conflations—the conflation of that which is desired with that which is good on the one hand, and that which is consensual with that which is desired on the other, we get this: whatever we consent to we must have desired, and whatever we desire is good. And although they often in fact operate in tandem, these are at heart two different sorts of inferences, and two different sorts of mistakes. The first mistake leads us to mischaracterize and misunderstand the nature of the harm occasioned by whatever we desire, and hence the nature of the harms occasioned by sometimes fully or passionately desired sex, such as the Lewinsky-Clinton affair. The second, though, leads us to mischaracterize and misunderstand the nature of the harm occasioned by sex we may or may not consent to, but *do not want or welcome*—hence, the target of sexual harassment, and targeted by sexual harassment laws.

Further, we might be more inclined to conflate the category of the consensual with that of the desired in the sexual context than in the nonsexual, for a reason peculiar to the sexual realm, and that is the sheer *ubiquitousness* of unwelcome but consensual sex. Women do, after all, at least in this culture, consent to sex that they don't erotically or hedonistically desire—and that is decidedly unwelcome—all the time. They do so for all sorts of reasons, good and bad: they do it for money, they do it out of friendship, they do it for long-term security, for affection, from habit, they do it because they want to become pregnant, because they want to get married, because they think it is their duty,[22] because their religion requires it of them,[23] because it is legally compelled,[24] because they are worried that if they don't their husband or boyfriend will be in an unpleasant snit, or that he will be obnoxious to the children, or that he will become angry or violent, or in order to be cool, hip, or liberated.[25] Given all this unwelcome but consensual sex, it is hard to see why unwelcome sex for a grade, or a raise, or a job, ought to be regarded as all that different.

Given the ubiquitousness and seemingly unproblematic status of so much unwelcome sex, how, then, do we make sense of quid pro quo sexual harassment law? One way to do so, endorsed by some feminist commentators, is to insist that sex for a grade, or a raise, or a job is somehow less consensual or more coercive than sex for affection, for domestic peace, for social status, or for cash.[26] This understanding of the quid pro quo branch of sexual harassment law—that sex for a grade or for a job or promotion is illegal because it is coercive—has the effect of explaining sexual harassment law, but it also has the effect, uncoincidentally, of maintaining our ideological commitment to the "welcomeness" of that to which we give our "true" consent: quid pro quo sex is illegal not because it is unwelcome—that would throw into question an awful lot of sex—but because it is subtly *coercive*, and therefore not truly consensual at all. This understanding—unwelcome sex that is sexual harassment is so because it is subtly coercive, not because it is unwelcome—has the effect, in short, of shielding the vast areas of sexual life in which women have sex for reasons other than sexual desire, from moral, much less legal scrutiny.

However, it also has the effect of mischaracterizing, and deradicalizing, the point of sexual harrassment law. Both prongs of sexual harrassment law—quid pro quo and hostile environment—are aimed at unwelcome sex, not nonconsensual or coercive sex, that happens in or around the workplace, with injurious consequences. The striking and radical insight that triggered the change in the law was *not* that some workplace sex is only seemingly consensual but is in fact coercive, but rather that some of the unwelcome sex that happens in and around workplaces is so injurious as to be actionable, and so inequitably and unequally harmful to women as to be fairly viewed as a violation of their civil rights. This claim does indeed rest on the discomfiting premise that "unwelcome but consensual" sex is not oxymoronic, or a null set. Women who consent either to sex at home or to a sexualized workplace that they do not desire, suffer real harms: the unity of desire, consent, and act, so central to liberal theory and society is severed, and at a deep and personal level. Their sense of autonomy, integrity, physical security, and independence suffers, if they are consenting to sex they do not want because they need either material or physical security from a man they do not desire. Their subjective sense of worth and identity, and hence their objective contributions and value as a worker, suffer, when they tolerate unwelcome sexualized workplaces. These harms can be (although of course they are not always) tremendously damaging, whether or not actionable, and the breakthrough in sexual harassment law was precisely that it brought these harms to public attention.

To see them, though, requires two uncomfortable shifts in perception: first, it requires us to see, or concede, ideologically, that some of what is legally consensual we do not welcome, and that some of those unwelcome environments in our world harm us. This alone is rough: it rubs against the grain of our consumerist inclination to equate that to which we consent with that which we welcome or desire. But second, it requires us to see that the unwelcome sex in which women often engage, or which women sometimes tolerate, might at times be damaging, even though it might also be consensual. Both these premises, I think, are at the heart of sexual harassment law. Both are true, both are important, and both are extraordinarily hard-fought gains. And both have been threatened, rather than sharpened, by the confused claims made on all sides regarding the nature of the Paula Jones case, what was at the heart of it, and why it failed.

## Juanita Broaddrick: Consent and Legality

Finally, the Juanita Broaddrick allegation. Juanita Broaddrick alleged that President Clinton forcibly raped her. After this allegation came to light, the legal consensus very quickly gelled not only to the effect that because of the passage of time the allegation couldn't possibly constitute grounds for impeachment—an unremarkable proposition—but that furthermore, the case would never have been prosecuted, even had it been brought at the time, because the evidence for it was too flimsy. It was, commentators opined, just a "he-said, she-said" fight, with nothing to tip the scales of justice toward a conviction.[27] But while the conclusion is right—the case would never have been prosecuted—the reason given is not right. The case would not have been prosecuted, but not because of the flimsiness of the evidence. There was as much or more evidence here as with the majority of fully prosecuted rapes: a reliable witness identification of an accused defendant, who allegedly committed a crime in full daylight, visible marks of injury, and contemporaneous complaints to third parties. Rather, and as Juanita Broaddrick fully understood at the time—indeed, as virtually everyone understood at the time—the case would not have been prosecuted not for lack of evidence, but because she had admittedly invited Clinton into her hotel room. It would not have been prosecuted, in short, because the sex was not viewed as rape. And it was not viewed as rape not because it did not fit the legal definition, but because he was in her hotel room by her invitation. Yet commentators routinely dismissed the relevance of the Broaddrick allegation as non-prosecutable, and explained its nonprosecutable quality not by reference to the fact that actually made it such—that she had invited him into the hotel room—but rather, on the basis of insufficient evidence.[28]

This iniquitous claim, widely stated and surely widely believed, clearly served a function: it permits us to maintain the illusion that sex is either consensual or nonconsensual, and that when it is nonconsensual, it is rape. It also permits us to maintain the illusion that when a woman refuses to consent to sex, either the sex does not happen, or if it does, it is rape: it permits us to maintain the illusion, that is, that a woman is in control of her sexuality. However, the claim that sex is either consensual, or if nonconsensual it is rape, misstates both legal and social reality, not only at the time of the alleged rape, but now as well.

First, on the law: at the time of Broaddrick's alleged rape, nowhere was rape defined as nonconsensual sex.[29] It is now defined as nonconsensual sex in very few jurisdictions;[30] most states continue to require both that the sex be nonconsensual and that it be forced. A number of feminist and liberal reformers and scholars have argued that rape should be defined as nonconsensual sex,[31] but for the most part it is not so defined now, and was nowhere defined as such when Broaddrick made her claim. Her refusal to consent did not transform the sex into a rape—even legally.

More importantly, however, the oft-repeated claim that if what Broaddrick claimed happened then she was clearly raped, and that it was rape because it was nonconsensual, rests on a misreading of social reality, which in turn makes the legal mistake seem natural. We are culturally committed to an on-off view of consent, and of its legal consequences: if a woman consents to sex, then it is legally unproblematic; if she doesn't consent to sex, then either the sex doesn't happen, or if it does, then it is rape. But this is wrong: it is not now nor was it then the case that if a woman does not consent to sex and the sex occurs anyway, that a rape has *therefore* happened. Rather, it must first be shown that the woman is legally, psychologically, and socially *capable* of giving her consent to, or withholding her consent from, the man she has accused of raping her. There is a sizable class of women, and a much larger one at the time Broaddrick made her allegation, who by virtue of their status are incapable of either giving or withholding consent to particular individual men or classes of men. When a woman in this class has sex without her consent, the resulting sex is not, by virtue of her nonconsent, rape. It is simply sex, and it is something that just happens. It is as natural, inevitable, and as legally and even morally inconsequential as the injury that results when a woman gets blindsided by a falling boulder, when she has neither "consented" to nor withheld consent from the accident.

Today, if we take at face value recent reforms in black letter law, this class of women is relatively small. It no longer includes, for example, as it did at the time of Broaddrick's rape, all married women raped by their husbands. However, it does still include, in about half the states, married women who are mentally retarded, married women who suffer from either a temporary or permanent mental disability, and married women who are drunk and who are sexually assaulted by their husbands: sex with these women is not consensual—they are all incapable of giving consent—but nevertheless, by virtue of continuing marital rape exemptions, such sex is not rape. They have neither given nor withheld consent. The sex was not consensual, but nor have they actively withheld consent. The sex was accordingly not rape. Their refusal to consent is not the act of will that triggers a violation of autonomy which in turn renders an offense criminal; rather, their refusal to consent is a function of their status as someone incapable of giving or withholding consent; someone who is essentially will-less. And although this is a relatively small class of women in doctrinal terms, in terms of practice, of course, the class is much larger even today: there are virtually no successful prosecutions of marital rape. One might reasonably infer that the lived, internal reality in many of these marriages is that much of the sex is nonconsensual but is not rape for essentially the same reason: the woman is perceived by herself and her partner as being incapable of giving or withholding consent.

At the time of the Broaddrick charge, of course, that class of women explicitly included all married women raped by their husbands: rape laws in Arkansas and everywhere else explicitly exempted from their coverage married women who suffered nonconsensual, forced sex with their husbands. But it is also clear that, at the time of her charge, that class of women implicitly (although not explicitly) included all women who could be closely *analogized* to married women—common-law wives and girlfriends, certainly, but also prostitutes, and most broadly, women on "dates," and, finally, women like Juanita Broaddrick who invited men into their hotel rooms. Women in this class stood in relation to the sex itself, when it occurred, not as someone who had power, autonomy, or control, and who accordingly had reason to complain when that power, autonomy, or control was overridden, but rather as someone who may or may not suffer while enduring a natural event: sex, in such circumstances, is not something to which one might or might not consent, it is something that just happens, something that one might enjoy, suffer, or just get through as best one can. This is how Juanita Broaddrick described her own reaction after the event.[32] She invited Clinton into her hotel room, and she realized too late that by doing so she had identified herself as a woman without power to give or withhold consent. Sex—violent, forced, and unpleasant—then happened. She could not "report" it, there was no criminality to report. She suffered it, as she would have a natural calamity.

This relation—of passivity to force—it should not be necessary to say, is harmful. It is a tremendous assault on women's autonomy, physical integrity, security, and emotional and spiritual well-being. The history of rape law cannot be told or understood until we come to understand the centrality of that relationship. It is a relationship, however, and a harm, that we will not even begin to understand so long as we maintain the delusional belief that it doesn't really exist: that women either consent to sex, in which case they must welcome it, or they withhold consent, in which case sex typically doesn't happen, but in the rare case that it does, it must be rape.

Neither of the prongs of this decisional dilemma are true. Consensual sex is not necessarily welcome (and welcome sex is not necessarily good). But just as important, nonconsensual sex is not necessarily rape. Perhaps it should be, but it is not. Where a woman is by legal definition or natural limitation incapable of giving or withholding consent, the nonconsensuality of sex, should such sex occur, does not render her a rape victim, or the victim of any crime. The sex itself renders her unfortunate, to whatever degree she suffered. The injury, though, leaves her without legal recourse; an accident victim, rather than a victim of a crime the state will regard seriously. She is passive and will-less, as much an object as it is possible to be.

## Conclusion

The discourse surrounding the sex at the heart of the President's impeachment correctly insisted on its legalistic irrelevance to impeachment, but in so doing it revealed a pattern of overreliance on consent as a marker of value, of desire, and of legality. We tend to assume, in a culture that has habitually commodified almost everything, that consent to a change or transaction renders the change a valuable one, at least for the parties involved. We also tend to assume that we consent only to those changes we desire, and we tend to assume that consent cleanly divides the legal from the illegal, at least in criminal law. All three assumptions are problematic in all realms of life, but they are demonstrably untrue of sexual relations: we do from time to time consent to and desire sexual affairs that are quite bad for us, and bad for us regardless of moralistic harms to the institution of marriage; we also at times consent to sexual encounters that we do not desire; and there are countless women who have nonconsensual sex but who are not victims of rape because of the status accorded them by law, not because they haven't had their autonomy violated. Maintaining these assumptions—taken jointly, we might call them the "consensual faith"—in the face of experiences to the contrary has badly confused not just our self-knowledge, but our understanding of the laws under which we live.

Affairs like the one between Monica Lewinsky and Bill Clinton are oftentimes both consensual and desired, and therefore neither rape, nor harassment, nor coercive. But they may nevertheless be harmful. Denying that leads us to either wrongly deny their potential for harm, or to wrongly insist on their coerciveness. Interactions like the one between Clinton and Jones might constitute sexual harassment, and if so, they constitute harassment because they are unwelcome, not because they are nonconsensual. Insisting to the contrary either leads us to blur the difference between unwelcome and nonconsensual sex, or to deny the unwelcomeness of the sex itself, again counterfactually. And lastly, encounters like the one between Clinton and Broaddrick, if it happened as she alleged, were clearly nonconsensual, but that fact alone hardly implies criminality. Rather, the nonconsensuality of the sex implied criminality only if she, as a potential victim, could first establish her bona fides as someone capable of giving or withholding legally meaningful consent to sex. If she couldn't—and at the time she was raped, she knew full well she couldn't—the event she endured was unfortunate, but not criminal. Failing to grasp these differences both illustrates and perpetuates our larger failure to comprehend not just the history but also the continuing complicity of rape law in the construction of sexual relations between men and women in this culture.

### NOTES

1. See Richard Posner, *An Affair of State: The Investigation, Impeachment, and Trial of President Clinton* (Cambridge: Harvard University Press, 1999); Jeffrey

Toobin, *A Vast Conspiracy: The Real Story of the Sex Scandal That Nearly Brought Down a President* (New York: Random House, 1999). See also Gore Vidal, "The Real Crime Is Going against the Will of the People," *Los Angeles Times*, August 12, 1998, B7.

See also, e.g., *CNN and Company* (CNN television broadcast, November 5, 1998); *CNN Crossfire* (CNN television broadcast, January 11, 1999); *CNN Crossfire* (CNN television broadcast, September 8, 1998); *CNN Saturday* (CNN television broadcast, October 8, 1998); *CNN Talkback Live* (CNN television broadcast, January 27, 1998); *The NewsHour with Jim Lehrer* (MacNeil/Lehrer Productions, October 7, 1998); *Rivera Live* (CNBC television broadcast, March 4, 1999).

2. See Posner, *An Affair of State*; Ken Gormley, "Impeachment and the Independent Counsel: A Dysfunctional Union," *Stanford Law Review* 51 (1999): 309; Randall K. Miller, "Presidential Sanctuaries after the Clinton Sex Scandals," *Harvard Journal of Law and Public Policy* 22 (1999): 647.

3. See, e.g., Charles J. Cooper, "A Perjurer in the White House? The Constitutional Case for Perjury and Obstruction of Justice as High Crimes and Misdemeanors," *Harvard Journal of Law and Public Policy* 22 (1999): 619; Jonathan Turley, "Congress as Grand Jury: The Role of the House of Representatives in the Impeachment of an American President," *George Washington Law Review* 67 (1999): 735; Jeffrey Toobin, "Terms of Impeachment," *New Yorker*, September 14, 1998, 32; Jeffrey Toobin, "Starr Can't Help It," *New Yorker*, May 18, 1998, 32.

4. See *Rivera Live* (CNBC television broadcast, February 24, 1999); *Rivera Live* (CNBC television broadcast, February 22, 1999), with Alan Dershowitz.

5. See Referral from Independent Counsel Kenneth W. Starr in Conformity with the Requirements of Title 28, United States Code, Section 595 (c), H.R. Doc. no. 105–310 (2d Sess. 1998).

6. See Christina E. Wells, "Hypocrites and Barking Harlots: The Clinton-Lewinsky Affair and the Attack on Women," *William and Mary Journal of Women and Law* 5 (1998): 151; Susan Estrich, "Clinton No Role Model for Feminists," *Denver Post*, August 28, 1998, B11; Susan Estrich, "Starr Abuses His Power," *Denver Post*, June 18, 1998, B11; Katharine Q. Seelye, "He Said, She Said—And They Clammed Up," *New York Times*, January 19, 1997, section 4, 15; Gloria Steinem, "Feminists and the Clinton Question," *New York Times*, March 22, 1998, section 4, 15; Gloria Steinem, "Yes Means Yes, No Means No, Why Sex Scandals Don't Mean Harassment," *Ms.*, May/June 1998, 62.

7. This is so basic that both Kenneth Starr and Catharine MacKinnon are in complete agreement on the point. See Referral from Independent Counsel, and Catharine MacKinnon, "Comments," Yale Conference on Sexual Harassment (forthcoming).

8. See *Jones v. Clinton*, 990 F. Supp. 657 (E.D. Ark. 1998).

9. Comments of Professor Karen Czapansky of Maryland Law School, *Mark Steiner Show*, WJHU, 88.1 Baltimore, Md.

10. "Kulturkampf" refers to a culture war—the state's attempt to "erase a normative subculture of its citizens." William Eskridge, "Democracy, Kulturkampf, and the Apartheid of the Closet," *Vanderbilt Law Review* 50 (1997): 435. The term gained recent popularity when used by Pat Buchanan in 1992 and by Justice Scalia in his dissent in *Romer v. Evans*, 517 U.S. 620, 636 (1996).

11. Toni Morrison, "The Talk of the Town," *New Yorker*, October 5, 1998, 31 (remarking that Clinton was the first black President).

12. See David E. Kendall, *Initial Response to Referral of Office of Independent Council*, September 12, 1998. Geraldo Rivera and his guests repeatedly stressed that the issue was really all about sex. See, e.g., *Rivera Live* (CNBC television broadcast, May 13, 1998); *Rivera Live* (CNBC television broadcast, March 2, 1999). See also *CNN Inside Politics* (CNN television broadcast, January 23, 1998).

13. See William J. Bennett, *The Death of Outrage: Bill Clinton and the Assault on the American Ideals* (New York: Simon and Schuster, 1999). See also *Hardball with Chris Matthews* (CNBC television broadcast, March 1, 1999), with William Bennett.

14. See Marcia Ann Gillespie, "The Backlash Boogie," *Ms.*, May/June 1998, 1; Anne Glusker and *Ms.* Editors, "Quote Unquote: On Bill, et al.," *Ms.*, May/June 1998, 20.

15. See Abiola Wendy Abrams, "Dear Monica," *Ms.*, June/July 1999, 80; Susie Bright, "Monica: The Beauty and the Brains," *Ms.*, June/July 1999, 73; Susan Jane Gilman, "Oral Report," *Ms.*, June/July 1999, 76.

16. See Jill Nelson, "The Pass on Paula: Was It Her Hair or What She Said," *Ms.*, May/June 1998, 64.

17. See *Burlington Industries v. Ellerth*, 524 U.S. 742, 747 (1998); *Meritor Savings Bank, FSB v. Vinson*, 477 U.S. 57, 68 (1986); Kathryn Abrams, "Postscript, Spring 1998: A Response to Professors Bernstein and Franke," *Cornell Law Review*, 83 (1998): 1257; Theresa M. Beiner, "The Misuse of Summary Judgement in Hostile Environment Cases," *Wake Forest Law Review* 34 (1999): 71. See also Yale Conference on Sexual Harassment (forthcoming).

18. See Robin West, "Authority, Autonomy and Choice: The Role of Consent in the Moral and Political Visions of Franz Kafka and Richard Posner," *Harvard Law Review* 99 (1985): 384; Robin West, "Submission, Choice, and Ethics: A Rejoinder to Judge Posner," *Harvard Law Review* 99 (1986): 1449.

19. See Niloofar Nejat-Bina, "Employers as Vigilant Chaperones Armed with Dating Waivers: The Intersection of Unwelcomeness and Employer Liability in Hostile Work Environment Sexual Harassment Law," *Berkeley Journal Employment and Labor Law* 20 (1999): 325; Steven L. Willborn, "Taking Discrimination Seriously: *Oncale* and the Fare of Exceptionalism in Sexual Harassment Law," *William and Mary Bill of Rights Journal* 7 (1999): 677; Yale Conference on Sexual Harassment (forthcoming). Susan Estrich was an early and influential proponent of this position in an early piece on sexual harassment law, in "Sex at Work,"

*Stanford Law Review* 43 (1991): 813, but has since apparently abandoned this position, perhaps as a result of the Clinton scandals themselves.

20. See Ellen Yaroshefsky, "More Than Sex: Why the Courts Are Missing the Point, an Interview with Vicki Schultz," *Ms.*, May/June 1998, 56.

21. See *Burlington Industries v. Ellerth*, 524 US 742, 747 (1998).

22. See Alan Wertheimer, "Consent and Sexual Relations," *Legal Theory* 2 (1996): 89.

23. See Mary Becker, "The Politics of Women's Wrongs and the Bill of 'Rights': A Bicentennial Perspective," *University of Chicago Law Review* 59 (1992): 453.

24. According to Lama Abu-Odeh (Harvard University), Islamic family law requires women to obey their husbands, which means, in part, that they be sexually available to them at all times.

25. See Sharon Thompson, *Going All the Way: Teenage Girls: Tales of Sex, Romance, and Pregnancy* (New York: Hill and Wang, 1996); Naomi Wolf, *Promiscuities: The Secret Struggle for Womanhood* (New York: Ballentine Books, 1998).

26. Susan Estrich, "Clinton No Role Model for Feminists," *Denver Post*, August 28, 1998, B11.

27. Katharine Q. Seelye, "He Said, She Said: And They Clammed Up," *New York Times*, January 19, 1997, section 4, 15.

28. See, e.g., *Fox Hannity and Colmes* (Fox television broadcast, March 3, 1999); *Rivera Live* (CNBC television broadcast, March 12, 1999); *Rivera Live* (CNBC television broadcast, March 1, 1999); *Rivera Live* (CNBC television broadcast, February 26, 1999); *Rivera Live* (CNBC television broadcast, February 25, 1999).

29. See Richard Posner and Katharine B. Silbaugh, *A Guide to America's Sex Laws* (Chicago: University of Chicago Press, 1996); Mary Becker et al., eds., *Cases and Materials on Feminist Jurisprudence, Taking Women Seriously* (St. Paul: West, 1994): 204–63; Joshua Dressler, *Cases and Materials on Criminal Law* (St. Paul: West, 2d ed. 1999): 378–403; Sanford H. Kadish and Stephen J. Schulhofer, *Criminal Law and Its Processes: Cases and Materials* (New York: Aspen Law & Business, 6th ed., 1995), 1099–155.

30. Michigan is an example of such "reform" jurisdiction. See Becker et al., "Taking Women Seriously," 219. See also Lynne Henderson, "Without Narrative: Child Sexual Abuse," *Virginia Journal of Social Policy and Law* 4 (1997): 479; Lynne Henderson, "Getting to Know: Honoring Women in Law and in Fact," *Texas Journal of Women and Law* 2 (1993): 41; Stephen J. Schulhofer, *Unwanted Sex: The Culture of Intimidation and the Failure of Law* (Cambridge: Harvard University Press, 1998).

31. See Susan Estrich, *Real Rape* (Cambridge: Harvard University Press, 1987).

32. See *Dateline* (CBS television broadcast, February 24, 1999), Juanita Broaddrick.

## Chapter 10

# Impeachment
## *A (Civil) Religious Perspective*

## *John Milton Cooper, Jr.*

Impeachment is one area of politics and government which inescapably impinges on America's civil religion—Constitutionalism. If anything separates American democracy from the way that it is practiced elsewhere in the world it is this quasi-religious reverence for the Constitution. This attitude is an object of some wonder and sometimes derision among foreigners and many American students of law and politics, especially those on the left side of the spectrum. The reverence for the Constitution carries with it a belief in a higher law and something above ordinary matters of politics. The term "ordinary" is not meant to be demeaning. War, peace, abortion, welfare, education, taxes—some deeply serious matters belong to "ordinary" politics. Constitutionalism is often derided by those who do not accept this distinction between political realms and who claim that it has been used as a cloak for entrenched interests.

Yet constitutional jurisprudence did serve, especially from the 1880s to the 1930s, as a defense for private property and business dealings from government regulation and oversight. Others, including myself, reject such derision of Constitutionalism both because the distinction between these political realms can be established and, moreover, because Constitutionalism has also served as a powerful tool for social justice and change. Twentieth-century experiences with civil rights and civil liberties are the greatest examples of this use of Constitutionalism. It is a doubled-edged sword that can and does cut both ways.

Few subjects, besides amending the Constitution itself, intrude on this sense of reverence for the Constitution and what are perceived to be its guiding principles more than impeachment. In fact, recent experiences with proposed amendments on such subjects as a balanced budget, school prayer, and flag burning raise questions about whether even amending the Constitution makes many people wake up to what is involved nearly as much as impeachment does.

This is not to say that impeachment automatically kicks in this reverence for the Constitution and for basic liberties. The Republicans in the House of Representatives evidently had little regard for those values, and the widespread revulsion against them sprang in part from the widespread belief that these politicians were transgressing a transcendentally significant matter for light and mean motives. By contrast, both the genuine and puffed-up solemnity of the Senate did attest to some feeling for the elevated matter at hand. Witness how the trial opened with the Chief Justice appearing to preside in his robe, the swearing in, the signing of the book as jurors. Then came the bipartisan retreat to the Old Senate Chamber, where Senator Robert Byrd spoke first and invoked the greats of that scene, quoting especially from Daniel Webster. Senator Christopher Dodd reminded his colleagues that this chamber had also been the scene of the violent assault on Charles Sumner. History was fairly dripping over the Senate, both the best and worst of that body's past.

When a question involves civil religion, I think one ought to approach it as he or she would approach any other religious subject. One ought to consult three sources—scripture, authoritative commentary, and experience—or history. In this case, scripture means the Constitution itself. What does this great text say on the subject? As is often the case when one consults scripture, the answer is "not much." The Constitution addresses the subject of impeachment only three times. First, in the last paragraph of Article I, Section 2, it says, "The House of Representatives shall chuse [*sic*] their Speaker and other Officers; and shall have the sole Power of Impeachment."

Second, in the sixth paragraph of Article I, Section 3, it says,

> The Senate shall have the sole Power to try all Impeachments. When sitting for that Purpose, they shall be on Oath or Affirmation. When the President of the United States is tried, the Chief Justice shall preside: And no Person shall be convicted without the Concurrence of two thirds of the Members present.

Third, in Article II, Section 4, it says,

> The President, Vice President and all civil Officers of the United States, shall be removed from Office on Impeachment for, and Conviction of, Treason, Bribery, or other high Crimes and Misdemeanors.

That is all the Constitution says. According to some notes from the constitutional convention, the Framers did consider adding a few other words to "high Crimes and Misdemeanors," but they did not. Why not? Why didn't the Framers say more? As well as anyone can surmise, the reason was that they did not think they needed to say more. The Framers evidently did not believe that they needed to be more expansive or specific on this subject because they were not doing anything new or remarkable here. This procedure for impeachment was, as everybody at the time recognized, copied from British practice: in Britain, the House of Commons impeached and the House of Lords tried. It is a truism to say that the Framers of the Constitution were torn between, on the one hand, imitating British practices and trying to improve upon them and, on the other hand, avoiding what they perceived to be the pitfalls and mistakes of British practices. That is the main reason why the United States has a system of separation of powers and a separately elected executive, rather than a parliamentary system of dovetailed powers and an executive chosen from the legislature.

With impeachment, evidently the Framers did not think they needed to tinker much. One reason was that several states had already adopted similar procedures in their own constitutions. It is good to remember that the convention that framed the United States Constitution in 1787 was a culminating, not an initiating, event. Constitution making was the favorite political sport during the 1770s and 1780s, and the "Great Convention" in Philadelphia was not so much a World Series or Super Bowl as it was a gathering of self-selected all-stars.

Both those points, about following English practice and previous state experience, are ones that Alexander Hamilton makes in the *Federalist*, Number 65. Here is the second religious source—authoritative commentary. On the subject of the Constitution, nothing rivals the *Federalist* for authoritative stature. To use analogies from Western religious traditions, the *Federalist* stands to the Constitution as the Talmud does to the Torah or as the Epistles do to the Gospels.

What does this overweeningly authoritative source have to say about impeachment? Again the answer is, not much. Just two numbers of the *Federalist*, 65 and 66, address the subject of impeachment, and the second of these mainly reiterates and elaborates on points made in the first. Both these numbers came from the pen of a single author, Alexander Hamilton. It is impossible, therefore, to say for sure whether his coauthors, James Madison and John Jay (who became the first Chief Justice), fully shared these views, much less expounded the views of other Framers. Actually, that single authorship really is not much of a problem, because what Hamilton has to say does not seem terribly controversial. Indeed, the simple fact that the authors of the *Federalist* did not say more about impeachment indicates that they didn't regard it as needing much elaboration or defense.

Three passages from these two numbers of the *Federalist* are particularly helpful in trying to understand what the Framers believed an impeachment and its ensuing trial should entail. First, from Number 65:

A well-constituted court for the trial of impeachments is an object not more to be desired than difficult to be obtained in a government wholly elective. The subjects of its jurisdiction are those offenses which proceed from the misconduct of public men, or, in other words, from the abuse or violation of some public trust. They are of a nature which may with peculiar propriety be denominated POLITICAL [*sic*], as they relate chiefly to injuries done immediately to the society itself. The prosecution of them, for this reason, will seldom fail to agitate the passions of the whole community, and to divide it into parties more or less friendly or inimical to the accused. In many cases it will connect itself with the pre-existing factions, and will enlist all their animosities, partialities, influence, and interest on one side or on the other; and in such cases there will always be the greatest danger that the decision will be regulated more by the comparative strength of parties, than by the real demonstration of innocence or guilt.

Here, Hamilton speaks to the basic conundrum of impeachment: Is it essentially a political or a judicial process? He answers, definitively, I think, that it is both. But his answer leaves the problem of how to combine the two processes. Further on, in Number 65, Hamilton also states,

The necessity of a numerous court for the trial of impeachments is equally dictated by the nature of the proceeding. This can never be tied down by such strict rules, either in the delineation of the offense by the prosecutors, or in the construction of it by the judges, as in common cases serve to limit the discretion of courts in favor of personal security. There will be no jury to stand between the judges who are to pronounce the sentence of the law and the party who is to receive or suffer it. The awful discretion which a court of impeachments must necessarily have, to doom to honor or to infamy the most confidential and the most distinguished characters of the community, forbids the commitment of the trust to a small number of persons.

There is more to this statement than just a procedural argument against having the Supreme Court conduct impeachment trials. Once more,

Hamilton is insisting on the political, as well as judicial character of impeachment. Right after this passage he goes on to note that if someone is convicted, then that person will be subject to criminal prosecution and trial, and he argues that this circumstance offers an additional reason not to have a court conduct the impeachment trial—because in the event of a conviction they may have to try the person afterward.

Finally, in Number 66, Hamilton repeats himself:

> This partial intermixture [of political and judicial elements] is even, in some cases, not only proper but necessary to the mutual defense of the several members of the government against each other. An absolute or qualified negative in the executive upon the acts of the legislative body is admitted, by the ablest adepts in political science, to be an indispensable barrier against the encroachments of the latter upon the former. And it may, perhaps, with no less reason be contended that the powers relating to impeachments are, as before intimated, an essential check in the hands of that body upon the encroachments of the executive.

At the risk of gilding the lily, let me say that this brief statement near the opening of Number 66 again shows how Hamilton, and presumably the rest of the Framers, viewed impeachment as both political and judicial.

That is what the *Federalist* has to say. Those statements help us gain an understanding of what the Framers of the Constitution intended impeachment to be. The statements make crystal clear impeachment's dual character as both a political and a judicial process. But these statements do not help us address the question of how to combine those two essential features in conducting an impeachment trial.

Finally, we must consult one other source in trying to relate impeachment to Constitutionalism. That is the actual history of impeachment—or, to use a nice eighteenth-century term that was familiar to the Framers, "the lamp of experience." What light does this historical lamp shed on impeachment?

Unfortunately, historical experience does not shed much light on impeachment either. The reason for its dim illumination is readily apparent. There simply is not that much experience with impeachment. Before 1998 and 1999, only one president had ever been impeached by the House and tried by the Senate. That was Andrew Johnson in 1868. Beyond that single, indisputably parallel case to the recent one, there have been only two other experiences with impeachment that help a little to understand what happened with Bill Clinton. These are the only impeachment and trial of a Supreme Court Justice, Samuel Chase, which occurred in 1805, and the Watergate experience, when Richard Nixon resigned after the House Judiciary Committee had voted to bring articles of impeachment against him, but before the full House could vote on those articles. Despite recent claims to the contrary, it is certain that the House would have voted to impeach Nixon and the Senate would have voted to convict him.

What light do these three episodes shed on the recent predicament? Let me take them up in a somewhat eccentric way: first, the Chase impeachment in 1805; next Watergate, and finally, Andrew Johnson. My reason for this peculiar choice is that I think that this ascending order best answers whatever relevance and revelation there is to be found.

First, the Chase impeachment. Contrary to what Chief Justice William Rehnquist has written in his informative book, *Grand Inquests,* I do not think that the Chase affair has much contemporary resonance. It happened early in the history of the Republic, less than twenty years after the ratification of the Constitution and establishment of the federal government. All the leaders then, including such demigods as Thomas Jefferson and James Madison and John Marshall, were still feeling their way and, to some extent, making it up as they went along. Moreover, the Chase impeachment did not involve his conduct on the Supreme Court, but rather his conduct as a trial judge when he sat on circuit courts, as Justices then did.

I agree with Rehnquist that Chase's acquittal was a good thing for the independence of the judiciary. Of the four articles that the Senate voted on, two did not even muster simple majorities, and none came close to two-thirds. Perhaps the only aspect of this episode that seems relevant to recent experience was the demonstration of partisanship. The Jeffersonian Republicans in the House were unquestionably out to get Chase, who was a rather nasty Federalist partisan, and his impeachment prefigured the inflamed partisanship that has surrounded later episodes. It should be noted that this was at a time when the party opposed to Chase commanded a large enough majority to convict him if it had held together. The point, of course, is that that majority did not hold together, mainly because the charges against Chase were so weak.

Next comes Watergate. Obviously, because impeachment was an aborted process in this instance, there are certain lessons that cannot apply to more recent or future cases. In a larger way, however, we can draw some important reflections from it. Basically, the prevalent view that the handling of Watergate makes a fine contrast to what happened later strikes me as correct. Then, I think they, the Representatives and the Senators and the Special Prosecutor, did things right about matters that their successors got wrong in 1998 and 1999.

On the matter of partisanship, the two episodes are a study in contrast. Of course, there was inflamed partisanship during Watergate. But consider what the source of the inflammation was: Nixon himself. With rare exceptions, the Democrats who controlled Congress were not out to get Nixon. Insofar as they acted in a partisan manner, they did so almost strictly in self-defense. Those partisan circumstances supply one of the two reasons why Senator Sam Ervin of North Carolina cut such a commanding figure. As an only slightly reconstructed Southern segregationist, whose state had gone for Nixon in both 1968 and 1972, Ervin had no partisan ax to grind against the President. The other reason why "Mr. Sam" assumed such heroic stature was that he so plausibly and luminously embodied a reverence for the Constitution. This was not just a matter of his demeanor during the Senate hearings, with his invocations of the Constitution. Representative Barbara Jordan behaved the same way, uttering a memorable invocation of Constitutionalism: "My faith in the Constitution is whole." Rather, for Ervin, it was that he was also a former North Carolina Supreme Court justice, and he had established himself in his previous eighteen years in the Senate as a stickler for legal rules and narrow constructions of certain provisions of the Constitution—albeit too often, sadly, in defense of segregation.

A few years ago, Archibald Cox, the special prosecutor whom Nixon fired in the Saturday Night Massacre, was asked to compare Watergate and Irangate. Cox answered that one of the major elements lacking in Irangate was that there was no "Mr. Sam." I think that the same contrast held true with the Clinton impeachment. Although Senator Byrd aspired to play Ervin's role, he did not enjoy Ervin's stature as a Constitutionalist nor did he argue along the same lines. There was also a similarity between the two episodes which actually masks a great difference. Both Cox and his successor, Leon Jaworski, kept their activities strictly separate from the House Judiciary Committee's impeachment inquiry. According to members of the committee on both sides in the Clinton impeachment, Kenneth Starr did the same thing, but Starr's role in promoting impeachment and his evident zeal to "get" Clinton robbed his conduct of legitimacy in the eyes of the public and a number of experts.

Finally, there is Andrew Johnson's impeachment and trial in 1868. During the Clinton trial many pieces in the newspapers and features on television recalled what happened then. Most of them dwelled on the contrasts between Clinton and Johnson. Except for being Southerners who had risen from humble origins, the two men had almost nothing in common. Johnson was a terrible politician and an unelected president who enjoyed only the most minuscule political support—none of which applied to Clinton. On the other hand, the partisan situation at that time was possibly even more inflamed than in recent years. The Johnson impeachment and trial came just three years after the end of the Civil War. At one point, one of the House impeachment Managers in the Senate trial waved a bloody shirt to remind his fellow Republicans where their loyalties lay and what they believed was at stake in Johnson's conduct.

By way of further contrast, the Republican opposition to Johnson commanded more than a two-thirds majority—enough strength to convict him on its own. There was no need for bipartisan support, and it took the defection of seven Republicans from the party ranks to acquit Johnson by a single vote. Johnson's acquittal came on two of the articles voted by the House, and the rest of the articles never even came up for votes. The Senate does not have to vote on all the articles presented by the House, although it did so in the Clinton trial. Johnson himself was summoned to appear at his trial but refused. Finally, as a quasi-courtroom drama, the 1868 impeachment produced even less drama than its 1999 counterpart. Except for the votes themselves, which were in doubt until the roll was called, all observers agreed that the Johnson trial was one of the most boring events that had ever taken place in Washington.

The overwhelming judgment of historians and legal scholars, including most recently Chief Justice Rehnquist, is that the right thing happened when Johnson got acquitted. Nearly everyone who has studied this event has concluded that it could have set a terrible precedent and wrought havoc with our system of government if Johnson had been removed from office. I question that conclusion, and I think some alternatives are worth considering before laying this consensus about the Johnson affair over its Clintonian successor like a blanket of judgment.

What really saved Johnson was reverence both for the Constitution and certain Senators' definitions of impeachment. The seven Republican Senators who broke with their party included two of the most respected Constitutionalists of that time. One was Lyman Trumbull of Illinois, chairman of the Judiciary Committee and author of the Thirteenth Amendment, and the other was William Pitt Fessenden of Maine, chairman of the Joint Committee on Reconstruction and principal author of the Fourteenth Amendment.

Two statements that Senator Fessenden made in the statement that he filed for the *Congressional Globe* (as it was then called) reveal his reasoning. First, he said:

> To depose the constitutional chief magistrate of a great nation, elected by the people, on grounds so slight, would, in my judgment, be an abuse of the power conferred upon the Senate, which could not be justified in the country or the world. To construe such an act as a high distant misdemeanor, within the meaning of the Constitution, would, when the passions of the hour have had time to cool, be looked upon with wonder, if not with derision.

Discounting the nineteenth-century style, this sounds a lot like recent defenses of Clinton and objections to his impeachment and trial. But Fessenden also said:

> To the suggestion that popular opinion demands the conviction of the President on these charges, I reply that he is not now on trial before the people, but before the Senate. . . . The people have not heard the evidence as we have heard it. The responsibility is not on them, but upon us. . . . I should consider myself undeserving of the confidence of that just and intelligent people who imposed upon me this great responsibility, and unworthy of a place among honorable men, if for any fear of public reprobation, and for the sake of securing popular favor, I should disregard the convictions of my judgment and my conscience.

What is unmistakable in Fessenden's statements is not only his invocation of the Constitutionalist faith but also his construction of impeachment as an almost purely judicial process, not really political at all.

But what about the Senators who voted for Johnson's conviction, who also made their statements? What did they have to say for themselves? To be sure, most of their statements betrayed more than a hint of the bitter partisanship that surrounded this affair, together with emotions that bordered on hatred of Andrew Johnson. That was not true of all their statements, however. One statement in favor of conviction came from Charles Sumner of Massachusetts, the eloquent and learned former abolitionist and the man who had been assaulted in the Old Senate Chamber in 1856.

Before he launched into a lengthy and impassioned indictment of Johnson himself, Sumner attempted to define the impeachment power. He ridiculed the attempt "to confound this great constitutional trial with an ordinary case at *Nisi Prius* and win for the criminal President an Old Bailey acquittal, where on some quibble the prisoner is allowed to go without the day. . . . Constantly we have been reminded of what is called our judicial character," whereas, Sumner maintained, a clear-sighted reading of the Constitution showed "that it [impeachment] is a political proceeding, before a political body, with political purposes; that it is founded on political offenses, proper for consideration of a political body and subject to a political judgment only."

Also, after reviewing English and American authorities and practices, Sumner defined high crimes and misdemeanors as any act through which "the Republic suffers or is in any way imperiled. Show me an act of evil example or influence committed by a President and I show you an impeachable offense which becomes great in proportion to the scale on which it is committed and the consequences which are menaced."

Sumner was clearly the polar opposite of Fessenden. His emphasis on the political character of impeachment left little or no room for the judicial element. It is worth noting what the most recent, quasi-authoritative commentator has said about this. In *Grant Inquests: The Historic Impeachments of Judge Samuel Chase and President Andrew Johnson* (New York: Morrow, 1992), Chief Justice Rehnquist comments,

> To Sumner, impeachment was much more like a vote of confidence in the government under a parliamentary system. The overriding issue for him was not whether Andrew Johnson had violated the Tenure of Office Act [the law in question], but whether Andrew Johnson should continue to be president in view of his repeated obstruction of the reconstruction policies of the Radical Republicans.

Rehnquist's interpretation deserves respect, not only because he is a learned man but also because of the office he holds. In the Constitutionalist religion, the Chief Justice is not quite a pope. He needs to get four of his eight cardinals to agree with him in order to claim infallibility. But, berobed as he is, sitting as the first among the equals of his similarly berobed Justices in that temple on Capitol Hill, he is the chief priest, and even when he speaks alone and off the bench his words carry weight.

Still, the more important question here is whether or not Rehnquist is right in dismissing Sumner's view of impeachment. I think not. Politics and policy differences inevitably play great roles in impeachment, and it was the intent of the Framers that they should. To reiterate, the problem is to find a satisfactory combination of judicial and political elements. Rehnquist is arguing that Sumner tilted too far toward the political side. But did he?

It is hard to imagine a wider and graver breach between the executive and the legislature than the chasm that yawned between Andrew Johnson and the congressional Republicans over Reconstruction policy from 1866 to the end of his term. Reconstruction policy was that time's equivalent of national security and civil rights rolled into one. It involved how, and on what terms, the nation would be put back together after the Civil War. Would the men who had tried to destroy the Union be allowed to resume their places of leadership in the South with only a symbolic slap on the wrist, as Johnson demanded? Or would loyalist outgroups from both races be encouraged to try to make fundamental changes in the politics and society of that region, as the congressional Republicans wanted? Reconstruction policy also involved how African Americans, newly freed from slavery, would participate in society. Would they be relegated to something less than full citizenship, some kind of peonage or semifreedom, as Johnson was willing to see happen? Or would they be permitted to exercise full political freedom and nondiscriminatory social relations, as, with varying degrees of commitment, the congressional Republicans desired?

Viewed in that light, Sumner's interpretation of impeachment looks much better. Indeed, it is closer to Constitutional correctness than is usually thought. True, his Republican opponents did set Johnson up by passing the Tenure of Office Act partly in order to have an impeachable offense. But that act also served the purpose of trying to prevent Johnson from sabotaging the implementation of Reconstruction through his appointments or removals, as he repeatedly tried to do. For all its sourness and its inside-the-Capitol quality, the Johnson impeachment concerned weighty affairs of state. If the political side of the Framers' intent cannot be legitimately exercised in such circumstances then this power under the Constitution may be a dead letter.

Indeed, that is what seems to have happened during this recent experience with a completed presidential impeachment and trial of a president. Because of the way that the Republicans in the House appeared to be acting for light and transient causes and almost entirely out of partisan spite, they reinforced the judicial side of impeachment at the expense of its political dimension. In part, Constitutionalism saved Clinton the same way that it saved Johnson. Apart from the undiluted partisanship of the proceedings there was the widespread sense that something more should have been involved here than merely obeying the law. Rather, the overriding question is what best serves the transcendent needs of our national interest and our system of ordered liberties—that is, what accords with Constitutionalism as it is interpreted at that moment.

The way that question gets answered does not always save a president, as it did Johnson and Clinton. The opposite happened in Watergate. Then, a sufficient number of Representatives and Senators "got religion"—that is, they recognized that these matters had moved beyond the realm of ordinary politics into something higher, and, in this civil sense, holier. Anyone involved in impeachment, especially presidents, acts at his or her own peril by not recognizing those stakes. That, I believe, is why Richard Nixon was effectively, though not formally, impeached and removed from office. He never seemed to realize that he had entered into a realm in which the rules and techniques of ordinary politics did not necessarily work. An apt comparison to Nixon's not "getting it" about Constitutionalism was Franklin Roosevelt's overwhelming and humiliating loss when he tried to "pack" the Supreme Court in 1937.

In sum, the light that the lamp of experience sheds on presidential impeachment is flickering and inconclusive. Constitutionalism played a varying role in the three instances. A radically judicial interpretation of the canon barely saved Andrew Johnson. Although commentators overwhelmingly judge that outcome a good thing, I do not think it was. His removal over such high-stakes issues as the consequences of having abolished slavery and the basis for rebuilding the Union might have set a good precedent for subsequent exercises of the impeachment power. Constitutionalism dovetailed with Democratic partisanship to save Clinton. I agree with the commentators who think this outcome was right. By Constitutionalist standards, the whole business was flawed and should never have gotten off the ground. The most salutary example is Nixon's, where Constitutionalism, as a respected minority of his fellow Republicans recognized, formed the basis for his removal.

The Watergate experience is an example of how the impeachment power ought to work. In fact, its formal incompleteness proves that point. If impeachment is working as it should, then any offending president possessed of good sense will resign and spare the country an unnecessary ordeal. The Clinton experience, however, has sent a bad signal about the use of this power. It was an abuse of a tool that should be seldom used, but which serves an absolutely legitimate and constructive function in the American system. That abuse makes it unlikely that a president will be impeached again in the foreseeable future. Some may say that with such a precedent Constitutionalism won. I disagree. The cheapening and misuse of impeachment in the Clinton affair was bad at the time and sets an even worse course for the future. Nobody and nothing won in this business, least of all properly practiced Constitutionalism.

# Chapter 11

# The Constitutional Politics of the Clinton Impeachment

## *Mark V. Tushnet*

The U.S. Constitution is incomplete. Even when read in light of their original understanding, its express terms do not define precisely the ways in which many functions of a modern state are to be carried out. Sometimes we fill in the Constitution's meaning by asking the Supreme Court to interpret it. Sometimes, however, we fill in the meaning by having the political branches—Congress and the president—develop what political scientist Keith Whittington calls *constitutional constructions*.[1] These constructions differ from the ordinary policy matters Congress and the president routinely address because they deal with fundamental questions of government organization rather than quotidian political concerns. In addition, constitutional constructions tend to provide solutions to problems of government that define relatively large-scale relations within the government and between the government and the people, and do so for a reasonably extended time period. Constitutional constructions are also political acts. They result from strategies adopted by politicians in response to the immediate needs of contending parties. Their content is therefore shaped by those needs.

The Clinton impeachment process—the entire set of events running from the Independent Counsel's Referral to the House of Representatives through the Senate's acquittal—was an episode in constitutional construction. But what exactly did Congress make of the Constitution during that process? I suggest that the process constructed the constitutional law of impeachment in two ways. It *legalized* the process, and it *trivialized* a House decision to impeach. These two constructions have different, and in some ways contradictory, implications for the future use of the impeachment power.

Probably the main constitutional characteristic of the impeachment process was its *legalization*, an intensification of aspects of impeachment law that have always existed. Nearly every participant addressed questions about the meaning of the Constitution's terms by referring to terms similar to those used in court-centered legal discourse. To answer the question, "What acts amount to high crimes and misdemeanors?" people asked whether the evidence established that Clinton's statements satisfied the criminal law requirements for perjury. To answer the question, "What standard of proof should be sufficient for the House of Representatives to impeach the President?" people asked about grand juries and trial juries, and about the proper role of prosecutorial discretion.

There is nothing inevitable about a legalized Constitution. One might have taken the issue in a presidential impeachment process to be a *political* one. Then the participants would ask whether the President's conduct was such that he should be removed from office because, for example, he had lost the people's confidence.

Legalizing the impeachment process had important implications for its outcome. Republicans legalized the process because they believed that doing so increased the chances that they would succeed in removing the President. Clinton's supporters accepted legalization because they understood that it made success less likely. Further, to the extent that a legalized impeachment process is the Clinton impeachment's legacy for long-term relations between Congress and the president, legalization may perhaps have reduced our ability to use the impeachment process as a device of purely political discipline. Perhaps removal need not be the goal of a House impeachment, as Jonathan Turley has argued,[2] but Turley believes that inflicting some political damage on a president is the alternative, and legalization reduced the scope of such damage.

The major political features of the impeachment process structured its course. The process occurred under conditions of divided government. The American people had chosen to be represented in Congress by a Republican majority and in the presidency by a Democrat. The Republican majority in the House and its Democratic minority were ideologically polarized and partisan, in the sense that defections from each side's majority were few. The Republican majority in the Senate was insufficient to ensure the President's removal if party lines held firm. Finally, throughout the process President Clinton retained such high levels of popular approval that few people took seriously the prospect of his removal from office. These political characteristics drove the legalization of the process.

We can begin by distinguishing between legal arguments that floated around the margins of the process, and those that were at its heart. Throughout the process people proposed actions that seemed to solve certain political problems, but that were rejected because they did not comport with widely accepted legalistic views. Early in the process, for example, a number of proposals for "censure-plus" were offered. Under them Congress would adopt a resolution censuring Clinton and imposing a significant financial penalty on him.

The idea of censure persisted through the process, but that of censure-plus did not. Censure-plus was defeated in part by the view of some partisan Republicans that the Constitution did not authorize censure and that censure-plus was an inadequate response to Clinton's misconduct. The argument against the constitutionality of censure alone was never strong, but the argument against censure-plus was. At first glance, it was a classic bill of attainder, the imposition by Congress of a penalty on a named individual for what Congress deemed his misconduct. Of course censure-plus would never have come about without Clinton's acquiescence, which distinguished it from the classic bill of attainder. But there was a decent constitutional argument against his power to accept a bill of attainder: It was argued that doing so would undermine the President's structural independence of Congress and no single president has the power to concede to Congress, on a matter that weakens the presidency as an institution. Again, some proponents of censure-plus described ways of enacting it that might have evaded the combined bill-of-attainder and separation-of-powers problems. Some people suggested, for example, that the President could make a "voluntary" contribution to the U.S. treasury as part of a political agreement that did not have the force of law. But these mechanisms obscured the clarity of censure-plus as a public, political, and law-pervaded means of expressing disapproval of Clinton's conduct.

Later in the process, law professor Joseph Isenbergh proposed an outcome that Republicans anticipating Clinton's acquittal might have favored. Isenbergh paid close attention to the Constitution's language. The House has "the sole Power of Impeachment." The Senate has "the sole Power to try all Impeachments," and "Judgment in Cases of Impeachment shall not extend further than to removal from Office, and disqualification" from other federal positions. Finally, "the President . . . shall be removed from Office on Impeachment for, and Conviction of, Treason, Bribery, or other high Crimes and Misdemeanors." According to Isenbergh, taken together these provisions supported the following process: The House could impeach Clinton for essentially any sort of misconduct, and, particularly, need not find that he had committed a high crime or misdemeanor. The Senate could then convict. But the Constitution mandates removal from office only when a president is convicted of a high crime or misdemeanor. The Senate had discretion to determine what punishment was appropriate for those convicted of other offenses. Isenbergh concluded that Clinton could be impeached and still remain in office. His proposal attracted a flurry of attention, but quickly died. Isenbergh's analysis did have support in the Constitution's text. It was so at odds with long-settled understandings about the scope of the impeachment power, however, that it could not be accepted within the process's legalized context even though it would have solved an important political problem the Republicans faced.

Censure-plus and Isenbergh's creative proposal were marginal to the impeachment process. Legalization went to its core as well. Consider both the substance of the articles of impeachment, and the standard of proof on which the House and Senate acted. The articles used thoroughly legalized terms, charging Clinton with the indictable offenses of perjury and obstruction of justice. The House of Representatives deliberately and without substantial controversy rejected a proposal to impeach Clinton for abusing his office in ways that did not clearly violate existing criminal laws, and for misleading Congress and the public over the period preceding the initiation of impeachment proceedings. Had the House seen impeachment as a political process it might not have rejected these wider charges.

The House of Representatives never clearly resolved the question of the standard of proof it needed before impeaching, but all the proposed standards derived from the criminal process. Some members thought they had to be sure beyond a reasonable doubt that Clinton had violated the law. Others believed that the House could act as a grand jury would, and impeach Clinton on finding substantial reason to believe he had violated the law. They would leave it to the Senate, acting as a trial jury, to apply the beyond-a-reasonable-doubt standard. By the time the case reached the Senate its conclusion was foregone, and little attention was given to the standard of proof. When the question arose, however, criminal standards were invoked. Prominent Senators used the language of reasonable doubt, and other Senators occasionally objected to the articles of impeachment on the grounds that they did not clearly identify, as a criminal indictment would, the precise items of wrongdoing with which the President was charged.

I could provide other examples of the legalization of the impeachment process, but these are sufficient to establish that it *was* highly legalized. The constructions developed during the Clinton impeachment were quite responsible, when considered as exercises in the kind of legalistic reasoning associated with court-centered constitutional discourse. Both censure-plus and Isenbergh's proposal were clearly problematic, although neither was plainly and grossly inconsistent with the Constitution. The only proposal that received less serious attention than it should have was law professor Bruce Ackerman's argument that an impeachment voted by a lame-duck Congress was constitutionally questionable.[3] Even there, Ackerman's proposal was probably mistaken in the form he offered it, because he framed his proposal as an argument about what the Constitution required rather than as one about the Senate's law of impeachment. In the end, the newly elected House endorsed the lame-duck impeachment by reappointing impeachment Managers, which was enough to satisfy Ackerman's constitutional concerns.

Seen legalistically, the view that House members were merely acting as a grand jury preferring charges to be resolved by the Senate was probably the only truly questionable position that was widely articulated and apparently endorsed by many House members. Both the history of impeachment and its current functioning probably demanded more of the House. Yet even here, the position is not entirely indefensible. In prior impeachments, including those of many judges, the House itself took evidence and was in a position to evaluate its substance, including the credibility of witnesses and the like. Clinton's impeachment was different because the House received the results of a substantial independent inquiry into Clinton's conduct. Under those circumstances, it may perhaps not have been legalistically unreasonable for the House to forgo its own investigation. Without such an investigation, however, it was difficult for the House to act as anything other than a grand jury.[4] The so-called trial in the Senate demonstrated the awkwardness of a trial in which essentially no evidence was presented. The House was in a similar position, and perhaps some members reasonably resolved their dilemma by applying the grand jury standard of proof.

Congress acted reasonably well within the framework of a legalized impeachment process. That does not resolve two additional questions, however: Why was the process legalized, and is a legalized impeachment process a constitutional construction we should find acceptable?

Legalization is particularly puzzling because it made it harder for the proponents of impeachment to succeed in removing the President. Of course the chance of removal was slight throughout the process, but legalization reduced it even further. The difficulties arose in the small and in the large. After structuring the impeachment process to resemble a criminal trial, supporters of Clinton's removal discovered that they had to prove the President's wrongdoing beyond a reasonable doubt. The Senate's unwillingness to expand the record beyond the one developed by the Independent Counsel made it essentially impossible to resolve conflicts of testimony regarding some aspects of the obstruction of justice count. The state of the record had Monica Lewinsky and Betty Currie disagreeing about factual matters whose resolution was important to determining whether the President had coordinated the concealment of evidence and thereby obstructed justice. Over the objections of the House Managers, the Senate rejected proposals to treat the trial as a real one, in which new testimony would be presented. The Senate insisted that the House Managers present new testimony only through videotaped material taken at depositions from three witnesses. The Managers apparently concluded that the political costs of deposing both Lewinsky and Currie would have been too great. Given the state of the record, a reasonable person could infer that Clinton had obstructed justice, but drawing that inference was hardly necessary. The criminal standard of proof beyond a reasonable doubt made it possible for Senators inclined by their partisan commitment to vote to acquit the President to do so without appearing to be driven solely by partisanship.

In addition, the President's lawyers adopted a strategy that made it quite difficult to be comfortable saying that the criminal standard of proof had been satisfied. In brief, they put on no factual defense whatever, while always refusing to concede the accuracy of the factual representations in the Independent Counsel's Referral and in the materials the House had presented to the Senate. Of course they had some opportunities to present a fact-based defense. As a strict matter of legalism one could say that having failed to do so they could hardly be heard to complain that Senators were finding their client guilty beyond a reasonable doubt on the basis of an incomplete factual record. But as a matter of juror psychology, the record's incompleteness impeded a finding that the criminal standard was satisfied.

More generally, legalizing the impeachment process disadvantaged the proponents of removal by taking some arguments away from them.

According to some jurisprudential analyses, the whole point of law is precisely to exclude from consideration some matters that would be relevant if the decision maker were to make a judgment about what was best, all things considered.[5] The exclusionary force of legalization was clear in the impeachment context. Proponents of impeachment may have been motivated by their judgment that President Clinton's behavior demonstrated his unfitness to continue in office. Their legalization of the proceedings, however, made it impossible for them to give that reason for Clinton's impeachment; rather, they had to say that he had committed a serious crime. In contrast, the opponents of impeachment could make the full range of arguments, legalistic and political or partisan. To the extent that removal could occur only if the public and the Senate were persuaded, the proponents of removal had fewer rhetorical tools than did its opponents.[6]

These strategic considerations might explain why the President and his lawyers would want to legalize the proceedings. But why did his opponents go along? Legalization seemingly made impeachment and removal from office exceedingly unlikely. The difficulty, of course, was that an openly partisan process would have made impeachment and removal entirely impossible. The proponents of impeachment were unable to break the hold of party affiliation even after deploying a legalized process: Only a handful of Democrats voted against the party majority in the House, and none did so in the Senate. Clinton was popular enough that a process in which partisanship was completely undisguised, not even covered over with the fig leaf of legalism, could have made almost no headway. Legalization gave Republicans some protective cover. When the process ended, they could say that they had not been pursuing a purely partisan course, but had merely been doing what the law required of them. Clinton's opponents, that is, found that legalization was the best they could do with the hand they were dealt.

In some ways, however, this argument simply pushes the question back one step. An unabashedly partisan impeachment process was doomed to failure; a legalized one was highly unlikely to succeed. Why then did partisan Republicans push the process so hard to a conclusion that, they should have known from the outset, was going to be quite unsatisfying to them? The reasons, I believe, lie in the structure of contemporary politics, that is, in the seemingly enduring characteristics of our current system of organizing a national government.[7] Here I focus on four of those characteristics.

First, the current constitutional order seems committed to divided government. We have experienced divided government for most of the modern political era, and Americans seem to find it satisfactory. Divided government means that the national government can act only when there is a reasonably strong bipartisan commitment to action; national policy will not rest on one side's position on highly contentious issues. Political scientists disagree about the precise reasons for the persistence of divided government. The best explanation appears to be that enough Americans like the results of divided government that they divide their votes when they can.

Second, the parties in Congress are highly partisan and highly ideological. The impeachment process illustrated partisanship when neither party experienced substantial defection from the party majority's position in both the House of Representatives and the Senate; defections from the Republican majority were proportionally greater in the Senate than in the House, but Senate Democrats voted as a bloc. And, contrary to the models developed by some political scientists, the parties are ideologically polarized; each party has been driven in the direction of its left or right wing rather than toward centrist positions.

Polarization results primarily from the processes of congressional districting and candidate selection. The Supreme Court's one-person, one-vote decisions took out of the districting process many traditional considerations that made it possible to have numerous congressional districts containing people with diverse partisan commitments. But they leave open one consideration that politicians love, partisanship itself. That is, politicians can draw district lines to ensure that each district has a clear partisan character for the foreseeable future. The Supreme Court's limitations on partisan gerrymandering are so loose that they place no significant constraints on it.[8] Most congressional districts, then, are either clearly Democratic or clearly Republican. And while districting cannot affect the Senate, there is some reason to believe that people choose to locate themselves in states whose political coloration is congenial to them. Districts will produce members of the House from the dominant party in each one, and migration will produce one-party Senate delegations. Who chooses that party's candidate? Not a party boss or machine. Instead, modern candidate-selection processes rely on party primaries to identify general election candidates. Those who vote in party primaries are more ideologically committed than those who do not. The candidates they nominate will be more ideological than the country as a whole (or even the district as a whole). Strongly liberal Democrats will confront strongly conservative Republicans in the House of Representatives.

Third, contemporary politics is highly personalized. Political scientists describe elections today as candidate-centered. Such elections encourage candidates to display their personal characteristics as grounds for election, in part because their affiliation with a national political party is less significant than in the past. Republicans descried what they called the politics of personal destruction when the impeachment resulted in the resignation of House Speaker–designate Robert Livingston. Because they believed that Democrats had perfected that politics when they blocked the nominations of Robert Bork for the Supreme Court and John Tower for Secretary of Defense, they found it impossible to resist the opportunity to practice the politics of personal destruction when Clinton gave them the chance.

The final ingredient in the present constitutional order is the way in which the nation moved from the New Deal and Great Society to a new system. Political scientist Stephen Skowronek describes these transitions in general terms that are quite illuminating.[9] According to Skowronek, one president will initiate a change in regime by developing substantial criticism of the previous system and sketching policy alternatives. This initiating president will be followed by others. Those from his own party will try to enact and extend the alternatives while also attempting to demonstrate their own distinctive leadership abilities. Those from the opposition party may practice what Skowronek calls a politics of preemption, in which they endorse the initiatives their party originally opposed, while tempering them somewhat.

For present purposes, these latter presidents are the most interesting. Skowronek points to structural reasons why they routinely get into real political trouble. Their opponents are furious that what they regard as their distinctive programs have been appropriated, or hijacked, by the other party. But even members of a preemptive president's own party are unlikely to be enthusiastic supporters of preemption. They come from districts where partisans of the older party positions remain powerful, and they are likely to be uncomfortable with the transformation of their party into one that resembles the other. A preemptive president, then, will face an enraged opposition and lukewarm supporters in Congress.

Skowronek's description fits the impeachment process nearly perfectly. President Clinton presented himself as a New Democrat who accepted most of the criticisms of the New Deal and the policy initiatives associated with the so-called Reagan Revolution. His famous "triangulation" policy was his way of developing political support in the nation by opposing congressional Republicans and, notably, congressional Democrats. Republican fury with Clinton antedated the impeachment process, and arose primarily from the fact that he successfully practiced the politics of preemption.

Under the circumstances, something much like impeachment was almost certain to occur. As Skowronek presciently wrote in 1993, with Clinton's recent election in mind, one "hallmark" of the politics of preemption is "the cultivation of independent political identities [by presidents], the exploitation of ad hoc coalitions, and the high risk of suffering the ultimate disgrace of impeachment."[10] Yet divided but ideological and partisan government and the politics of preemption may make impeachment nothing more than an ordinary part of politics.

In this sense, the current structure of politics trivializes the impeachment power. Knowing the likely result in advance, ideological House Republicans could satisfy the demands of their partisan constituencies without having to face a public outraged at the actual removal of a popular president from office. House Republicans found that the impeachment was cost-free. They might reasonably have seen the outcome of the process as a success rather than failure. For them, Clinton's impeachment was almost a "no harm, no foul" proposition. Their Senate counterparts, in contrast, had to extricate themselves from a politically difficult situation. But they managed to do so with relatively little damage to their political positions.

For that reason, the precise circumstances of the Clinton impeachment did not destabilize the political system.[11] Because the outcome was a nearly foregone conclusion, political life could go on unimpeded after the termination of the process. Obviously there were interim costs, as Congress and the President focused nearly exclusively on the impeachment process rather than on other, arguably more important public policy concerns. And some of those interim costs may be irretrievable. Some observers have suggested, for example, that the Administration was unable to devote enough time to building support for the Comprehensive Test Ban Treaty during the impeachment year, leading to its rejection by the Senate in 1999. Still, looking at the political system from a long-term perspective, I think it reasonable to conclude that the impeachment process did not, and will not, make much difference to the overall structure of that system.

Finally, it seems worth noting that the stakes in the impeachment process were actually quite small. Prior presidential impeachments were large-scale struggles between Congress and the President over which branch would dominate the national political process. Andrew Johnson was impeached because he insisted that the President had the primary role in setting policy. Congress rejected his Reconstruction policies that, in its view, conceded far too much to the South's secessionist elite. It made Johnson's effort to control the federal bureaucracy the occasion for his impeachment. Although Johnson remained in office, many historians believe that for decades the presidency was subordinated to Congress.

Richard Nixon's resignation in the face of impeachment occurred in a similar struggle for power over national policy. Nixon had refused to spend money Congress had appropriated and had conducted a war in secret and without significant concession to congressional sentiments regarding its termination. Congress seized on the Watergate episode to assert its primacy, or perhaps more accurately its coequal status, in the national lawmaking process. And again, the balance between President and Congress established in the Nixon impeachment held steady for a few decades.

In contrast, all that was at issue in the Clinton impeachment process was who would occupy the presidency. On the policy level, Clinton had already conceded much to his Republican adversaries. Because of divided government, Congress and the President already shared power. And because Republicans rightly believed that the present constitutional order was an outgrowth of the Reagan Revolution, they had no particular interest in displacing presidential with congressional domination of the national government. All they wanted was a Republican president. The Clinton impeachment process, then, raised no large-scale issues. It presented a simple question of personnel. And there too there was not much at stake. Clinton's removal would have put in office Al Gore, whose policies were indistinguishable from Clinton's.

A trivialized impeachment need not destabilize the government, then, but its legalization might be troubling. Perhaps in the abstract the impeachment power should be reserved for occasions when fundamental issues about political organization and individual liberty arise. But the structural sources of the Clinton impeachment suggest that it might become routine, as ideological and partisan Congresses confront presidents in a divided government.

Trivialization may make impeachment more likely, while simultaneously reducing its significance. Legalization, in contrast, might actually be undesirable. It will force real political disagreements into a rigidly legalized framework. Partisans who consider a particular president unfit for office will search desperately for criminal offenses that can be the legalized hook for his removal, and will never talk about their political reasons for thinking the President unfit.

Consider, for example, one of the charges against Clinton that was eliminated from the proceedings, that he had misled his Cabinet, Congress, and the American people for several months. The charge was dropped because misleading the people violates no criminal law. And yet, it seems to me, a president can indeed demonstrate unfitness for office by misleading the people. One can reasonably believe that Richard Nixon should have been removed from office because he misled the American people about whether U.S. forces were engaged in hostilities in Cambodia, for example. Similarly, one can reasonably believe that Ronald Reagan's public statements about the Iran-Contra affair showed either that he pursued in private a policy he rejected in public, or that he did not understand the policies members of his administration were pursuing, and that in either event he demonstrated unfitness for office. The legalization of impeachment forecloses the opportunity to engage in a productive public discussion about how damaging to our fundamental institutions it is for a president to mislead the public. There is nothing wrong with an impeachment focusing on the Watergate break-in, or on the violation of criminal law in connection with arms shipments to Iran and payments to the Contras, or on perjury and obstruction of justice. Legalization is problematic, however, when it precludes impeachments focusing on anything else, when much else could properly be the subject of an impeachment.

Here too the small stakes in the Clinton impeachment process make a difference. Andrew Johnson was engaged in a course of conduct that demonstrated a large-scale disagreement between him and Congress both over Reconstruction policy and over who should control its direction. Congress enacted a statute restricting Johnson's power over his Cabinet selections, knowing that Johnson would violate the statute, and used the violation to trigger his impeachment. Legalization in that form did not preclude consideration of the larger issues raised by Johnson's conduct. Republicans could not develop a similarly productive legalization in the Clinton impeachment process precisely because there were no larger issues at stake.

Future impeachments may be both more frequent and no matter of special constitutional concern because the House trivialized impeachment. But the legalization of the impeachment process may make it more difficult to retrieve a sensible construction of the impeachment power as something to be used as a tool of political discipline when political leaders lose the people's confidence. It may be impossible to specify standards for impeachment, or constructions of the term *high crimes and misdemeanors,* that satisfy legalistic requirements. Ordinarily, but perhaps not always, mere policy disagreement will be insufficient to justify impeachment and removal. Ordinarily, but perhaps not always, Congress will be able to find some preexisting criminal statute that a president who ought to be removed has violated, or may enact one that will trigger removal. What the impeachment process needs is people who will exercise good judgment as statesmen and stateswomen in determining how and by whom the nation can best be governed. Lawyers are not always good statesmen and stateswomen, however. The legalization of the impeachment process may reduce the possibility that good statesmanship will rule. That reduction may be the most important constitutional legacy of the Clinton impeachment.

### NOTES

1. Keith E. Whittington, *Constitutional Construction: Divided Powers and Constitutional Meaning* (Cambridge: Harvard University Press, 1999).

2. Jonathan Turley, "Senate Trials and Factional Disputes: Impeachment as a Madisonian Device," *Duke Law Journal,* vol. 49 (October 1999): 1–146.

3. Bruce A. Ackerman, *The Case against Lame Duck Impeachment* (New York: Seven Stories Press, 1998).

4. For a critique of the Independent Counsel statute on the grounds that the provision requiring the Independent Counsel to refer matters to the House of Representatives places the House in precisely this position, see Julie O'Sullivan, "The Interaction between Impeachment and the Independent Counsel Statute," *Georgetown Law Journal,* vol. 86 (July 1998): 2193–264.

5. Joseph Raz and Frederick Schauer are the primary proponents of this so-called exclusionary theory of law. See Joseph Raz, *The Authority of Law: Essays on Law and Morality* (New York: Oxford University Press, 1979); Frederick F. Schauer, *Playing by the Rules: A Philosophical Examination of Rule-Based Decision-Making in Law and in Life* (New York: Oxford University Press, 1991).

6. I have argued elsewhere that these effects can be seen in a number of other areas in which constitutional construction occurs outside the courts. See Mark V. Tushnet, *Taking the Constitution Away from the Courts* (Princeton: Princeton University Press, 1999), 109–10.

7. I develop the argument in the succeeding paragraphs in more detail in

Mark Tushnet, "The Supreme Court, 1998 Term: Foreword—The New Constitutional Order and the Chastening of Constitutional Ambition," *Harvard Law Review*, vol. 116 (November 1999): 29–109.

8.  See *Davis v. Bandemer*, 478 U.S. 109 (1986).

9.  Stephen Skowronek, *The Politics Presidents Make: Leadership from John Adams to George Bush* (Cambridge: Belknap Press, 1993).

10.  Skowronek, *The Politics Presidents Make*, 444.

11.  For an expression of concern about the overuse of impeachment, see the essay by Cass Sunstein in this collection.

# Part III

# Shaping Public Opinion

# Chapter 12

# Ontology in the Clinton Era

## *Andrew D. Weiner*

It depends on what the meaning of the word "is" is. If "is" means "is and never has been," that is not—that is one thing. If it means "there is none," that was a completely true statement.[1]

If you were writing a book about cynicism, the sentence, "it depends on what the meaning of 'is' is" would make an excellent epigraph.[2]

Even though I'm not writing a book about cynicism, but only a response to the memory of things past, I find this quotation from Louis Menand's essay an even better epigraph, for the cynicism that interests me here is the cynicism of the press and, even more, the news media that most of us tend to turn to in moments of perceived national crisis. One of the most interesting developments in the whole impeachment process was the casualness with which precision in language became something to be mocked, to be dismissed as a cynical attempt to manipulate not reality but the discourse allowed on the public stage. When the President's lawyers tried to make the case that what the President did does not fit the legal definition of perjury, editorials in major newspapers mockingly dismissed their arguments as merely "legalisms," apparently on the theory that since we all "knew" that he had lied, these attempts to draw meaningless distinctions could only be meant to confuse us. The only "kiss" commentators today do not regard with disdain is an acronym, "Keep it simple, stupid"; it signifies their contempt for those who would try to confuse the public with complicated language or suggest that language needs to be complex because reality is complex.

This insistence that "is" must be "is" marks the distance we have come since the revival of rhetoric as an art of persuasion in the Renaissance. The rhetorical culture of earlier centuries believed that language could help us come to agreement about complex issues; our media culture seems not to want agreement (what would they spend their time endlessly discussing if consensus were ever reached?) but rather tries to reduce reality to twenty-second sound bites accompanied by striking visuals. To judge by what we see on television, we live in a society where "balance" is to be achieved in the crossfire between totally opposed positions upheld by dogmatic partisans chosen because they would never disrupt that balance by acknowledging that the other side could make a persuasive argument or even make them change their minds (an act once the mark of a mind capable of learning new things but which is now labeled a flip-flop in sign of its new place as an indicator of political weakness).

As one who regularly spends a considerable amount of time talking about the wonders of the universes that Shakespeare's plays reveal to us, Menand's statement immediately made me think of Shakespeare's play *Twelfth Night*, a play about the adventures of twins separated by a shipwreck, each fearing the other drowned. Viola, the one whose situation receives the most consideration in the play, disguises herself as a man, dresses as her brother was when their ship sank, and seeks service with a Duke, Orsino, who is in love with a Countess, Olivia, who has vowed seven years of mourning for the deaths of her father and brother. Orsino takes Viola, now called Cesario, into his service, thinking her a man, and makes her his ambassador to Olivia, who, after being made wise about the foolishness of excessive grief by Feste, her wise fool, proceeds to fall in love with Cesario, who has, naturally, fallen in love with Orsino. Into this simple situation eventually comes Viola's twin brother Sebastian, who again, naturally, is immediately assumed to be Cesario by Feste, who has been sent by Olivia to seek Cesario. When Feste finds "Cesario" (Sebastian, of course), he is rebuffed:

> *Feste:* Will you make me believe that I am not sent for you?
> *Sebastian:* Go to, go to, thou art a foolish fellow, Let me be clear of thee.
> *Feste:* Well held out, i' faith! No, I do not know you, nor I am not sent to you by my lady to bid you come speak with her, nor your name is not Master Cesario, nor this is not my nose, neither. Nothing that is so, is so.
> (*Twelfth Night*, IV.i.1–8)[3]

Irritated because Cesario is stubbornly denying the obvious, Feste cynically suggests that Cesario's denial is a palpable lie, as plain as the nose on Feste's face.

Soon, however, Feste is himself asked to dissemble. Malvolio, Olivia's steward, whose sense of decorum leads him to chastise others for excessive drinking and singing in the house of one who is in mourning (he has missed a news bulletin concerning the end of Olivia's mourning), has been led to imagine himself the beloved of his lady, the Countess Olivia, and while he is deeply engaged in his fantasy of political promotion to Count Malvolio, those he has rebuked convince Olivia that Malvolio has gone mad and must be locked up in a dark place until he is cured. Since madness was thought to involve demonic possession, Feste is ordered by the conspirators to pretend to be a minister come to cure Malvolio.

> *Maria:* Nay, I prithee put on this gown and this beard, make him believe thou art Sir Topas the curate. Do it quickly. I'll call Sir Toby the whilst.
> *Feste:* Well, I'll put it on, and I will dissemble myself in't, and I would I were the first that ever dissembled in such a gown.

> *Sir Toby:* Jove bless thee, Master Parson.
> *Feste:* Bonos dies, Sir Toby, for, as the old hermit of Prague, that never saw pen and ink, very wittily said to a niece of King Gorboduc, "That that is, is." So I, being Master Parson, am Master Parson; for what is "that" but "that," and "is" but "is"?
> *Sir Toby:* To him, Sir Topas. (*Twelfth Night*, IV.ii.1-18)

Feste, amused by the folly under way, wisely comments that as the world goes, whatever people think is true—based upon whatever evidence is presented to their senses, be it nothing more than a costume to disguise them—is true, even when, as in this case, it isn't.

As the play shows us how easily the complexity of life can overwhelm our sense of what is, Olivia rebukes Sebastian, whom she thinks is Cesario, for not returning her love; when Sebastian shows himself to be more interested in her love than she had expected, she promptly offers to marry the now-willing man of her desires. And they go to the church with the *real* Sir Topas (who of course is actually only an actor); after they are wed, Sebastian is assaulted by some other characters who think him the not very manly Cesario (the woman pretending to be a man whose part is actually being played by a prepubescent boy, as are all of the "women" in the play); when he defends himself (offstage), they come running and bleeding onstage, where they find "Cesario" whom they have just fled from, already present but in disgrace with Orsino, who thinks that Cesario has betrayed him by making love to Olivia. When Sebastian enters shortly after, the two twins are finally together onstage before everyone at the same time, leading to general wonderment and Orsino's comment that reality is more complicated than he— or anyone else on stage—had thought:

> *Orsino:* One face, one voice, one habit, and two persons /
>    A natural perspective, that is and is not. (*Twelfth Night*, V.i.213–14)

The multiplication of possibilities caused by the existence of the same person as both male and female turns a triangle into a polygon: both Orsino and Olivia can end up with a "Cesario" of their own as soon as "Cesario," returned to "his" own natural sex by donning her own feminine dress, can satisfy Orsino that she is indeed as beautiful a woman as she was a man. Life as depicted in the play, clearly, is a more complicated business than anyone had realized up to this point in the play.

Comparing the resolution of Shakespeare's play with the play of the actors in the impeachment drama, one can understand why all concerned— actors and audience alike—wished life could be as "simple" as art and tried to make it so. The press, initially expecting to see a simple morality play, were outraged when Clinton defied their expectations and refused to resign in shame: clearly he had no shame or he would not have defied their predictions that he would have to resign within a week were he once to be shown to have engaged in "hanky-panky" of any sort with Monica Lewinsky. The special prosecutor, who had known all along that Clinton was guilty of something, was overjoyed that Clinton's sin was now as plain as the nose on his Pinocchioed face and sent to Congress a report that Clinton was pretty much guilty of everything (or at least of something) and ought to be impeached for smoking cigars (among other things). House Republicans, who would have to vote to impeach a sitting president for something, released the whole of the Starr Report, hoping everyone would be as disgusted with Clinton's disgusting sexual proclivities, only to discover that others seemed intent on publishing reports of their own sexual proclivities: Newt Gingrich resigned in the expectation that his multiyear affair with a young female government employee was about to be exposed; his successor, Speaker-designate Livingston, made a speech denouncing the President's immorality, then promptly revealed his own and resigned. Several other Republican leaders, ignoring the maxim that once is tragedy but twice is farce, likewise either excused, denied, or apologized for all sins published, about to be published, or imputed.

With all charges against Clinton reduced to two, the next scene in the morality play turned farce opened in a Senate anxious to do anything but deal with either the House's bill of particulars or, for that matter, the House Managers: that the President's poll ratings, violating Republican laws of moral gravity, kept rising the more charges they hurled against him, made it unlikely that many—or perhaps even any—but certainly not enough Democratic votes could be found to convict and rid them of this villain. The trial was presided over by a Republican Chief Justice who had been so impressed by a costume worn by the Lord Chancellor of England in a performance of Gilbert and Sullivan's *Iolanthe* that he had his robes modified in imitation of the Lord Chancellor's, apparently forgetting that in *Iolanthe* the Lord Chancellor had begotten a child out of wedlock upon a fairy and that he desired to marry his own ward without his own consent, much like William Jefferson Clinton, who allowed oral sex to be performed upon his person without, apparently, either giving his consent or enjoying it. As the President's ratings continued to climb, the trial became more and more of a political liability for those conducting it, and in the end, not even a bare majority could be found for either of the two charges. With not the slightest abatement of anger or disgust, the House Managers slunk back to their lair, and the country was forced to listen to the waves of punditry that came flooding in.

Rather than drown in that flood, however, I wish to consider in the light of this epiphanic narrative, not how we got there but how we might go there again. On the front page of the *Wisconsin State Journal's* "Your Forum" section for January 23, 2000, the headline proclaimed, "America's Demand: One Honest Man." Yet, as if to remind us of Democritus's quest, the letters section on the next page contained four responses to the editor's decision to drop the weekly column by Doctor Laura Schlessinger, a tough, no-nonsense moralist (who had recently been angered and, one assumes, embarrassed when nude pictures taken of her some years earlier were posted on the Internet). One reader demanded that the paper reverse itself: "I see you've dropped Laura Schlessinger's column. I am very disappointed in that decision. It's interesting that you seem to have room each Sunday for the cheap, left-leaning garbage of *The Capital Times* in the 'Your Forum' section, but no room for the deep truths Schlessinger discusses in her column. Where's the balance? Is the *State Journal* headed to the same mediocre trash heap as *The Capital Times*?" Yet another reader applauded her disappearance: "I was disappointed to read the two letters from readers who were very angry that you dropped Laura Schlessinger's column. I support your decision. I find Schlessinger to be a foolish prejudiced woman, whose columns were full of half truths, and increasingly, out and out lies. I, for one, won't miss her." If America cannot agree on the question of whether Schlessinger is one honest woman, how can we ever expect to find "One Honest Man" to be President when the conventions of electioneering require that the candidates, after resisting as long as humanly possible (perhaps a week or two), begin calling each other liars (which requires a visit to the Crossfire where experts will insist that they are and are not)? Nor is it just people who read screeds by columnists like Laura Schlessinger who seem to have trouble defining their terms.

Two recent books on the impeachment, Richard A. Posner's *An Affair of State: The Investigation, Impeachment, and Trial of President Clinton*[4] and Alan M. Dershowitz's *Sexual McCarthyism*, demonstrate the same lack of success in reaching uniformity. For Posner, the question of Starr's culpability in leaking grand jury materials is more or less irrelevant:

> If there were leaks by the Independent Counsel's office . . . they were part of the Independent Counsel's public relations battle (which he lost) with the White House's slander machine, and so in retrospect they are inconsequential. . . . [B]ecause the Independent Counsel's office achieved nothing by its leaks (if it did leak, which has not yet been established), it is difficult to see how the President can complain, especially when his own lawyers were part of the campaign of slander directed against the Independent Counsel's office. At worst, the disclosures of grand jury testimony were premature. (74)

For Dershowitz, however,

> From the time Monica Lewinsky was given full transactional immunity, the obvious target of the grand jury has been President Clinton, though Kenneth Starr seems to acknowledge President Clinton cannot be indicted while serving as President. Accordingly, Kenneth Starr has misused the grand jury to obtain evidence and testimony for inclusion in a report to Congress that will be made public. The implications of using a grand jury to produce a report that standing alone may cause severe legal, political, and personal consequences creates a dangerous precedent and threatens to impinge the basic liberties of our adversarial system. (192)

These two distinguished legal scholars, one an important jurist, the other a well-known civil libertarian, might just as well be talking about two different cases and two different Kenneth Starrs.

Can we avoid these impasses of opinion against opinion? Probably not. If the testimony of my students tells me anything, it tells me that our schools are teaching our students that every American has the right to his or her own opinion and that all opinions are, more or less, equal. Can we avoid public displays of name-calling? Probably not. So long as television is more interested in what is visible than in what is significant, so long as campaigns leave debates and extended discussions in the snows of New Hampshire, substituting expensive political advertisements for answering unlimited questions at town meetings, the quest for answers will inevitably migrate to the TV spot ad noisily trumpeting the simplistic and to the bellowing hosts of talk (or attack) radio. By forcing the complex into a simple (if not simple-minded) form, we deny life the possibility of becoming a thing of ordered complexity and force it to appear as its messy old self. Stately Plump Buck Mulligan insisted to Stephen Dedalus in James Joyce's *Ulysses* that distinguishing between things that look alike but serve different functions is important. We too need to learn to make water when we make water and tea when we make tea, to expect the art we create to have a shape and the thing we encounter in the world around us to be much messier. In art, our fools can be wise; in life, it is more realistic to expect that those who brandish their wisdom like a club with which to beat the rest of us are foolish indeed. The consequences of not doing so are all too clear.

At the end of *Twelfth Night*, when the complexity of life is revealed, a great deal of wonder breaks out. To Olivia, it is "Most wonderful!" (V.i.223) that the world has in it enough of such goodly creatures that both she and Orsino can get what they want. Our world, however, seems more and more to operate on the assumption that if I have something then no one else can have it, and to offer us nothing more wonderful than the sight of our leaders and our "experts" on leaders and leadership trying to find lower and lower depths of sense and behavior to which to plummet.

NOTES

1. Quoted in Alan M. Dershowitz, *Sexual McCarthyism: Clinton, Starr, and the Emerging Constitutional Crisis* (New York: Basic Books, 1998), 29.

2. Louis Menand, "After Elvis," *New Yorker*, October 26 and November 2, 1998, 167.

3. All citations to Shakespeare's works are to the Electronic Edition of *The Oxford Shakespeare*, ed. Stanley Wells and Gary Taylor (London: Oxford Electronic Publishing, 1989).

4. Richard A. Posner, *An Affair of State: The Investigation, Impeachment, and Trial of President Clinton* (Cambridge: Harvard University Press, 1999).

# Chapter 13

# All We Had to Do Was Rationalize the Sex

## *Linda Denise Oakley*

Yes, President Clinton lied, but he lied about sex—consensual sex. For those who opposed impeachment, the fact that the President lied was never more than half the story. The other half, the important half, was the lie itself. For the supporters of impeachment, just the opposite was true. No matter what the President had lied about, the indisputable fact was that he had lied under oath. The fact that his lies were about sex had no bearing on their case. Their gigantic impeachment case against the President had been designed to rivet public attention to one fact in evidence: he lied.

Thus the case for impeachment, as it was put to the American public, held that when President Clinton lied under oath his lies were high crimes punishable by impeachment and removal from office—because he was President. This was a difficult impeachment strategy. The impeachment supporters' case required nothing less than successfully using the President's words to show him to be a liar without granting importance to what he had said.

At the end of the day, the hard-earned failure of the perjury and obstruction case against the President was a no-brainer. Any careful observer of the twenty-four-hour-a-day spectacle being played out on television, on-line, on talk radio, and in print would have seen that large segments of the public refused to ignore the sex. And why should they? The supporters of impeachment seemed obsessed with the President's sex life. Thanks to them, most of us ended up knowing more than we wanted to about the sexual appetites of the President.

The public literally was given every detail about the sex that the President had lied about. Few people know as much about the sex life of their closest friends. Giving the public detailed accountings of the President's sexual misconduct should have purchased public acceptance of the condemnation of President Clinton by the supporters of impeachment. As it turned out, publicizing the President's sexual misconduct made it possible to explain away his sexual misconduct as just another story about sex and power. A story, I might add, that was made only slightly less interesting when it was disclosed that the President was not the only married man elected to high office who had an impressive track record with young women.

Clinton-haters aside, for many people the psychosexual nature of the case against the President was core. Since there appeared to be little else, we were left to assume that if the supporters of impeachment could have made their case against President Clinton with less salacious evidence they would have. But without alternative evidence of misconduct, anyone who believed that the President's only offense was a stupid sexual affair could have found it easy to oppose impeachment. With a little motivation it was relatively easy to find a psychosexual explanation for the President's misconduct.

This is not to suggest that there was a lack of good nonpsychosexual reasons to oppose impeachment. Rational voters still consider the impeachment of an elected president to be a dangerous, no-win situation. For this reason alone, removing the President of the United States from office should not be easy when the case against the President *warrants* this action. Public opposition to the questionable case against President Clinton could have been foreseen.

Second, using impeachment to damage a political enemy is a grievous insult to voters. No one can honestly say that the legal case against the President had not been carefully designed to humiliate him and ridicule the people who voted for him. Since few elected politicians thought it wise to insult the large number of voters who continued to support the President, that job was left to high-priced media stars.

Third, the punishment of impeachment must fit the crime. President Clinton could not be impeached for being a bad man or a bad husband. He could only be impeached for being a bad president. Few people were likely to support removing the President from office under circumstances that might not be sufficient to cause anyone else to lose his or her job.

And lastly, although it took a few years, frugal voters took note when the moment finally arrived at which an almost perfect negative correlation could be calculated between the money being spent to prosecute the President and the legal merits of the impeachment case against him.

Once the sordid sexual details became common knowledge, public curiosity seemed to give way to public disinterest. Gradually, it appeared that the impeachment case against President Clinton was essentially devoid of national or legal importance to anyone other than Clinton-haters. Our voyeurism having been satiated, we turned away from impeachment. Always prepared to follow a popular trend when they find one, the media easily replaced their somber impeachment commentary with wicked cartoons, jokes, and depictions of public burnout.

Legal and political scholars will spend the next decade sifting the ashes of the Clinton impeachment trial. Hopefully they can figure out what was supposed to happen, what actually was accomplished, and why. In the meantime we are left with an interesting question: Why did the public reject the Clinton impeachment case when the case had been custom designed to purchase public acceptance?

Social-psychological theory would suggest that the public could not accept the case against the President. The public could not accept the case as presented by the supporters of impeachment because in the United States, when the question is sexual, the answer is sexual. Yes, President Clinton lied about sex, but it was the kind of sex we could rationalize.

## Public Opinion versus Public Opinion

Public reaction to the President's sexual misconduct appeared to be neutral whereas public reaction to the case for the impeachment of the President appeared to be political. A nationwide ABC poll conducted in 1999—after the Senate found the President not guilty—showed a 60 percent public approval rating for the Senate vote. The very same ABC poll also indicated that 56 percent of the people asked believed that the charges brought against the President were serious enough to justify putting him on trial. That opinion poll also asked if anyone was interested in hearing more about the impeachment case. Most people (81 percent) said they were sick of it.

A CBS/New York Times poll conducted the same year asked Republicans, Democrats, and Independents to answer similar questions. Asked if they thought the charges against the President were serious enough to warrant removing him from office, 28 percent of Republicans, 85 percent of Democrats, and 63 percent of Independents said no. Asked if they thought the impeachment process had been a true investigation or politics, 58 percent of Republicans, 91 percent of Democrats, and 80 percent of Independents said the impeachment was politics. Polls conducted the same year by CNN/Time, Fox News/Opinion Dynamic, and Gallop/CNN/US yielded similar results.

Starting practically the day after the Paula Jones 1994 press conference, at which she alleged that a motel room encounter years earlier with then-Governor Clinton caused her mental duress and violated her civil rights, nearly every major media organization has conducted and published opinion polls about the case. Add them up and the poll numbers indicate three persistent lines of incompatible public reactions: the public opposed impeachment, the public was offended by the President's sexual misconduct, and Republicans supported using impeachment to remove the President from office.

## Psychological Agility

Bullet-proof rationalization of the President's sexual misconduct could lead to public opposition to his impeachment which, in turn, would make it possible for an observant U.S. Senate to end the impeachment trial. Rationalization is a simple yet powerful psychological tool used to manage anxiety.[1] According to Karen Horney,[2] a contemporary of Freud, the psychological meaning that difficult circumstances may hold for the persons involved is proportionate to the anxiety that the circumstances may generate. Difficult circumstances alone need not generate anxiety. But difficult circumstances perceived as dangerous can generate intolerable anxiety.

President Clinton's impeachment trial was dangerous. If the supporters of impeachment had been successful, the nation and the White House would have been thrown into a state of chaos that no one could welcome. If those who opposed impeachment prevailed, the dignity of the office of the U.S. presidency and the voting public would suffer. And may we all agree that the sexual misconduct in question could not have been more dangerous. In fact, there appeared to have been more danger than sex.

Horney and her peers defined rationalization as the invention of a reason or an attitude or an action, the motive of which is not recognized. Since we now understand that anxiety is often the motive for such invention, the modern definition of rationalization can be simplified to mean giving an acceptable explanation.[3] If for no other reason than to escape the inherent dangers of impeaching the President of the United States, the American public had good reason to rationalize the President's sexual misconduct.

One of the neat things about a psychological tool like rationalization is that one may be fully aware, partially aware, or completely unaware that one is experiencing anxiety or using rationalization to manage anxiety. One need not recognize a source of anxiety as such, or recognize one's own anxiety, or recognize one's rationalizations for what they are. In this regard, the psychological mind is remarkably efficient. When people have to deal with dangerous circumstances, psychological agility is a necessary but not always sufficient predictor of success.

I submit that the ever agile but increasingly anxious American public needed to rationalize themselves, Congress, and the President out of the dangerous impeachment mess. Given the documented hound dog sex life of President Clinton and the scary medieval prosecution tactics that were being used to get him, applying an acceptable rationalization for the President's sexual misconduct seemed better than the alternative.

### When All Else Fails, Follow Instructions

Disposable sex with young lovers is a traditional perk enjoyed by powerful men. Margaret Mead[4] summed it up well when she proposed that each society must solve the question of sexual competition among males. Mead's instructions were clear. Whatever the agreed-upon social solution is, that solution must reduce the risk of competing males killing each other off or monopolizing the desirable lovers.

Mead observed that the Western solution to the problem has been to concede unrestricted sexual license to males who have obtained enough power to wipe out most of us. Very little has changed since Mead's day. Whether the power is political, economical, physical, or social, enjoying and then disposing of a sexual partner remains a socially accepted measure of personal power among U.S. males.

Unfortunately for President Clinton, Ms. Lewinsky either was clueless about the nature of her role as his power-perk or she believed that her charms as a young lover would, if not intoxicate, at least remain in demand. Ms. Lewinsky apparently was confident that the President would not discard her. Events soon made it impossible for Ms. Lewinsky to escape this unhappy ending to her adventure.

As any pissed off discarded young lover might, Ms. Lewinsky redirected her devotion to the tasks of raising hell and reeking havoc in that most sacred of sacred temples of male power, the White House. Unfortunately for President Clinton, Ms. Lewinsky's weapons of choice were hours of girl-talk phone conversations with trusted friends and her well-cared for blue party dress.

Unfortunately for Ms. Lewinsky, the published accounts of her sexual encounters with the President of the United States made it easy for voters to rationalize the President's misconduct as a traditional story of sex and power. Had the record shown that the President and the intern were truly in love, instead of reacting with public anxiety, an outraged American public may have acted to politically destroy the President. Even male British royals find it difficult to successfully pull off that stunt.

Because President Clinton fully understood the way the story goes, he publicly declared his lack of love for Ms. Lewinsky by referring to her as "that woman." With those two harsh words, President Clinton claimed his male rights of power. And so it was. The deal between the man and his voters was done. The American public and the U.S. presidency would survive the impeachment trial, and Mr. Clinton and Ms. Lewinsky would be left to their own resources. To keep their end of the bargain, all the American public had to do was rationalize the sex.

## The Power of Social Psychology, the Promise of Reform

Lawyers, philosophers, and pundits may puzzle over the public's seemingly ambivalent reaction to the impeachment case against President Clinton. When viewed from lofty intellectual heights, the President was charged with legal crimes that should have been sufficient to turn the American public against him. Yet despite his having been exposed as a fool deserving of the worst possible fate, non-Clinton-haters seemed unwilling to play a supporting role in either his prosecution or his scandal.

But when examined through the lens of social psychology and the political climate of the day, the public's ambivalent reaction to the Clinton impeachment case begins to make sense. No one should be surprised when the public chooses to identify *with* a person when they see that the government is using its limitless resources to destroy that person. Normal self-interest ensures that the public will do nothing that might encourage this form of government. And the sorry truth is that so many people have cheated—and lied—that it would be almost impossible for the public to high-hat Clinton's cheating and lying. Even people who have not and would not cheat and lie might be unwilling to make either a high crime.

Given how easy it was to rationalize the President's sexual misconduct and given the absence of a compelling case for impeachment, the public rightly perceived that they had little to gain from turning against President Clinton. Given the national political climate at the time, those who opposed impeachment may have believed they stood to benefit from giving President Clinton political protection, albeit passively so.

Just before becoming the poster child for stupid powerful men, President Clinton was speaking on behalf of ordinary people when he called for reform of the U.S. health system. Speaking at a fall 1993 White House press briefing, one year before the Paula Jones press briefing, Clinton said that one of the central reasons he ran for President of the United States was to try to resolve the issue of health reform. Clinton said we must preserve what's right with the health system such as the close patient-doctor relationship, the best doctors and nurses, the best academic research, and the best, most advanced technology in the world. But he believed we could keep what was right with the system and still fix what was wrong.

The 1993 Clinton Health Security Act proposed six principles of reform. Principle 1 proposed that health coverage could never be denied or dropped. Principle 2 proposed that healthcare payment should be based on healthcare costs rather than market prices. Principle 3 proposed improving the effectiveness of the health system by having more health promotion and illness prevention services to help people stay well. Principle 4 proposed that consumers be able to choose their doctor and choose their health plan. Principle 5 proposed a single system of paperwork and payment. And lastly, Principle 6 proposed that, without exception, everyone must pay into the system.

Had Clinton's six principles been adopted, the U.S. health system would indeed have been reformed. Most notably, people with conditions requiring healthcare would not be denied services because they were already ill. Health system profiteering would end. The U.S. health system would not lead the world in selling costly disease treatments to those who could afford to pay. Fraud and waste would no longer be hidden under pages of incomprehensible forms. And if everyone paid for healthcare, everyone would become a stakeholder in the system. Fewer people would feel entitled to misuse and waste services in order to exploit a system they experienced as indifferent to their needs.

The list of charges against President Clinton did not appear to include attempted health reform, but the 1994 movement to impeach the President closed his 1993 health reform agenda. Or did it? President Clinton's generation of middle-aged boomers might continue his health reform movement and, once again, change the way America lives. They may just be the generation who can do it. For boomers didn't learn about no coloreds signs from textbooks, they lived them. Boomers didn't learn about body bags. They lived them. Boomers saw the fifties and sixties for what they were, a time to imagine change, a time to make change happen. Then, it was civil rights and war. Now it's health.

Instead of segregated restaurants, we have a segregated system of healthcare that is closed to the poor. Instead of young men and women dying in war, we have one of the highest infant mortality rates in the world. The wealthy elite may prefer to continue to debate *if and how* healthcare might eventually come to be reformed, and the Clinton proposal for reform may have been silenced, but the conversation continues.

Today, when a hospital prohibits the use of RN on the name tags worn by Registered Nurses this seemingly unremarkable strategy accomplishes a valuable hospital objective. It makes it all but impossible to figure out how many nurses the hospital employs. Years ago, many hospitals elected to cut the number of RNs they employed to the lowest number possible as a means of shifting health service costs. These cuts maximized the patient workload for RNs by establishing heavy nurse-to-patient ratios and twelve-hour shifts, with the possibility of mandatory overtime.[5]

Predictable RN burnout further decreased the pool of RNs willing to work in hospitals. Today it is not uncommon to find family members and friends of hospitalized patients literally staffing the bedside of their loved one around the clock. They feel they have to do this because there are too few hospital RNs, and those few are overworked. In an attempt to do something about the problem California[6] became the first state to pass legislation requiring the Department of Health Service to set standards for safe nurse-to-patient ratios in hospitals.

Today, in 2000, Wisconsin Congresswoman Tammy Baldwin[7] has joined the growing ranks of elected public officials calling for health system reform. Her issues include what she has called the systematic price discrimination practices of drug companies. The results of her commissioned study of Wisconsin seniors showed that, when compared to the prices being charged to favored customers, seniors were being charged prices 83 percent to 201 percent higher.

According to Marcia Angell,[8] drug price discrimination is only a symptom of a much larger problem. Angell says the problem today is capricious drug pricing, noting that Americans regularly pay as much as twice what Europeans and Canadians pay for the same drug. In Angell's opinion, the standard industry response to questions about drug prices is a dismissive claim that high prices reflect high market value and a fair return on high-risk investment in new drug development. But as Angell points out, most of the high-risk new drug research is paid for with federally funded research grants. Her conclusion is that "an industry so important to the public health and so heavily subsidized and protected by the government has social responsibilities that should not be totally overshadowed by its drive for profits."[9]

Today, most managed healthcare organizations list professional mental healthcare services in their brochures, but they are not required by law to make mental health services available at anywhere near parity with physical health services. Instead, a person seeking professional mental healthcare for a disorder as common as depression, for example, may first have to meet with a screener. The screener's job includes determining whether the person is suffering from an illness or suffering from life, a distinction that may be lost on the person who is suffering.

The managed care viewpoint is that life stress is not a disorder that requires treatment. Maybe so, but life stress today is the leading cause of preventable mental disorders in children, adolescents, and adults. Health services aimed at preventing disabling stress-related disorders such as binge drinking, adolescent depression, and domestic violence seem the decent thing to do. As it stands today, families are left to pay the painful social costs of preventable stress-related disorders.

Today, racial and gender disparity in the U.S. system of healthcare is still tolerated. Health researchers report that regardless of income, education level, or presenting symptoms, African Americans and women routinely receive less healthcare than European Americans and men.

Kevin Schulman[10] and his colleagues have conducted a tightly controlled study of race and gender differences in situations in which physicians decided whether or not to recommend cardiac catheterization for actors posing as patients with chest pain. The researchers found that blacks and females were significantly less likely than whites and males to be referred for this definitive cardiac examination. The researchers attributed the racial and gender disparity they found to the unconscious *personal* bias of the MDs who participated in the study. But a similar California[11] study of the health records of real Asian, black, Latino, and white patients concluded that racial and gender bias in healthcare is *systemic*.

In the California study, despite similarities in insurance coverage, age, diagnosis, and general health, people of color, particularly blacks, and females received high-tech care (e.g., kidney transplantation, total hip replacement, and coronary bypass) significantly less often than did Latinos, Asians, and males. The researchers offered several carefully worded explanations for the racial and gender disparity, including the possibility that different care did not necessarily mean less care. Yet their leading conclusion was that having insurance and being admitted to a high-tech hospital might not insure that people of color or women received high-tech healthcare.

Given the peerless resources of the U.S. system of healthcare today, you would think that the system would be highly effective. That more people than not benefit. But yet another World Health Organization (WHO) study of healthy life expectancy has shown that America continues to spend more on health than any other country but only ranks twenty-fourth in citizen healthy lifespan. The top ten countries were Japan, Australia, France, Sweden, Spain, Italy, Greece, Switzerland, Monaco, and Andorra. Canada ranked number twelve. Despite the poor ranking of the U.S. system, according to WHO researchers the world's healthiest people continue to be wealthy Americans.

The U.S. system of healthcare is not broken—it just doesn't work for everyone. The question is, should it? This is the conversation that Clinton's proposal for health system reform started, and this is the conversation that continues today. Will the U.S. health system meet the basic needs of everyone, or will we continue to be the marketplace where the best disease treatments in the world are sold?

Am I suggesting that as far as the public was concerned, President Clinton lied about sex but told the truth about their problems with the health system? Am I suggesting that the public may have declined the Republicans' offer to remove Clinton from office because they owed him some kind of weird social psychological debt for his health reform movement? Am I suggesting that if you're a tall good-looking man with an important job you can get away with anything? Yes, I am suggesting the above. The Clinton impeachment case was too big and too complex for anyone to be certain as to what did and did not affect its outcome. The same reasoning justifies including my suggestions in our conversations about the case.

## Living in the Clinton Impeachment Afterworld

So what were the impeachment outcomes? Clinton was not removed from office, but his powers as a leader were revoked. The Office of the Independent Counsel closed. Hillary Clinton ran for the Senate in New York. Paula Jones married and divorced. Linda Tripp was acquitted of illegal wiretapping charges. Monica Lewinsky left Washington.

Had the supporters of impeachment been successful in their efforts to remove Clinton from office, their triumph would literally have rewritten the book of high stakes political wargames. As it turned out, the game had no winners, only players. No one can deny that President Clinton was hit with everything and anything that could be thrown at him. But like it or not, the system worked, the defenses held, the status quo was maintained.

Of course we have to expect that for years to come, politicians and watchers of the political scene will display Clinton's impeachment case as evidence of all that is wrong with this country and all that must be done to make things right. For everyone else, I suspect that the measurable public aftermath of the Clinton impeachment case may be of much smaller proportions. Which is not to say that the impeachment case was not a big deal. It was a very big deal. But it was big the way a summer action film is big. Like a summer action film, the impeachment gave us an incredible sound track, hot images, and a music-video story line. But like an action film, when the show is over, it's over. There really isn't much to talk about. You either liked the way the impeachment ended or you didn't. Still, it was a hell of a show.

And although it might appear that nothing of value was accomplished, life in the Clinton impeachment afterworld offers everyone something new to fear. I doubt that I am the only voter who now fears having to endure the personal confessions of future political candidates bravely telling tales on themselves in the odd hope that by spilling their guts they will be less vulnerable to their political enemies.

Before the Clinton impeachment case, a candidate for public office wanted voters and political opponents to know his or her position on the issues of the day. Running a clean election campaign meant building grassroots relationships with voters strong enough to carry the candidate to victory and open new doors to leadership. Clean candidates were those who were prepared, mature, and qualified for public office based on their training, experience, and wisdom. They worked to substantiate their political vision by representing and serving the voters well. If voters were interested in education, for example, candidates made sure that their position on education was informed by the facts and tested by the discourse of public debate.

OK, so maybe this political wonderland didn't even exist before Clinton. But I fear living in a Clinton impeachment afterworld in which political candidates do little more to run for elected office than to clean their soiled personal lives in public and complain about the lack of disclosure by their opponents. My fear of having to endure the personal confessions of politically correct candidates does not mean that I've given up all hope of ever being able to vote for a political candidate who is not a weasel. I count myself among the majority of voters who care very much about the character of the man or woman I give my vote to. But in the afterworld of the Clinton impeachment case will you and I, as voters, bother to make the distinction between personal character and personal history?

Suppose we take the personal history of political candidates, and we learn every young, dumb, or questionable thing every candidate has ever done. Would this get us better government? Or would the mere threat of having one's personal history used for political sport become a poison pill that no one in his or her right mind would wish to swallow, thereby effectively closing access to high elected office to everyone but those to the manor born?

In conclusion, I guess it would be too much to hope that politicians might do their jobs and stop investigating each other. Senate Republicans have already demanded that the Attorney General name a special prosecutor to investigate whether Vice President/Democratic presidential candidate Al Gore *misled* prosecutors in his answers to their questions about his 1996 democratic fund-raising activity.

The take home message I offer is a simple one. Excluding war, I can't think of a more dangerous presidential political agenda than health reform. The health industry is the biggest business there is and a lot of powerful people like it that way. Just before stepping into a political death trap of his own making, President Clinton said the health system needed to be reformed and he took actions that made it clear his intentions were serious. I have to wonder whether President Clinton would have had to spend years defending himself in various courts of law had he stopped talking about health reform. If he had not led the national conversation about health reform would we have heard about him and Ms. Lewinsky or any other woman?

NOTES

1. Rollo May, *The Meaning of Anxiety* (New York: Ronald Press, 1950).

2. Karen Horney, *The Neurotic Personality of Our Time* (New York: W. W. Norton, 1937).

3. Linda Denise Oakley and Claudette Potter, *Psychiatric Primary Care* (St. Louis: Mosby, 1997).

4. Margaret Mead, *Male and Female: A Study of the Sexes in a Changing World* (New York: W. Morrow, 1949).

5. *The American Nurse*, publication of the American Nursing Association (July/August 2000).

6. Doug Willis, "California Gov Signs Nurse-to-Patient Ratio Bill," *Capital Times*, November 12, 1999.

7. Tammy Baldwin, *Reports on Health Care in the 106th Congress: Putting Patients First* (2000).

8. Marcia Angell, "The Pharmaceutical Industry—To Whom Is It Accountable?" *New England Journal of Medicine*, vol. 342, no. 25 (June 2000).

9. Angell, "The Pharmaceutical Industry," 1904.

10. Kevin A. Schulman et al., "The Effect of Race and Sex on Physicians' Recommendations for Cardiac Catheterization," *New England Journal of Medicine*, vol. 340, no. 8 (February 1999).

11. Mita K. Giacomini, "Gender and Ethnic Differences in Hospital-Based Procedure Utilization in California," *Archives of Internal Medicine*, vol. 156 (June 1996).

# Chapter 14

# Perjury and Impeachment
## *The Rule of Law or the Rule of Lawyers?*

## *Lawrence M. Solan*

It was a bad year for the Rule of Law.[1] In fact, the 1990s was a bad decade for the Rule of Law. Through Court TV, the world saw legal gamesmanship relegate to a back seat the question of whether O. J. Simpson really killed his former wife and her friend. Then, beginning with the sensational disclosure of the Monica Lewinsky story in January 1998, and ending with President Clinton's acquittal before the Senate in February 1999, we were treated to a year in which the following three themes recurred on an almost daily basis:

First, a mendacious President sought to maintain his office and his credibility by deceiving the public and by making false and deceptive statements under oath. He said he didn't lie, but he did lie, even about that. Later, his lawyers did the only thing they could do: they defended the President by attacking the lawyers who were prosecuting him. The strategy proved effective.

Second, the year's events made most of us admit that we regard some lies as worse than others, even when they are made under oath. A moralistic minority said no: a lie is a lie. The minority rightly understood that the stakes were high in this debate. If we write crisp laws but evaluate conduct in fine gradations, we find ourselves in an inevitable double bind. Applying the law evenhandedly will cause us to act unfairly in some cases. But applying the law flexibly according to a set of values outside those articulated by the law itself is to compromise the Rule of Law as the determinant of social norms. To resolve legal disputes we would need both laws and a set of unarticulated, unenacted values. The very thought of such a thing offended some people and left others confused.

Third, lawyers involved in the events behaved so miserably that it became difficult to consider the President's conduct much worse than theirs. In the grand jury, prosecutors quizzed the President on his obligation to testify forthrightly, and then tried to trick him with one deceptive question after another. Kenneth Starr's tactics were so abusive as to shock the conscience of most Americans. His defense of this conduct—that prosecutors routinely act that way—did even more to damage popular confidence in a Rule of Law. The House Managers, in the role of prosecutors, pursued theories that the facts did not support. And let us not forget the President's lawyers, who did what they could to make sure that someone other than the President was on trial in the media.

I don't have much to add to the record about the President's conduct. I more or less accept those facts as Richard Posner describes them harshly in his book, *An Affair of State*.[2] I would like to devote this essay to the other two issues: the extent to which we even have a Rule of Law and the conduct of the legal profession in enforcing it. Some of what we saw during the Clinton affair reflected a confluence of events not likely to recur. Much of it, however, repeats itself every day in one way or another. If we take it seriously, it should cause us to rethink some very basic assumptions that underlie our system of law.

## The Rule of Law

Public debate of Clinton's legalistic approach to perjury pervaded the proceedings. Clinton relied heavily on the Supreme Court's narrow definition of perjury in its 1973 decision, *Bronston v. United States*.[3] The federal statute defines perjury as a statement made under oath on a material matter that the person "does not believe to be true."[4] It says nothing about the literal truth or falsity of the statement. In *Bronston,* the Court added a "literal falsity" requirement. Samuel Bronston had filed for bankruptcy. During his examination, he testified under oath that he did not have any Swiss bank accounts. He was then asked: "Did you ever?" He answered, "The company had an account there for about six months, in Zurich." In fact, he also had an account there earlier. The questioner took the bait, and did not ask the appropriate follow-up questions. The Supreme Court held that this was not perjury. Bronston's answer was misleading but not false, and Bronston did not believe it to be false when he gave it. No wonder Clinton thought so highly of this opinion.

It would have been perjury had Bronston said, "No, the company had one," instead of simply, "The company had one." This seems like a very thin reed on which to base a distinction between innocent and criminal conduct. The two scholars who have written about perjury from a linguistic perspective, Peter Tiersma[5] and Steven Winter,[6] make this point using Grice's theory of conversational implicature.[7] According to Grice, people employ a cooperative principle in communicating with one another. We try to convey new information in a helpful way, and assume that those speaking to us are doing the same. Bronston took improper advantage of the cooperative principle. He assumed that the questioner would infer that his statement about the company's bank account meant that he didn't have one personally. Rather, he was adding information about his company just to be cooperative. Bronston's ploy worked, and the Supreme Court held it to be legal. Tiersma and Winter both criticize the Court for rewarding him so. While I take a more generous view of *Bronston*, I agree with their analyses.

The work of another philosopher of language, J. L. Austin, also explains what is troubling about *Bronston*. It was Austin who first developed the theory of speech acts.[8] According to this now-familiar perspective, we perform acts through our speech, just as we perform acts through physical movement. Examples of speech acts are promises, threats, questions, and statements. One thing that defines certain speech acts is the effect that they have on the minds of others, which Austin called their *perlocutionary effect*. For example, we *persuade* people when we have in some way caused them to have a particular state of mind with respect to a proposition. *Deception* is also a concept whose meaning depends on its perlocutionary effect. We deceive people by causing them to believe something to be true although we know it to be false.

Just as there are many ways to promise or to persuade, there are many ways to deceive, only one of which is outright lying. We all know this intuitively, which is what makes the *Bronston* defense morally troubling, and what made Clinton's legalistic style offensive even to many of his supporters. What seem to be two ways of performing the very same act—the act of deception—are treated differently under the law.

While Austin and Grice suggest that *Bronston* draws too fine a distinction, work by other linguists and psychologists suggests that the law does not distinguish finely enough. Most people were relatively forgiving of Clinton for lying about his sex life, even under oath. They were willing to blame the system for allowing him to be asked such questions. Furthermore, some dishonest statements feel more like lies than do others. To see how, let us look at experiments conducted by two linguists, Linda Coleman and Paul Kay.[9]

Coleman and Kay claim that people are most certain that a statement is a lie when three criteria are met: the statement is literally false, it is made with knowledge of its falsity, and it is made with an intent to deceive. When all three of these elements are present, everyone calls it a lie, and when none of them are present, no one does. What happens when only one or two of them are present? Consider the following Clintonesque story that was part of their experiment.

John and Mary have recently started going out together. Valentino is Mary's former boyfriend. One evening John asks Mary, "Have you seen Valentino this week?" Mary answers, "Valentino's been sick with mononucleosis for the past two weeks." Valentino has in fact been sick with mononucleosis for the past two weeks, but it is also the case that Mary had a date with Valentino the night before. Did Mary lie?

Note that Mary's statement is literally true, although intended to deceive.

On a 1–7 scale, from "very sure it is not a lie" to "very sure it is a lie," this story scored an average of 3.48, close to the midpoint of 4.0. Of 67 subjects, 18 thought it was a lie (scoring a 1, 2, or 3), 42 thought it was not a lie (scoring a 5, 6, or 7), and 7 subjects could not say (scoring a 4).

How can we explain this array of responses? Coleman and Kay argue that lying is a graded category. Some statements are better examples of lies than are others. How good a lie a statement is depends on the number of features of lying in the statement, and how we weigh the particular features present. This explanation follows from the pioneering work in the 1970s by the psychologist Eleanor Rosch, who performed a set of experiments that showed people to have a highly nuanced sensitivity to how well an object fits into a category.[10] To most people, ostriches are bad examples of birds and robins are good examples.

Prototype theory offers explanations for both Coleman and Kay's results, and people's reaction to Clinton's conduct. In both cases, some but not all the elements of the prototypical lie were present. As a result, subjects equivocated about whether Mary lied, and the public was not sure what to think of Clinton's conduct. If this is really how we think, then it challenges Rule of Law values based on a legislature enacting clear rules in plain language that we should all obey or face the consequences, as Winter points out in his forthcoming book.

Another, equally troubling explanation for Coleman and Kay's results assumes not that lying is a graded category, but rather that it is defined in the minds of most people more or less as written in the federal perjury statute: making a statement the speaker knows not to be true.[11] In this account, uncertainties about whether a particular statement is a lie arise from problems we have applying the definition to particular situations. If someone is certain that his statement is false, but it turns out to be true, did he still "know" that he was making a false statement? More to the point for Mary and Clinton, in deciding whether a statement is not true, should we limit our concept of "statement" to the actual words that were said, or should statements include their predictable perlocutionary effects? If people differ with respect to their answers to these questions, then we would expect some to consider Mary and Clinton to have lied, others to consider them to have told the truth (leaving aside lies that Clinton unequivocally made), and still others to be unsure. U.W. Law Professor Carin Clauss's example of a criminal lawyer who dresses her client up in a suit for trial to create the impression that the client is a respectable member of society engages many of the considerations raised thus far. Most would not consider this a lie, although some might be tempted because it is possible to consider dress a "statement" of sorts.

I conducted an informal replication of Coleman and Kay's study with a group of undergraduates at Princeton. The mean response approximated Coleman and Kay's. I then presented the students with the following alternative account:

> I do not think that Mary lied. However, if I say that she didn't lie, I might be implying that I think Mary was being honest. I don't want to imply that Mary was being honest, so I'd rather say that she lied, even though I don't think this was really a lie.

Most of the students preferred this statement, which suggests that people distinguish conceptually between lying and other forms of deception, but are uncomfortable distinguishing between them morally.

How morally bad we consider a deceptive act to be depends in part on the social context in which it occurs. We have a rich everyday vocabulary for describing lies that we do not judge to be morally wrong. As Winter points out, we speak of "fibs," "white lies," "stretches," and "exaggerations." In contrast, we have a relatively impoverished vocabulary for describing statements that are true, but morally just as bad as lies. Perhaps "half-truths" is the best example. This asymmetry may account in part for the willingness of subjects to call Mary's statement a lie while feeling that it really wasn't one.

204 LAWRENCE M. SOLAN

It may well be that both accounts contribute to everyday intuitions. Prototype theory tells us that Mary and Clinton behaved in a way that includes the most important features of lying. For that reason, they should be held morally accountable. The definitional approach, on the other hand, explains why most people do not believe that Mary and Clinton really did lie. The psychologist Philip Johnson-Laird has argued that our concepts contain both types of information: prototypes and defining features.[12] Johnson-Laird's approach explains why many people can simultaneously believe that Clinton did not lie, and that his conduct sufficiently resembled a lie to make him morally culpable for lying. It also explains why many people could forgive Clinton so easily while still thinking him to be a liar: Clinton's dishonest conduct was in furtherance of his effort to keep his private life private, to save himself and his family terrible embarrassment, and to maintain his presidency. As noted above, how unacceptable we find an untruthful statement depends on the context in which it is made.

None of this is good news for traditional Rule of Law values, a fact that Clinton's opponents grasped intuitively. It suggests that the law is too pat for the complexities of everyday life, if we care about being fair. The only solution must lie in the exercise of discretion in as judicious a way as possible, which is exactly the conclusion that so many would avoid.

## The Rule of Lawyers

On August 17, 1998, President Clinton testified before a grand jury. The testimony was videotaped to make it available to a grand juror who was absent. When the House of Representatives received the tape the following month with Kenneth Starr's impeachment report, a fight broke out over whether the tape should be released for public viewing. Everyone believed that the grand jury testimony would show Clinton in a bad light, thereby enhancing public support for impeachment which, at that time, was very thin. The Republicans, who held a majority in the House, prevailed, and the tape was aired. Curiously, after people saw the President testify, his ratings rose. The standard explanation for this miscalculation is that both parties had underestimated him. While there might be some truth in that account, it is just as likely that everyone had overestimated the lawyers.

After some preliminaries, the testimony begins with pages of questioning about the meaning of the oath. For example:

*Question:* You have a privilege against self-incrimination. If a truthful answer to any question would tend to incriminate you, you can invoke the privilege and that invocation will not be used against you. Do you understand that?

*Clinton:* I do.

*Question:* And if you don't invoke it, however, any of the answers that you do give can and will be used against you. Do you understand that, sir?

*Clinton:* I do.

*Question:* Mr. President, do you understand that your testimony here today is under oath?

*Clinton:* I do.

*Question:* And do you understand that because you have sworn to tell the truth, the whole truth, and nothing but the truth, that if you were to lie or intentionally mislead the grand jury, you could be prosecuted for perjury and/or obstruction of justice?

*Clinton:* I believe that's correct.[13]

The questioning continues in this vein for quite some time. The prosecutor purports to be concerned about truth. Maybe he is. But he is also concerned about power.[14] He has made it clear that the President must behave in a certain way or risk prosecution. That is, the prosecutor has engaged in the speech act of *threatening*. I don't think anyone who sees or reads this excerpt could miss that point.

Typically, we have little trouble with government lawyers exercising this kind of power. If the grand jury had been convened to investigate a smuggling ring, and the prosecutor issued these thinly veiled threats before asking a witness whether he had ever carried certain substances into the United States from abroad, we might expect the witness to invoke his Fifth Amendment privilege, or tell the truth, or face the consequences of lying.

But this situation was different. The grand jury inquiry was about whether the President had been dishonest in the Paula Jones proceedings. Although Clinton clearly lied in his *Jones* deposition, the perjury case against him was weak because the Lewinsky affair was not a material issue in that case. By requiring the President to testify about his earlier testimony, the prosecutors could hope to provoke the President into committing a new crime. It is not unconstitutional for law enforcement agents to question a witness about an activity that is not prosecutable, and then to prosecute him for answering falsely.[15] But most of us are uncomfortable with the manufacturing of crimes in this manner, especially in political circumstances.

Most importantly, I believe, the prosecutors committed the same misdeeds of which they accused Clinton, but they did so in the name of the law. Consider, for example, the following exchange:

> *Clinton:* I believe at the time that [Lewinsky] filled out this affidavit, *if she believed that the definition of sexual relationship was two people having intercourse, then this is accurate.* And I believe that is the definition that most ordinary Americans would give it.
>
> *Question:* But you indicated before that you were aware of what she intended by the term sexual relationship.
> *Clinton:* No, sir. I said I thought that—that this could be a truthful affidavit. . . . When she used two different terms, sexual relationship, if she meant by that what most people mean by it, then that is not an untruthful statement.
> *Question:* So your definition of sexual relationship is intercourse only, is that correct?
> *Clinton:* No, not necessarily intercourse only, but it would include intercourse, I believe.[16]

Or consider this example:

> *Clinton:* And that if you go back and look at the sequence of events, you will see that the Jones' lawyers decided that this was going to be the Lewinsky deposition, not the Jones deposition. And given the facts of their case, I can understand why they made that decision. *But that is not how I prepared for it.* That is not how I was thinking about it.
>
> *Question:* You've told us you were very well-prepared for the deposition.
> *Clinton:* No, I said I was very well prepared to talk about Paula Jones and to talk about Kathleen Willey.[17]

In both instances the prosecutor attempted to mislead a witness at best, and to lie at worst. Of course, lawyers do not take the oath so they do not commit perjury when they use such tactics. But that is my point. The legal system is structured so that lawyers control the discourse. They sometimes use this power to engage in speech acts of threats and deception. They often violate the cooperative principle, just as Bronston did, hoping that an intimidated or inattentive or impatient witness will agree to their dishonest characterizations. Sometimes it works, although it didn't with Clinton.

Moreover, the cost-benefit analysis sometimes used to justify such tactics did not apply in this case. It is one thing to argue that the system must tolerate prosecutorial lack of candor in order to convict rapists and killers. It is quite another to argue that the system must tolerate prosecutorial lack of candor to convict a party for lack of candor. In many ways, then, the Clinton impeachment provided an excellent test. The moral force of the law would have to earn its position of priority in the public mind. It failed to do so.

The excerpts from the grand jury would be less troubling if they were aberrational. We could simply applaud Congress for allowing the Independent Counsel statute to expire. From my many years of litigation experience, however, I do not believe they are aberrational. Lawyers behave that way all the time. And the less likely they think they are to be caught, the more likely they are to behave that way.

Lawyers are least likely to get into trouble for dishonest conduct toward witnesses when the conduct occurs during a deposition in a civil case, where no judge is typically present. The Federal Rules of Civil Procedure and the local rules of many courts concern themselves much more with lawyers making improper objections to proper questions than with witnesses being misled or abused by lawyers. Cases in which the issue arises generally deal with whether an objecting lawyer should be sanctioned for instructing a witness not to answer a dishonest or otherwise abusive question. The defending lawyer argues that the question was deceitful. The questioner cites rules that require witnesses to answer questions subject to objections. Typically, the defending lawyer wins. But the risk is all on her.[18] The system takes very little interest in sanctioning a lawyer for asking misleading questions, especially at a deposition. As Jeffrey Toobin points out, Clinton benefited from this structural bias by having a judge present at his deposition to sustain certain objections, an advantage that Paula Jones did not have when she was treated shabbily in her earlier deposition.[19]

There are exceptions. Courts will sometimes dismiss an indictment that the prosecutor obtained through deceitful questioning of witnesses before the grand jury. The misconduct must be egregious, but it does happen.[20] Similarly, cases have been dismissed when prosecutors, at trial, attempt to discredit a witness the prosecutor knows is telling the truth in order to create a dishonest impression of what happened. Again, these cases are rare.[21] And in recent years the courts have become protective of children who are subjected to misleading questioning, and of defendants whose freedom may be lost as a result of children's responses to these questions.[22]

For the most part, though, the system does little or nothing to sanction lawyers who act dishonestly with witnesses. It may not always be a wise tactic to trick witnesses. And it may not succeed: objections to such questions are almost always sustained at trial. But most often, apart from the most egregious cases noted above, nothing else happens. Lawyers are never prosecuted for deceiving witnesses.

For most people who saw it, then, the Clinton grand jury testimony confirmed what they already thought of lawyers: people who wield enormous power, and then abuse it by acting dishonestly. That, to me, is among the saddest aftermaths of the impeachment. In a recent Gallup poll[23] asking people to "rate the honesty and ethical standards of people in different fields," lawyers ranked thirty-seventh of forty-five professions based on the percentage of respondents answering "very high" or "high," barely beating out gun salesmen. Only telemarketers and car salesmen got more "very low" votes. The impeachment proceedings only served to reinforce these views.

In fact, all the impeachment proceedings were riddled with evasive and deceptive conduct by lawyers. Posner points out some of the worst of them by Clinton's lawyers and supporters. These include silly evidentiary arguments and slanderous attacks on opposing counsel to distract both the public and the decision makers.[24] But Posner is too gentle with Clinton's opponents. House Republicans, acting as prosecutors in the Senate, pursued theories that any forthright person would have abandoned.[25] And Starr's conduct included evasive testimony before the House Judiciary Committee, replete with well-placed lapses of memory;[26] misleading statements to the public through the press;[27] and misleading statements to a United States Court of Appeals,[28] the kinds of conduct he wanted punished when done by others. As I said, it was not a good year for the Rule of Law.

## The Rule of Lawyers and the Rule of Law

When we put the two parts of my analysis together—our uncertainty about what the law means and the terrible conduct of the lawyers—*Bronston* seems quite sensible. It says that we will prosecute people for perjury only when traditional rule of law values are most transparent. This should inhibit much of the incentive for prosecutorial abuse of the perjury statute, and reduce the amount of judicial discretion required to determine whether perjury has occurred. It should also reduce the potential for hypocrisy in punishing borderline perjurers without acknowledging the system's uncertainty about what it is doing, as complete candor would require.[29]

However, all this comes at some expense. It comes at the expense of our not punishing equally deceitful acts the same. It comes at the expense of our lowering our expectations of witnesses to match our expectations of lawyers. It comes at the further expense of our finally abandoning the innocent notions of a Rule of Law that is at once both flexible and clear, an ideal about which Cardozo fantasized, but understood was just a dream.[30]

On April 12, 1999, Judge Susan Webber Wright found Clinton in contempt of court for his dishonest conduct in the *Jones* litigation, which had already been dismissed.[31] The case was not unique in that regard. Courts sometimes hold parties in contempt for their dishonesty. This decision is admirable. In a sense, it was one of the few victories for decent conduct in the entire ordeal.

Judge Wright also referred Clinton's conduct to the Arkansas Supreme Court's Committee on Professional Conduct for potential disciplinary action. As this essay goes to press, the Committee has responded by recommending that Clinton lose his license to practice law, the most severe sanction available for attorney misconduct. The lack of candor by so many lawyers who participated in the Clinton ordeal may make this the perfect time to decide whether we want to raise the stakes so high. If we do, we should, of course, do it for everyone.

#### NOTES

1. I am grateful to Len Kaplan, Myron Rush, Peter Tiersma, Spencer Waller, and Steven Winter for discussion and comments. I also wish to thank Cori Browne, Antonella Galizzi, and Robyn Schneider for their valuable assistance.

2. Richard A. Posner, *An Affair of State: The Investigation, Impeachment, and Trial of President Clinton* (Cambridge: Harvard University Press, 1999).

3. 409 U.S. 352 (1973).

4. 18 U.S.C. 1621.

5. Peter M. Tiersma, "The Language of Perjury: 'Literal Truth,' Ambiguity, and the False Statement Requirement," *So. Cal. L. Rev* 63:373–431 (1990).

6. Steven Winter, *A Clearing in the Forest* (Chicago: University of Chicago Press, forthcoming).

7. H. Paul Grice, "Logic and Conversation," in P. Cole and J. Morgan, eds., *Syntax and Semantics 3: Speech Acts* (New York: Academic Press, 1975), 41–58.

8. J. L. Austin, *How to Do Things with Words* (Cambridge: Harvard University Press, 1962).

9. Linda Coleman and Paul Kay, "Prototype Semantics: The English Word *Lie*," *Language* 57: 26–44 (1981).

10. Eleanor Rosch, "Cognitive Representations of Semantic Categories," *Journal of Experimental Psychology: General* 104: 192–233 (1975).

11. The linguist and philosopher Anna Wierzbicka defines "lie" that way. See Anna Wierzbicka, *Semantics: Primes and Universals* (Oxford: Oxford University Press, 1996).

12. Philip N. Johnson-Laird, *Mental Models: Towards a Cognitive Science of Language, Influence, and Consciousness* (New York: Cambridge University Press, 1983).

13. The transcript of the President's grand jury testimony ("Grand Jury Transcript") appears in Communication from the Office of the Independent Counsel, Kenneth W. Starr ("Starr Report"), Appendices to the Referral to the U.S. House of Representatives 453, Tab 16, 456–58 (September 18, 1998).

14. For analysis of power in the lawyer-witness relationship, see John M. Conley and William M. O'Barr, *Just Words: Law, Language, and Power* (Chicago: University of Chicago Press, 1998).

15. The Supreme Court recently upheld this practice in *Brogan v. United States*, 522 U.S. 398 (1998).

16. Grand Jury Transcript, Appendix, 473–75.

17. Grand Jury Transcript, Appendix, 510–11.

18. See *In Re: Folding Carton Antitrust Litigation*, 83 F.R.D. 132 (N.D. Ill. 1979).

19. Jeffrey Toobin, *A Vast Conspiracy: The Real Story of the Sex Scandal That Nearly Brought Down a President* (New York: Random House, 1999), 161–62.

20. See, e.g., *United States v. Roberts*, 481 F. Supp. 1385 (C.D. Cal. 1980).

21. See, e.g., *United States v. Barham*, 595 F. 2d 231 (5th Cir. 1979).

22. See, e.g., *State v. Michaels*, 136 N.J. 299, 642 A.2d 1372 (1994).

23. Gallup Social and Economic Indicators—Honesty/Ethics in Professions, http://www.gallup.com/poll/indicators/indhnsty_ethcs.asp.

24. Posner, *An Affair of State*, 125, and throughout the book.

25. After the defense had put on its case in the Senate, during which it scored points on such issues as the timing of Vernon Jordan's contacts with various people, Senator Edwards asked the House Managers whether there were any statements in or omissions from the exhibits that the Managers had used "that you believe, in the interest of fairness or justice, should be corrected at this time." Representative Hutchinson answered: "We are not aware of any corrections that need to be made

on any of our exhibits we have offered to the Senate." Transcript of Senate Impeachment Trial, January 22, 1999, Question 42. Representative Hyde subsequently explained, "You may disagree with us, but we believe in something."

26. For example, Congresswoman Lofgren asked Starr whether he had discussed the possibility of a tape recording on which a woman claimed to have had sexual relations with Clinton. She used her entire time on this issue. At first, she asked Starr if he would provide the information in writing. Starr replied: "Well, I am happy to consider any question, and if it is viewed as germane to—what is before you, if this is an effort to try to search my recollection and to see if there is something that perhaps I'm not able to recall." Later, he promised "to evaluate" the question. At the end, he said he would have to take time to "search my recollection." It was clear throughout that he had no intention of providing the information that was requested. U.S. House of Representatives, Impeachment Inquiry, Hearing before the Committee on the Judiciary 121 (Serial no. 66, November 19, 1998).

27. Impeachment Inquiry, 182–84. Starr had denied in the press that his office had asked Lewinsky to wear a wire to tape conversations with the President. Both Lewinsky's grand jury testimony and the FBI agent's notes of his meeting with Lewinsky state otherwise.

28. On June 29, 1998, Starr told a panel of the United States Court of Appeals that Clinton's privilege arguments concerning his confiding in government lawyers based on the possibility that impeachment proceedings would be brought were "too remote" to be considered. Starr said, "It is premature for this court to look down the road and look at impeachment." Stephen Labaton, "Lewinsky Case and 'Privilege' Fought in Court," *New York Times*, June 30, 1998. Three days later, on July 2, Starr applied *ex parte* to another panel of the Court of Appeals to unseal grand jury testimony to be sent to Congress as part of an impeachment report. His request was granted on July 7. Starr Report, Appendices to the Referral 10, Tab B.

29. See Roy Sorensen, "Vagueness Has No Functions in Law," in *Legal Theory* (forthcoming).

30. Benjamin N. Cardozo, *The Nature of the Judicial Process* (New Haven: Yale Univesity Press, 1921).

31. *Jones v. Clinton*, 36 F. Supp. 2d 1118 (E.D. Ark. 1999).

# Chapter 15

# Impeachment and Enchanting Arts

## *Eric Rothstein*

Why revisit the "Clinton Scandal," wading waist-deep in the yellow con-
fetti of previous punditry? Well, free from calls for clairvoyance or for
calming jitters about The System's death rattle, one might inquire what
we gained from Impeachment besides another slam-bang episode in a
Punch-and-Judy show. And gain we did. To doubt it is to embrace the
Hack's dictum in Swift's *Tale of a Tub*, that true felicity lies in being well
deceived. We gained hostile caution about politicians, journalists, and
other chattering classes. Americans also gained, I'd say, insofar as their
disenchantment went beyond simply being fed up. That is, they gained
insofar as they felt a different, more profound disenchantment, Max
Weber's *Entzauberung*. My argument is this: During the Impeachment
Spectacle, energy spilled from one model of politics to another. The awe-
some wheels of government turned out to be the stage effects of disrep-
utable wheelers and dealers. One could best accommodate this fact, still
watchful of Washington's power over our lives, by being *entzaubert* rather
than fed up. Politics could make sense through a new cognitive model
that junks magic, myth, and mystification, thus disenchanting the staging
of events. By aestheticizing what's staged, we learned, one can evaluate
the actual running of the government pragmatically. This cognitive
model, I'll suggest, could alter American politics, without having to dis-
place all other models, work for everyone, or get adopted in toto.

By the 1990s in America, multiple cognitive, moral, and aesthetic
stances everywhere competed for legitimacy. In doing so, they kept elabo-
rating a trading floor for values, an options exchange. On that trading
floor, legitimating arguments and legitimated interests met, mingled,
vied, and swapped energies. This produced strangely complex problems
of appraisal. The typically nineteenth-century formation of Kierkegaard's

*Either/Or* (1843) cast moral and aesthetic allegiances as existential, exclusive alternatives, along the ancient lines of a rivalry between duty and pleasure or community and self, lawlike codes of principle. In living one's real life, though, moral and aesthetic practice are nearly always a both/and, cooperating as applied skills. Since they resemble each other in structure, they often seem to stand over against the cognitive, in rivalries like heart and head or value and value-free. Separately and together they also depend on cognitive stances as to truth, belief, knowledge, and opinion. None of these standards—the true, the good, and the beautiful, so to speak—has its own simple legitimacy, let alone simple ways of legitimating the particulars that fall beneath it. On this complex trading floor for values, the Clinton imbroglio was staged.

Staging fit admirably with current politics, a branch of the service industry, advertised by testimonials and come-ons. Politicians get fitted out to be the optimal stand-ins for themselves: they thus vend themselves as representatives of their constituents (with capacities as to programs, responsiveness, savvy, and energy) and as representations of selves with glamour, aura, and gravitas. By 1998 the various media had long been highlighting the backstage dressers, such as spin doctors, pollsters, and PR experts. We'd all learned how to see politics as marketing and theater. In talking about the portrayal of roles in literal theater, a director has remarked that we can say this: that an actor playing Hamlet is not not-Hamlet.[1] The actor's doubleness draws one into a doubleness of one's own, as viewer and participant. Thus we're complicit with the make-believe. From and over the structure of the occasion, audience and actor produce an antistructure of responsive performance. So with first-rate politicians. That's why pressing the flesh is electric: it's the moment of real presence when Hamlet and not not-Hamlet (or, for Washington Republicans in 1998, Macbeth and not not-Macbeth) closely coincide in a single, present, image-bearing body. The figure can pass from a public prop into a private, make-believe, participatory-game prop, with our keeping a double awareness as in theatrical or fantasy experience. The pathology of extreme passion for or against President Clinton may arise in part from his genius at just such deep, flexible impersonation of "himself." Correspondingly, Impeachers tried to dissociate a "real," fleshy, rapacious Clinton from the President as a satisfactory public prop—hence the heaping on of prurient detail in Starr's report.

Even if this were not true, staging would have had to take place. However much propelled by hatred, power politics, and money, the prosecution's tribunal had a communal, emotive, ceremonial function. The staging, though, was hard. After learning too much about the President and nearly enough about the press and Congress, most Americans found the case against Clinton flimsy. He'd had an adulterous consensual liaison with a much younger woman. He'd publicly lied about it. He also deceitfully answered one line of questions in a lawsuit. But all the clamor about official or financial wrongdoing had led nowhere for the (ironically named) Independent Counsel. Nor was the liaison itself so strange: since 1911 operagoers have wept at a candied form of this scenario, *Der Rosenkavalier*, where a thirty-plus married princess relinquishes her hot, cute sex life with a boy of seventeen. Who doesn't know that irrespective of gender and social status, the middle-aged typically crave the youth they've lost and the youthful crave the worldly glamor still unattained? Both often crave the intimate abandon of sex as a mode of access. Many of us have felt such cravings and recognize too, not only from ourselves, that at times people react to them recklessly. Out of such personal knowledge came clarity: however reckless he was, Clinton didn't coerce or harass the eager, sexually canny Lewinsky. Both parties did suffer great abuse, but not from each other. As to the lawsuit, it looked political or extortionist; the questions about sex, malicious and immaterial. Understandably, the public asked what Jeffrey Toobin says "baffled future citizens" will ask: "He was impeached for *what*?"[2]

With so meager a case, media and political impresarios depended on aesthetic effects, and still more so given the President's high public approval. To fatten fact and morality (or its pharisaic proxy), they promoted the sensuous delight of public spectacle—isn't that the delight that spectacles induce?—to render unholy the private sensuous delight relished by the aptly named Mr. Blythe (the birth name of Clinton). For appealing to a mass culture, the impresarios chose kitsch as Walter Benjamin defined it, "art with a 100 percent, absolute and instantaneous availability for consumption."[3] One digests kitsch so fast and so fully, it primes the appetite for more. Kitsch, I suspect, has always been one's best bet for mass evaluative appeals. It undoubtedly was best in a cultural environment where high-glamour industries catered to and for "the society of the spectacle," "the empire of fashion," or such like. One can see why the Impeachers ended up spotlighted on their minarets, loudly proclaiming veracious ethical ends for the giddy, addictive sex-and-gossip farce they had advertised.

How, one asks, could sleazy hanky-panky hatch high crimes and misdemeanors? The anti-Clinton faction owned a dramatic model, Watergate, but no sufficient plug-and-play scandal to set the model whirring. To create one, they deployed two modes of Weberian legitimation, law and charisma, the latter as simulated by media effects. By ornamenting the plot with tradition, Weber's third mode, they hoped to make it portentous. Clintonites cooperated for their own ends. As to charisma, they reasoned, the President had plenty. As to law, his misdeeds looked trivial, misdemeanors in the modern sense.[4] Both sides summoned talking heads of academia for the solemnity and lore of tradition. In the media, the annals of America poured into a synchronous national past: Andrew Johnson's trial; presidential mistresses (Lucy Mercer, Kay Sommersby, Judith Exner); Jefferson's offspring; and, in the *ubi sunt* tradition, sibylline Founding Fathers. To these inflationary remembrances, Chairman Henry Hyde single-handedly added Bunker Hill, the Vietnam dead, and with reliable decency, Auschwitz.

This scheme might have failed Clinton's enemies no matter who had handled it. Because it demanded values with both aesthetic and moral force, energies supposedly in aid of truth had to shuttle between asymmetric realms of value. They're "asymmetric" because the traffic flow among these realms is one-way. Truth and morality *can* infuse the aesthetic. Artworks gain by verisimilitude, by eliciting virtuous pride, altruistic tears, or generous indignation. In contrast, our code of cultural labors disavows judgments of morality and truth that rest on aesthetics, on beauty, eloquence, glamour, and glitz. This asymmetry—that nonaesthetic values may inflect the aesthetic, though not vice versa—always threatened the balance on which the didactic showmen of Impeachment relied. Far from overcoming the aesthetic-to-ethical asymmetry, they worsened it. When little energy could gather at the weak ethical pole of the Impeachers' case, structures of judgment and value shared by ethics and aesthetics slid fast toward the aesthetic. Clinton's behavior may have been tawdry, adolescent, and narcissistic. He made many Americans squirm. But if we impeached on a squirm quotient, the White House would need a turnstile.

Besides, Clinton exercised power well, most polled Americans believed. Who would take over for him? The zealot's glee or crocodile tears of the Impeachers made plain that they looked for quick kicks, fast bucks, and steel muscles, just what they damned the Clintons for. Then too, serious moral life entails "sincerity (including an absence of self-deception)" as "a fundamental prerequisite. . . . Indeed, in some respects sincerity in the exercise of the elemental capacity to *describe* a moral problem may be even more important to moral choice than the possession of a developed judgment."[5] If self-deception as well as willful fraud counts as insincerity, Clinton's tormentors had no "elemental capacity" for description. Yet their only hope lay in their power of description. The prosecution's dream plot exhibited a just natural order of truth uncovered. De jure in this plot, the pillory and exile follow crime. In fact, the plot sloughed any "natural" order when the prosecution team became selves—rancorous, interested actors with suspect motives—not stewards of the standard judicial model of lawful process. Just so, another image of natural order, moral and political health, looked bogus once people saw Starr's scalpel as a dagger. One can see why in this case many Americans, missing "moral life" and "moral choice" in politicians, might have turned to thoughts of fiction, a useful category for antics of insincerity. Cognitive activity depends greatly on pattern recognition and the cues that let one perceive an object or event as part of a pattern. Indeed, cognitive activity may always and only be cued pattern recognition.[6]

To replace the judicial model, then, a new model had to do three things: clarify events, reduce the unease of instability, and yet, as long as the furor seemed to impinge significantly on American life, keep people attentive to what might be consequential goings-on. The simplest model was that of the talk-show tabloid. America of the 1990s gobbled up personal squalor. Commonly, sex spiced the *pièces de résistance*, whether in politics, daily life (a wife who sliced off her husband's penis, a sportscaster who bit women's buttocks, and a celebrity who butchered his wife), or both (a former presidential candidate who touted his Viagra-spurred erections). The tabloid phenomenon, and more broadly an often unwanted loss of privacy to everyone, helped reveal the Impeachers' outrage as fake or as lip-lickingly obsessive. Starr's mirror image, Larry Flynt, could duly report Impeachment to be a fantasy of domination. Fittingly, unlike most "respectable" American journalists, the crass pornographer Flynt exposed by far the most scandalous abuse in the "scandal," its gross, integral hypocrisy.

But talk shows and tabloids don't pursue a plot. The aesthetic model does. As an easily available model, it could track the intricacies of Impeachment. It also finessed the issue of people being conned, and it relieved the problem of asymmetry. In it, as of course in tabloids and talk shows, moral clamor mostly served the drama rather than vice versa. The general pattern that had these virtues recurred in movies, television, and pulp fiction, including post-Watergate and Iran-Contra political movies and books. The public could easily recognize it from appropriate cues. The aesthetic model was rewardingly "natural," adequately stable as to value, and unabashed about how to take its truth claims. It could replace the disorientation that the Impeachment show induced, yielding a set of responses that would give us an immediate, pleasing sense of understanding. When the uneasy balance between the moral and the aesthetic in Impeachment slid toward the latter, then, the public had available an apt, variously reinforced aesthetic model that responded to its needs. A pattern and cues now awaited successive new elements. Adroitly, the President enhanced the life of the aesthetic model when he let it be known that he kept at his executive duties, compartmentalizing Impeachment as an isolable, enclosed, and effectively private system. He treated its woes as something he had brought on himself as a man, not as a president. This ploy rebuilt the split wall between public and private so as to isolate his self-serving foes as intruders on the wrong side of it.

An aesthetic model sharpened attention to the structure of Impeachment. That's because, roughly speaking, the propositions of artworks are true or false only within the context of the work itself. Serendipitously, this particular celebrity-sex story had a structure of rich fictionlike elements that affected the ambit and force of true and false. The *res* that Americans entered *in medias* incorporated structural analogues like a well-made plot: Bill betrayed Hillary; as a result Monica Lewinsky betrayed Bill; thence Linda Tripp betrayed Monica; consequently, the media betrayed Tripp as a frowzy false friend and fink. Simultaneously, members of the print and talk media betrayed each other, therefore themselves, as of Tripp's ilk. Confirming their place in the aesthetic scheme, media stars and anchorpersons pursued their incessant, greedy chatter, *hm hmm*ing and *tsk tsk*ing, fawning, spiteful, venal, and treacherous. Like the politicians staging Impeachment, all protesting à la Paula Corbin Jones that they weren't that kind of girl, journalists who mounted this spectacle were soon part of the action too. Watching plays comes so near participating in them as to make this move easy. One got a show like a Restoration comedy revamped by Tom Stoppard for cable TV.

The more people savored this show trial as entertainment, the more the model's internal structure knitted so as to reward their using it. Predictably, the political accusers impersonated the sinner they damned. The adversarial case itself required the trope of high and low: since *he*, B. C., sank into beastliness, *they*'d rise majestically into an aggregate vox populi. However, they botched even being whited sepulchers. In their own

modes Clinton's foes repeated all his alleged sins—libido, deceits, eva-
sions and stonewalling, and obstruction of justice. If Chairman Henry
Hyde's committee, through the Starr Report, slipped us the lowdown on
Clinton's so-called "zipper problem," then cruel fate shone a torch on the
youthfully indiscreet Hyde's codpiece problem and the anointed Speaker
Bob Livingston's worse one. Once Chairman Dan Burton called the President a condom—he said "scumbag"—we *had* to learn that Burton, he
who eschewed condoms, begot a bastard child. The snap of Monica's
peremptory thong echoed in the fleshpot where Speaker Gingrich wal-
lowed with a congressional aide. Allegory dictated that the aide be named
Callista: in myth Zeus (here read Gingrich ascendant) impregnated the
nymph Callista though she was pledged to the goddess of chastity,
Artemis (here read Gingrich the family-values homilist). Even the robe of
Chief Justice William Rehnquist, who presided over the Senate trial, was
uncanny in being styled after the Lord Chancellor's in Gilbert and Sullivan's *Iolanthe*. Not only does *Iolanthe* ridicule Parliament, it also stars an
aging, "highly susceptible" supreme official, the Chancellor, in love with
one of his wards, aged nineteen.[7] In Impeachment as in a good play, of
course, one grasped the idea without having to see all the parallels and al-
lusions. The texture of events kept rewarding the casual, not only the
scrutinizing aesthete.

Helped by an invaluable public service, the "outing" of leading sexual
hypocrites, the public caught on to other hypocrisies. The President's enemies imitated him in teetering on legalisms, toying with the truth, and
calling on spin doctors. Some of those who piously recalled George
Washington's cherry tree had once hoped to raise an admitted perjurer to
the Senate, Oliver North, and did raise another, Gingrich, as Speaker.
Children-Church-and-Kitchen patriarchs keened for harassed women.
Republican shows of chivalry jarred with Starr's bullying Lewinsky's
mother, Clinton's secretary (a black woman), his captive Susan McDou-
gal, and the single mother Julie Hiatt Steele. The covert operator who
chucked tidbits under the table to a slavering press—wasn't that also
Starr, who insisted that his team leaked and suborned only within standard operating procedure? The Republicans solemnly swore that Clinton
had shamed us before the world. Yet the Impeachment process itself did
that, to judge by unprecedentedly public support for him from major foreign leaders. When Clinton's selfish folly challenged the GOP to outdo
him, they did. They invoked a universal moral code so as to undo univer-
sality and forfeit national consensus. At last, at high noon on Lincoln's

Birthday in 1999, they lost even a Senate majority for the two charges left from the original four. As fits the stock plot, Clinton's dizzy enemies found that "purposes mistook" had "fall'n on the inventors' heads"—and hoist by their own petards, their defeat grew by their own insinuation (*Hamlet* 5.ii.395–96, 3.iv.207, 5.ii.58–59). Outrage died, for moral sentiments depend on breached expectations. Here all moral or ethical expectations had collapsed, freighted by the repetition and ubiquity of styles of misbehavior.[8] Aesthetic expectations, though, were handsomely met.

Why might the President gain in public opinion and his foes sink? The structural patterns I've mentioned have a larger dimension. Because aesthetic performances have semiautonomous structures, one reads them in the context of their grounds of internal difference. When the President's enemies flattered his sins through imitation, difference was visibly grounded in power alone. The moral disparity between him and them first ceased being moral, then ceased being a disparity. Republicans' slogans, sound bites, and scabrous revelations let everything be seen as spin. That normalized Clinton's stagecraft. An accurate everybody-does-it argument normalized his misbehavior within a too familiar sex-and-violence story. If sex had deep-sixed his principles, relentless violence demolished the Republicans'. So strong was their will to power that they impugned the integrity of the Joint Chiefs of Staff over Middle East bomb raids (December 1998)—this from jingoes who daily slicked down their hair with Smith & Wesson oil! While they aligned President Clinton with sanctified veterans, their massive pursuit of citizen Clinton aligned him with other darlings of theirs, the religious cults, gun merchants, OSHA-rule scofflaws, and Utah paramilitary groups about whose oppression by the Feds they had speechified. At last the party of free markets coerced bloc voting. It made Tom DeLay, Dick Armey, and Henry Hyde look like a Tom, Dick, and Harry for the whole GOP.

To interpret an instructive civic spectacle, I've proposed, one employs familiar patterns to assort cognitive, moral, and aesthetic values. Impeachment developed so many glitches, plot clichés, and serendipitous twists as to wrench it loose from its impresarios. It came within the gravitational pull of a common fiction. That altered its force as truth and morality. Since the new model gave its users rewards and relief at low cost, public curiosity increased while, and also because, the perceived truth value and seriousness of the events dwindled. In this way, the conditions that got super ratings for "District of Columbia 20500" also led it to be discounted. People kept reading about it and watching it; they also kept saying that they were sick of the scandal. At this a sneering press went on dumping a slurry of "news." I suggest that people meant what they said. The to-do fascinated them as lurid docudrama. It repulsed them as an overblown exhibition of vileness among those on whom they had to rely. How too was one to understand enraged Americans, some of them still at it in this volume, who bypassed presumptions of innocence? Or those who debased Lewinsky to a fanged vamp or an underage puppet of *tempora* and *mores*? What of those who foretold a national apocalypse? People could accept such passionate extravagances as apropos to addictive melodrama and still be sick of having them trotted forth seriously.

Staunch partisans, of whom there were many, did and apparently still do endorse such stuff. Pro- and anti- knew how to roll events, any events, down the slope of their biases. The less partisan public too was hardly of one mind. For my argument, that does not matter much. People commonly use different cognitive models, successively and/or differentially weighted, to interpret a set of events. That's exactly why a newly available interpretive resource helped so greatly with a high-pressure, polarized issue about which citizens were supposed to make up their minds. For an aesthetic model to leaven one's attitudes, one didn't have to subscribe to it. Even those who refused it knew that its widespread use gave it *prima facie* respectability. These conditions logically led to its dissemination. On the evidence of polls, jokes, newspaper columns, and cartoons the aggregate public moved toward the available model that promised best (as I have operatively defined "best") to array and process what they saw and heard. What I envision is a Doppler shift, but seldom a full about-face. In the mix of interpretive options, ever more weight fell on a fictional pattern for the neat, dovetailing story.

Suppose this is true. Then, using the aesthetic mode, Americans saw not honesty, duty, and selflessness but their representations. As I suggested near the beginning of my discussion, this was plausible in the political life of the 1990s. What are the gains from this event? In what follows, I'll propose that the potential gains are great. By controlling Impeachment's representations as fiction, Americans improved a new way to organize political knowledge. Citizens learned the value of distancing actual political events by pretending that they were make-believe. Indeed, at another level, these events really were make-believe. Seeing and deploying the artifices of fiction helped Americans divide reality from its mystification, other people's imposition of narratives upon them. If I'm right, not only the practical skills here, but also the model itself, with its cues, may be a splendid legacy for disenchantment, *Entzauberung*, even to those who rejected the model in 1998–99. The functional interplay between political truths and political fictions has suddenly grown more open to reflectiveness and change.

Over the history of Western cultures, a principle of thrift has accompanied disenchantment: people have stored displaced magic in a new category, the aesthetic. This has allowed them to draw on aesthetic magic without contaminating what has needed logical or naturalistic treatment. As the mystifying artifices of media technology have complicated this division of labor, we've increasingly tried to regulate their powers of confusion. In this arms race, we build defenses and reward spies, while the media beef up their weaponry. Cooperatively, though, we and they expose their gimmicks, we for the sake of control and they so as to woo us into amity with them. Overall, their display of a demystified "magic" of passing techno-illusions has made an awareness of illusion into a standing *caveat emptor*. Because of the reciprocity between illusion and disillusion, I'd argue, we're better at regulating the technology of myth. Overwhelmingly, Americans now function just fine in a society with many narrative options as to plot, meaning, feeling, and likely trajectory. They couldn't do that if they lacked acumen and deftness in deciding which narratives to deploy when, and how to deploy them. How could they live in an ad-mad culture if those same ads, the mostly visible machinery of illusion, had not trained them in the arts of hedging belief?

This analysis runs counter to, for example, Jared Diamond's chattering-class claim that American children endure "devastating developmental disadvantages" from "being passively entertained by television, radio, and movies."[9] No doubt then, reading books to children has for centuries been tantamount to poisoning them with lead. But except as ideological cant (Diamond poisoning?), why suppose that people just sponge up fictions they see or hear at any age? Does a sitcom or animated cartoon produce EEG flatlining? Instead doesn't it help one get the hang of the U.S. Senate chamber? We have excellent reasons to assume that people treat mass fictions the way modern life encourages us to treat practically everything, as information to be processed and assessed. In the course of sifting, processing, and assessing the information we glean from factoids and stealthy frauds as well as popular fictions, I'm arguing, we—from childhood on—learn profoundly about coping with the world. This includes know-how as to a metadiscourse, a metaconsciousness about truth claims.

During over fourscore years of Public Relations, pundits have often sensibly worried about the docile hoi polloi. Walter Lippmann thought

(1927) that public consent was manufactured by "an intensification of feeling and a degradation of significance."[10] In support of this, shortly thereafter one could point to the Third Reich: an aestheticised Nazi politics "is one of the established topics of scholarly research on German and international fascism." Here "a form of worldly temporal power and a juridical legal form combine[d] with an aesthetic form" so as to stage "a harmonious national community."[11] Mythic politics, charisma, the heroic leader, and PR hit their peak. This scenario bears a family resemblance to those of many state occasions, including the grave pomp of Impeachment. Yet what's risky here is *Zauberung*, political myth-making and eager credulity. It's not aestheticization. The valence of aestheticization is fully reversible: in the 1930s enchanted Germans took the heroic performance for reality, and in the 1990s disenchanted Americans, accustomed to the forging of myth, grasped the reality that heroic "reality" was really performance. In the Impeachment Spectacle, Americans displayed a public independence of judgment historically rare when the powers-that-be wheel out the hoods, the whips, the stocks, the gibbets, the branding irons, and the indictments. Most of the nation didn't just black the bluenoses' eyes and spurn the pundits, it dispensed with the axioms of heritage. In 1998, Lippmann's formula produced public *dis*sent. When aestheticized, the spectacle lowered the risk of enchantment. It sharpened the public nose for fraud. It also located the parties in complex but clearly visible webs of value. It individuated events and enhanced *situated*, discretionary comprehension. Interpretation through skills, know-how, and pattern recognition led to skepticism about the rules of the law to which the Impeachers urged obedience and obeisance.

My argument has focused on how Americans read Impeachment, and why; and on the benefits from their having done so. The events, I've said, lent themselves so rewardingly to aesthetic patterning as to create aesthetic distance. That distance let the public see events in an orderly, proportionate way; it let them be increasingly skeptical without having to be cynical; and, crucially, it freed them from being told what to think. Thus we experienced adulthood and enlightenment as Kant famously equated them: "Enlightenment is humankind's emergence from its self-imposed immaturity," *Unmündigkeit*, the perpetual need for parenting.[12] Myth was okay when the Union was weak, the melting pot was needed, and most of the populace was barely schooled. Having passed that stage, we can simulate it only by purchasing a commodity, a Big Daddy or Nobodaddy role model. Daddy promises, if religiously used, health, wealth, and inner peace. With its distrust of voters and its hierarchic communitarian bent, American political culture peddles this product. It puffs spiritual gas into select persons who bulge larger than life, a collective sublime like balloon figures in a holiday parade. Now that Impeachment and our experience of media exposure have degassed these swells for the moment, I suggest it might let us go on demythologizing our history and politics.

Once we stopped clutching at notions of our Executives as candidates for eternal statuary, that is, the aesthetic model might keep us grown up. We could redefine jobs, using a disenchanted, radical, anti-Platonic, and pragmatic concept of the government. Specifically, we'd treat charisma, aura, larger-than-life, and rituals of veneration as aesthetic effects. In 1998–99, turning national fantasy into an aesthetic theme, Americans could critique the fifteen-month run of *The Merry Monica; or Sin on Bended Knee*—or was it, honoring Gingrich's Georgia home, *Naughty Marietta*? One might have reasonable hope that our adulthood can continue. Not only has media exposure trained us to maintain an ongoing metaconsciousness about truth and illusions, but also much demythologizing, requiring no aesthetic effects, had already occurred by the end of the twentieth century. Medicine, law, academia, and the military had moved, irregularly, toward professionalism without an aura. One expects deeply knowledgeable doctors and generals. We don't smirk at people as diagnosis wonks or summon them to battle from the plow. In politics too, then, one might expect that meaning would be increasingly weighed by professional competence, as in law, medicine, and the rest. Perhaps from a now tattered privacy at least a space for privacy, with acknowledged impunity, can be rescued.

Like other animals with pecking orders, we may never scrap idols and aura. Impeachment showed that *entzaubert* adults don't need to. After we know that idols are commodities, we can transport them into a locale of absorption, distance, and transience. The disposable fetish, I suggest, may be the invention Americans need most. Today, singularly fiction-ridden commercial activities supply such commodity idols—in 1998, say, Mark McGwire and Sammy Sosa, whose titanic home-run battle sold tons of souvenirs. Such phenomena add a consumerist twist to Benjamin's "kitsch," "art with a 100 percent, absolute and instantaneous availability for consumption." Democracy and consumerism, which rose together in the modern West, suppose that evanescence inheres in the object, whether the piece of goods happens to be a politico or his peruke. Through enlightenment, *Mündigkeit*, we can turn one class of objects, reflectively, into passing consumables. I mean the class of objects that satisfy general ego-centered desires. Many central, indispensable values and relationships require durable loci. Objects of ego-centered desires don't. By their nature, the desires remain; by their nature, the objects that slake them are fungible. Examples include erotic indulgences from flirting to sexual flings (Clinton and Lewinsky), sports events, tourist attractions, and experiences of the arts. Though enthralled by artifices of presence, the consumer knows the transience of the affair, the game, the holiday, the performance. At their best these leave us their psychic ghosts, a residuum of adjusted feeling and experience. So it is, for adults, with heroes. Within democracy and consumerism, one can beget serial proxies as off-the-shelf heroes and shooting stars who strut and fret for a Warholian quarter-hour. As we have done just that, sentimental, father-knows-best public guardians have moaned. Gone are the gracious, graceful heroes of yesteryear. Gone is the afterglow of the passé idol, callously abandoned. One might prefer less hand-wringing and more applause for our adulthood.

I've conjectured that for a central batch of sociopolitical practices we can enjoy but fence off daydreams. We can do so with a new template, enabled because the values of such practices are traded among various interests. If Impeachment did convert politics into art of a familiar genre, we now have an exemplar of this template in action. The new model for pattern recognition arose from the act of interpreting a closed narrative, the interlocked events of 1998–99. From witnessing and appraising this closed, eerily well-structured narrative, Americans realized an open *meta*narrative. It improves our access to some old useful functions by relocating them in a new, disenchanted, antinostalgic matrix where meaning resides in competence. That's enlightenment. Disenchantment, metaconsciousness, and consumerism appear to have kept advancing during our time. Therefore one has some reason to hope for political enlightenment. How well in fact we'll cleave to it, who dares predict? As the loud acrobats, beasts, and clowns of Impeachment 1998 demonstrated, history's plot lines are formidably contingent. What one *can* predict is that we American citizens will need such disenchantment. The *Fin-de-Siècle* Circus didn't put paid to the gaudy and the seamy, to fakery, self-righteous pontification, and mean obsession. We know we can rely on our politicians and our press to carry on those traditions.

NOTES

1. Richard Schechner, *Between Theater and Anthropology* (Philadelphia: University of Pennsylvania Press, 1985), 110–13.

2. Jeffrey Toobin, *A Vast Conspiracy: The Real Story of the Sex Scandal That Nearly Brought Down a President* (New York: Random House, 1999), 400. I am indebted to Toobin for some of the details below, particularly about Henry Hyde and Paula Jones.

3. Walter Benjamin, *The Arcades Project*, trans. Howard Eiland and Kevin McLaughlin (Cambridge: Belknap Press, 1999), 395 (K3a, 1).

4. Constitutionally misdemeanors are crimes exclusive of treason and those for which English law prescribed forfeiture of land and goods. See David M. Walker, *The Oxford Companion to Law* (Oxford: Clarendon Press, 1980), s.v. "felony," "misdemeanor." In the later eighteenth century, "crimes" and "misdemeanors" were, "properly speaking," synonyms. See William Blackstone, *Commentaries on the Laws of England*, 11th edition (London: 1791), 4: 5.

5. Michele M. Moody-Adams, *Fieldwork in Familiar Places: Morality, Culture, and Philosophy* (Cambridge: Harvard University Press, 1997), 128.

6. The point is most powerfully made by Howard Margolis in *Patterns, Thinking, and Cognition: A Theory of Judgment* (Chicago: University of Chicago Press, 1987); and *Paradigms and Barriers: How Habits of Mind Govern Scientific Beliefs* (Chicago: University of Chicago Press, 1993).

7. The age gap between the ward, Phyllis, and the Chancellor's lone child, Strephon, chimes with that between Clinton's intern and his lone child. Monica, born 1973, is six-and-a-half years older than Chelsea (1980); Phyllis at nineteen—she comes of age in two years—is younger than Strephon, "nearly five-and-twenty." *The Annotated Gilbert and Sullivan*, ed. Ian Bradley (Harmondsworth, Mx.: Penguin, 1982), 1: 179, 199.

As to allegory, what friendly trope dictated that Paula Jones, who adjudged Clinton's phallus short, should have sprung from the self-styled minnow capital of the world?

8. I'm following the analysis of moral emotions in R. Jay Wallace, *Responsibility and the Moral Sentiments* (Cambridge: Harvard University Press, 1996), 12.

9. Jared Diamond, *Guns, Germs, and Steel: The Fates of Human Societies* (New York: W. W. Norton, 1997), 21.

10. Quoted in Stuart Ewen, *PR! A Social History of Spin* (New York: Basic Books, 1996), 157.

11. Thomas Lischeid, "Male Performance Hysteria: Book Burning in Nazi Germany and the Avantgarde," *Die verletzte Diva: Hysterie, Körper, Technik in der Kunst des 20. Jahrhunderts*, ed. Silvia Eiblmayr, Dirk Snauwaert, Ulrich Wilmes, and Matthias Winzen (Köln: Oktagon, 2000). I have slightly modified Christiane Spelsberg's translation, 200, of the German original in the same volume, 193.

12. I've slightly modified Ted Humphrey's translation of Immanuel Kant, "An Answer to the Question: 'What Is Enlightenment?'" (1784), *Perpetual Peace and Other Essays on Politics, History, and Morals* (Indianapolis: Hackett, 1983), 41.

# Chapter 16

# A Year after the Acquittal in the Impeachment Trial

## *Lawrence Joseph*

The President's more reflective side emerges late in the day. For example recently, at a fund-raiser at the Waldorf-Astoria, while Luther Vandross was singing *Evergreen* for him, the President whispered loudly to those at his table that this was, he thought, the greatest love song of the last twenty-five years. Yes, members of a remote country Pentecostal church in Alexandria, Louisiana, were told after a performance of Handel's *Messiah* (a portrayal of the life and death of Jesus, during which, Mr. Clinton said, he cried continuously), yes there was, there was a period of time, a day or two at least, when there was some question whether he would finish his second term. It was close to midnight. The President was standing beside the church's pastor, the Reverend Anthony Mangun, and a group of former drug addicts and convicts who'd put their lives back together through religion. During the heat of impeachment, Reverend Mangun and his wife dropped off a recording of an uplifting song and some biblical readings at the White House, gifts that helped the President get through the tough times. "He said," said the President, "'I know you. You are my friend. We have raised our children together. I love you. I was there when you were going up. If the ship starts to sink and other people start to bail out, you call me. I want to go down with you.'" The President then gave Reverend Mangun what was described as a bearhug. At an appearance before the American Society of Newspaper Editors—clearly irritated by the line of questioning—"I'm not ashamed of the fact that they impeached me," the President said of the vote of the House of Representatives to send charges against him to the Senate. "That was their decision, not mine. And it was wrong. As a matter of law, Constitution and history, it was wrong. And I'm glad we fought it. That has nothing to do with the fact that I made a terrible mistake"—no specific mention was made of his affair with Monica Lewinsky—"of which I am deeply regretful. I've struggled very hard to save my relationship with my wife and my daughter, I have paid quite a lot. I think that an average, ordinary person reviewing the wreckage left in that would say that I paid for that. And I should have paid for it. We all must pay for our mistakes." The settlement of the sexual harassment suit filed against him by Paula Corbin Jones had cost him half his life savings, even though, he emphasized, he'd won the case. The questions put to him by Paula Jones's lawyers, he said, were asked in bad faith. Jones's lawyers knew the answers and knew—"something hardly anybody ever points out"—the questions they were asking had nothing to do with the lawsuit. Asked about the possibility of a presidential pardon if Robert W. Ray, who has succeeded Kenneth W. Starr as the Independent Counsel investigating the President, chooses to indict him on charges of perjury and obstruction of justice after he leaves office, the President, in slow measured tones, pounded the lectern with his fist. "NO. NO. I don't have any interest in that. I have no need to be pardoned. And I am prepared to stand before any bar of justice I have to stand before. But"—his voice rose in anger—"just once I'd like to see someone acknowledge the fact that this Whitewater thing was a lie and a fraud from the beginning, and that most people with any responsibility over it have known that for years." In the March 13, 2000, issue of the *New Yorker*, Rebecca Mead, in the "Talk of the Town," noting the President's appetites "for cream puffs as well as for comestibles," mentioned that Julian Niccolini, managing partner of the Four Seasons restaurant, was surprised to read in the *New York Times* about an elaborate dinner—lobster salad with caviar-cream dressing, a duo of stuffed saddle and roasted rack of lamb with tomato-spinach compote and rosemary-lemon polenta, apple tarte-tatin—prepared for President Clinton by another restaurant, Daniel, on a recent Thursday evening. Mr. Niccolini was surprised because later that evening the Four Seasons prepared a dinner for the President of tuna tartare with beluga caviar, roast filet of lamb with truffle sauce and sauteed spring vegetables, and a dish of mixed berries. "After the main course," Mr. Niccolini added, "he cleaned his plate with his bread." According to Daniel's banquet director Anthony Francis, the President was at Daniel less than an hour, twenty minutes of which he spent delivering a speech to the dinner guests, sixty-six members of the Democratic National Committee. Yet he managed to eat every scrap of his appetizer and his main course. (He ordered his tarte-tatin to go.) Driven, then, thirteen blocks south to the Four Seasons, the President, Mead reported, settled in for a three-hour blowout and gabfest, leaving for Chappaqua (with another doggie bag, containing a slice of key lime pie) at twelve forty-five in the morning. In the *Wall Street Journal*, former Ronald Reagan speechwriter Peggy Noonan says that the Department of Justice's actions concerning custody of the six-year-old Cuban Elian Gonzalez may be explained by the fact that Fidel Castro has been blackmailing President Clinton with secret phone intercepts. Item: In the *New York Times*, under the caption "Public Lives," "A Loyal, Oathful D.O.B. (Defender of Bill)," James Carville, "the self-described 'loudmouth' political consultant and Clinton defender," says: "It's what I call my comma: James Carville, comma, Clinton's sex defender, comma. . . . After all, without him I wouldn't have an obit! I wouldn't have a comma! I wouldn't have anything! . . . Ask people who's that guy and he's not the guy who wrote four best sellers, not the guy who ran the successful presidential campaign here or in Israel or wherever. . . . He's the guy who defended the guy who got in trouble. I wish it never happened. But wish in one hand 'n spit in another, and see which one fills up faster." "Hound dog! Ain't nothing but a hooooooooound dog! That's what Clinton is. Crying all the time!" an employment law lawyer, management side, from Jefferson City, Missouri, says over lunch at Vong, laughing. The word "courage" is repeatedly invoked, Joan Didion observes in her essay, "Uncovered Washington," in the *New York Review of Books*. Midge Decter, a Director of the Independent Women's Forum, praises Henry Hyde's "manliness." Watching him and "his merry band" on television during the impeachment trial had caused her to recall "whole chunks" of Rudyard Kipling's poem *If*. A commercial: "A word about impotence from Pfizer, the maker of Viagra." When seen: February 14, during the Daytona 500 on CBS. Former Senator from Kansas, 1976 Republican Vice Presidential candidate and 1996 Republican Presidential candidate, Robert Dole, is seated in an armchair: "Courage, something shared by countless Americans, those who risked their lives, those who battle serious illness. When I was diagnosed with prostate cancer, I was primarily concerned with ridding myself of cancer, but secondly, I was concerned with possible post-operative effects like erectile dysfunction, E.D., often called impotence." And the point Bob Dole wants to make is this. "There are many treatments available for E.D., so my advice is, get a medical checkup. It may take a little courage, but I've always found that everything that's truly worthwhile always does."

Former presidential advisor Dick Morris, describing his last telephone conversation with Mr. Clinton in January 1998: "The second or third thing that I said to him was—I said it occurred to me that I may be the only sex addict you know and maybe I can help you. . . . Then he said, 'You know, ever since the election, I've tried to shut myself down, I've tried to shut my body down, sexually, I mean. But sometimes I slipped up and with this girl I just slipped up.' And I said, 'I know. You know, addicts fall off the wagon.' I said, 'This is an addiction just like drugs or alcohol and you just have to recognize it and fight it.'" In an article by Alexandra Jacobs, "Enough! The Overexposure of Sex Is Ruining the Mood for Everybody," in the *New York Observer:* "'I see sex as kind of the newest art form,' said the bustling Ms. Alison Maddex, who is 33 and Camille Paglia's girlfriend. 'Sex and technology are the art forms of the new millennium!' One twenty-eight-year-old heterosexual male who works at MTV said that about eight months ago, after a period of furious dating, he decided to stop seeing anybody and stop having sex. 'I decided that sex was just kind of stupid, the whole thing. For a while, there was a lot of masturbation and that kind of thing, but now I don't even do that. I just kind of will it away. Not having sex makes me feel stronger and mentally clearer. I don't know—energy you know, chakras—I don't know exactly what's involved, but, by not having sex at all, I feel like you become a more intense person somehow.'" When Kenneth Starr left his job as a partner in the Washington office of the Chicago-based law firm of Kirkland & Ellis, he was at the top of the earning range of partners. (Starr joined Kirkland & Ellis in 1993; he had been Solicitor General in the administration of George Bush.) Although Starr was named Independent Counsel in 1994, he maintained his partnership until 1998, when he took a leave of absence from the firm to devote himself full-time to the Monica Lewinsky investigation. In 1999, members of the top earning group at Kirkland & Ellis were paid approximately two million dollars each; in recent negotiations, Starr was offered about eight hundred thousand, which is at the bottom of the firm's partner salary range. Mr. Starr's former position as Independent Counsel is apparently not perceived by his partners as having enhanced his ability to "eat-what-you-kill" (a legal term that means a partner is compensated on the basis of how much business he or she generates for the firm). In an article by T. Z. Parsa, "The Drudge Report," in *New York* magazine: "'It was a much more social and friendly atmosphere before,' says another large-firm partner. 'There were a lot of good old functioning alcoholics back then—the three martini lunch really happened. You'd go out and get all the gossip and then come back and work. Unfortunately, the nature of the work doesn't allow that anymore.'" One big-firm associate says: "There are a few of the old guys still around wearing bow ties and leaving the first button on their suit sleeves unbuttoned to show that they are the real deal. There's this one guy who is always saying I should come to his club to play squash, and I'm like, You have to be kidding me. I'm this kid from Staten Island. The pinkie rings and the white hair, you know—nice guys, but you want to shake them and say: Hey, listen—I've been here for three days straight, and I smell terrible. There's nothing clean and noble about this stuff. It's down and dirty, like Uncle Lou's retail. It's business, baby, so let's not pretend." In a letter to the *New York Review of Books* about a review in its pages by Ronald Dworkin, Professor of Law, New York and Oxford Universities, of his book *An Affair of State*, Richard Posner, Chief Judge, United States Court of Appeals for the Seventh Circuit and Senior Lecturer, University of Chicago Law School, writes that Dworkin "whacks my view of the proper approach to deciding whether a president should be impeached." No ideal in the impeachment debate has been invoked more often than the rule of law. The President's critics (paraphrasing Dean Anthony Kronman of the Yale Law School) charge that he lied under oath, violating one of the essential conditions of the rule of law, the requirement that anyone formally sworn to tell the truth in a legal proceeding do so, even if the truth means possible prosecution and certain embarrassment. To allow an oath taker to be the judge of whether and to what extent his oath shall be respected is to substitute the rule of men for the rule of law. The President's defenders (again paraphrasing Dean Kronman) deny that he committed perjury, however incomplete and misleading his testimony may have been. They also seek to take back from their enemies the immense authority associated with the ideal of the rule of law itself. The remorseless pursuit of technical infractions by a politically motivated prosecutor armed with limitless resources must be seen as the destruction, not the vindication, of the rule of law. Item: Thomas Friedman in the *New York Times*. "Yup, I gotta confess, that now famous picture of a U.S. marshal in Miami pointing an automatic weapon toward Donato Dalrymple and ordering him in the name of the U.S. government to turn over Elian Gonzalez warmed my heart. They should put that picture up in every visa line in every U.S. consulate around the world, with a caption that reads: 'America is a country where the rule of law rules. This picture illustrates what happens to those who defy the rule of law and how far

our government and people will go to preserve it. Come ye all who understand that.'" There are some who say that during the past year, while
the President's domestic travails have all but eclipsed news of anything
else, the nation's foreign affairs have slid into a worrisome, muddlesome
mess. Nicolas Von Hoffman: "Seemingly, no camel driver, resting his
dromedary in a gorge in Afghan-istan as he makes himself a cup of tea,
can be free from the vague thought that one of Mr. Clinton's cruise mis-
siles may be winging up the self-same canyon to foreshorten his life or
livelihood. . . . As it is, Mr. Clinton looks like a gutless politician ready to
kill noncombatants in other countries rather than risk the lives of his
own soldiers. That may wash with the yahoos whom he plays to with as
much zest as do the Republican members of the impeachment committee, but it is contemptible." How about the vast, virtually unchecked influence of money on presidential politics? It wasn't until 1995, you know,
that the Internet as we know it began to exist. "And like dreams, the experience of the Web is intensely private, charged with immanent meaning
for the person inside the experience, but often confusing or irrelevant to
someone else," Ellen Ullman writes in an excerpt of an essay in the May
2000 issue of *Harper's Magazine*. "It was the fall of 1998. I was walking toward Market Street one afternoon when I saw it, a background of bril-
liant blue sky, with writing on it in airy white letters, which said: now the
world really does revolve around you. The letters were lower-case, soft-
edged, spaced irregularly, as if they'd been skywritten over a hot August
beach and were already drifting off into the air. The message they left behind was a child's secret wish, the ultimate baby-world narcissism we are
all supposed to abandon when we grow up: the world really does revolve
around me. What was this billboard advertising? Perfume? A resort?
There was nothing else on it but the airy, white letters, and I had to walk
right up to it to see a URL written at the bottom; it was the name of a
company that makes semiconductor equipment, machinery used by
companies like Intel and AMD to manufacture integrated circuits. Oh,
chips, I thought. Computers. Of course. What other subject produces
such hyperbole? Who else but someone in the computer industry could
make such a shameless appeal to individualism? The billboard loomed
over the corner for the next couple of weeks. Every time I passed it, its
message irritated me more. It bothered me the way the 'My Computer'
icon bothers me on the Windows desktop, baby names like 'My Yahoo'
and 'My Snap'; my, my, my; two-year-old talk; infantalizing and con-
descending." March 6, 2000, in a speech to a conference on the "new

economy" at Boston College, the Chairman of the Federal Reserve repeated his message that the wealth being created in the stock market is creating more demand than the economy can satisfy. Investors took notice. They sent the Dow Jones industrial average down 196.70 points, to 10,170.50. Mr. Greenspan even took some air out of high-flying technology stocks, helping send the Nasdaq index down 9.94 points, to 4,904.85. The same day it was announced that Former Treasury Secretary Robert E. Rubin would be paid more than $15 million (not including options for one and a half million shares of stock) this year in his position as one of the top three leaders of Citigroup, according to a new filing with the Securities and Exchange Commission. This statement by Treasury Secretary Lawrence Summers, quoted in the *New York Times*: "When history books are written 200 years from now about the last two decades of the 20th century, I am convinced that the end of the cold war will be the second story. The first story will be about the appearance of emerging markets, about the fact that developing countries where more than three billion people lived have moved toward the market and seen rapid growth incomes." The rapid growth of per capita income perhaps, but how about the distribution of income (which has worsened both within and between countries as globalization has proceeded), environmental destruction, the loss of biodiversity, labor or human rights? Economists have predicted that the largest intergenerational transfer of wealth in history—approximately $12 trillion—will take place in the United States from the mid-1990s until 2020. One third of the money will go to 1 percent of the baby boomers, who will receive about $1.6 million apiece. You know, there's a law of the conservation of violence, don't you? All violence must be paid for. The structural violence exerted by the financial markets is, sooner or later, revealed in the form of depression, alcoholism, drug addiction, suicide, and other forms of severe physical and mental disorders. A whole host of major and minor everyday acts of violence. Shouldn't those who think of themselves as intellectuals be directing their energy against those corporatists, politicians, and lawyers who openly ally themselves with the interest of anarcho-economic forces which undermine the existence of a civil state from within? Item: September 20, 1999, the *New York Observer*, under the caption "Entertainment City," in the section "Party Space," beside a photograph with her mouth open: "MONICA. MEETER and GREETER. I'LL AUTOGRAPH MY BOOK. I'LL SHAKE EVERY HAND IN THE HOUSE. I'LL BE THE LIFE OF YOUR PARTY. FOR A PRICE. CALL ME AT 1–800–542–0420

X295." Item: Thursday, April 20, 2000, the *New York Times,* under the caption "Campaign Briefing. Republicans": "Governor George W. Bush has been sued by the former head of the Texas Funeral Service Commission, who said that Mr. Bush had impeded an investigation of a company that had contributed to his campaign for governor. The former official, Eliza May, filed a lawsuit last year asserting that she had been wrongfully fired for investigating the company, Service Corporation International. On Monday she amended her suit to include Mr. Bush. Service Corporation International, one of the world's largest funeral homes and cemetery operators, is headed by a Bush family friend and campaign contributor, Robert Waltrip. Ms. May was investigating possible violations of funeral home regulations. She was fired after Mr. Waltrip met with a top Bush aide, Joe Allbaugh, to complain about the investigation, the suit says. . . . Ms. May is a former treasurer of the Texas Democratic Party."

# Part IV

# Religion

# Chapter 17

# An Un-Christian Pursuit

## *Stephen Toulmin*

Few episodes in recent American history have polarized opinion as sharply as the Clinton-Lewinsky affair. On the one side, a self-conscious, self-righteously Christian fraction of the electorate banded together to condemn the President for his escapades with Ms. Lewinsky, and for his attempts to conceal, misrepresent, or even deny them. On the other, a less ostentatiously "religious" fraction found many details of President Clinton's behavior more distasteful and perjurious than sleazy, but they were turned off even more by the manner in which Special Prosecutor Kenneth Starr, Linda Tripp, and their allies pursued their investigation. It struck them as disproportionate, even prurient. This second group rarely offered an outright moral defense of the President's conduct: at best, they dismissed it as politically trivial, if not purely private. Still, their response to Prosecutor Starr's procedures was basically sound. Indeed, this essay will argue, their moral sentiments were more in accord with the Christian tradition as it has existed historically, than those of today's self-styled "Christians." By traditional standards, we might say, the energetic pursuit of William Jefferson Clinton by the Starr Chamber was not just unfair, but positively un-Christian.

This claim may sound extreme, but the case is clear if we consider two prefatory points. First let me quote a historical essay entitled "Sins of the Tongue: Bill Clinton, Ken Starr, and Traditional Christian Values," written in the fall of 1998 by Debora Shuger of the U.C.L.A. English Department:

> Given that the vast majority of Americans describe themselves as Christians, many of whom will try to understand the Lewinsky matter according to Christian values and principles, it seems important to know what these might be.

What, then, are we to understand by Christian values and principles? That question is too rarely asked. Most Americans assume that the views stated by their preachers are historically well founded, and see no need to explore the strength of their support, let alone challenge them. This remains the case even when there is substantial disagreement among preachers from different parts of the Western Church: not just between Protestant and Catholic teachers, but among different varieties of Protestants. So we may begin by looking at the historical relationship between popular American assumptions about Christian ethics and the classic traditions of earlier times.

I begin with a chronological truism. The period from the lifetime of Jesus up to the Protestant-Catholic divide in the sixteenth and seventeenth centuries covers more than three-quarters of the historical span of Christianity: the subsequent centuries of the Western Church are at most one quarter of that history. This at once gives rise to Dr. Shuger's question,

> How closely do popular ideas of Christian Ethics today reflect the carefully thought out positions of theologians and confessors in the Medieval Western Church? And if there are differences between them, what is their significance?

Can we assume that twentieth-century theologians have come to understand the mind and teachings of Jesus better, as a result of living so much later than he did? Or have we, perhaps, lost some of the spirit of charity embodied in truly Christian life and conduct for their first fifteen hundred years? If we are anxious to resolve our moral quandaries in a solidly grounded way, these questions must be taken seriously, and some serious historical research cannot be avoided. As we shall find, the things that come to light as a result of quite simple research may be quite surprising.

Lutheran teachers today, for instance, rarely trouble to remind us that Luther himself regarded marriage as a civil contract, which a prudent Church should take care not to get too involved in: the sacramental view of marriage was foreign to his ways of thinking, as it was to much of the medieval Church. Before the Reformation, customary practices over weddings, and the public acknowledgment of matrimonial unions, resembled those still associated with (say) "common-law marriages" in Scotland or Texas more than they do the standard Church weddings of today. It was courteous to ask the parish priest or minister to attend the event, to register it in the parish records, and even give it a blessing, but that was all.

The change in the social and ecclesiastical view of marriage from civil ceremony to sacrament is only one of the changes in Church practice that resulted from the struggle between the rival Christian churches between 1550 and 1700. The only reason it became as embedded in later attitudes as it did was that a spirit of extremism overtook many parties to this dispute. Catholics and Protestants competed to be "Holier than Thou"; and their intellectual ambition was less to show their superiority in loving-kindness, as to prove the certainty and correctness of their ideas. The ideological goal of the Religious Wars was thus to establish the intellectual as well as spiritual authority of the Church. For extreme Protestants, the enemy was Popery, as it still is for Ian Paisley in Northern Ireland, or at Bob Jones University in the United States. For extreme Catholics it was Heresy, as it is to this day for those who insist on the unique *magisterium* of the Vatican in matters of Faith and Morals. The continuing controversy between these extreme views—notably after the French Revolution—encouraged dogmatic censoriousness rather than inquiry, let alone honest doubt.

At this stage, another preliminary point is worth making. Oddly enough, Western commentators on world affairs find it easier to recognize the side effects of religious controversy and extremism on other religions than they do in the case of Christianity itself. In discussing Islamic beliefs and customs (say) they can often adopt an intelligently critical attitude that acknowledges the historical differences between the Islam of the Quran and that of the late twentieth century, between the Sunni, Shiite, and other branches of the religion, and between the local doctrines that popular preachers insist are "Islamic" in one country or another in the Muslim world today.

Faced with Islamic customs we find puzzling or horrifying—ranging from the insistence on the wearing of veils to surgical excision of a young girl's clitoris—we are open to the idea that these are not truly Islamic obligations, imposed by the text of the Quran or other generally revered texts, but manifestations of local conservatism that have been preserved in parts of Africa and Asia as a result of their authority's being misinterpreted. Who is strictly in the right? Conservative Iranian mullahs who object to young women playing soccer before male spectators? Or the Taliban of Kandahar, who object even to male soccer players wearing shorts?

Muslim scholars in Mali, for instance, admit that clitoral surgery is not strictly speaking required by Islam; but at once add that Islam tolerates it, because it is an effective way of controlling women's sexual appetites. So, long-standing social traditions, however repulsive to onlookers, come to be understood by the general public as having an Islamic authority that local scholars may admit they do not have. (Recall that Descartes himself recognized that no Euclidean theory of ethics was available, and saw conformity to local customs as a prudent alternative.) Meanwhile, fundamentalists who enroll in "Armies of God" are convinced that they will die as a way of achieving the goals of Islam, though their own goals confuse nationalism of a strictly Western kind with slogans borrowed from Islam.

Now we can return to Clinton and Lewinsky. If we take a truly historical position, we must begin by admitting that all kinds of sexual pleasure outside matrimony were regarded by the medieval casuists and moral theologians as sinful; but "sinful" was one thing, "illegal" something else altogether. They all called for confession and penitence, but the actions confessed to in acts of penance were not at once made common property. On the contrary, they were offered to God, through the intermediation of the confessor, as an occasion for the penitent to seek to amend his or her manner of life. At the same time, sexual peccadillos were so common and variable that confessors needed guidance, and a complex taxonomy of these acts—attributed to an imaginary couple called Titus and Bertha—entered the course of instruction for would-be confessors. So much for the goings-on in the White House: if Christian decency had been respected, nothing more need have been made known to the general public.

To go further, it is not just that no more *need* have been made known to the general public, but that the publicity given to the Clinton-Lewinsky affair was precisely what historical Christian ethics was meant to prevent. Suppose we put the distinction between law and morality—state interests and Church concerns—in center stage, and ask whether, morally speaking, there were any limits to the questions an individual could be required to answer to the state authorities, under threat of punishment (*sub pœna*)—as distinct from thoughts or actions he or she might be expected to confess through his or her confessor, under a vow of secrecy—there is once again something to be learned. Here, Dr. Shuger's essay draws our attention to some important distinctions, which call in question the actions not just of Linda Tripp, but also of Kenneth Starr himself.

> [F]rom the Middle Ages through the early modern period, both Roman Catholic and Protestant teaching upholds as a fundamental principle that no one is compelled to reveal his own secret sin (*nemo tenetur detegere turpitudinem suam*), and correlatively, that no one—including judges and

prosecutors, no matter how "special"—has a moral right to compel another person to disclose his or her private shameful acts.

As authority for this view, Shuger cites the eminent Protestant divine, William Ames, who wrote in 1639, "he whose offence is hidden has . . . as yet right to preserve his fame that it should not rashly be laid open. Neither is it the part of a judge to search into hidden faults." And she adds:

> Ames here follows the medieval canonists, who had argued for the *nemo tenetur* rule on the ground that a court of law is not a confessional: "private and shameful acts" . . . are matters for the penitential forum, not public tribunals.

From the outset, the goings-on between Mr. Clinton and Ms. Lewinsky were, surely, just the kinds of "private and shameful acts" traditional Christian ethics reserved for the confessional, and were not to be made a matter for prosecutorial inquiry:

> As Richard Helmholz's study on the privilege against self-incrimination makes clear [Shuger continues] canon law prohibited the courts from scrutinizing the intimate details of a man's personal life. [In this respect] it defended a theological right to privacy.
>
> Both Catholic and Protestant writers argue against compelling people to answer specific incriminating questions under oath because virtually no one will tell the truth. Ames thus declares that it is "against nature [to expect] that any man should betray or defame himself." To put someone on oath, and then ask if he has masturbated or committed adultery [mortal sins according to traditional Christian theology] is merely to "give occasion of horrid perjuries." It is not just weak, unprincipled men who lie on such occasions. Hence, as Helmholz points out, canon law forbids bringing charges of perjury "based on false answers to formal questions" even when false answers were given under oath.

The moral theologians of earlier centuries based their analyses on an understanding of human foibles, frailties, and defensiveness that had as much room for the real lives of Bill and Monica as it did for the hypothetical lives of Titus and Bertha. It is as though they had exactly foreseen what we have now lived through.

What, then, are traditionally minded Christians to say when this theological right to privacy is disregarded? What kind of moral offense is committed by those who demand public answers to private questions? The historical record is unambiguous:

Traditional Christian moral theology does not view attempts to hide one's private sin and shame, even when those attempts involve perjury and equivocation, as grave sins. What it does view as a very grave sin is *detractio*: disclosing another human being's private sin and shame in order to ruin his good name or otherwise bring him into discredit. To harm someone by making damaging allegations against him is a sin against charity, whether or not the allegations are in fact true.

If one is told a secret, which, if made public, would [in Ames's phrase]

> be hurtful to another's soul, body, credit, or estate, he which doth reveal it without cause sinneth as well against justice as charity.... Because the unjust revealing a secret hath in it oftentimes the pernicious violations of trust, friendship, and honesty, therefore it is not only in the common esteem of men, but in the Scripture also, reckoned amongst the most odious sins.

Let sincere Christians, who care about the lessons of traditional teaching, think carefully about Shuger's conclusion:

> What Mr. Starr, Ms. Tripp, and the press have done in the Lewinsky matter is, from the perspective of traditional Christian moral theology, at least as sinful, as immoral, and as wrong as what the President did, and yet only he has been made to squirm, confess, beg forgiveness, and eat humble pie.

> Mr. Clinton's behavior is not evidence for the erosion of Christian values; Christians have been committing adultery and lying about it for centuries. The erosion lies elsewhere: in the transformation of charity from a theological virtue to a tax deduction; in the fact that we apparently no longer consider savaging another's reputation, betraying the confidence of a friend, compelling someone to publicize his hidden faults, and then punishing him for not cooperating in his own disgrace, stripping a man of dignity and privacy by putting the juicy details of his private life on the Internet, to be sins at all.

In short, what the moral theologians of the high medieval period called *detractio*—what lawyers today know as "defamation"—was, from the traditional Christian viewpoint, "a very grave sin." It was, in a word, *Un-Christian*. Will Kenneth Starr's successor, Robert Ray, care any more for the truth about historical Christian values than Mr. Starr and his earlier associates seem from the record to have done? That still remains to be seen.

# Chapter 18

# Abuse of Power as a Cultural Construct

## *Lawrence Rosen*

Politicians and pundits alike were mystified by the public support that President Clinton maintained throughout the impeachment process. With favorable job ratings at near record highs and no popular outcry for the President's removal ensuing from their own jeremiads or analyses, commentors frequently characterized the American electorate as puritanical or cynical (with varying degrees of hypocrisy attendant on either state), or simply more offended by the Special Prosecutor's actions than by those of the President.[1]

But there is at least one other explanation that may account for the President's support, one that draws together many of the emphases that pervade American political and personal life and thus gain force by reverberating through a host of cultural domains. For what may have been at issue, in no small part, was the belief held by many Americans that, in the absence of any underlying act tantamount to a criminal offense, Bill Clinton did not appear to be a man who abused his official power. To understand what "abuse of power" means in this broader cultural sense it is necessary to consider a set of interrelated issues—from the distinctive American style of struggling against temptation, to the linkage this implies to the concept of character, to the place that hypocrisy occupies in the American moral imagination, to the implications of federalism as the relinquishment of personal freedom. As measured against these cultural criteria President Clinton was not, I believe, seen by the majority of Americans as an abuser of power. It may have been this larger cultural view that ultimately supplanted any legalistic concept of high crimes and misdemeanors as the defining feature in the popular political imagination of an impeachable offense.

The Constitution does not list "abuse of power" as grounds for impeachment.[2] Indeed, the House of Representatives avoided returning charges against the President for abusing his office through any unspecified noncriminal actions. Yet lurking behind both statutory language and formal charge may lie an idea that resonates through the whole of popular political culture and constitutional faith. Though poorly articulated (as indeed the entire affair demonstrates) and perhaps (like pornography and injustice) more clearly felt than defined, the abuse of power as a cultural concept would appear to embrace several distinguishable elements.

In the American cultural view, abuse of power is an attribute of a person rather than the characterization of a single act. Indeed, it is the repetition of acts that, at some unspecified point, converts into a feature of an individual's overall character. In this sense, Americans are implicitly more committed to the ideas of Hume than they are to those of Kant, for while they recognize with the latter that fairness requires some opportunity to assess the risks attendant on one's conduct they tend toward the former's view that blame should attach to an individual if inappropriate acts point to undesirable character traits. We may have laws that permit strict liability offenses, and we may punish people even though they are ignorant of the law, but popular sentiment (as indicated in everything from moral assertions and political support to jury nullification and popular ideas about child rearing) supports the idea that the act must say something about the person if it is to be regarded as more than an idiosyncratic event. This linkage to character will, as we shall see, be crucially bound up in religious ideas that permeate American popular culture.

To constitute abuse the differential of power must, in addition, be seen as largely inescapable: Only when this is so can any particular victim stand as representative of the larger public. If there are other ways to get around the powerful—particularly if they operate through established institutions that, formally or informally, are touted as checks on the powerful—it is far more difficult to overcome the ethos of personal responsibility in asserting a claimed abuse of power. This sentiment is evident in numerous cultural domains: In economic competition, when market dominance is perceived as restraint of trade; in familial life, where the public can identify with the abused spouse or child on whose behalf others can finally see no way out; in love, when one party plays on the emotional weakness of another in ways that outsiders can empathize with as a form of being trapped; and in politics itself, where the secretive exercise of power (as in Watergate) contravenes the image of fair competition for desired ends.

Not surprisingly, then, the commonsense view of abuse of power also seems to entail the idea that the alleged abuse must be aimed at personal or partisan advantage, rather than constituting action that might be justified as being in the public interest. The injury, however, cannot be simply personal. For it is part of the very discrepancy in power that while the offender avails himself of some individual gain the victim must seem to be the commonweal rather than a particular person or party. Watergate could, therefore, appear not as an act against the Democratic Party by Nixon and his operatives but as an act against the public. By contrast, Iran-Contra or the questionable way in which George Bush committed American troops to combat in Panama and the Gulf War could easily be portrayed as acts on behalf of the public rather than unalloyed personal advantage. But just as character is revealed through a course of action so too, in the popular evaluation of the abuse of power there must be preconditions, suggestive of a course of conduct, to those acts that direct attention to possible abuse. This is, in a sense, a corollary to the view of abuse of power as a character flaw. For example, a great many Americans, including members of his own party and those who voted for him, had long thought Richard Nixon capable of the events connected with Watergate: The image of "Tricky Dick," based on everything from his earliest congressional campaign to perceptions of his mannerisms and tone, made plausible his involvement in Watergate in a way that, as we shall see, the sobriquet of Clinton as "Slick Willie" and his earlier sexual exploits only became firmly rooted in his most ardent opponents. Where abuse of power is involved, the question "Is he likely to have done this thing?" becomes converted into "Has he shown the character of one who does such things?" and "Have we, as a consequence of his character, been placed in a situation of moral vulnerability by him?"

Moral vulnerability, of course, connects with the idea of hypocrisy as it affects any judgment of abuse. Hypocrisy is, however, an even more subtle and ambivalent notion in American religious and cultural thought than most commentors appreciate. Well before the Lewinsky affair broke, Charles Krauthammer had expressed the view that not only are most politicians hypocrites but so is the public at large—"And thank God for it."[3] Krauthammer's point was that since we all inevitably possess vices, it is far better that we should err in our behavior than that we should fail to express, in however backhanded a fashion, the values we favor in leaders but fail to live up to in our own lives. "The choice," he argued, "is not really between a society of vice or virtue—we will never have the latter. The choice is between a society of hypocrisy or cynicism." But the logic of culture is not the logic of philosophical distinction. In fact, as events surrounding Clinton's actions suggest, the choices are more complex. For if one is to be characterized as an abuser of power, one must oneself be seen as a hypocrite and the acts themselves as acts of hypocrisy. If these conditions are not met—as they were not in the popular view of President Clinton's conduct—the powerful figure himself will not be seen as having fallen short of the requisite standard for abuse. In this rather involuted cultural scheme, where charges of hypocrisy may seem like endless and ever-receding images cast up by facing mirrors, hypocrisy actually vanishes from view as an attribute of culpable public character if it is not rooted in a long-standing reputation for saying one thing and doing another in ways that threaten the public weal. The very privacy of Clinton's sexual behavior and the problematic nature of the women's participation in it inured the President from charges of hypocrisy without his supporters feeling, given the cultural logic at work, that they had fallen into cynicism.

Indeed, the cultural logic of hypocrisy, like that of character, may only become evident if one looks at those aspects of religion that play a prominent role in the configuration of American moral concepts. The argument has often been made that, in the Weberian sense, all Americans are Protestants: We imagine ourselves to have failed in some deeper moral sense, for example, if we do not work hard and succeed, and (regardless of particular faiths) we are all the heirs to a dominant set of values that are connected to Protestant notions of personal responsibility for moral self-fashioning. Clearly these elements are present in the ways in which we formulate our images of character and honesty, and clearly they played a distinct role in the public evaluation of President Clinton. Indeed, several very concrete aspects of Baptist/Evangelical Protestant thought played a key role in the public assessment of the President—elements whose broader existence in American culture may have been insufficiently or incorrectly perceived until the events precipitated by Clinton's actions brought them to the fore.

In what is arguably the dominant form of Protestant culture in America, the problem of humankind's sinful nature is approached neither by sacramental cleansing nor expiation through good works but by the demonstration that one is indeed constantly struggling against temptation. There is no expectation that one will overcome such forces in any permanent way; to the contrary, the expectation is of occasional relapse. What matters is not the achievement in this life of a settled goal but the demonstration that one is grappling with this very human condition.

Process, in a sense, is both more important and more realistic than result. Failure of character is the failure of an individual to continue this struggle. Abuse of the powers that inhere in each person is evident when one gives up the fight against temptation: It is the process of showing that one is fighting against sin (or, in somewhat more secularized terms, human failings) that proves one is not abusing one's God-given powers, not the achievement of any specific (and necessarily momentary) result. Bill Clinton not only made his private life public (as Jean Elshtain properly notes) but used it to show that he was struggling against downfall. Character is shown through such private battles publicly portrayed, and the victim of one's propensities is now the common man of character whose privacy is turned inside out so that the private is the terrain where scripted (indeed, scriptural) moral resistance is played out. What to Elshtain and others may seem contemptuous behavior to women is taken the next cultural step to personal repentance and the public demonstration of a very private struggle against the fall.

Bill Clinton was no more hypocritical than the culture he incorporates in this respect. Whether it is in the revelation of the problems with drink and drugs and gambling in his own family or in the use of religious figures and appearances before Evangelical congregations, Clinton was partaking of— indeed was deeply implanted within—this vision of the human condition. The overtones that informed his public demonstration of his struggle came from numerous sources within this Protestant culture, particularly as represented in the forms common to the American South. Standing before the public as before a congregation, his statements and his stance were those of the sinner combating his nature, subject to no single authority in this world, and giving witness to that self-reliance and self-fashioning which lie at the heart of American Protestantism's vision of the point of contact between personal salvation and public morals.

Clinton, like other sinners, could, therefore, demonstrate his attachment to the requirements of Evangelical assumptions in ways that reverberate through the whole of American—and particularly Southern—cultural representations. Baptists and other Evangelicals, like most Americans, are neither cynical nor relativistic: They do not accept the notion that moral elites formulate the categorical terms by which all moral actions are to be guided. Rather they are given to the contextualization of morals. Baptist churches, which exploded in growth following the eighteenth-century Great Awakening of Calvinism, stood for the idea of each individual's personal encounter with God and that creeds should emerge from below rather than be imposed by a Church hierarchy. The risk, as Emerson had said, was that every man might become his own Church, but the repercussion was also that each individual was not reduced to a single role and a single set of moral certainties. Indeed, compliance with morality may actually require certain transgressions, specific instances often being cited to show that compliance with inflexible moral categories may lead to harmful consequences. In contemporary popular culture one sees these types of dilemmas portrayed in television series about doctors or policemen or lawyers whose humanity lies in their traversing simple imperatives; in popular songs, where lack of certainty accompanies the "right" way to act toward one's lover; in religion itself, where redemption is not linked to singular acts that partake of moral certainty. Southern literature, in particular, often turns on the availability of alternative roles that the character can assume and hence the appeal to alternative sources of authority, rather than transgression of dominant authority, as the best available means to resolve a moral dilemma.[4] Clearly, Americans would not want the threshold for justified transgression to be set too low, but where life and law do not map onto one another very exactly—as, in the popular view, they rarely do—the acts of one's opponents may justify raising the level beyond which criticism of one's own acts take full effect.

Bill Clinton could, therefore, partake simultaneously of these cultural emphases by showing that he was struggling with temptation, that he was employing his own will in addressing his failings, and that this struggle—which for anyone has to be accompanied by public demonstration—must be regarded as largely private. To those Evangelicals who, as one interviewee told a reporter, envision the human condition as "a struggle between dignity and depravity," there remains a real tension between bringing such matters into the domain of the political in the first place.[5] For to link oneself to the criteria of public morality is both to yoke oneself to the values of that domain and to undercut the need to carry on the struggle outside of all constraint. This ambivalence is deeply writ in American Evangelical Protestantism as part of the central notion of voluntarism itself, where the unconstrained individual quest for salvation takes precedence. The strength and weakness of this position in the American context has been described by one commentor, who says of Baptist voluntarism:

> That voluntarism also sees its integrity and spontaneity fatally compromised whenever the state intrudes into the realm of religious conscience.

Voluntarism has its weaker side in becoming the passive reflection of a surrounding culture in surrendering slowly and unthinkingly to what one author has called the "cultural captivity of the churches."[6]

Ironically, then, American Evangelism is at once so embedded in that culture of voluntarism it has helped spawn that it cannot be separated from American culture—including political culture—at large, even though the values the two have come to represent may at times contradict the very idea of being constrained by any specific form of state-sanctioned moral certainty. I must, therefore, disagree with Father Neuhaus when he says that Clinton "never rose above his origin" and "plays to the pit" such that the entire affair tells us nothing about the American character. To the contrary, it tells us a great deal about how Americans approach the whole issue of character and why, in no small part, their answer to that question never resulted in loss of support for the President.

Indeed, we are constantly forced back to the question of character as a general concept in order to understand the cultural process that the Clinton impeachment entailed. For, in addition to being the symbolic summation of the meeting of action and will, character also implies a particular relationship to power. Frequently Americans speak of someone who demonstrates good character as one who sticks to his or her own beliefs notwithstanding adverse personal consequences, and we seek to encourage this capacity by placing as few restraints as possible on individual expressions of this commitment because we believe that it is for the good of all that each should be so free. Similarly, we see character in this sense as itself a check on the abuse of power inasmuch as each person may, without harming the common good, be the source of an alternative moral authority to that of the state.

Such a conceptual system is also related to the paradox of federalism as a projection of one's personal situation, for in the common view what one gives over to the state is more an individual than a collective power: One projects moral attributes onto the state (and its primal figure, the President) in such a way that a test of abuse becomes a test of both character and its effects on one's own freedom. When all these attributes become associated with the dramatic circumstances of a single individual—whether in literature, warfare, or the enactment of political and personal conscience—it is the struggle that becomes the end every bit as much as the particular outcome. Bill Clinton embodied all these cultural precepts and challenged the assumptions they embrace. The result was not only a demonstration of the power of American cultural ideas about character but a remarkable affirmation of the associated concept of abuse of power.

When, therefore, voters say that they are indeed more concerned with a candidate's character than with his or her capabilities, they are giving voice, in shorthand expression, to a complex cultural idea. Commentors who tell us to "forget . . . theories on presidential character. Look at the real question: competence,"[7] may, therefore, be missing what character means in this cultural context. A better indication of its meaning may come from such statements as that made to a reporter by a factory worker who said of her own approach to candidates: "Actually, I look for who has the best character, who has my best interests at heart."[8] At first blush it might seem that equating or conjoining someone else's character and one's own best interests is either contradictory or hypocritical. But again, culture makes leaps that logic does not always encourage. And here the idea that one's own best interests are tied up in another's character, as we have been analyzing it culturally, makes a great deal of sense for Americans. For if character, revealed by struggle against one's nature, implies that one does not abuse power over others, and that the avoidance of abuse is central to one's own ability to fashion a moral stance that is not dependent on one formulated by the state, then self-interest and another's character do indeed get summarized within a single concept and achieve material expression in just such events as the President's impeachment. Kenneth Starr's elaboration of the sexual details of the Clinton-Lewinsky affair in his Referral to Congress not only backfired (as Robert Gordon points out) as morality: It also backfired as proof of abuse of power. For while categorical moralism may seem to pervade both the criminal code and the far right's view of proper conduct, mainstream low Protestant thought emphasizes the process of moral self-evaluation and supports a far more situational vision of the human condition.

Abuse of power, then, is an indispensable category to understanding impeachment, and no amount of legal fine-tuning or bipartisan agreement on specifics will either replace or limit it in the popular imagination. Like many cultural ideas it may not be readily articulated by those whose lives are informed by it, but that does not mean it is any less central to their sense of the orderliness of their world. Being cultural, a concept like abuse of power can garner its force by resonating through a host of domains, and thus can serve as a hedge against seeming hypocrisy because it draws domains together rather than being subject to conceptual segregation. The Clinton impeachment tested this felt sense of abuse of power and showed quite clearly that neither Clinton nor his detractors understood it—Clinton because he could have "confessed" to the affair and there would have been no public pressure for impeachment because it was not seen as an abuse of power; the Republicans because they became legalistic and had no way to tie their legal categories to the popular assessment of the situation. Richard Posner is typical among commentors who miss the force of culture when he argues that Clinton may have seemed clever in admitting to moral wrongdoing, thus freeing the Republicans to go after him on legal grounds.[9] In fact, both Clinton and his opponents misread the public precisely because what was at work, in the absence of an underlying crime, was a cultural and not a political concept. Neither sincerity of contrition nor cleverness of approach can escape the nested web of categories by which the larger sense of character and abuse are understood: Whatever our individual judgments of the man or his acts, culture cannot be written out of the equation when one is inexorably locked into a situation that itself cries out for just the sort of ordering that is of the essence of the cultural process itself.

There is an error that is not uncommon among novices who sail in tidal waters: They assume that they should bring their boat up into the prevailing wind in order to bring it safely to its landing. But in most instances it is the less visible tide that is controlling the boat, and failure to appreciate the old adage that "the tide is king" has, particularly in more turbulent conditions, brought even those sailors who have averted its effects under benign conditions to a tangled and undignified end. The analogy is apt. For just as unapparent tide wields power over more apparent wind in the sea, so too, when it comes to understanding presidential impeachment, commentors and public figures alike may do well to consider the admonition that "culture is king—ignore it at your political peril."

NOTES

1. Throughout the entire process surrounding the investigation, impeachment, and trial of the President about two-thirds of the public continued to give him a favorable job rating.

2. The second proposed article of impeachment of Richard Nixon did not specifically employ the term "abuse of power" but did characterize his use of federal agencies to pursue his political opponents as "contrary to his trust" and a "violation of his constitutional oath." See Emily Field Van Tessel and Paul Finkelman, *Impeachable Offenses: A Documentary History from 1787 to the Present* (Washington, D.C.: Congressional Quarterly Inc., 1999), 261–63. The term has

been used in the impeachment of federal judges, where the constitutional standard may differ from that applying to a president inasmuch as Article III, Section 1 mandates that federal judges hold their offices only "during good behaviour." See, e.g., the impeachment of District Judge George W. English in 1926. Van Tessel and Finkelman, *Impeachable Offenses*, 144–52. The term "abuse of power" has not, therefore, become the subject of legal parsing in the same way as "high crimes and misdemeanors" even though, as argued here, it constitutes a key concept in the popular political imagination. In the Clinton impeachment several scholars who appeared before Congress or published comments on the process did argue that, as one of them put it, impeachment should be limited to "serious abuse of official authority." Geoffrey R. Stone, "Moral Zealotry Is a Worse Crime," *Chicago Tribune*, February 20, 1999, 22. However, this view is not unambiguously sustained by a reading of the constitutional text itself.

3. Charles Krauthammer, "In Praise of Hypocrisy," *Time*, April 27, 1992, 74.

4. I am particularly grateful, in thinking through this issue, to the presentation by William H. Simon on "Moral Pluck" and the comments made in response to it by Robert Ferguson in the Columbia Law School faculty workshop series in the spring of 2000.

5. Alan Wolfe, "Under God, Not Indivisible," *New York Times*, February 27, 2000, WK17. Wolfe also notes that Paul Weyrich, who coined the term "moral majority" and heads a Christian conservative organization, recently voiced the frequent strain in Evangelical involvement in politics when he told his followers that perhaps it was time to pay less attention to politics and "to separate themselves from this hostile culture." It is also worth noting that while the actual vote in the House on the articles of impeachment followed partisan, rather than religious, lines, religion did play a significant role for some Congressmen. The entire relation of religion to politics in this context clearly deserves closer cultural analysis. See Bill Broadway, "Impeachment Raises Questions of Faith: Analysts See the Influence of Evangelical Christianity in Republican-Led Vote," *Washington Post*, January 9, 1999, B10.

6. Edwin Gaustad, "Baptist Churches," in Mircea Eliade, ed., *The Encyclopedia of Religion* (New York: Macmillan, 1987), vol. 2, 63–66 at 66.

7. Garry Wills, "A Better Way to Test a Candidate's Mettle," *New York Times*, November 10, 1999.

8. Nicholas D. Kristof, "Voters Say Character, Not Issues, Is their Concern in Race for White House," *New York Times*, February 12, 2000, A13.

9. Richard A. Posner, *An Affair of State: The Investigation, Impeachment, and Trial of President Clinton* (Cambridge: Harvard University Press, 1999), 140.

# Chapter 19

# Bill Clinton and the American Character

## *Richard John Neuhaus*

That the country would be better off stuck with him rather than having removed him from office was, many thought, the clinching argument of Dale Bumpers, former Senator from Arkansas, during the Senate trial. "If you have difficulty because of an intense dislike of the President, and that's understandable, rise above it," Bumpers exhorted the Senators. "He is not the issue. He will be gone. You won't. So don't leave a precedent from which we may never recover and almost surely will regret.... After all, he's only got two years left."[1] That the impeached President was not the issue in an impeachment trial was among the more curious assertions in this curious affair.

But it is true that the public contention was about more than Bill Clinton. For a year and a half we have been treated to seemingly endless discussion about what all this means for our constitutional order, our political culture, and, inevitably, "the American character." In this reflection, it is the last question that is of particular interest.

Until I came across an old video of the program, I had quite forgotten that at the beginning of January 1993, I had done an extended one-on-one interview with Robert MacNeil of what was then the *MacNeil-Lehrer NewsHour* about the impending Clinton presidency. Asked by Mr. MacNeil what I expected, I answered: "I think what I expect, and maybe what I wish as well, is that he will continue on a trajectory [of] trying to move the Democratic Party into, if not the center, at least into conversational distance with most Americans. I think he has taken the lessons of the 1972 McGovern debacle very much to heart, and he could have a real opportunity, especially when he speaks of a new covenant with America, to engage in a new kind of political discourse."

It is hard to remember that a "new covenant" was a theme of Clinton's 1992 campaign. Not many days later, I watched with friends the news conference following his inauguration, at which he announced that he was rescinding the Reagan-Bush executive orders that placed pitifully modest restrictions on government support for abortion, and said the military should be open to gays. He was hardening the lines. In words that have been frequently quoted back to me since then, I remarked to friends, "Mark my words. We are watching a man stumbling through the rubble of a ruined presidency." Nobody could know all the ways he would stumble, nor how sordid the rubble would be, but the impending ruin, I believe, was evident from the beginning.

The Clinton news conference took place on the anniversary of the *Roe v. Wade* decision, the very day that tens of thousands were marching in the streets of Washington to give life a chance. There was nothing in Clinton's words about his famous propensity for feeling their pain, nor even the slightest gesture of ambivalence about abortion. Completely absent was any reference to a "new covenant," or reaching out to create a "national conversation" about who we are and intend to be. For Clinton, it seemed, the thousands of marchers, and the majority of Americans who are morally troubled by abortion, did not exist. His commitment to "reproductive rights" was adamant. It is the only promise that he was to keep.

Mendacity has been the chief mark of this presidency. His friends and political allies have said that he is a remarkably good liar. Obviously, that is not true. A good liar does not have a reputation for being a good liar. After meeting with Clinton early in the presidency, my colleague James Nuechterlein described him as "serially sincere." Clinton seems to be persuaded, it is observed, that he really means whatever he is saying at the time. I don't know if that is true. Did he believe what he was saying when, in January 1998, he told the American people he had never had sexual relations with Miss Lewinsky? Perhaps it is true that he did, depending on what the meaning of "is" is.

But what does this tell us about "the character of the American people"? After all, they elected him, and did so twice. Not by a majority, to be sure, but by enough to secure his claim to the office. The failure of the political process to remove him from office has been turned by some into an indictment of the character of the American people. The people, we are told, got the President that they deserved. In 1976 Jimmy Carter campaigned by promising America a government as good as its people. Now it is said that America has a government, or at least a president, as bad as its people. That, I believe, is a conclusion not to be lightly accepted.

A most doleful conclusion about the American character was announced by Paul Weyrich, President of the Free Congress Foundation, on February 16, 1999, and has been the subject of widespread commentary.[2] Weyrich is an old warhorse of conservative causes, and in the late seventies he was the one who suggested to Jerry Falwell the name "moral majority." Now he has concluded that it was all a dreadful mistake. "What Americans would have found absolutely intolerable only a few years ago, a majority now not only tolerates but celebrates." Until now, he says, "we have assumed that a majority of Americans basically agrees with our point of view." "I no longer believe that there is a moral majority. I do not believe that a majority of Americans actually shares our values."[3] Politics had failed, Weyrich suggested, and it was time to withdraw from the public square.

To the extent that Weyrich and others are issuing a caution against the dangers of politicizing religion and are underscoring the limits of what can be achieved through politics, their statements should be welcomed. But it is more than that. Their position reflects a painful deflation of political expectations that can only be explained by a prior and thoroughly unwarranted inflation. In addition, it purports to know much too much about the character of the American people.

In October 1998, Andrew Sullivan offered one liberal reading of what the Clinton affair had revealed about conservatism. In a *New York Times Magazine* article, "Going Down Screaming," he depicted conservatives as embracing a neo-Puritanism that increasingly rails against a decadent culture.[4] *First Things*, he said, is "the spiritual nerve center" of a new conservatism of "moral righteousness" (he meant self-righteousness, of course) that sounds increasingly like a twisted replay of the radicalism of the sixties. Alan Wolfe, a sociologist then at Boston University, directed interviews of two hundred suburbanites and concluded in *One Nation, After All* that America is a country of more or less happy liberals. He, too, has had fun with Weyrich and those making similar claims, noting the similarity with sixties radicalism, and suggesting that we may be witnessing the breakup of the alliance between economic conservatives and the "moral regulators" in the Republican Party.[5]

Sullivan and Wolfe illustrate the uses to which some put what they took to be conservative despair of the American character. Writing in the *Wall Street Journal*, Paul Gigot challenged this conservative reading of the American character:

> Conservatives used to understand that all political change is slow, that in fact it ought to be slow, and that the task of political persuasion is never

done. Russell Kirk, who forgot more about American culture than Mr. Weyrich remembers, liked to say that "There are no lost causes because there are no gained causes." Conservatives can't save America by becoming anti-American.[6]

(Actually, it is Kirk quoting T. S. Eliot, but the point stands.) Similar arguments were made within the worlds of evangelical Protestantism. Charles Colson, for instance, writing in the mainline evangelical publication, *Christianity Today,* urged that this was no time to withdraw, that the tide of the culture war was turning in a direction favorable to the causes cherished by evangelicals.[7]

Among conservative heavyweights, few carry more weight than William J. Bennett. Seven months into the Monica Lewinsky phase of the continuing chronicles of the Clinton scandal, he published *The Death of Outrage: Bill Clinton and the Assault on American Ideals.* The book is an exemplary instance of the venerable genre of the jeremiad, made more effective by his fair-minded statement of opposing arguments. Bennett's conclusions, however, offer naught for our comfort.

> What explains this seeming public indifference toward, and even acceptance of, the President's scandals? The explanations most often put forth include very good economic times; scandal fatigue; the fact that a tawdry sexual relationship makes people queasy; the President's hyperaggressive, relentless, and effective spin team; the inclination to withhold judgment until more facts are known or give the President the benefit of the doubt; the fact that there are few leaders in any realm (religious, business, and the academy among them) who have articulated the case against the President; and the fact that Republican leadership—the Loyal Opposition—has been quiescent and inconsistent in its comments about the Clinton scandal, apparently afraid of voter backlash. These are plausible explanations. And still. I cannot shake the thought that the widespread loss of outrage against this President's misconduct tells us something fundamentally important about our condition. Our commitment to long-standing ideals has been enervated. We desperately need to recover them, and soon. They are under assault.[8]

Seven months later, after the impeachment and Senate acquittal, Bill Bennett publicly opined that he had been forced to the conclusion that his most doleful analysis had been vindicated, that he had for years been wrong about the American people, that maybe he was simply out of touch. In a *Wall Street Journal* article he reviewed again the arguments offered to exculpate the American people, and he found them wanting.

"These wishful assertions do not square with reality," he said. Restating the articles of indictment against a nation that had lost its capacity for outrage, he wrote, "These are unpleasant things to realize. But it is the way things are, and it is always better to accept reality than merely wish it away. . . . There is no escaping the fact that Bill Clinton's Year of Lies— told and retold, not believed but accepted—has been an ignoble moment for a great people."[9]

Many blamed the year of horrors on the media. The media made us do it. That was the suggestion of Lewis Lapham, the editor of *Harper's*, for example. His wrap-up reflection was portentously titled "Exorcism," and he began with the line from *Troilus and Cressida:* "Take but degree away, untune that string. And, hark, what discord follows!"[10] The electronic media, said Lapham, have untuned the string of public reason. Citing Marshall McLuhan as his authority, Lapham asserted that the habits of mind derived from the electronic media have deconstructed the texts of civilization founded on the print media, which led him to the thought that "maybe the argument at the root of the impeachment trial was epistemological, not moral."[11]

Lapham seemed to be not entirely without sympathy for the congressional Republicans who "objected to the society's order of value and wished to overturn it."[12] But in the kingdom of the camera and celebrity, it is simply too late for that. Since they couldn't impeach the electronic culture, it is understandable that conservatives turned on Clinton. "Who better to bear the blame for everything else that has gone so badly wrong in the once happy land of Christian print?"[13] Many commentators on the Clinton affair, on both the left and right, came back to the supposedly omnipotent media. Against that explanation, it was pointed out that the yellow and feverishly partisan papers of a century ago were hardly more conducive to calm deliberation. But the news came more slowly then, and the positions advocated, no matter how partisan, had a modicum of continuity.

Yet the electronic media are not omnipotent, and we let ourselves off the hook by thinking otherwise. Were it up to the television networks— and almost all the prestige print media, for that matter—many things would have been very different in recent history; for instance, Reagan and Bush would never have been President, we would not have prevailed in the Cold War, there would certainly be no prolife movement, and Clinton would not have been impeached in the first place. Whatever the forces at work, it will not do to say that the media made us do it.

Many commentators spoke of the Clinton affair having created a sleazy subculture that transfixed the public. A more apt image is that of people watching with fascinated disgust as an unstoppable toilet backed up into their living room. There are those who know such things should not happen, and even plumbers who used to fix matters when they did. The *New York Times,* for instance, the old gray lady of public rectitude. But that was a long time ago. For some years now she has been telling us to get used to the backup—in the form of transgressive art, obscenity as free speech, gay sex, and, of course, the unlimited license to kill unborn children. But the Clinton eruption momentarily startled her into sobriety. She had some very severe things to say about his behavior. An editorial of September 12, 1998, declared that, until the Starr report, "no citizen—indeed, perhaps no member of his own family—could have grasped the completeness of President Clinton's mendacity or the magnitude of his recklessness."[14] Clinton will be remembered "for the tawdriness of his tastes and conduct" and for producing "a crisis of surreal complexity."[15] Then, most ominously, "A President without public respect or congressional support cannot last."[16]

Yet when it came to the crunch point of impeachment and conviction, the *Times* and others took FDR's tack: "He may be an S.O.B., but he's our S.O.B." From 1992 on, journalists were in on Clinton's game; they saw the wink and the nudge, and entertained one another with the feats of their man, "Slick Willy." Then, quite abruptly, in January 1998, they became the game, and they were furious. Not furious enough, however, to abandon their S.O.B. Most were prepared to circle the wagons against the attacking neo-Puritans, while letting Clinton know in no uncertain terms that they were not at all happy about his forcing them to defend the indefensible.

Others seemed to relish the call to battle on Clinton's behalf. At impeachment time, artists and intellectuals rallied at New York University. The persecution of Clinton had "all the legitimacy of a coup d'etat," said novelist E. L. Doctorow.[17] Toni Morrison, Elie Wiesel, Arthur Miller, Arthur Schlesinger, Jr., and hundreds of others cheered. "Vietnam is almost the last moment I can think of until now when intellectuals, writers, and artists have really raised their voices in a chorus of protests," said novelist William Styron. Happy days are here again. "There's the smell of brimstone in the air," warned legal philosopher Ronald Dworkin, sending a frisson of terror through the crowd. Todd Gitlin, loyal archivist of radicalisms past, opined, "For years, the intellectual left has been deeply divided over identity politics. Here's an issue on which they can agree, and there's relief."[18]

Harvard's Alan Dershowitz had his own distinctive contribution to the solemn process of public deliberation:

> A vote against impeachment is not a vote for Bill Clinton. It is a vote against bigotry. It's a vote against fundamentalism. It's a vote against anti-environmentalism. It's a vote against the right-to-life movement. It's a vote against the radical right. This is truly the first battle in a great culture war. And if this President is impeached, it will be a great victory for the forces of evil—evil—genuine evil.[19]

No matter what he had done, it was either Bill Clinton or the Fascists.

"Where is the outrage?" asked Bob Dole in 1996.[20] It was there. But it was outshouted by the outrage directed against those outraged by Bill Clinton. The loudest shouters with the biggest bullhorns were in his corner. The winners of Nobel and Pulitzer prizes rally at NYU, not in Colorado Springs, Colorado. They have nothing but contempt for what the *Times* calls the "process of public deliberation." How could you trust a public that includes millions upon millions, perhaps even a majority, of conservatives? They elected Reagan, didn't they? There's no telling what they would do next time, given half a chance.

Polling data, of course, played a large role throughout the affair. "Approval ratings" were often confused with the sentiment that he should not be thrown out of office, a sentiment shared by some notable anti-Clinton conservatives who thought removal from office would be dangerously disruptive for the country. But even if the so-called approval rating was cut in half, what were those who held him in contempt supposed to do? Storm the White House and throw him out physically? Anyway, as Dale Bumpers might have said, it was only a matter of months before his term expired. Plus, storming buildings and disrupting meetings is not what conservatives ordinarily do.

As to what "the American People" really think, the American people have been and, God willing, will be around for a long time. They are not instantiated in responses to a telephone poll that interrupted the watching of a basketball game, or by a question asked as they're leaving the mall. Yes, it is objected, but the polls are generally accurate about many things, such as predicting who people will vote for. Good for the polls. What does that have to do with what people think about marital fidelity, adultery, lying under oath, rape, and the meaning of "high crimes and misdemeanors"? About some of these things people think very deeply in ways that cannot be caught by a polling question; about others they have not thought at all, which does not prevent them from having a "response" to be registered.

It is not true that the American people "knew what they were getting" when they elected Clinton in 1992 and again in 1996. Richard Cohen of the *Washington Post* again: "Here is a President who has been like no other. If I told you three years ago—even two years ago—that the President was having sex in the Oval Office with a young intern, you would not have believed me. In fact, I would not have believed it myself. The rumors, I thought, were the work of his worst enemies—crazies, mentally unstable."[21] And so with sex-stained dresses, and keeping Yassir Arafat waiting or chatting with Congressmen on the phone while being serviced by Monica. And now the allegation of rape. If he had reported such things, says Cohen, "You would have called me deranged, a perverted pundit. No one does that." Yet it all happened. "You can look any of this up. But you could not make any of this up."[22] Of course there was earlier evidence of Clinton's moral delinquencies, but it is not to the discredit of the minority of Americans who voted for him that they wanted to give him the benefit of the doubt. They turned out to be wrong, of course. They did not know what they were getting.

### Pulpit Prophecy and Pandering

A question persistently asked through all this, especially by Clinton opponents, was, "Where are the voices of religious leadership?" I was asked that again and again, and was a little puzzled about what people expected from religious leaders. They apparently thought clergy should be leading the outcry against presidential perfidy, issuing jeremiads that rattled the rafters and brought the miscreant to book. Most clergy likely thought it was not their business to prescribe what ought to be done about the prodigal President; that was a job for the politicians.

An important factor in the relative absence of clerical expressions of outrage is that there was no real public dispute about the gross immorality of what Clinton had done. It was not necessary to call in moral experts to certify that his behavior was outrageous. Even many of his sycophants were outspoken in deploring his shamelessness, recklessness, infidelity, habitual mendacity, and related moral deficiencies. The question of what was to be done about it quickly became a political and legal matter. Part of the political equation was to determine whether Clinton was appropriately contrite, at which point the clergy were invited in to certify the state of his soul.

Many religious figures expressed doubts about Clinton's contrition. After his disastrous televised "apology" of August 17, 1998, Clinton convened a clutch of clerics in the White House to testify to his being truly sorry. The National Association of Evangelicals declined the invitation, explaining:

> NAE leadership decided no representative would attend the breakfast because there would not be an opportunity to express a prophetic voice. The paradigm of the Old Testament prophets was that they went to the palace to speak God's word to the King with a call to repentance. . . . NAE did not relish the distinct possibility that it would be considered by the media as part of the President's "amen corner."[23]

Religious publications, for the most part, pulled their punches. The liberal *Christian Century* fretted about the quality of his contrition; the evangelical mainline *Christianity Today* said Clinton's actions had "rendered this Administration morally unable to lead,"[24] but stopped short of calling for resignation or removal; *America*, the Jesuit weekly, was in Clinton's corner and expressed satisfaction that the bishops had remained largely silent during the entire affair. In September, Bishop Anthony Pilla, then President of the National Conference of Catholic Bishops, said it was up to the constitutional process to determine the proper response to what Clinton had done.[25]

Already by October 1998, the heads of the Southern Baptist Convention, the Reformed Church in America, and other denominational leaders, including some liberal Methodist bishops, had publicly called on Clinton to resign. On October 9, a most respectful letter to Clinton signed by hundreds of religious leaders and coordinated by the Institute on Religion and Democracy calmly laid out the reasons why he should resign. In sum, hundreds if not thousands of clergy of some national prominence publicly called for resignation or removal. This received almost no attention in the media and, of course, no response from the White House.

Resignation was, literally, unthinkable. All those who were thinking about it apparently did not exist in Bill Clinton's mind. In an interview on March 31, 1999, Dan Rather asked the President on *60 Minutes II*:

> "Did you ever consider resigning?"
> "Never."

"Never for a second?"

"Never, not a second, never, never."

"Never entered your mind?"

"Never entered my mind. . . . I wouldn't do that to the Constitution. I wouldn't do that to the presidency. I wouldn't do that to the history of this country."

Clinton went on to say that he was honored to have had an opportunity to defend the Constitution and to teach morality to America's children, but he also bore no grudges against his persecutors. "I realized that particularly in the last year, if I wanted people to give me forgiveness, I had to extend forgiveness. . . . And I have worked very hard at it. I have had very powerful examples. I look at a man like Nelson Mandela who suffered enormously." And so forth. This takes the breath away. It is crazily Christian in a surreal way, a moral jujitsu whereby he is more sinned against than sinner, but is prepared to forgive those who tried to hold him accountable for what he did. "Forgive them their trespasses as we forgive ours."

## Judgment Day

In December 1998, more than two hundred university and seminary teachers of religion signed a "Declaration Concerning Religion, Ethics, and the Crisis in the Clinton Presidency." This became the basis of a book, *Judgment Day at the White House*, edited by Gabriel Fackre of Andover Newton, that will be an invaluable document for the study of this period.[26] The declaration and most of the essayists did not explicitly call for Clinton's removal, but did offer incisive criticism of the political manipulation of Christian themes of contrition and forgiveness. Of particular interest is an essay by Edward P. Wimberly of the Interdenominational Theological Center, Atlanta, from the viewpoint of "African-American pastoral theology." The overwhelming black support for Clinton, he observes, is similar to the pattern of "settling" among black women. That is, they don't expect much from a man and are glad to settle for what they can get. The "almost unanimous" support for Clinton, Wimberly says, is reinforced by his sharing "a small-town, folksy, rural style with black preachers and Southern white politicians."[27] Nor does it hurt that he, too, depicts himself as a victim. He may be an S.O.B., but . . .

*Judgment Day* reprints a notable essay by Shelby Steele of Stanford University, "Baby-Boom Virtue," which is, I believe, helpful in understanding the moral confusions surrounding the Clinton debacle. His generation, says Steele, won its rebellion against parents who defined virtue in terms of personal responsibility, largely in the sphere of family, work, and religion. The boomers subscribe to "virtue-by-identification." It is a matter of identifying with the right causes and with those who identify with the right causes. "But iconography of this sort," Steele writes,

> is even more effective in its negative mode. Because it represents virtue, it also licenses demonization. Those who do not identify are not simply wrong; they are against virtue and therefore evil. Any politics of virtue is also a politics of demonization, and this has been a boomer specialty since the 1960s. . . . We could not have had a Bill Clinton without the generational corruption that allowed virtue to be achieved through mere identification.[28]

Generational generalizations such as Steele's are suggestive, but I continue to be disinclined to blame Bill Clinton or the failure to remove him from office on the American people, or even on the boomer generation. The liberal claim that conservatives in their disappointment have turned anti-American does not, Paul Weyrich and a few others notwithstanding, bear close examination. The January 1999 issue of *Commentary* asked seventeen prominent conservative thinkers whether, "read as a barometer of the national temper," the November elections and the reaction to the Clinton scandal tell us much about America. Among the questions asked was this: "What is your own sense of where, on moral matters, the public stands?" Six (including William Bennett) thought we had received bad news about the American character, one was undecided, and the ten others put the blame elsewhere, mainly on the ineptitude of Republican leaders. A month later, the *Weekly Standard* ran a similar symposium with twenty-one participants (two overlapping with the *Commentary* symposium) and the blame-America count, as I read it, was no more than five out of twenty-one.

Bennett, Weyrich, Kimball, Gertrude Himmelfarb, and a good many others have drawn such doleful conclusions, but I am not persuaded. So what have we learned from all this? One thing we have learned is what might happen if we had an MTV President. We never had one before. The political philosopher Leo Strauss liked to say that the American system was built on foundations that are low but solid. The Clinton presidency was built on foundations that are low and sordid. For all his successes in life, it seems that Bill Clinton as a person never rose above his origins. That is a difficult subject not untouched by the delicate question of class, but the fact is that Clinton plays to the pit.

Like none who held the office before him, the MTV President has exulted in playing to the pit in a populism not of policy but of appetite. In an orchestrated slander against a woman on whom Clinton tried to force himself, and with whom he later settled out of court for a huge sum, a Clinton media lackey spoke of the trash that turns up when you trawl money through a trailer park. It is a fitting image of this presidency, and the trailer park is not just Arkansas, for every state and every community has a subculture that wallows in being pandered to, even as the panderer wallows in their gratitude for his being one of them.

Again, the approval ratings during that period should be viewed with robust skepticism. A strong case can be made that they reflect feminists and those intimidated by them, for whom the only issue is abortion; diehard liberal Democrats and leftists on the commanding heights of culture for whom conservatism is pure evil; big labor, especially in education and other parts of the public sector, for whom the alternative to Clinton is catastrophe; and blacks who are pitiably grateful for the assurance that Master feels their pain. Add in the very large number of sensible Americans who found the whole thing repugnant and just wanted it to go away, plus those who feared that removal from office would dangerously destabilize the country and the economy, and one ended up with those high "approval" ratings.

What happened beginning in January 1998 does not tell us much that is worth knowing about "the American people." The fact is that nothing like this has happened to us before. If it is allowed to happen again anytime soon, we might have to reconsider the dark ponderings about the American character that have gained such currency. The most hopeful thought is that enough Americans have learned from this experience never again to entrust the presidency to a person of such reckless habits and suspect character. But that hope comes with no guarantee.

Meanwhile, we have a president who is guilty of perjury, witness tampering, the obstruction of justice, and sexual predation, including, it seems, at least one alleged rape. Quite likely there will be more unsettling disclosures about the man and his presidency. But, in what was presented as the clinching argument of his loyalists during the impeachment trial, Bill Clinton will soon be gone in any case. Until somebody comes up with a better idea, the course of wisdom is to pray for the nation while averting our eyes as much as public duty permits from the sorry spectacle of a man stumbling through the rubble of what remains of a ruined presidency.

NOTES

1. R. W. Apple, Jr., "Clinton Defense Concludes by Weighing Admitted Sins against Good of Nation," *New York Times,* January 22, 1999, A06.

2. Paul Weyrich, Free Congress Foundation letter, February 16, 1999 (mailed to several hundred conservatives around the country). See, e.g., Ron Fournier, "Conservatives Sees U.S. Cultural War," *AP Online,* February 16, 1999. See also Craig Gilbert, "As a Top Conservative Cries Defeat, His Colleagues Disagree: Weyrich Provokes a Storm with His Declaration that the 'Culture War' is Lost," *Milwaukee Journal Sentinel,* February 28, 1999, 6, in which Weyrich is quoted as saying that the culture has suffered a collapse of "historic proportions."

3. Weyrich, Free Congress Foundation letter, February 16, 1999.

4. Andrew Sullivan, "Going Down Screaming," *New York Times Magazine,* October 11, 1998, section 6, 2.

5. See Alan Wolfe, *One Nation, After All: What Middle Class Americans Really Think about God, Country, Family, Racism, Welfare, Immigration, Homosexuality, Work, the Right, the Left, and Each Other* (New York: Viking, 1998).

6. Paul A. Gigot, "New Right Now Sounds Like Old Left," *Wall Street Journal,* February 19, 1999, A18.

7. Charles Colson, "The Sky Isn't Falling," *Christianity Today,* vol. 43, issue 1 (January 11, 1999): 104.

8. William J. Bennett, *The Death of Outrage: Bill Clinton and the Assault on American Ideals* (New York: Free Press, 1998).

9. William J. Bennett, "What We've Learned," *Wall Street Journal,* February 10, 1999, A22.

10. Lewis H. Lapham, "Exorcism," *Harper's Magazine,* March 1, 1999, 12.

11. Lapham, "Exorcism."

12. Lapham, "Exorcism."

13. Lapham, "Exorcism."

14. See Editorial, "Shame at the White House," *New York Times,* September 12, 1998, A1.

15. "Shame at the White House."

16. "Shame at the White House."

17. Ronald Radosh, "Bring on the Impeachment Squeeze," *Newsday,* December 20, 1998, B05.

18. Quotes cited in this portion of the essay are from speakers at a rally held at New York University Law School, organized by Americans against Impeachment. See, e.g., Patricia Cohen, "To the Barricades, 25 Years Later," *New York Times,* December 19, 1998, D1; Bret Louis Stephens, "The Impeachment of William Jefferson Clinton: . . . While His Supporters Blame 'Swiny People,'" *Wall Street Journal,* December 16, 1998, A22.

19. See Rally at New York University Law School; see also David Gelernter, "Why Impeachment Drives 'Em Nuts," *New York Post*, December 31, 1998, 33 (similarly quoting Dershowitz in an appearance on *Geraldo Rivera*).

20. See, e.g., Bill Thompson, "Hello? Anybody Home Here?" *Cleveland Plain Dealer*, November 2, 1996, B11.

21. Richard Cohen, "The Untouchables," *Washington Post*, February 23, 1999, A19.

22. Cohen, "The Untouchables."

23. Mark Tooley, "Pro-Clinton Clergy Won't Play Nathan to Bill's David," noting that leaders of the National Association of Evangelicals shunned a White House meeting to avoid appearing supportive of Clinton. *Insight*, vol. 14, issue 37 (October 12, 1998): 28.

24. Editorial, "The Prodigal President," *Christianity Today*, vol. 42, no. 11 (October 5, 1998): 36.

25. Catholic and other responses, *Catholic Trends*, September 19, 1998.

26. Gabriel J. Fackre, ed., *Judgment Day at the White House: A Critical Declaration Exploring Moral Issues and the Political Use and Abuse of Religion* (Grand Rapids, Mich.: W. B. Eerdmans, 1999).

27. Edward P. Wimberly, "African-American Pastoral Theology," in Fackre, *Judgment Day at the White House.*

28. See Shelby Steele, "Baby-Boom Virtue: Public Positions Matter More than Private Ones," *Wall Street Journal*, September 25, 1998 (page references not available online).

# Chapter 20

# The Clinton Scandal
## *Law and Morals*

## *David Novak*

The Clinton scandal is supposed to have been an event that shows the essential difference between conservatives and liberals in the United States, especially their different views of the relation between law and morals. All conservatives are supposed to have been in favor of the impeachment of President Clinton because of his affair with Monica Lewinsky and his subsequent lying about it under official interrogation. For them, it seems Bill Clinton's conduct constitutes a "high crime and misdemeanor," calling for nothing less than removal from office by law (and further prosecution as a private citizen). Liberals, conversely, are supposed to have been opposed to President Clinton's impeachment because his affair with Miss Lewinsky was only a private indiscretion, and even his cover-up was only an individual fault, but neither the "high crime" nor the "misdemeanor" that the Founders had in mind as grounds for the official removal of the President of the United States from office. Whereas "Mr. Clinton" may have committed a minor sin, "President Clinton" certainly did not commit a major crime. Bill Clinton's trial, for both sides, was supposed to be either a victory or a defeat. And the victory or defeat was supposed to be a moral one.

In fact, though, the trial provided no moral victory or defeat for anyone at all. It seems to have been only a political defeat for conservatives. Unlike the great trials in history that did provide significant moral victories and defeats, this trial only showed once again the amazing good luck of Bill Clinton to survive moral and legal assaults designed to finish him off politically once and for all.

The trial did show another political fact: all conservatives were not in favor of Clinton's removal from office by means of a trial. Since more Americans consider themselves conservatives than liberals (thus we have the pejorative "L" word, but not an equally pejorative "C" word in current political rhetoric), if all or even a large majority of conservative Americans had really agreed with the self-appointed spokesmen of American conservatism in the Republican Party, this would probably have swayed enough Democratic Senators to have joined their Republican colleagues in the successful removal of Bill Clinton from the presidency.

I am one of those conservatives who did not and does not (and probably will not) follow the leadership of the Republican Party, especially in calling for President Clinton's political death. And I do not think I am unique in this respect. In my view, these Republicans have a poor conservative philosophy, and they have a poor grasp of the moral beliefs of most Americans. This poor combination turned the whole Clinton affair into a political boomerang for the Republicans and, by implication, for all conservatives who are assumed to be Republicans themselves. At the level of the most basic public opinion, for example, many Americans sympathized with Bill Clinton as the object of a political witch-hunt, and regarded Ken Starr as someone like Inspector Javert pursuing Jean Valjean in Victor Hugo's *Les Miserables*. In other words, the punishment seemed to be way out of proportion to the crime. The pursuit of Clinton seemed to be an act of political vengeance for his undeserved popularity with the American people.

In spite of the philosophical irrelevancy of the Clinton trial (and all it involved), there are indeed fundamental philosophical differences between conservatives and liberals about the very nature of civil society (of which the government is not the only institution, but only the most official one). Nevertheless, the basic triviality of the whole Clinton affair makes its trial an unworthy locus for the airing of philosophical differences. They deserve something more than what most Americans regarded as a soap opera. (James Carville, the Democratic Party strategist, was probably right when he said that most Americans were convinced that the whole thing was about sex.) As such, let this brief reflection of mine be an occasion for this conservative to at least try to spell out what one of these fundamental differences between conservatives and liberals *really* is, and why the Clinton trial seriously obfuscated it rather than clarifying it. Indeed, this obfuscation has been politically significant despite the trial itself being quite trivial, even comical. Most people seem to think it was a waste of public time and money, and that it embarrassed the United

States government, maybe even the whole American people, before the world. Conservatives should have picked a better fight through which to make their philosophical case. So, what were the errors of the conservatives, and what can we learn from them?

The first error is that too many conservatives see *the* fundamental difference between themselves and the liberals to be that conservatives affirm a moral foundation for politics and law, while the liberals deny any such foundation at all. This leads them to assert that they are moral whereas their liberal opponents are amoral. Accordingly, they see themselves as affirming "right over might" in general, whereas their liberal foes have no moral foundation at all for their political and legal positions and, thus, they only act to increase their own personal power and pleasure. These conservatives usually see Bill (and Hillary) Clinton as the prime example of such an amoral liberal. And whereas a merely "immoral" person can be redeemed and restored to his or her position in society after proper penalty and penance, an amoral person is deemed beyond redemption, being somebody from whom society must be ever protected by means of his or her permanent banishment. This, of course, turns the trial of Clinton into a sort of public expiation. His demise would now finally atone for the American sin of electing a man like him to the presidency in the first place. And lest this moralism, even the demonization of the political opposition, be thought to be the error of conservatives alone, let us not forget what the liberals did to Robert Bork.

This approach to the conservative-liberal divide is not only untrue, it is dangerous for its capacity to destroy occasions for rational moral debate in a democratic society. It is untrue because all political and legal debates (except, perhaps, those dealing with legal technicalities) are moral debates, that is, they are clashes between rival moral visions. Therefore, these rival visions should have enough of a general commitment to rational persuasion, *within which* they have the possibility of persuading others of the rational superiority of their specific moral vision. Optimally, those others are one's own moral opponents; more realistically, however, those others are the large number of people who are at present undecided about where they ought to stand on many major moral issues. Accordingly, a constitutional democracy should be a rationally constituted society, however irrationally its citizens and officials often speak and act.

As for this conservative view of liberals, it is well to remember that Plato showed long ago that even those who proclaim "might over right" do so due to their conviction that it is right to follow those whose power seems to make them wise and beneficent rulers of society (*Republic*, 339C). Thus it is dangerous for the state of democratic public discourse to brand one's political opponents "amoral," because such an accusation destroys the occasion for a rational exchange of ideas by banishing the group one ultimately wants to persuade or philosophically defeat. Without this respect for the most "other" of others, who are one's philosophical adversaries, political discourse cannot rise above the level of propaganda. The political health of democratic society requires the increase, not the decrease, of such occasions for reasoned dialogue whether in politics or law. In Clinton's case, the conservatives engaged in legalistic overkill, which many regarded as mean-spirited, irrational, and undemocratic.

Conservatives of all stripes have been ready to condemn Mr. Clinton because they (we) believe that the personal morality of all citizens, and especially that of our officials, is a matter of public concern. Although personal virtue is no guarantee of political wisdom, it ought to be taken as a necessary condition thereof. In Mr. Clinton's case, his adulterous relationship with Miss Lewinsky, coupled with his admitted deception of Mrs. Clinton, should have led him to voluntarily resign his office, even before being confronted with the evidence by Mr. Starr. That would have been the honorable thing to do. But, as we all now know, Mr. Clinton is not an honorable man.

This is based on the conservative view that the social contract lying at the heart of constitutional democracy, from which our moral duty to obey the law of the state derives, can endure only when it is made and kept by persons who can be trusted to keep their word, a serious instance of which are their marriage vows. For conservatives, personal moral standards, which emanate from a higher source than their own desires and are ultimately enforced by that same source, are presupposed by the state and its law. Sometimes the state even enforces that morality, but even here it does not claim that morality as its own creation. Following these assumptions, conservatives insist that the personal moral conduct of leaders of the state be exemplary, and that these leaders not be exempted from them based on a notion that high political rank entails low moral privilege.

Liberals believe that personal morality is a matter of privacy, which should only be of concern to the private parties involved in any violation of it. Thus in the Clinton-Lewinsky case, the adultery they committed together should be of concern only to Mr. Clinton, Mrs. Clinton, and Miss Lewinsky—and whatever the source of their personal moralities there might be. Society, in its legal role, should be concerned with cases where someone has been harmed against his or her will. Based on this criterion, Mr. Clinton and Miss Lewinsky cannot claim any public adjudication of their dispute since both of them entered their relationship as consenting adults. Neither of them was coerced by the other. As for Mrs. Clinton, who has been involuntarily harmed by her husband's adultery (having been deceived and humiliated), public adjudication would only be appropriate if she were to exercise her right to sue him for divorce. However, since Mrs. Clinton has chosen not to exercise this right, but has chosen (at least legally) to "stand by her man," society cannot very well act on her behalf. In fact, many people believe that had Hillary Clinton chosen to divorce Bill Clinton at this time, public opinion would have been so sympathetic to her that it would have forced him to resign his office. Yet even if that had happened, many liberals would not have regarded a "messy divorce" and the reason for it as sufficient grounds for the public to legally remove a president from office. As for Bill Clinton's lying about the whole affair, many liberals excuse that on the grounds that his private life should never have been so minutely investigated in the first place.

The second political error of the Republican Party acting as a conservative party was to assume that a large majority of the American people agree with their view that the revelation of private vice is sufficient grounds for the most severe public condemnation of a public official possible. The fact seems to be, however, that many Americans believe that one's private life, especially when it involves sex between consenting adults, is not a matter of much public concern, if any at all. Bill Clinton understood that better than anyone when he presented Ken Starr (and Henry Hyde and his colleagues) as a fanatical invader of his privacy. Perhaps Clinton remembered how Richard Nixon, the last President driven from office, was so feared because he had invaded the privacy of citizens for the sake of his own political power. For Americans, privacy is so important that even the President can get a good deal of sympathy when his own privacy (in Clinton's case the privacy of the White House) seems to have been violated.

What this also shows is that the Republican Party is a marriage of temporary political convenience between two very different groups: one, social conservatives interested in more public regulation of personal morality; two, economic libertarians interested in less public regulation of capitalism. What brought these two groups together seems to be a nostalgia for an earlier time when personal, even private, morals were considered to be a matter of public concern, and economics a matter of individual initiative. Contemporary liberalism became the common enemy of this political marriage because it seems to have radically reversed the public-private balance. Now personal morality is left to individual initiative and economics is assigned to greater public scrutiny.

Nevertheless, the Clinton affair, especially, illustrates how the social conservatives have been coopted by the economic libertarians. Witness the success of the Republican Party in convincing many middle-class Americans (the moneyed upper class never needed any such convincing) that the government should be "gotten out of your business." In other words, the right to private property has been emphasized at the expense of the right of society to control the economy. However, the right to private property is part of a larger right to personal privacy per se. As such, the libertarian philosophy of individualism leads one to conclude that if the government does not belong in your business, it certainly does not belong in your bed—where many more people than those with much property to protect and maintain think one's most important business is really being conducted anyway. That explains why the uncritical subordination of many social conservatives to the economic libertarians in the Republican Party has led to many libertarian victories, but few if any conservative ones.

The defeat of the Republican attempt to unseat President Clinton demonstrates that the Republicans cannot successfully use a conservative issue like personal morality as a means to remove a democratically elected president from office. They will have to find another means for their ultimate vision of dismantling the liberal welfare state. Conservatives should learn from this defeat how the misuse of their moral vision for the political cause of the Republican Party might well lead to a further unraveling of the so-called "Reagan coalition." The libertarians had no good reason to be offended by Clinton's personal morality. And considering that the probusiness policies of his Administration are so similar to those of the Reagan and Bush Administrations, libertarians could hardly be very opposed to Clinton for economic reasons either.

The third error of conservatives shown by the Clinton affair is that they have misjudged the economic philosophy of their libertarian colleagues in the Republican Party. For libertarians, the reason for emphasizing the private character of economics is because everyone has a right to use and enjoy the work of his or her hands—or money. With this emphasis on the right to pleasure, it is no wonder that libertarians cannot be in favor of greater public control of personal (especially sexual) morality. Any expression of such favor could only be for the most instrumental reasons, namely, saying so to get the political support of social conservatives.

For conservatives, on the other hand, the purpose of the economic order is not the right to pleasure but the duty to work and build up the world. Coming out of biblically based traditions, the conservatives see work through individual initiative as being redemptive. God has assigned the earth to humans "to work it and to keep it" (Genesis 2:15). God "did not create the earth to be a wilderness but as a dwelling place did He form it" (Isaiah 45:18). Humans are to be God's partners in the creative development of the earth and its resources. As such, there is also a social interest in the economic order, namely, the public encouragement of hard work from which the society as a whole benefits. A work ethic requires a restrained personal life, which was shown so clearly in the social vision of our Puritan ancestors. (And that Puritan work ethic was not confined to our English ancestors alone.)

So the same society that seeks to limit private vice also seeks to expand private initiative in the area of work. Once the economic order is perceived to be for the sake of private pleasure (a society of consumers of wealth rather than one of creators of wealth), there is no essential connection between the economic order and the order of personal morality. Too many conservatives have forgotten how hedonistic the United States has become. Few of our ancestors would have regarded the purpose of their hard work to be the accumulation of enough money to enjoy a Caribbean cruise or a weekend in Las Vegas.

The task for conservatives after what can only be seen as the Clinton fiasco is to better understand the moral condition of the American people and to clarify their (our) philosophical principles for the sake of addressing that condition. The place to begin addressing that condition is the family. Indeed, conservative concern over the personal conduct of Bill Clinton centers around the compromise of his familial role as a husband, and by extension to his role as a father. (Hillary Clinton was certainly deceived and humiliated; Chelsea Clinton was certainly humiliated too, not to mention being given a frightening view of what kind of fidelity she might expect from a husband.) That is, Clinton's conduct offends our sense of family values. One then ought to connect a proper family morality to the political and economic health of society, that is, how it contributes to what almost everyone would consider to be the common good.

Liberals have a very bad time dealing with the family at all. For them, there seem to be lone individuals at one end (hence their obsession with the rights of individuals alone) and the state at the other end. The purpose of the state is to maximize conditions for the exercise of individual liberty (hence their obsession with the duties of society alone). But where does the family come into the picture? Is the family an individual matter? If so, why should liberals be so concerned these days about extending governmental control over the way individuals raise and educate their children? Is the family a public matter? If so, why should liberals be so concerned that private individuals be allowed to define any relationship they want to be "family"? This confusion often manifests itself in a confusion about the relation between law and morals. Is the family primarily a moral (which is for liberals a private) issue, or is the family a legal (which is for liberals the only public) issue?

Conservatives ought to see the relation between the private and public realms as a relation between families and society. Society can be seen as first the economic order and then the governmental order. Lone individuals need only be seen totally separate from their families for the purpose of the assignment of legal responsibility. (Thus children are not legally responsible for the crimes of their parents, for example.) People act primarily for the sake of their children, who are their future, and thereafter for the sake of bringing honor to their parents, who are their past. They want to be able to provide for their children, and they want their children to be proud of them because of their contribution to the overall common good of society. That is why familially motivated people are usually highly productive in the economic sphere. They want to build something for their children in the present and leave them something for their future as their parents left them something before.

This is quite evident when one looks at segments of the American population who are mired in what seems to be perpetual poverty. In many such cases, one sees several generations of dysfunctional families, especially families where the father has absented himself and has thus forsaken his responsibility to his children and their mother. And in fact, even in cases of wealth, we have seen the dissipation of great fortunes because of equally dysfunctional families. More often than not families break up because of adultery—or even incest. In both cases, society has suffered, economically and politically. Even at the level of youth crime, there is a much greater likelihood that a child coming from a one-parent home or a no-parent home will break the law and endanger others than will a child from a traditional two-parent home, that is, where the parents take joint responsibility for their child's upbringing by conducting an ordered and substantial family life. Indeed, Bill Clinton's dysfunctional childhood family life (especially having lost his natural father and having an abusive stepfather) might well have contributed to his own immoral behavior as a husband and as a role model for his daughter (as Hillary Clinton has publicly admitted).

Since strong family life makes such an important contribution to the economic and political health of society, in return society should do everything possible to encourage strong family life and, conversely, do everything possible to discourage the weakening or destruction of family life. This includes such things as making it possible for parents to educate their children the way they see fit, which means making the type of education that best develops their own family values economically feasible through school vouchers or tax credits. On the negative side, it means working to outlaw elective abortion, seeing it as the most serious form of child abuse being practiced today. That should be done either by overturning outright the *Roe v. Wade* Supreme Court decision of 1973, or by legislatively and legally whittling down the range of cases in which *Roe v. Wade* can be invoked as a precedent. When these programs are rationally conceived, and when they avoid demonizing of the opposition, they are worthy projects for conservatives, and they promise some degree of success. One should see the moral struggle of America as one between familial responsibility versus individualistic hedonism. Conservatives should try to tip the balance in favor of family over individualism. In many cases, in order to do this, we will have to break ranks with the economic libertarians who see the making of money as an end in itself rather than as an occasion for exercising social responsibility.

The problem with the political behavior of too many conservatives in the Clinton scandal is that they wasted their time in a public forum that had no chance of yielding any good results for conservatives—or for the nation as a whole. Because of this waste, conservatives have made it harder for ourselves to get a proper hearing in a public forum where we really do have the opportunity to present a higher moral vision of human being and society than the current *Zeitgeist*, one that might be listened to and not laughed at. In the case of the Clinton scandal, it is Bill Clinton and those like him who got the last laugh—at our expense.

# Part V

# The Political Is Personal

# Chapter 21

# The Spectacle and the Libertine

## David Kennedy

What was going on last year anyway?[1] Monica, Clinton, the Republicans: some kind of freight train through our collective life, massive, unavoidable, by turns exciting, gripping, and then gone, as suddenly as it had come. A year ago an interdisciplinary Monica festival like this would surely have convened a full house, and look at us now. The incandescent spotlight cast then on the chattering classes has been switched off, the cud chewers of the academy have returned to pasture.

I must say I've had a hard time figuring out just what cud to chew, chastened that our ephemeral pop-cultural phenomena should turn out to be, well, ephemeral and pop-cultural, resistant to the weight of interpretation and analysis. It all seemed very meaningful at the time, and I remain convinced that Monica was basically good for the country. But maybe the whole thing was simply very present, a thrilling presence, less a "distraction" from other pressing matters than the breaking through of sound, sight, and feeling onto an otherwise cloudy cultural and political surface.

There is no shortage of explanations, interpretations, and reactions to what happened, just as there was no shortage of commentary at the time. Take only the questions of politics and sex: the Clinton Impeachment retold as a story about the maneuvers of politicians in a legal regime, the Bill-Monica (Hillary) Affair as a story about the machinations of men and women in institutions and families, evaluated in every sort of social, moral, legal, and religious frame. People have attitudes about things like "What the nation's first impeachment trial in more than a century meant for our institutions." We get conclusions like "Congress did its duty," or "the presidency has been compromised," "the Republicans went too far," or "the Democrats will stop at nothing," or "someone politicized what is properly legal," or "legalized what is properly political," and so forth. And there are reassurances that, in the end, our institutions worked rather well, even as any number of reform proposals, from proportional representation to term limits, elbow their way onto the event's ample coattails. People have attitudes about things like whether Bill and Monica's adventure was or was not sexual harassment, or exploitative, or demeaning, or adulterous, attitudes which are every bit as nuanced as Bill's own analysis of whether it was "sex" at all. And there are reassurances that, in the end, the American people showed good sense about the whole thing, just as there are numerous proposals about what Bill and Monica—and for that matter Hillary and Linda and all the bit players—should, in fact, have done. Once it all got going, no one could move without stumbling into a tar pit of moral and political and legal interpretations.

In books like this, one can certainly revisit this terrain. I'm sure the event did (or, as some of our authors argued, did not) have one or another consequence of this sort, and there is nothing wrong with getting a bunch of academics together to try to sort it all out. But monumentalizing last year's experience into these molds loses a lot of wax. And it was great wax, even where it prefigured this meltdown into meaning—there is just something different about it before it turns to bronze.

In today's academic world, it has been the traditions of "cultural studies" which have held onto the wax most aggressively, resisting the pull of our most familiar interpretive machinery while simultaneously expanding its range. In cultural studies, the ephemeral, the low, the random, and the rote can all be grist in the mill of meaning. These broad historical-cultural readings do open things up, and the results can sparkle with wit and wisdom. But I am wary to turn Monica over to the mavens of cultural studies—their practices can be at once too earnest and too glib.

For all its zip and buzz, much of cultural studies today remains a redemptive practice—emphatic while looking down the microscope that these little things do *mean* something. Although we know that reading the surface can also efface it, there is gravitas in being savvy this way, reformatting the lofty and the base in the key of history, a world of mythical antecedents and hidden political effects. Somehow Culture already knew all this and now embraces all this, understands all things and, ultimately, judges all things. It is *pleasurable* to ask what it all means, for our "system," for our "Constitution," things which go up and down like stocks, and for which cultural studies might provide a helpful index, folding the speculation of yesterday's talking heads into the measured paragraphs and bright narratives of significance.

Robert Gordon suggests that we should think of the Clinton Scandal as an enormous populist deliberation about sex and politics and the Constitution, a sort of legislation from below. Expansive historical reading—legislation from, as, culture. He seems right—there *was* deliberation and most everyone participated and afterward we *had* legislated together, about adultery and phone sex, about the President and the Congress, about the media and the public will. More *was* going on than the operation of a separation of powers scheme, and it makes more sense to align last year with other great moments of popular legislation—prohibition perhaps, or withdrawal from Vietnam—than to see it merely as one more Constitutional Crisis or Impeachment Trial.

But last year was more intense and less certain than populist legislation. We might better line it up with Anita Hill and O. J. Simpson and Lindberg's Baby, with the Gulf War and Waco and the national election process, with Elian Gonzales and Mrs. Simpson and Sally Hemmings, with Louise Woodward, Tawana Brawley, the Death of Diana, or the Chicago Seven. The line to Monica runs through Oscar Wilde and Scopes, through the Rosenbergs and McCarthy and Watergate. These spectacles take more than an instant—an assassination, a moonshot—they seem to take deliberation and a narrative unfolding. These offer more than the catharsis of collective empathy or condemnation—this is not Dahmer or McVeigh, or even the Unabomber. For this sort of spectacle there needs to be debate, at best the intense enactment of debates at once dormant, even unspeakable, but unsettled.

When these events get going, the result is more than legislation. We feel a welling up of ambivalence, a flood of uncertainty and conflict. Many people feel an intense personal engagement with media images and issues of which they may have hardly been aware. These events multiply the scandalous—one thing seems outrageous to some people, to someone else it is something else which outrages, soon one's indifference to the other's outrage is outrageous, and so on, until the original scandal is lost under layers of reaction and failures to react. Much of cultural studies, much historical study—work like Gordon's—takes us into the heart of this second process. But even the best work leaches the ephemeral and the uncertain from our great public spectacles, ironing out the contradicted meanings which gave rise to this grand cultural legislative moment in the first place, off-loading the intensity we experienced. I was not surprised to learn that the very word "sincere" once meant without wax.

There were certainly big public spectacles like this before 1950, but we remember them only dimly, as a vague disturbance, a diversion, a footnote for

the vagaries of popular enthusiasm. Spectacles disappear from History, unless, like Dreyfus, they become connected with the Real Politics of the day.
Otherwise they are slowly replaced by depressions and wars, by presidents
and proclamations, judgments and legislation. Unless the historian means
to say, with a wink of surprise, amusement, irony, "*meanwhile* people were
preoccupied with this kind of thing." This forgetting is not surprising. Spectacles expend themselves into meaning. The social body smooths its feathers, tucks away the loose ends of our experience, fading the intensity and
ambivalence which first made it vivid. For last year's events, this is well un-
derway, the whole complex business reduced to an impeachment, a President, the Clinton Scandal. Efforts like ours here are less about remembering
than forgetting.

There is another side to cultural studies, however, which can ruffle up
the feathers again, often by leaning against our taking all this too seriously. This is the cultural studies which opposes meaning, stands against
interpretation, the cultural studies of irony and loopy calls for self-refer-
ence to innoculate against anyone thinking you're taking anything too seriously. Relax, chill, be happy, it's all just culture—and the word *just* does
an amazing work, brutally denying us the importance of our earnestness.
But this "just" is never just just. The cultural studies of the "just" offers
lots of flash, a babble of academic winks and nods accompanying, masking, counteracting the somber timbres one hears as new pieces are
chipped and fit into Culture or History. We wink because we know how
silly it all really is, how much of the real is really ritual, of the canny really
cliché. We wink at *their* folly—they think they are thinking, struggling,
seeking, when we know they are speaking the lines of a thousand plays,
novels, stories. "All the world's a stage" might itself be a cliché, but not
when we're the only ones who know it, when the actors go on thinking
they're real. It's so dear, so droll, when all they would have had to do is
take a few more literature courses, and they would have known too, and
none of this would have turned out quite this way. Would not have
turned out this way because, really, if sensible well-educated people like
us were out there on stage we know what we'd do—the right thing. This
last is the sound of the nod which follows the wink.

Let us set both cultural studies traditions to one side, both the muse
and the bemused. My own inclination is neither to drag Bill and Monica
into meaning, nor to push meaning aside, leaving it hidden and unspo-
ken—the knowing nod of what would have happened had they only
known what we all understand but needn't say. I mean the term "specta-

cle" to help resist a knowing celebration of the surface, as also an erudite plumbing of the depths. I want to keep it light, but not half-baked. The spectacle is surface, ceremony, culture, and cliché. But the fantasy that we'd escape all these roles once cast in them, that we could play Hamlet in the tabloids without being Hamlet, is just that.

Against the hidden convictions of the glib, I mean to foreground the intense and awkward feelings one has *in* spectacle. Role playing, when you do it, is more than an ironic gesture. In spectacle, there is something abject about our relations with one another. Sometimes the intensity itself is, at least retrospectively, a bit embarrassing—but even at the time, it feels odd to be so intensely present, alive, concerned, and at the same time see ourselves living forth what we recognize as a role. The spectacle offers less the experience of meaning making than the awkward, unsettling collective experience of cliché-being. And it's uncanny to feel both commitment and cliché.

You'll feel this better if we focus on Monica, returning her to the center of the story. Let's call it The Monica Scandal, the Monica Affair, Monicagate. Just say her name now—Monica. Monica Lewinsky. Monica Monica Monica. Saying her name aloud—try it in a restaurant these days—produces a weird feeling, somehow embarrassing, conjuring words like wallowing, obsession, unseemly, and sentiments like how-could-she, how-could-we. I want to hold that feeling, place a magnetic field around it, at once a bit giddy and childish, but also tawdry and uncertain.

What *was going on* last year anyway? What were we all *doing* exactly? Not just watching, certainly. Maybe peeping, peeping together, but more part of the action than that. Talking about Monica, all the time, reading the stories. Obsessively. All those facts—not just the blue dress and the cigar, but exactly what he said when she told him she needed to know if he cared, and how many minutes it took the first time, and how long they talked on the phone afterward. We had *views* on these things. I was on the shuttle from New York to Boston the day the Starr Report came out, and the scene was an ad for the *New York Times*, every passenger holding a copy aloft, avid about the finest print.

Is there a word for performing something together which is and is not a role, which loses track of the line between being and being a cliché? All surface, but not just surface? Could we call it sex? Or "spectacle." Let's place these grand media events in line with other liminal rituals, circumcision, initiation, graduation, marriage, orgasm. The spectacle can be very small-scale, like a summer camp talent contest we'd rather forget. Or perhaps like that show-and-tell at school when you brought altogether the wrong thing—or, more troubling still, when what you brought was, inexplicably, just exactly right and all the school was for a moment your stage . . . and then it was later at lunch, and you took it out of your satchel again so someone, probably not your best friend, could take one more look, maybe even asked you what it *meant*, and you really didn't know, and maybe you made something up, and everyone knew it hadn't been like that at all, and later still, on the walk home when you tried to make sense of these two moments, and you couldn't.

If you've been to a wedding or a circumcision or a fraternity hazing, if you've had sex, you know what I mean. Something happens, something big and connected and social—but there is also the mountain of absurd detail, the struggle against the risible, the weird particularities of *this* wedding. If you've been in a wedding, even gotten married, you will re-member the intensity of being for that minute *the one* who is getting married, even as you see yourself strangely turned into this other person, the *bride*, the *groom*. Look at the next wedding picture you see framed on someone's mantle, there is something embarrassing about having been—what, exactly—so *young*, so . . . neatly fit within the convention, or so ill at ease with it, or so idiosyncratic. In a way, you can't shake the feeling, you can buy the whole package and let the photographer lead you up the aisle or you can struggle to make each detail meaningfully your own, and you will have performed yourself into a wedding either way. It won't do to re-member the wedding as a commitment, a transition, a tradition—but we also can't dismiss it with a knowing wink and the suggestion that sensible people like us would know never to find ourselves there. To see the wed-ding as spectacle embraces heartily at once its intensity and its silliness, affirms it whole, while struggling not to be capsized by wake from the ocean liner of meaning it drags behind.

We need a better taxonomy of the spectacle, just how does it work? I am convinced the key lies less in the event than in our posture toward it. There *is* something here of the deliberative, something populist, ab-solutely. The spectacle can be read, lives do get rearranged—afterward these people are *married*, Monica is on television, Hillary is running for the Senate, Bill is entering into history. I've also heard people invoke tra-ditions of drag or camp as a posture toward the spectacle, to capture a confounding at once of meaning and identity. There *is* something here of drag, of not just watching, but performing, dressing up as oneself who is also something or someone else. A spectacular practice with consequences, a serious practice which expends itself into the spectacular. But just as the spectacular exceeds the deliberative, so it also demands more than the camp of the outsider, the ironist, the drag queen, the conscientious interpretation resister. I want a posture which affirms both what is and is not, which holds the itchy surface, the momentary, collective situation of performance, holds the leftover feelings, unseemly against the memory of all that intense involvement. When we look at the spectacle, then as now, when we adopt the posture toward it of spectacle, we can't help wondering how we got so carried away. Where was our cynical consciousness? What is it, exactly, to be carried away? To embody the form, to rise to the level of cliché.

Choreographer Mark Morris says something unique happens at a live performance, with live music, hard chairs, sweating bodies. You are all together and for a moment you all know that whatever is happening is really happening, now. He says this happens because you don't know what will happen, don't know more deeply than in the most absurdly unpredictable film. But watching a film is also an experience in real time, and even in real life we mostly do know what will happen. Apparently O. J. and the white Bronco changed network television, bringing home to everyone in the business what CNN had discovered: the power of poor production values, of live reporting, and the Right-Now story. But when you see the dramatic aerial shot, a white Bronco on a highway, it turns out you do know what will happen actually, and that is part of the riveting pleasure—you know the police will eventually catch the white Bronco and maybe someone will shoot someone and maybe they won't, and you have a prediction, probably a pretty good one. You are interested—you are in some way—because you know. If you looked at the decision rules (majority in the House, supermajority in the Senate) and the party configurations and the polls, you also knew what would happen in the impeachment trial. Knowing, predicting, interpreting was to be present. And even in dance, you know. You come into being as audience as this knowledge melts into the performance—they'll play music, some of it you will recognize, or know, or think you know, or play yourself, people will dance, you will, or will not, give yourself over to the piece, will or will not use the time wisely to reevaluate your to-do list. Of course someone *might* fall off the stage, just as O. J. might commit suicide, or Clinton might be impeached, but probably they won't.

As Walter Dickey pointed out, the longer the Monica Affair went on and the more intensely we became engaged with it, the more we found ourselves turning into talking heads, strangely aware that each of our most earnestly felt interpretations was but a line, that we were somehow being spoken to by the affair. Even, and perhaps especially, when we were at our most jaded and seen-it-all-before. Part of the unseemly residue arises here. The name Monica is madeleine to a feeling, but it is not she who disturbs. The sound of her name returns us to the posture of spectacle, to our collective realization that we have met the artificial, and it is us.

This feeling is not at all the contentment we feel when sagely reminded that Monica and Bill and the Republicans, followed at every step by the press, the commentators, and the public, trudged through the oldest scripts in the books. To know that it was all, after all, "just" culture comforts us. It leaves lying there the implication that all these players, ourselves included, *should* obviously have been doing something else, that we knew that then as we know it now. But what should they/we have been doing? Getting on with the nation's "real" business? Minding our own business? Expressing really original points of view, really new ideas and perspectives? Coming up with something really shocking? These are also staged things, mythical things, things performed in a lexicon.

Authenticity, the Real, the Avant-Garde. When we invoke them, we are promising a performance, or, better, performing a familiar promise. Even, I'm afraid, when the promise is staged on a field of pain and death. Or love. I remember a wonderful Quaker wedding in which everyone struggled to be moved to say what they really felt, including the bride and groom. No ceremony here, and yet, didn't it also sound vaguely familiar, a kind of homey Hallmark hodgepodge? And yet wasn't it also moving, not just vagary but vow?

Cultural studies of the earnest and the glib hardly exhaust the range of academic conventions for thinking about the spectacle. There is a whole world of demystification and critical narration, of alienation effects and personal testimonials. In their own way, these also comfort, gently separating the wheat of meaning from the chaff of display. We could say the spectacle is entertainment, an elaborate narcotic circus to placate the proles of the new Imperium, while down below, or backstage, the big boys do the really dirty work of power. We could say the spectacle performs a social function, persuading the people that everything else is real (when you know it's not really real). We could say the spectacle legitimates the state apparatus, persuading us that at least our institutions worked (when they really don't/didn't work). Or we could say the spectacle soothes us, lulls us into passivity by suggesting that in the middle of our meaningless consumer existence there is something real after all (when really there isn't, or this isn't). We could say the spectacle's very spectacularity reassures us that our own lives are truly lived. We Witness, therefore We Are (when really we are not). Or we could say that the spectacle, deliberative theater, teaches us that Politics "R" Us (when really they aren't). These are all fun stories to tell. We can stand outside, lamenting from the desert that Watergate is *not* a scandal, Campaign Finance is *not* a scandal, that Monica and O. J. are *not* important. *People*, we can implore, *it's all a delusion*. The real scandal is AIDS or poverty or simply your own narcotic stupor in front of the television. Wake Up America.

But the peculiarity of the spectacle lies neither in its escape from the script, nor in its escape into the script. The spectacle functions as a theater of affirmation among players who experience one another staged as real. In such moments we are not the each-one-unique snowflakes of the humanist imaginary, deluded into collective unconsciousness. The spectacle lets us lay down the pretense of individuation, or permits us to rise up and embody the promise of particularity, as a script, a type, a point of view. In the spectacle we enact for one another our deepest and most shallow roles—blow ourselves up into Michelangelo-sized cartoons, stretched across the Sistine ceiling of our imagination. We can be "law" to their politics, good sense to their carelessness. We can be "the people" and, for that moment, they can be "government," just as we can be "men" or "women" or "interns" or whatever. In the spectacle we experience the power and pleasure of the most expansive self-generalization, but we also know that we are just the boy who brought an antler back from Yellowstone to show the class, that they are just our classmates, the teacher just a nice lady playing at pedagogy.

In spectacle we are all somehow always already demystified, we know and don't know that this is all there is, this moment of loss is, in a word, as good as it gets. It is not surprising that in spectacle we judge one another's performance more firmly than their presence. Precisely not the attitude of our critical academic conventions, piercing the veil of performance to show us the real. We ask whether Clinton's contrition was well played, did he "sound" presidential, was Hillary convincing as Tammy Wynette, standing-by-her-man? Of course we are also intrigued to know what The President Is Really Like, and there was an entire second level of commentary here—what did Hillary Really Think, and so on. But this went on one tier below the theater of how-they-performed, like tabloid fascination with whether Matt Damon and Ben Affleck really are friends beneath more serious commentary on their performances and artistry. There is something scandalous in attention to the "real"—what did you really think about Monica, what does the scandal *really mean* for our Constitution? Far from redeeming our moment of giddy collective artificiality, these gestures steal its thunder. The real is an issue, not an alternative. A promise, a performance. It is somehow unseemly, base, to ask if Monica had an aftermath.

Thinking about the events of 1998 as spectacle keeps this experience before us, continuing the spectacle not simply as a diversionary shimmer, but as living terrain for enacting identities and competing over stakes and insisting on what we both want to be right and know as rite. Let us put the spectacle—all of us—in the same frame with our "analysis," let our posture now continue our posture then. For this, the spectacle offers a vocabulary, roles, positions—offered them then and offers them now. With Monica-Bill you can come into your own as a liberal centrist, feel nobly marginal, practice disdainful lines about the moral majority and then suddenly find yourself at the center of a mainstream chorus. You can think you were 1/3 and turn out to be 2/3, and you will give the whole thing a positive review, unless of course you preferred it over on the cultural edge. Just as you can think you were President and turn out to be Husband, and so forth. You can know and display yourself as the Christian Right, stand ready to assail the media, only to find in their sanctimonious judgments your only real echo. Disorienting, a bad feeling. Is this social legislation? Interpretation from different "points of view" duking it out over who gets in the history book? Yes, but also the making real of different identities, the intensification of being which comes when the wax firms the first time as a model. And knows itself as wax.

Being an internationalist, I thought I would say something about the foreign reaction to the whole thing. If you read around in the foreign press, you find all sorts of things. Recaps of savvy commentary from Washington, odd local preoccupations, restagings of classic arguments about America and the Rest of the World. Are we puritan or not? If they think we are and they're not, it sounds one way, where they think we're not and they are, it comes out another. Nations coming into being through mythic differentiations. My favorite foreign clipping was serious speculation in the Egyptian press about whether Monica was an Israeli agent sent to derail Clinton's efforts to pressure Israel on settlement with the Palestinians. Monica turns out to be an ink blot. Or, better, the spectacle pours us each out as blot for the other.

My favorite line in the Starr Report came in a footnote dangling just where it became clear that there was, actually, no evidence of a quid pro quo nexus between White House support for Monica's job search and her testimony about the affair. Still, the footnote told us, this remained terribly unfair to all the other interns who would not get such favorable letters of recommendation. You can just hear the indignant voice of someone coming into being as a recently graduated law clerk: impeach that man, he writes letters of recommendation which *are not based on the candidate's merit.*

That's the law clerk—but what about me? The Monica Spectacle brought and brings me into being as a Libertine. The Libertine is a role, a position, a set of lines, into which one can constitute oneself in relation to an audience. Here might be one: Monica did more for Libertinism than anyone since the Marquis de Sade. A senior colleague of mine put it to me less gently, before he trailed off, chuckling: "that woman did more for the blow job than . . ."

"Doing something" for Libertinism, or, I suppose, for the blow job, doesn't mean creating more favorable conditions under which appropriately serious national Libertine lobby groups can translate populist consensus about the scandal into real legislative accomplishments in Congress. Although I suppose it could. But Libertinism is not just a position about sex—it is also a position about government, about the centrality and seriousness of society's meaning machine, about what I have been calling the spectacular.

During the 1992 campaign a postcard appeared at gay bookshops and resorts depicting a beaming Bill and Al standing together with buff torsos and cutoffs, flies open just a suggestive bit. Bill has his thumb hitched in the pocket of his jeans, dogtags hang around his neck, his arm loops comfortably around Al's waist. The top. Sporting a string of beads, Al has his arm around Bill's shoulder and looks like the cat that ate the canary. It's a nice shot, very gay-friendly. Something anyone could identify with. Part of the allure is the feeling that Clinton and Gore wouldn't have minded the joke, might even have been kind of proud to be shown so buff. Something about the generational change of that election, something about their style, something about their embrace of the "gay vote." It was a spectacle, a coming into being of a generation.

I remember a hotel ballroom dinner with a thousand blue-chip gay donors to the first Clinton-Gore campaign—tear-jerking videos, smarmy speeches. The only camp table was a bunch of straight folk, queers coming into the spectacle as voters, citizens, potent sources of campaign cash. Serious articles about whether there were now more gays than Jews in key primary states. There is nothing wrong with trying to translate this feeling into legislation. I suppose, it's a feeling made to be monumentalized and lots of people tried. And we got "don't ask don't tell." And the Defense of Marriage Act. And the feeling, the feeling of coming in as out, was gone. Libertinism locks its fingers around that feeling—even if it is a bit tawdry and awkward, won't shoehorn properly into a party platform. If you can't see the scandal as spectacle, if you insist on dismissing it glibly or embroidering it into meaning, you also can't see it as a Libertine. The Libertine is brought into being in the moment of abjection and ambivalence which stands right at the brink of the descent into meaning and history.

Of course the Libertine has lines about sex, sex-affirming lines. The Libertinism shares a lot with sex-positive feminism and queer theory. Adultery happens. Clinton and Monica didn't do anything wrong. Those would be Libertine lines. Sex-positive doesn't mean any sex any time anywhere is good. Clinton and Monica's sex might have been a terrible idea for him, for her, might have hurt people, including people he/she/they didn't want to hurt. Someone might well not want to have an affair, or become involved with a married man. But it isn't morally wrong or depraved or degraded. Those are other people's lines. For the Libertine, it is simply true that people do follow their desires, and it's generally a good thing. There are risks, you have to calculate, and you can be terribly wrong and pay a high price. People you love can pay a high price. But the price is paid because you were wrong, not because you were bad.

Libertinism is, ultimately, not about sex, comes not to judge what sex is good and what sex is not. It is a posture about judgment about sex—a posture not *against judgment*, any more than the spectacular stands *against interpretation*. The Libertine struggles to keep the vibrating edges of sexual possibility—the structured paradoxes into which the sexual repeatedly falls—on the table. There is an affirmation, a kind of positivism or realism—people will/do follow their desires. There is a pull, a tendency, a default among a range of positions, a default position in a vocabulary, to affirm what happens, to demand that people, oneself, others, accept the consequences of their own and others' desires. But there is just beside it an intense agnosticism about whether it worked as sex, whether it was worth it, what it meant. Maybe it was a terrible idea, a mistake, something to regret, to suffer, in the face of which one must be stoic, whose consequences one can only yearn to reverse. Maybe it was just great, for Monica, for Bill, in spite of everything, or because of everything. And maybe it was no big deal at all, either way. People routinely decide about these things, individually and together. They make cost-benefit calculations for themselves, other-regarding evaluations, paternalist judgments. For the Libertine, moreover, there is no reader of last resort, no place from which we could know if this was desire, was sex, was good, was mistaken. Not Bill, not Monica, not Hillary, not even Barbara Walters, and certainly not the Libertine. We/I/they just don't know, didn't know for certain then and still don't. The Libertine remembers about sex what we know of the spectacle—the experience that one knows intensely, that one is sure, is the canary in the coal mine.

For the Libertine, reading the Monica Spectacle was a terrific experience. There were the bad guys, but then there was Monica. A woman's sexuality and sexual pleasure affirmed. Not just his pleasure, but her pleasure. The very definition of what sex "is" put up for grabs. Fetish practices affirmed as sexual by the country's leading conservative moralists. Sex which was not always reciprocal or parallel, but seemed nevertheless desired and enjoyed. But the more the Libertine talked, the less edgy it became, and the more the Libertine fell into the banalities of knowledge and norms. The *Wall Street Journal* at one point observed with amusement that liberals already thought of Clinton as the first black president—broken home, saxophone, Southern accent and food preferences—what would be next, Clinton as the first gay president? Well, yes actually. Multiple sexualities, public sex, the blow job, the cigar, the closet, the scandal, the universal insistence that it was fine as long as it was *private*. Starr shouldn't ask and Bill shouldn't tell.

As the Libertine became less a posture and more a position, it was easy to confuse the Libertine and the Civil Libertarian. Still, the Libertine tries not to rely on the distinction between public and private to privilege or shield the private. The Libertine shares with feminism the insistence that the private is political. Even when it doesn't result in legislation. Public sex. Sex in the Oval Office, at work, while *talking to a Senator about a bill.* Now that's Libertine. In what it says about sex, and what it says about Senators and bills and the quotidian practices of government. My favorite bumper sticker to emerge from the scandal read simply, "Honk if you're having sex with the President." I hope a lot of people honked. I hope Hillary honked.

But I am afraid they didn't. I'm afraid the only honks were derisive, affirming the sticker's edge, the wedge. Of course the Civil Libertarian might affirm public sexuality when it is expressive, as a form of speech, perhaps. Sex could be political if they were somehow trying to convince somebody in government to do something, or trying to change public opinion, about something government was about, well then, OK. But sex *qua* sex. Well, no.

For the Libertine, sex is political even, maybe especially, when it's cut off from speech and persuasion. And it can be affirmed as sex, does not need a procedural privilege or analogic reinterpretation as quasi-governmental, an affair of the mind rather than the body. For the Libertine, to be affirmed, sex needs neither to be disentangled from everything else and placed alone in a private cabin, nor to be transformed into something else. It can simply be, and the Libertine defaults to its affirmation. But what is it? Ahh, here again, we can't be sure—identifying sex turns out to be as complex as evaluating it.

Take the blow job. People do it, people deny it, people deny it's sex. You can come into being as a lesbian in that moment's irritation that anyone should "deny" that oral sex is sex, in rage about the preeminence assigned heterosexual genital intercourse. You can come into being as a woman—straight, gay—in that moment's worry about the centrality of a penis, the incapacity it attributes to two women, to woman, in the insult, the shame—at some horrible level, one buys into it. You can come into being as a man, or a woman, in the dozens, but probably not hundreds, of different ways a blow job can be wired into our sexual imaginary. Submission, control, the pleasures of sex which is not sex, service, the prolegomena, the aftermath, the substitute, the homoerotic which is not homosexual, and more. Maybe he just wanted her to be quiet. Maybe she just wanted to stop talking, wanted something to do while he chatted with the Senator. Maybe she was just bored. If we keep the blow job outside sex, do we protect it or demean it? Protect her or demean her? Protect him or demean him? Would it be better if we pushed it on to center stage?

It is interesting to ask what Monica thought, what Bill felt, what Hillary and Bill's deal had been as to the blow job, and so forth. But even if we could know, if they're sure, we can't be. To find the sex in the story, we need models and roles and types, just as we did to judge. Analogies—the model of males and females perhaps, the models of pornography, of the Bible, of *Esquire* or *Elle*. Perhaps all sex is fetish—or all fetish sex. Maybe sex-with-the-President is never sex, or all sex-with-men is with the President. For the Libertine, sex can be a transaction between individuals, who come to it with objectives, entitlements, dignities, and negotiate a practice. It can also be far messier, embedded, interactive, among people who are already connected, whose egos float back and forth, who come into being as individuals, as groups, through, around, against their evolving sexual practice. That it is modeled, that one comes into sex by coming into role as sexual, for the Libertine says nothing about whether it is good or bad. In identifying, judging, having sex, there is an aporia, a delicious and delicate coming together of model and its dissolution. The intensity, the coming into being and the loss of being, the residue of shame, the recollection of pleasure, that we, I, you, did that, went there. That we knew ourselves, to ourselves and, if there were two, to one another, as that which is sex. And know our sex, come into ourselves as model.

Sex may not escape modeling, but for the Libertine, sex, model sex, sex-as-model, has specificity. Its own rules and roles, which can't simply be borrowed from the contract, the parliament. It is common just now to think that sex is no good unless it's one man-one vote. Reciprocal. Equal. Dignified. Rational. Chosen. Safe. If, for example, men and women are too unequal for these standards to be met, sex simply cannot be good, or perhaps cannot be sex. Or if some people do not, cannot, know their own hearts—subalterns, who can't speak, or women, for whom the power to choose lies too deeply beneath the coercions of the everyday to be trusted—then they should not, even cannot, have sex. Or better, women can have sex but no one can have it with them, or all the sex they can have is false sex, sex only for men. Or *all* that they have is indignity. To be sexual is to be raped, to experience only the surplus beyond pleasure which we call dignitary injury. Equal. Rights.

For the Libertine, sex on your knees, sex which is not reciprocated, sex by yourself, by yourself with another person, sex in a dog collar, sex when the parties are not equal in status and wealth and salary and job grade and beauty and age and height, can also be sex. Even sex that women want can be sex. For the Libertine, sex doesn't have to be equally chosen or equally desired by all the parties, may not even be chosen at all. You needn't require consent, needn't reimagine sexual partners as autonomous transactors to eliminate coercion. Compulsion, obsession, sex when you can't stop yourself. The Libertine leans toward it, wants to, defaults to its affirmation. Say yes to abjection. Shame. Vulnerability. Inequality. Danger. Lean toward the sadomasochist, the fetishist, the happy couple at home on a Sunday afternoon. Still, coming into knowing, into judgment—in short, coming—great as it can be, is also a loss. The Libertine knows, judges, even comes, against his Libertinism. Comes when he chokes his canary.

And all this develops over time, cycles back, the canary breathes again, and you choke it again, or someone else does that for you. You can bargain about it, and be quite confident, but once the river flows. . . . Sex leaves loose edges and frayed thoughts. They don't fit back into a neat story of right and wrong, of dominance and submission, of love or betrayal. And other people get involved, and things take new shapes. And the man you knew denies you.

Lots of sex-positive readers stayed with Monica and Bill until he denied her. "I never had sex with that woman"—what a schmuck. But had he denied her before? Habitually? "Always already?" Can you get involved with the President without yearning to be denied? Can a blow job ever be affirmed? Or can denial, like the blow job, be erotic? Does it matter what she wanted? Or what she thought? Were they vulnerable to one another? Was he? Was she? Having sex with the President? Having not-sex with the President. With the not-President. Or were they both alone there in the Oval Office. Onanistic, on the phone. Masturbation, anonymous sex, sex by yourself with someone else present. It happens, the Libertine defaults to affirm. But it can be a terrible mistake, you can be wrong, people can get hurt. Just like in the missionary position at home with your spouse.

And can we imagine that in sex we know all this? In the dissolution of self, the loss into and of the other, we know that we don't know? Perhaps. Perhaps sex is simply spectacular. The question is what posture to take toward this unknown, and toward the intense desire, the pressure, the will to know, to intuit, to interpret. *We want to know.* "Was it good for you?" Was it sex, for me, for anyone. Perhaps we should hold a conference, ask some academics, figure out what happened, who came, *what it all meant.* Here the Libertine gets off the bus. He knows the crash to come.

At the start of the Clinton era, Libertinism was on the rise. Bill and Al were on the postcard, flower children in power. Gay men with gay women. Too bad Tipper was so down on rock and roll, and Hillary did seem a bit earnest, but women today, women after Women's Studies, can be like that, and still the situation was basically good. We might contrast the early Bill-Al image with an image of George Bush and Dan Quayle which came out about the same time. George holds Dan by the hair across his knee and slaps his butt to the caption "Now—how do you spell Potato?" Somehow a different spectacle. We don't think they would appreciate the joke.

But as the presidency wore on, the feeling wore off. In the middle years we find a new set of images on the postcard stands. Bill and Al are now dressed in leather shorts and fetish gear, wearing collars labeled slave and master. It's a complex image—and it's not clear they would appreciate the joke. Al seems happy enough in handcuffs, but Bill's hands are firmly at his side, his mouth set. He's tolerating it, but he's not enjoying it. And in the follow-up card he appears alone, his body in the sharp angles of a sax player on a long riff, and his hands are in the cuffs. Fighting back? Enjoying it? Is it sex? Maybe his hands really are tied, and it's all just a metaphor. About the vast-right-wing-conspiracy, or the constraints of governing, or the fate of Libertinism as the nineties fade back into the fifties.

The scandal breaks and Bill's not with Al any more, but alone with the Republicans and Hillary and the press. Al has disappeared and cute George denounces Bill, and everyone says they are just positively scandalized, and anguished and disappointed. He told us. And it wasn't true. He was Married, and he . . . Suddenly it's all prayer breakfasts and serious family time. He says he didn't do it and it wasn't sex and he's really sorry. For the Libertine this denial marked the beginning of the end, the end of sex and spectacle. Here the beginning of a Libertine morality?

Something about Bill's denial turned their sex into an anonymous encounter, and the Libertine at first leans to affirm—but this time it didn't seem fine. Not because of some general rule against anonymity and denial or a requirement of mutuality. And not because it's the men who deny and the women who need affirmation—there is something anonymous in sex with The President, and women might well hide their pleasure under a denial. No, simply because it apparently went wrong, for her, for him, although that is also just my interpretation. And here is the point—it pushed me over into interpretation. Of course, for all I know they were getting off on the intrigue, the intensity of being denied, reinterpreted, exposed. But I no longer thought so—the ambivalence, the intense uncanny feeling, it had moved on for me, and we were now deep in aftermath. Something touched me deep inside. I even thought about his widowed bride, and that day, I'm afraid my own canary died.

Oddly, for some time Starr keeps the Libertine facts before us. And by the end of the scandal, in some way Monica is all that is left standing. The postcard stands depict Hillary with a whip and a sadistic laugh, and you don't think she appreciates the joke any more than George and Dan. In fact now she's in the same scene with Nancy Reagan and Barbara Bush. The card is entitled "First Ladies Club." Hillary and Nancy sport leather—Nancy more playboy bunny, Hillary more nineties dominatrix, Barbara in jogging shorts, brassiere, and sensible pearls. The objects, not the subjects, of Libertinism.

Monica Lewinsky. Libertine Hero. There's Barbara Walters asking her in all earnestness if she didn't agree, looking back, that it had all been pretty degrading. Unreciprocated, on her knees, with the President. Well, actually, she said, no. It wasn't degrading. It was a mistake, but you just had to be there. It was human and touching, and we really had something nice. She describes Bill sucking in his stomach when he opens his trousers as a cute moment of mutual vulnerability, and remembers talking with him about her life and his.

Through all that she was put, somehow she never lost that fresh dignity; she managed to embrace abjection and shame and humiliation without conceding that all that had happened was anything other than human. Maybe I see the world through rose-colored glasses, but somehow our cities seem full of young Monicas. The students and waitresses and sales personnel, there's her haircut, her lipstick, and above all, her firm sexual confidence.

I hope they also share mantras with Monica. It doesn't have to be private or pretty, can be laced with power and pain, but that doesn't mean it's not fun, not human, not really me, and not really him or not really her. And anyway, not "really"? What's that? Last year Monica and Bill and all of us together made a spectacle of our nation. It was great. Let's not screw it up by trying to turn it into legislation, popular or otherwise.

### NOTES

1. David Kennedy is Henry Shattuck Professor of Law, Harvard University. This talk was delivered at an interdisciplinary conference at the University of Wisconsin Law School on February 5, 2000 entitled "Aftermath: Conversations on the Clinton Scandal, the Future of the Presidency and the Liberal State." My thanks to Len Kaplan and Beverly Moran for the invitation to participate in the conference, and to Yishai Blanc, Brenda Cossman, Dan Danielsen, Karen Engle, Janet Halley, and Duncan Kennedy for conversations about Monica and related matters.

# Chapter 22

# The Political Is Personal

## *Beverly I. Moran*

My introduction to Bill Clinton was through the 1992 Democratic primaries. The field was filled with second stringers as the heavy hitters—Al Gore, for example—sat out the season thinking George Bush unbeatable. The traveling road show filling my television left me convinced that all Bill Clinton wanted was the presidency. That is, despite his reputation as a policy wonk, it wasn't about policy, stupid, it was about winning.

My insight began with healthcare. At first, healthcare was not on Bill Clinton's radar screen. But when Bob Kerry began gaining ground, Bill Clinton appropriated the issue. Of course, that choice might have signaled candidate Clinton's leadership by demonstrating his ability to recognize and act upon new information, but my sense was different. Incorporating healthcare successfully undercut Kerry, whose own campaign relied too heavily on that single theme. Thus, I saw a candidate who found a winning slogan, not a man won over by an idea. If my view was correct then it was less likely that the Clinton White House would commit to the things that I cared about because so many of those issues came with political costs. As the primaries and the election proceeded, I saw nothing to diminish that fear.

At first, the new Administration seemed set to prove me wrong. On the day President Clinton proposed letting gays serve in the military, I remember swearing that I would support him for the rest of his term. My father served in a segregated army and both my parents were victims of the Red Scare. I grew up in Spanish Harlem where hard times made women dream of marrying Merchant Marines. In my world of poor kids with a lot to give and nowhere to turn, a military career allowed youngsters to risk their lives to support their families. As a child of the working class, I was appalled that people feared for their jobs either because they were homosexual or because they were merely accused. This feeling was heightened by the knowledge I gained through my work with Lambda Legal Defense and Education Fund that homosexual charges are often employed to harass service women who repel heterosexual advances. In other words, I knew that there were real people who wanted to serve their country and their families even to the point of giving their lives for whom this Order meant everything. For me, this wasn't abstract politics. It was about the lived lives of real people who needed and deserved protection. Of course, the Order died before implementation and was replaced by the infamous "Don't ask, don't tell." That at least one man has died as a result of that policy was to be expected. So much for my oath of allegiance to a Clinton presidency.

After four years of disappointments too numerous to name here, I was glad to spend the next election season abroad. When the scandal began, I knew less than most of the rest of the world. My introduction to President Clinton's troubles was in Eritrea, in a crowd of Americans watching satellite TV. Buried between news from the Middle East and the erupting war in (the then) Zaire, there was a brief clip showing a finger-shaking President declaring he "never had sexual relations with that woman."

No one cared. Not a comment was made.

Our lack of interest was typical. Even in Eritrea, we had heard it all before. Hadn't he never had sex with Gennifer Flowers, nor with his high school sweetheart, nor with Miss Something in the back of a Cadillac? In my time in Eritrea, I don't recall a single mention of the Clinton scandal.

When I returned to America, I found myself—for a brief moment—in a new position. For an instant, my views were in line with the American majority. Given my pent-up feelings against the President, this was strangely exhilarating. I would like to feel in step. Here was my opportunity. Knowing nothing more than that the President had lied to the press about an affair, I concluded that America faults no man for fictionalizing his sex life.

But as I learned more and events unfolded, my days with the majority were over. My doubts became questions. Questions raised by my life in America as a law professor, a woman, a working-class person, and a black. Questions about why this crisis failed to inspire us to act on important issues of law, politics, and morality.

### *The Law Professor Questions*

#### Whatever Happened to Lying?

My personal low point occurred as I watched the President's televised deposition. When I heard "It depends on what your definition of 'is' is," I thought: "This man is a master." My shame at that moment still haunts me. Here I am, a law professor, responsible for training honest public servants. Yet I reacted with admiration. I saw artful advocacy, not obfuscation. If I didn't need a definition of "is," I could have used some guidance on how to define "lie."

My failure prompted me to reconsider the 1962 film *Advise and Consent*.[1] The difference between that fiction and my reaction illustrates how far we have traveled in our understanding of the meaning and importance of truth.

*Advise and Consent* is set in a Senate confirmation hearing for Secretary of State where the nominee (Robert Leffingwell) is blindsided by accusations of former communist cell membership combined with punishing a student who knew his past, first by failing that student in a political theory class, and then, years later, by having him fired for entering a tuberculosis sanatorium.

In his defense, Robert Leffingwell demonstrates that:

- the informant was never his student,
- a nervous breakdown, not tuberculosis, caused the dismissal, and
- rather than harm the fellow, he found the sick man a new position after his return from the insane asylum.

Leffingwell's nomination is back on track. Yet, immediately upon leaving the Senate Chambers, he implores the President to drop his name from consideration. It turns out that he was once a member of a communist cell. Because of this old indiscretion, the nominee declares, "Mr. President, I want to withdraw my nomination—I lied at the hearing."

The Chair of the Senate Confirmation Committee learns Leffingwell's secret. His response is also: "Leffingwell lied under oath."

The people in *Advise and Consent*'s fictional world were not saints. Many used any available weapon—from strong arming to blackmail—to achieve their goals. But they all knew that Leffingwell had lied. The mid-century public this film spoke to would accept nothing less. Even the characters who supported confirmation never suggested anything to the contrary.

But in our era, there is no lie. Leffingwell never denied communist cell membership. Instead, he avoided the issue. By attacking his nemesis with the truth on collateral issues, he diverted attention from his own acts to others'. After what we've seen, how can we fault this strategy? It is certainly a step up from forcing words into only arguably personal meanings.

As with the rest of the Clinton scandal, we are forced to ask why we went along with the most artful dissembling of all, the conviction that a lie is not a lie.

As an academic, I fear that one reason we can't see public lying is that we already turn a blind eye toward semiprivate lying. Plagiarism and other forms of cheating are rarely punished. It is not just that detection is hard. It is also difficult to get support. Who has time to fight? There is no reward for standing against bad actors. We follow the easy path for ourselves, so why not for others?

### Do We Want to Tolerate So Much Prosecutorial Power?

For me, the most disappointing public reaction to the Clinton scandal was the cry against so-called prosecutorial misconduct. Unlike some, I do not believe that Ken Starr's actions were beyond reproach. In fact, much of what Starr did was awful. However, I argue, as Frank Tuerkheimer does here, that the investigation was mostly routine.[2] The House Republicans tried to make this point when they paraded convicted perjurers before the cameras. They hoped that seeing ordinary people imprisoned would help us punish the President.

I had a different hope. I trusted that, as daily evidence of prosecutorial zeal was piped into our living rooms, the Clinton scandal would raise our consciousness about state power.

In this, we were both mistaken.

Eric Rothstein asserts that the scandal produced at least one positive result: an America beyond deified presidents.[3] If this is true, the proof lies somewhere besides public reaction to the Independent Counsel. Instead, that reaction reveals our willingness to accept different justice for different people.

Whatever was done to the President is routinely done to ordinary people. The major difference is that presidents have the money and power to expose wrongdoing. Yet even rage against Ken Starr failed to translate into a critique of prosecutorial power. Instead, the protest remained focused on the President and his friends.

This was a lost opportunity. If, for example, the Clinton scandal had fired our imagination the way that DNA testing is now helping challenge the death penalty, then it might have been worth all the effort.

## The Woman Questions

### How Did We Forget Paula Jones?

For David Kennedy, Monica is the fifteen-minute girl of the Clinton scandal.[4] Her willingness to be open and playful with the leader of the Free World. To sink to her knees and read *Leaves of Grass*. To admit to romantic fantasies and to being charmed when he pulled in his stomach. To initiate sex and then have it freely. For Kennedy, the heart and soul of the scandal is Monica's place in the sexual vanguard.

My attention belongs to Paula Jones. The everywoman who managed to make the system work for her. Whatever happened to Paula Jones? How did she lose her centrality to these affairs? What can her journey teach us?

The first and most telling lesson is that, while Americans love show trials, we are not particularly interested in learning from them. It is as though the *History Channel* were our most popular form of entertainment and yet no one had heard of World War II. Information dances across the screen without being absorbed or acted upon. If we paid attention, would we change what we see?

### Paula Jones Accomplished an Almost Impossible Task. Are We Obligated to Make That Task Easier?

Let's make the comparison among contemporary American sex scandals.

As Robin West points out, the one rape claimed against President Clinton has received only the briefest interest.[5] Even Juanita Broaddrick's supporters only hope that she keeps her good name.[6]

Kathleen Willey is condemned as a liar.[7]

Anita Hill was well positioned after the Thomas hearings, but she spent most of her post-Thomas years in self-enforced silence. In the smiles and thank yous and invitations to a man whose behavior haunted her. When she finally spoke, Anita Hill became a lightening rod for unrelenting hate with none of the safety the White House affords.[8]

And then there is Paula Jones.

If she graduated from high school, no one says. She worked in small state government in a small-time job. She had no particular connections or political friends. State employees brought her to a hotel room where the Governor showed her his penis and she

- found friends who could help her,
- fired the lawyers who told her to take the money without the apology,
- was called every type of whore and liar,
- changed her looks,
- hit the talk shows,
- influenced history, and
- managed to get the President's friends to pay most of her attorneys' fees.

Can we ask for a better modern-day heroine?

## Where Was the Outrage over the Dismissal of Paula Jones's Lawsuit?

In the heat of litigation, Bill Clinton became the first sitting President to tour Africa.[9] His trip was well received on the continent but, what most Americans remember from that journey is how he beat drums to celebrate the dismissal of Paula Jones's lawsuit.[10] It was certainly one of my biggest shocks. Not just the public callousness of his action but the result itself left me momentarily baffled.

I am not a civil rights attorney. I admit to knowing nothing about sexual harassment law. But I am an attorney and a working woman. As an attorney I knew that a dismissal by summary judgment was the judge's way of saying that, assuming that everything Paula Jones said was true, she still had no basis for relief. As a casual consumer of the news media, I knew that her claim was that Bill Clinton had exposed himself. As a working woman, I wondered how the head of an organization, *the Governor of a state*, could display his penis to an employee without creating liability.

By now, the Supreme Court has provided further guidance on this issue and a number of books explain the now overturned rules that temporarily kept Paula Jones from pressing forward.[11] Yet I still wonder why the dismissal stirred so little protest even from those who accept that, based on controlling precedent, the judgment was correct.

John Cooper and Mark Tushnet both point out that the impeachment process took a turn toward legality that was not preordained by either the Constitution or our political history.[12] Robert Gordon asserts that the scandal illustrates our tendency to legalize morality.[13] The nonreaction to the summary judgment dismissal against Paula Jones shows another side of our cultural push toward legalization. The side that accepts legal rules without question as though law controlled us rather than the other way around.

We often accept undesirable results while noting ways to avoid similar outcomes in the future. For example, some claim that the Clinton scandal will make federal courts rethink civil suits against sitting presidents.[14] Yet this thinking was hardly evident in public discourse about Paula Jones. There was no great outcry (particularly on the left) that a working woman had no redress if *all* her boss did was expose himself.

Have labor and the Democratic Party so abandoned working women that an act that could lead to arrest if committed in a street is not important enough to create liability if committed in the workplace?

## The Working-Class Questions

### Are We Too Prone to Judge Sexual Harassment Claims Based on Status?

If liberals can find Clarence Thomas's behavior outrageous while dodging what it means if Paula Jones's story is true; if Republican indiscretions can force resignations as conservatives proclaim themselves the country's moral force; if, in predicting a person's position on the evidence, the essential thing to know is not *what* happened but *who* was involved; then we are using status to judge sexual harassment claims.

Human beings have employed status-based justice systems for thousands of years. They are certainly efficient because, when status completely controls outcomes, women like Paula Jones don't try.

Is that the lesson? That we don't want women like Paula Jones to try? We certainly put enough barriers in their way. Just by requiring self-prosecution we make the already emotional task of fighting harassment expensive and difficult as well.

304 BEVERLY I. MORAN

Yet one charge against Paula Jones is that she used a conglomeration of right-wing groups to help press her suit. Well, what was she supposed to do? Go up against the President of the United States with Plaid Stamps? If we truly wanted to clean up the workplace, we might start by finding ways to handle harassment claims that prevent money from turning women into pawns. But that might put feminists at odds with the Democratic Party and, as Elizabeth Rapaport discusses, after this scandal that shift seems unlikely.[15]

### Has Class Become the Great American Sin?

Perhaps the clue to how we want to handle harassment is found in the way the American people reacted to various claims against President Clinton. Richard Neuhaus discusses the shock conservatives felt at how much we tolerated. Before the scandal, the right wing believed that it represented the *Moral Majority*.[16] But when neither adultery, perjury, nor rape aroused the masses, these spokesmen were forced to reevaluate their beliefs about popular morality.

By their nature, status-based justice systems tend to favor the well-positioned over the hoi polloi. Because of this tendency, they generally operate outside public opinion. Yet in this very public conflict, majority opinion was crucial. Harsh terms had to speak to large numbers of people from all parts of the country with divergent social and political views.

President Clinton is a fine politician, a man who knows how to speak to us. If any group can reach the American people, it is the Clinton team. His supporters' attacks on Paula Jones imply that the two most objectionable qualities in America today are being poor and unattractive. Forget about politics or morality. The greatest modern American sins are looking bad and working for twice the minimum wage.

Surely the President's mother was called trailer trash more than once during his childhood. Yet his associates used that label against Paula Jones without fear. They used it because they knew it would work, and what does that say about us?

### *The Black Question*

Even more than the failure to give Paula Jones her due, black people's reaction to the Clinton scandal baffled me. This bewilderment draws me uncomfortably close to many of the conservative authors in this volume. I too want to know how I could have been so wrong about "my" people.

It was especially strange that blacks were the President's greatest supporters. My initial reaction suggested that a different response was equally plausible.

First, I was outraged when candidate Clinton made a point of distancing himself from black constituents by attacking the hip hop entertainment at a Jesse Jackson rally.[17] This disgust increased as he made another bow to the right by attending a mentally retarded black man's execution.[18] Each day's news confirms what blacks knew at Rickey Ray Rector's death—that capital punishment kills blacks at higher rates than whites and far more innocent people than it should.[19]

As president, Bill Clinton's dismissal of Dr. Joycelyn Elders and his failure to support Lani Guinier were two more reasons for my problems with his Administration.[20]

But the healthcare debacle and the destruction of welfare were most significant. As Linda Oakley points out, every black American has a destitute family member who often suffers from income insecurity combined with uninsured medical expenses.[21] Yet at the same time that welfare reform and the lack of a national healthcare program made these problems more likely, the Clinton Administration failed to stop the ongoing attack on affirmative action and the continuing decline in affordable public education thus narrowing two major paths for blacks escaping poverty.[22]

In terms of the sex scandal, I did not see black people as a natural presidential constituency. As a group, we are generally conservative about sex because we suffer more from the consequences of risky behavior.[23] Philosophically, we tend toward a strong (often fundamentalist) Protestant ethic.[24] Black children suffer from broken homes often caused by infidelity. All this leads me to believe that blacks are unwilling to condone adultery.

Next, blacks are more subject to arrest and prosecution than whites.[25] Thus, we understand the penalties for subterfuge. I suspected that, having received heavy-handed treatment ourselves, we might demand the same for the President.

Black women are more likely to work outside the home and so are presumably more familiar with sexual harassment in the workplace.[26] I thought black women might sympathize with Paula Jones and with Betty Currie who was forced to deal with the implications of her boss's affair.

Finally, the President's cliched use of Vernon Jordan and Betty Currie recalled old-fashioned Gothic Romance novels where dashing young scions on dilapidated plantations use colored Uncles and Mammies to hide their unseemly affairs.

Clearly these factors were not important to the majority of black people.

So what was going on in black America?

In terms of candidate Clinton, there were at least three easily understandable factors at work.

First, the candidate was different from the President. The candidate was going to bring healthcare to the masses, promote peace, support civil rights, and protect income security. For people who need government protection, candidate Clinton hit the right notes.

Next, what was the alternative? In the year before the election, George Bush placed Clarence Thomas on the Supreme Court and sponsored the Gulf War. Given our overrepresentation in the military and Thomas's record on civil rights, Bush's pre-election strategy played against black interests without a prior record generating goodwill.

Finally, black American culture is filled with stories of people saying one thing in order to disguise a completely different intent. A historical illustration is found in black spirituals containing elaborate escape plans imbedded in talk of the hereafter.[27] A more recent example is found in the many black people who believed that, once on the Supreme Court, Clarence Thomas would reveal himself as a civil rights champion. In this thinking, the world is a treacherous place where words must often disguise true aims revealed by action.

In other words, he got the benefit of our doubt.

So what if candidate Clinton made some noise about a meaningless campaign entertainment? Jesse Jackson was not going to be president no matter what Bill Clinton said. As for Rickey Ray Rector, he was going to die whether or not Governor Clinton attended his execution. The important thing was that, once in office, black people believed that Bill Clinton would be a better president than George Bush. In this, we were probably quite accurate.

How blacks were able to accept President Clinton's actions in office is somewhat harder to explain. It may be that we believed he fought the good fight. That without him, welfare would have disappeared sooner. That the failure of universal healthcare and his distancing from Elders and Guinier were caused by the need to appease powerful conservatives who would have taken more if they could. He wanted to do the right thing, he tried to do the right thing, but our efforts don't always succeed and neither did his.

The Clinton sex scandal, however, challenged many important black values. With our four-hundred-year-old history, the black community takes sexual abuse seriously. Thomas Jefferson's connection to Sally Hemmings is no love story for us. If there is a collective black subconscious, then it surely contains images of young girls servicing old men in big White Houses. So why did the Clinton sex scandal leave us cold? Because we thought it was all pretext.

There are many stories of sexual abuse in black American culture. Rape in the big house is only one.

An equally compelling image is of a man falsely accused in order to punish him, often for no more than walking the earth. Some of these cases are well documented, others are only known within families. More than once, these false accusations have leveled whole towns and killed hundreds of people.[28] Further, the women in these narratives often fit Paula Jones's public stereotype as heavily made up, working class, uneducated, and Southern. Thus, antipathy overrode possible class identification.

Another picture in black consciousness shows government agencies using real sex acts in order to punish outspokenness, as in the FBI investigations of Dr. Martin Luther King, Jr.[29]

As these tales circulate within black communities, they teach us that sexual misconduct is often claimed for illegitimate reasons against innocent men.

These stories bear witness to one more reason for black people to buy into the Clinton worldview, that is, the belief that white people routinely engage in unseemly sexual behavior combined with subterfuge. In the false accusation stories, for example, the charge is often explained as a cover for illicit sexual activity between whites. In addition, keep in mind that black communities traditionally housed the bordellos and drug parlors white people use.[30]

The black view of white sexuality, and what white people consider appropriate behavior, is informed by these experiences. Thus, many of us questioned why seemingly normal white behavior was suddenly being penalized. When these factors were added up the denials rang true and the actual misconduct was forgiven as simply being part of white culture and as mere pretext for penalizing a liberal social agenda. If the crime itself was bogus, then rejecting the punishment was appropriate. Rather than wish condemnable harm on others, blacks were willing to stand against injustice.

Yet none of this explains why blacks were at the forefront of the Clinton defense. Why did our ministers and politicians seem so eager to man the barricades? For me, this is where Vernon Jordan, (the by then dead) Ron Brown, and Betty Currie become so important. One aspect of black culture that translated into almost unconditional support for President Clinton is that black Americans love white people who we believe love us.

I don't know how many times I heard that, whatever the details, it was enough that Bill Clinton had black friends. It didn't matter how he treated those friends or how he used them. When the President needed help, he turned to Vernon Jordan. That was more than enough to solidify his credentials as someone who liked us. And we returned the compliment.

And that is the most dangerous move of all. Because we are such outsiders, we compromised our moral vision, and perhaps our self-interest as well, in return for a seat at the table. In this we are no different from the feminists, environmentalists, and labor advocates who ignored their concerns and supported the President. The black American public and its leaders gave Bill Clinton and the Democratic Party a gift in return for a hope. Now we need strategies to demand a fair return.

*Conclusion*

The Clinton era is drawing to a close. Yet the aftermath remains. That is this scandal's blessing. It allowed us to see our politics, law, and culture with all the spotlights gleaming. Every flaw was revealed. But will our enlightenment lead to action?

What brought us here was very human and requires a human response. I have tried to offer such a response by tying my concerns to my life in America as a law professor, a child of the working class, a working woman, and a black.

As a law professor I ask what we think about lying and the reach of prosecutorial power. Those practices are not confined to this scandal. Nonetheless, the scandal paraded the consequences of those acts across our television screens. Our confusion over what constitutes lying, much less perjury, makes me ask whether we can find ways to bring honesty back into public life.

The prolonged investigation against Bill Clinton, his family, and associates made us recoil from the specter of state power. Will we recognize that the American Revolution was a cry for limits on state power, especially power turned against individuals? Will we take that idea and use it to limit what prosecutors do to ordinary citizens?

As a child of the lower-working class, this drama reminds me that class is the last great American sin. We allow calumnies based on working-class status that would repel us if linked to race or sex. Will this scandal finally release the working class from its role as the bearer of our social contempt? Or will we continue to base our judgments on the package and not the person?

As a working woman, I wonder what we learned from another working woman's attempts to maintain a lawsuit for sexual harassment. At the very least, we now know how much it costs to go forward, both in terms of time and money. We also know that those costs mean that some women will have to rely on others to pursue their actions. For those who saw Paula Jones as a tool of the right wing, I ask what we can do to free women from the financial and emotional burdens of protecting their rights.

Finally, as a black I wonder whether a seat at the table is enough. Are more Cabinet appointments all we desire or do we want real change that can move us forward economically and socially? Can we maintain a political agenda and a special relationship to people who are not coming through with meaningful social reforms?

Yes, this was a very human event. If we avert our eyes to the human costs it extracted, we have no one to blame but ourselves.

### NOTES

1. *Advise and Consent* (Otto Preminger Films, 1962).

2. See Frank Tuerkheimer, "Comparing the Independent Counsel to Other Prosecutors: Privilege and Other Issues," this volume.

3. See Eric Rothstein, "Impeachment and Enchanting Arts," this volume.

4. See David Kennedy, "The Spectacle and the Libertine," this volume.

5. See Robin West, "Sex, Harm, and Impeachment," this volume.

6. See Dorothy Rabinowitz, "Juanita Broaddrick Meets the Press," *Wall Street Journal*, February 19, 1999, A18.

7. See Andrew Cohen, "White House Has Willey on the Ropes," *Globe and Mail*, March 20, 1998, A12; Mary Leonard, "Women Who Accuse Men of Sexual Misconduct Are Often Portrayed Negatively, Prompting Mental Experts to Recommend: Don't Complain, Don't File Charges, Just Keep Quiet," *Boston Globe*, March 22, 1998, E1.

8. In 1997, Anita Hill reflected on the Thomas hearings in Anita Hill, *Speaking Truth to Power* (New York: Doubleday, 1997). See also Anita Hill, "A Matter of Definition," *New York Times*, March 19, 1998, A21; Larry Riley, "Hill Says Thomas Should Be Quiet," *Indianapolis Star*, June 29, 1998, B01.

9. See James Rupert, "Clinton Visit Paid Off, Africans Say: Dialogue Improvement Cited, but Many Push for Tariff Cut," *Washington Post*, May 22, 1999, A13.

10. See James Bennett, "Clinton Marks a 'Vindication' with a Guitar," *New York Times*, April 2, 1998, A5.

11. See, e.g., Vincent Bugliosi, *No Island of Sanity, Paula Jones v. Bill Clinton: The Supreme Court on Trial* (Los Angeles: Library of Contemporary Thought, 1998); Richard A. Posner, *An Affair of the State: The Investigation, Impeachment, and Trial of President Clinton* (Cambridge: Harvard University Press, 1999).

12. See John Milton Cooper, Jr., "Impeachment: A (Civil) Religious Perspective," this volume, and Mark Tushnet, "The Constitutional Politics of the Clinton Impeachment," this volume.

13. See Robert W. Gordon, "Legalizing Outrage," ths volume.

14. See, e.g., Robert J. Spitzer, "Clinton's Impeachment Will Have Few Consequences for the Presidency," *PS: Political Science and Politics* (September 1999): 541, 542–43; "The Damage Done," *Economist*, January 2, 1999, 15; John Farmer, "Courting Disaster: We're Still Sorting Out the Mess Made by the Judiciary's Entry into the Political Fray," *Star-Ledger* (Newark, N.J.), February 7, 1999, 001; Bill Straub, "On to the Senate," *Cincinnati Post*, December 22, 1998, 20A; Rosemary Roberts, "Suing a U.S. President Can Become a Sport," *Greensboro News and Rec.*, June 30, 1999, A11; R. K. Shull, "This Is No Way to Run a Country," *Indianapolis News*, December 21, 1998, D01.

15. See Elizabeth Rapaport, "Sex and Politics at the Close of the Twentieth Century," this volume.

16. See Richard John Neuhaus, "Bill Clinton and the American Character," this volume.

17. See Ronald A. Taylor, "Clinton Campaign Not Aimed at Blacks," *Washington Times*, June 29, 1992, A4.

18. See Christopher Olgiati, "The White House via Death Row," *Guardian* (London), October 12, 1993, T018; Christopher Sullivan, "Death Penalty Cases Test Fairness of Clemency Mercy," *Los Angeles Times*, August 29, 1993, A13.

19. See David Cole, *No Equal Justice: Race and Class in the American Criminal Justice System* (New York: New Press, 1999), 132–41; Paul Butler, "Affirmative Action and the Criminal Law," 68 *University Colorado Law Review* (1997): 841, 882–84; Raymond Bonner and Marc Lacey, "U.S. Plans Delay in First Execution in Four Decades," *New York Times*, July 7, 2000, A1; Sandy Grady, "Morality of Capital Punishment Staring Bush Squarely in the Eye," *Milwaukee J. Sentinel*, July 2, 2000, 04J; Sally Kestin, "Death Penalty Errors Vex State," *Sun-Sentinel* (Fort Lauderdale, Fla.), June 19, 2000, 1A.

20. See Martin Fletcher, "Clinton Sacks His Health Chief in School Sex Furor," *Times* (London), December 10, 1994, available in 1994 WL 9199700; "NAACP Has Hero in Guinier," *San Diego Union-Tribune*, July 14, 1993, A6.

21. "Compared to whites, minorities are almost twice as likely to be unin-

sured and are far less likely to have a regular source of care. Minorities also live with a disproportionate burden of sickness and death from a variety of diseases when compare[d] to whites." Anita Lienert, "Inequities Medical Access for Minorities Lags: Poor Find Haphazard Care Meted Out Along Racial, Socio-Economic Lines, Experts Say," *Detroit News,* June 25, 2000, 08.

22. See William G. Bowen and Derek Bok, *The Shape of the River: Long-Term Consequences of Considering Race in College and University Admissions* (Princeton: Princeton University Press, 1998), 94–95; Kevin Merida, "Worry, Frustration Build for Many in Black Middle Class: Growing Worries among Black Middle Class," *Washington Post,* October 9, 1995, A01.

23. See June Dobbs Butts, "Sex and the Modern Black," *Ebony,* September 1997, 96 (discussing how blacks under forty have a more open view of sex).

24. Participation in Pentecostalism has shown a marked increase by blacks. See Kenneth Estell, *African American: Portrait of a People* (New York: Visible Ink Press, 1994), 232, 237. In addition, participation rates for blacks in the Roman Catholic church and Islamic mosque has increased. See Estell, *African American,* 237.

25. See Cole, *No Equal Justice,* 41; Butler, "Affirmative Action and the Criminal Law," 841–42; Steven A. Drizin, "Juvenile Justice System Tilted against Minority Youths," *Chicago Daily Legal Bulletin,* May 12, 2000, 5; Christi Parsons, "Race Report Singles Out Illinois for Drug-Conviction Disparity," *Chicago Tribune,* June 8, 2000, 1.

26. See *Black Americans: A Statistical Sourcebook 2000* (Boulder, Colo.: Numbers and Concepts, 2000); Beverly I. Moran and William Whitford, "A Black Critique of the Internal Revenue Code," *Wisconsin Law Review* (1996): 751, 794–95 (discussing studies showing that married black wives are more likely to work than their white counterparts).

27. See Estell, *African American,* 228; James Weldon Johnson, from Preface to *The Books of American Negro Spirituals,* in *Signifyin[g], Sanctifyin', and Slam Dunking: A Reader in African American Expressive Culture,* ed. Gena Dagel Caponi (Amherst: University of Massachusetts Press, 1999), 45, 52–53.

28. See Duncan Campbell, "Remembering the Night That Tulsa Burned," *Guardian* (London), June 2, 2000, *available in* 2000 WL 21818205; Jeff Dickerson, "Coming Clean Unsavory History: Across the Country, People Are Facing Up to Brutal and Violent Acts of the Past," *Atlanta Journal and Atlanta Constitution,* March 12, 2000, F1.

29. See "FBI's Hidden Agenda: Files on King's Top Aide Reveal Elaborate Witch Hunt," *Newsday,* July 12, 1999, A04.

30. See George Chauncey, *Gay New York: Gender, Urban Culture, and the Making of the Gay Male World, 1890–1940* (New York: Basic Books, 1994).

# Chapter 23

# Dropped Drawers
## *A Viewpoint*

## *Drucilla Cornell*

At first I was a bit troubled by being asked to write a response to the Clinton impeachment process. I watched as little as possible of the impeachment proceeding on television, and I completely avoided the Monica Lewinsky interviews. Why go there when you can watch *Moonstruck* for the 9,782nd time? For those who know the movie, this might give you some sense of my sexual and romantic tastes. And as for public purposes, that's all I want you to know. I followed the "politics of sleaze," as it was often referred to in the media, only enough to reach a judgment as to whether or not Clinton should be impeached.

My bottom line as a matter of constitutional law, shared by many of the other commentators in this volume, is that Clinton did not commit an impeachable offense. So for legal reasons, and political and ethical reasons, I was glad to see the impeachment defeated. But that conclusion does not mean that I approved of Clinton's behavior. I believe he made a fool out of himself and publicly humiliated his family. My heart went out to Chelsea, who was making a big transition in her life as she was going off to college. This transition is difficult enough without having to handle endless public displays of your father's sexuality. Still, it is important to keep personal ethical judgments about Clinton's behavior separate from the constitutional issue of impeachment.

But my focus here is on another matter at hand inevitably raised by the Clinton scandal. What is a feminist to do when a president is so consistently caught with his drawers down that even those of us who did not want to look could not help but see him exposed? Are there serious ethical, political, and legal issues that Clinton's behavior raises, particularly for a feminist? I think there are many such issues—too many to address in a short commentary. So I will focus on one. What should be the feminist attitude toward the renewed commitment to public civility called for by the philosopher Thomas Nagel in the wake of the Clinton scandal? Let us face it: many of those who were against the impeachment of the President blamed feminists for paving the road for sexual McCarthyism. Sexual harassment laws, in particular, have been singled out. Accusations against the effect of sexual harassment laws have often been misguided, or downright wrong, about what the law of sexual harassment is in this country. But this misperception aside, such laws have been indicted in the public imagination anyway for having had dire effects, one being that Clinton's sexual life should have been open for public review. Broadly construed, the accusation has been that feminists have undermined the important values of sexual freedom and expression. After all, John F. Kennedy was a known philanderer, and the press and the public did not seem to care.

So what has changed since then? One answer is that the "femi nazis" have successfully created an all-guns-blaring assault on male sexual freedom. No man is safe if he even dares to say, "you look nice today," in a workplace or any other public forum. But are feminists in any way to blame for legitimizing the graphic exposure of the most intimate details of a public official's personal life, and endangering male sexual freedom more generally? My answer to this question is that certainly the feminism I have advocated does not participate in that assault.

Indeed, as a feminist, I join with Thomas Nagel in his call for public civility, and for the protection of the moral and psychic space in which we can live out our fantasies and play with different sexual personae. I have named that space the imaginary domain[1] and have argued that it is exactly the protection of this kind of moral and psychic space that should inform our law of sexual harassment. But Nagel is not limiting his discussion to the law and its effects. He is making a more general point about our culture, and why we should ethically aspire to insure a social and cultural life that does not force us to expose aspects of ourselves that we would rather conceal. I do not agree with some of Nagel's specific descriptions of what has happened with our culture. For example, I disagree with him when he states that "Forty years ago the public pieties were patriotic and anticommunist; now they are multicultural and feminist."[2] Perhaps we travel in different circles, but frankly my experience has been that feminism is often disparaged. Do not misunderstand me, I do not want pieties offered to a feminist, but a little respect for what feminism has accomplished is always nice. Neither do I agree with him that we should not turn gay and lesbian marriage into a public issue. Indeed, I have been a strong advocate for making this a public issue.

But despite our disagreements on some of his conclusions, he is on to something ethically important. Indeed, in light of the recent public attention to Mayor Giuliani's personal life, Nagel's call for public civility seems even more urgent. I am no fan of Giuliani's. In fact, I disagree with almost all his major policies, and have often joined in public protests against them. Yet I agree with him that whatever his relationship with his good friend "is," it should have been considered his own business and that his "friend," who did not choose to live a political life, should not have had to face public exposure of her love life. Nor should Donna Hanover have had to have the intimacies of her marriage splashed all over the paper. It is hard enough to build and maintain relationships without having to give public interviews and answer intrusive questions about them.

So let me turn to Nagel's call for public civility, and to why feminists can be his allies. In Nagel's words,

> The public gaze is inhibiting because, except for infants and psychopaths, it brings into effect expressive constraints and requirements of self-presentation that are strongly incompatible with the natural expression of strong or intimate feeling. And it presents us with a demand to justify ourselves before others that we cannot meet for those things that we cannot put a good face on. The management of one's inner life and one's private demons is a personal task and should not be made to answer to standards broader than necessary. It is the other face of the coin: The public-private boundary keeps the public domain free of disruptive material; but it also keeps the private domain free of insupportable controls. The more we are subjected to public inspection and asked to expose our inner lives, the more the resources available to us in leading those lives will be constrained by the collective norms of the common milieu. Or else we will partially protect our privacy by lying; but if this too becomes a social norm, it is likely to create people who also lie to themselves, since everyone will have been lying to them about themselves since childhood.[3]

Nagel insightfully notes that forced public exposure, either by law or social pressure, actually feeds repression by cutting us off from the personal freedom we need to demarcate our own boundaries between our public persona and the other personae we live out within our intimate and sexual lives. For Nagel—and again I agree with him—we need to lead our lives as if some of our personae were invisible or effectively masked by our public face, even if we know that it is a fantasy and that we can never neatly divide those personae. Public personae always take some toll on us. Again to quote Nagel,

> At first it is not easy to take on these conventions as a second skin. In adolescence one feels transparent and unprotected from the awareness of others, and is likely to become defensively affected or else secretive and expressionless. The need for a publicly acceptable persona also has too much resonance in the interior, and until one develops a sure habit of division, external efforts to conform will result in inner falsity, as one tries hopelessly to become wholly the self one has to present to the world. But if the external demands are too great, this problem may become permanent. Clearly an external persona will always make some demands on the inner life, and it may require serious repression or distortion on the inside if it doesn't fit smoothly or comfortably enough. Ideally the social costume shouldn't be too thick.[4]

Whether or not we will be weighed down by social costume to the point that it actually drowns some of us under its burden, is undoubtedly related to the rigid enforcement of gender norms. There is clearly more freedom now for women and gays and lesbians to work through their own division between a public persona and their intimate selves. If one's sexuality is simply closeted as it was for so long—and let us face it, as it continues to be for gays, lesbians, transvestites, and the transgendered—then the freedom to shape what we want to display and what we want to keep to ourselves is effectively undermined. My argument for the moral and the legal right of the imaginary domain is that we desperately need the moral and psychic space to draw these boundaries for ourselves and to rework them as we see fit. I would argue that it is a fantasy that we can ever consciously or precisely know how we have separated ourselves from our public persona. But it is a necessary fantasy for the protection of our freedom, and more broadly, for our psychic ability to claim ourselves as a unique person who is something more than what meets the public eye.

Now, Nagel recognizes that feminism has at least played some role in loosening the hold of rigid gender identities, and therefore has helped to create a more tolerant sexual environment for women, which he believes is now part of our culture. He applauds, for instance, the end of the sexual double standard between men and women, which he admits was helped along by widespread contraception and the right to abortion. We, at least, need to remember who was and continues to be responsible for sex education for young women, including the provision of birth control materials. Feminists. Let us not forget that Margaret Sanger went to jail over and over again for no other reason than for demanding birth control *for women*. Her written materials and contraceptive tools were censored as obscene. Who is still at the forefront of the battle to maintain the right to abortion against the assault by the right wing? Feminists. The end of the double standard did not simply come about. It took thousands, if not millions, of women to fight for the conditions that would allow them sexual freedom. I know, because I was right there, in the nationwide mobilizations for the right to abortion.

So feminism deserves credit at least for the more tolerant environment Nagel describes and seeks to protect. As I have also argued, over and over again, one of the most important aspects of the second wave of feminism is that it challenged the imposed masquerade of femininity.[5] We need to claim our moral and psychic space to reimagine and represent the meaning of our sexual difference. Of course there are social costumes[6] for men and regulated norms of masculinity too, as much of the recent writing on boys and men has shown.[7] In no way do I want to trivialize the suffering of men under rigid norms of gender identity and imposed heterosexuality. I believe that it is real enough. The moral and legal space afforded by the imaginary domain is for everyone and therefore an expression of the generous spirit of a feminism that respects sexual freedom. The only restriction on the imaginary domain is the "degradation prohibition,"[8] which means that people must actually be treated as less than persons by someone else's expression of their sexual personae. For instance, if a straight white man believes that he is only free if the world is cleaned up of gay men, and advocates that therefore they should be denied all their civil rights, his expression of his sexual identity is curtailed. On the other hand, two gay men sitting in a restaurant do not simply by their appearance degrade a heterosexual couple in the sense of denying them their personhood and the rights that flow from it. It is one thing to be offended; it is another thing altogether to be degraded by being denied the status of a person. In a sexually tolerant society we may all have to put up with forms of sexual behavior that offend us. Mere offense should not be allowed to undermine the crucial value of freedom. Thus I agree with Nagel that even in sexual harassment law we should allow "the toleration of sexual feelings," and that this toleration "should include a certain margin of freedom for their expression, even if it sometimes gives offense, and even though it will often impose the unpleasant task of rejection on its target."[9]

Nagel wants to extend this kind of toleration to heterosexual men, even obnoxious heterosexual men, and that follows for me as a matter of principle. After all, the imaginary domain is for the obnoxious as well as the charming. However, as Nagel also notes, despite their own struggles few, if any, men would like to change their lot and become a woman. Some, of course, undergo surgery in order to do so. Still, as a matter of culture, Nagel rightfully points to the pervasive idea that it is somehow better to be a man; somehow men are superior even if the reasons for their superiority keep changing as the former ones are challenged. For example, in a recent *New York Times* article, Andrew Sullivan returned to the age-old argument that testosterone gives men the edge in almost all forms of public life.[10] Feminists have argued against blaming hormones for the inequality of women over and over again, and I am sure some feminists will take on his recent revival of that argument.

Although I agree with Nagel that the double standard has been undermined, there remain significant differences in the public treatment of men and women's sexuality. Women are more likely than men to be disparaged simply by an appeal to their "sex,"[11] or by the stereotypes about it. One of the political tasks of the second wave of feminism was to educate women about our bodies so that we could explore and enjoy our sexual difference, and free ourselves from internalization of the way our "sex" is viewed as a mark of inferiority. As Simone de Beauvoir reminded us long ago, for most men sex and subjectivity are one.[12] It is much harder to disparage a man simply by pointing to a stereotype of his sex.

Sexual harassment law certainly has played some role in correcting the perpetuation of this difference between the way in which men and women's sexuality is viewed by the public eye. To return to Nagel, I also want to argue that one ethical justification for the recognition of sexual harassment as a moral and legal wrong—yes, when properly defined to protect sexual freedom—is Nagel's own conception of public civility, and the corresponding protection from forced exposure of one's intimate life. Think, for example, of the case of Teresa Harris, a fairly recent and well-known sexual harassment case. She landed a job in a firm as a manager. Of the six managers Harris was the only woman to be employed in a managerial capacity who was not directly related to the owner. She loved her job but she eventually had to quit. Why? Her boss Hardy would not leave her sex out of her job. He would call her a "dumb-ass woman"; he would frequently suggest he and Harris start "screwing around." When she completed a big deal, her boss said in front of a number of workers,

"What did you do, Teresa, promise the ASI bugger Saturday night?" And on, and on.[13] Now, I am sure Nagel would have no trouble agreeing that her boss Hardy's behavior did not meet his standards of public civility.

And it is easy to see the ethical wrong in Harris's case exactly in Nagel's terms. As we have seen, Nagel argues that we need the space protected in order to develop a public persona; to work through which part of ourselves we turn over to the public gaze, and which part we will seek to shelter in our intimate lives. What happened to Teresa Harris was that she could not keep up her public face because of the constant barrage of comments about her "sex." Indeed, I would go so far as to argue that it is exactly this kind of barrage that makes it difficult for women to sustain a public persona. Sexual harassment law reasonably construed allows women, and any others who are affected by such bombardment against their sexuality, the moral and psychic space to form a public persona, to present it, and separate that persona from others they seek to articulate within the intimate aspects of life.

Women have historically been more vulnerable than men to having their sex used to undermine their attempt to develop the public persona that is necessary, as Nagel argues, for us to survive in the rough and tumble of the outside world.[14] There is no doubt that for centuries in the West, women were not supposed to appear as public figures. To attempt to have a public persona was a contradiction in terms. It was going out in drag. And despite the change in climate about what it is appropriate to say about women's sexuality in public spaces, we continue to be more subject to sexual speculation that trivializes our accomplishments. We all know what forms this trivialization take: "We don't have to listen to her because she is a dyke," "She's only advocating that position because she's too unattractive to 'get laid,'" or alternatively, "We don't have to take her tenure file seriously because she slept with all the men that wrote for her." When we have to constantly struggle to keep up a public persona against other people's fantasized projections of who we are sexually, it can seriously affect the way we experience public space. As Martha Nussbaum has noted,

> Prominent women are treated differently from prominent men. There is a tremendous amount of misogyny in our intellectual culture (in both America and Europe), and in the general popular culture. It is extremely difficult to get a hearing for your ideas (and your heart and soul) without it all being turned into something about your face and your sex life. I mean, I think and argue that people are embodied substances, and I do deliberately

write like one. I want my readers to know that this is an author who has felt grief and love and anger. But that doesn't mean that I am inviting people to investigate my personal life—any more than Seneca was, when he described his own emotions in his philosophical text. There is, however, an insatiable appetite for stories about prominent women, and I have increasingly found myself wanting to be a Garbo-like recluse.[15]

It is a long struggle to separate sexual shame from the expression of our sexual difference. This is why feminists who insist on the importance of freedom are willing to undertake the difficult task of delineating the relationship between sexual freedom and equality for all of us when it comes to the way we orient ourselves to our lives as sexual creatures. There is an important reason for us to affirm Nagel's call for public civility. The reason is that sexual freedom, and some degree of public civility, are intertwined with one another. In part because we all need to develop a public persona, as Nagel so rightfully notes. I leave you with a small dream of mine. That dream is that men will keep their drawers on in certain obviously public places, and that we will no longer have to talk about it because we can all take such behavior for granted.

NOTES

1. For my suggested reform of sexual harassment law so as to render it an ally of women's sexual freedom, see Drucilla Cornell, *The Imaginary Domain: Abortion, Pornography and Sexual Harassment* (New York: Routledge, 1995), chapter 4, "Sexual Freedom and the Unleashing of Women's Desire," 167–225.

2. Thomas Nagel, "Concealment and Exposure," *Philosophy and Public Affairs* 27 (Winter 1998): 3, 24.

3. Nagel, "Concealment and Exposure," 19–20.

4. Nagel, "Concealment and Exposure," 7.

5. See Drucilla Cornell, *Beyond Accommodation: Ethical Feminism, Deconstruction, and the Law*, new ed. (New York: Rowman and Littlefield, 1999), Introduction, "Writing the Mamafesta: The Dilemma of Postmodern Feminism," 1–20.

6. See generally Anne Hollander, *Sex and Suits* (New York: Alfred A. Knopf, 1994).

7. See, for example, Susan Faludi, *Stiffed: The Betrayal of the American Man* (New York: W. Morrow and Co., 1999). For a discussion on the sexual dilemmas of young boys, see Adrian Nicole LeBlanc, "The Outsiders," *New York Times Magazine*, 22 August 1999, 36.

8. For a longer discussion of the degradation prohibition, see Cornell, *The Imaginary Domain*, 8–13.

9. Thomas Nagel, "Personal Rights and Public Space," *Philosophy and Public Affairs* 24 (Spring 1995): 83, 106.

10. Andrew Sullivan, "The He Hormone," *New York Times Magazine*, April 2, 2000, 46.

11. For my distinction between sex and gender, see Cornell, *The Imaginary Domain*, 5–7.

12. See generally Simone de Beauvoir, *The Second Sex*, trans. H. M. Parshley (New York: Vintage Books, 1974).

13. For a further discussion of Teresa Harris's case, see Cornell, *The Imaginary Domain*, 207–11.

14. See generally Joan Scott, *Only Paradoxes to Offer: French Feminists and the Rights of Man* (Cambridge: Harvard University Press, 1996).

15. Martha Nussbaum, "Thinking in Public: A Forum," *American Literary History* 10 (Spring 1998): 1, 60.

# Conclusion

## The Penultimate: The Meaning of Impeachment and Liberal Governance

### Leonard V. Kaplan

> "My child, child of an old man—Antigone / where are we now? / What land, what city of men? / Who will receive the wandering Oedipus today? / not with gifts but a pittance . . . / It's little I ask / and get still less, but quite enough for me. / Acceptance—that is the great lesson suffering teaches, / suffering and the long years, my close companions, / yes, and nobility too, my royal birthright." Oedipus speaks thus at Colonus.

"Where are we now?"[1] This is not merely a question of place but of spirit. The recent impeachment and trial of William Jefferson Clinton provides an instructive point of departure for analysis because it captures the interaction between our law and our morality. The Clinton impeachment defines political, cultural, and legal limits to liberal toleration in a very concrete situation, with an explicit concern with sex, lies, and the manipulation of media and state power. And with a cast of living players. Around this event we may become anthropologists and see the tensions, if not the contradictions, in the liberal state. In one way or another, all the essays collected here present perspectives on our liberal institutions and culture.

In the following discussion I use two metaphors to attempt to integrate the various perspectives that are represented in these essays. I am also after bigger game. These essays represent at their best—and I think they are very good—partial glimpses into liberal culture and liberal modes of governance. Even the concept of liberal is problematic because not all liberal states and cultures are the same. Further, certain issues seem to me to be intrinsic to the human condition and are not merely a consequence of the liberal apparatus, law, and/or culture. Any jurisprudence worth consideration must try to distinguish between what is shaped by liberal institutions and what seems to be endemic to human existence itself.

One metaphor goes back to the origin of political theory, and can be found particularly in Greek discourse and in Jewish theology and practice. This metaphor I am calling pollution, or in Greek terms, miasma; it could also be called contagion. Did the Clinton impeachment process create more pollution for our political discourse, for the legitimacy of our legal and cultural institutions, or for our everyday social relations? The pollution metaphor operates as a hermeneutic for a mythopoetic analysis. *Oedipus at Colonus* and *Oedipus Rex* are two texts that illuminate the pollution problem for Western political theory and anthropology. The liberal state depends for its very operation on a certain degree of discretion from state officers, which necessarily entails a certain degree of corruption in the form of mistakes, lying, favoritism, stupidity, and downright theft. At some point this corruption—a form of pollution—threatens the legitimacy of liberal governance. It is our intellectual job and our pragmatic job to make sure that history neither repeats itself nor takes the form of an authoritarianism that has been called "fascism with a friendly face."[2] There are no procedural safeguards which by themselves can protect liberalism from degradation.

Pollution is central to the stories surrounding Oedipus. The citizens of Thebes "knew" that, to mix literary texts, "something was rotten in the state of Denmark" or rather, in Thebes. Sophocles was telling us that the plague was caused by Oedipus's "transgressions." He was telling us that the Thebans were right, that behavior in the polity could pollute the very structure of everyday existence.

Another perspective necessary for bringing intelligibility to the Clinton scandal is what I am calling structural analysis. Against the poets, Plato in *The Republic* and *The Laws* presented structural analyses on how to shape a polity so as to allow it both to flourish and to allow citizens to find their appropriate place within the particular mode of governance. Both modes of analysis—the metaphor of pollution and the seemingly more scientific idea of structural analysis—can help enlighten (1) our understanding of the significance of the Clinton impeachment, and, perhaps even more importantly, (2) tell us something about the future of our particular liberal state.

This penultimate essay is concerned with what the Clinton impeachment and its cultural reverberations teach about liberal law and culture. Will the impeachment turn out to be only a factoid with respect to Clinton's place in history, a symptom of something basically wrong with liberal culture and law, or the baseline for future struggles concerning our political and cultural norms?

## Providing Context

One meaning of the concept of postmodernism is that any attempt at textual coherence is a rhetorical artifice. Postmodernism cannot exist as a rhetorical or conceptual device short of its dependence on the various meanings of modernism. Modernism, with respect to texts, assumes a beginning, middle, and end. They stand by themselves. They reveal themselves in the dialectic between the given and the reader. This is what modernism teaches. Postmodernism disputes such coherence. Even those of us who are convinced that there is something correct about the notion that the world cannot be contained in conceptually neat ways, that knowledge and the world are both of a piece and problematically related, strive toward an illusory coherence despite ourselves.

Each of the essays here captures the personal intellectual positions of the respective commentators. Each is valid from the perspective of the particular author. Each represents only one voice. Liberalism as a hallmark demands toleration. We accept speech as free in the marketplace of ideas. However, we divorce free speech from active practice. One can say almost anything if there is some community that supports that saying.[3] However, one cannot do almost anything. In fact, what one can do is much more severely limited than is generally understood, particularly with respect to institutional transformation. What happens, then, is that speech becomes more strident as the likelihood of consequence from it grows more constrained.

In his classical analysis of Balinese society, Clifford Geertz illuminated the cultural interactions through the medium of one cockfight: their commitments, their deep play, their bonds of friendship toward themselves and their willingness to befriend strangers, their relationship to official legal structures, their sense of personal identity.[4] In short, Geertz's account offers the classical structural functionalist story about culture and political form, one that resonates with conviction and truth. Geertz's analysis of the cockfight showed how deep play reflected and shaped law and politics in Bali.

But Bali seems a more homogeneous society than our own, one with a different, more intelligible set of relations between the folk culture and the legal-state structure than the liberal, postmodern globalized state in which we live. The Clinton impeachment is more than deep play. Bali and its cockfight represents a simple case in a simple society. Geertz writes an elegant essay, using this one event to integrate the cultural and social. But my concern in understanding and commenting on these essays is with a polity that defies such coherence and elegance. The impeachment represents a significant psychosocial moment for the contemporary liberal state that must be approached, as it is in this volume, through philosophic, theological, aesthetic, and legal discourse.

The Clifford Geertz of the cockfight continues to teach, but in his more recent work, he provides postgraduate instruction on how to deal with complexity and textual structure. He helps us to refine our collective awareness of the problems of reading culture and making ethical and political judgments thereon. As "culture," "the liberal state," "society," "community," and "identity" have all become worn concepts, Geertz calls for more textured readings of state, society, culture, identity, and difference in a world that presently resists any easy theoretical grasp.[5] For Geertz, and for us, these abstract terms both demand concretization and yet seem to defy our capacity to make them continually heuristic. Such overdetermined complexity was reflected in the Clinton impeachment and trial.

I was not a Clinton fan. Clinton's 1992 decision to return to Arkansas to symbolically preside over the execution of a brain-damaged person did not endear him to me.[6] His callous abandonment of his friend and nominee Lani Guinier again was exemplary, for me, of deficiencies in his character.[7] More institutionally, the "New Democrats" led by Clinton seemed less progressive than the former (Nelson) Rockefeller wing of the Republican Party. No, Clinton did not represent my political preferences. But I did not want him impeached, much less removed from office. Nor did I want him to resign. In the game that played out, I became a fan rooting for my side in the battle with the Manichean forces of light and darkness. Is this an irrational position on the politics of impeachment? I root *against* the Dallas Cowboys, although they are commonly regarded by their fans at least to be America's team. For many of us, politics was reduced to fandom during the Clinton impeachment process. More intro-spectively, I think, I came to identify with Clinton. He was just so much more likable than his adversaries. "Considered judgment" in our cultural and legal debates is frequently so motivated. Psychological identifications and rationality are often confounded. Even after reflection, I am not sure that I could separate my "identifications" from my reasons for agreeing with most of the commentators in this volume that Clinton should not have been impeached. Americans, perhaps like the Greeks, enjoy the *agon*.[8] But for us, the *agon* becomes a game as well as a conflictual strug-gle. We don't like to lose. Some resentment concerning Clinton's survival as president can be attributed to the American unwillingness to lose.

My primary concern here is with what the impeachment experience reveals about the condition of law in our liberal state. I explore the topic through an examination of the special forms of discourse deployed by a set of worthy intellectuals who have responded to the invitation leading to this volume: "Present your candid analysis of what the Clinton im-peachment meant, continues to mean, and might mean for the future of our state." I am guided by a professional awareness that each author pro-vides something of significant worth for discovering the meaning of the impeachment experience. Where the authors significantly disagree, the reader has the opportunity to consider whether or not the disagreement is personal and says something about the nature of deeper conflicts in liberal discourse. Those disagreements reveal sometimes evident, some-times subtle, fissures in our liberal polity. The question becomes whether or not these disagreements can be successfully reconciled, or whether they point to true contradictions in the constitution of our liberal state.

Before proceeding further with summarizing remarks, I should, at least in preliminary fashion, highlight the salient facts that triggered our cockfight. Monica Lewinsky made oral love to Bill Clinton in a small area, the size of a proverbial closet. Lewinsky, by all accounts, desired the act, may well have inspired or initiated it, and took some pleasure in it. Clin-ton, presumably, enjoyed her ministrations. She was not coerced, cer-tainly not in any strong sense of the term. She became frustrated by her partner's seemingly adolescent behavior in not consummating a more satisfying lovemaking act. Clinton claimed that he had no sexual relations with Lewinsky. For all we know, in his mind, she wasn't a person, just a mouth. Therefore, from his subjective stance, he did not have a rela-tionship with her. Oral sex can be one of the most intimate, loving acts open to a participating couple. Alternatively, it can be a psychologically detached, alienated act of narcissistic gratification. My guess is that Clinton felt a certain affection for Monica.

These events, and the ensuing public relations and legal battles, were viewed by some as a moral struggle and by others as bordering on farce. After all, who could have imagined that when Woody Allen's character ironically commented in *Husbands and Wives* (1992) on a student's paper entitled, "Oral Sex in the Age of Deconstruction" that he would be assigning a title to a political sociolegal treatise.

This cockfight starts with an act of love, whether mutual or self-regarding, and not with the aggressiveness of the Balinese cockfight, where male roosters are trained to kill each other for sport. As long as the sex act between Bill and Monica remained covert, it fit the District of Columbia's ethos. Women have performed sex acts, outside marriage, with notable federal politicians throughout our history. The behavior of John Kennedy and Lyndon Johnson are only two recent presidential examples that most people considered adulterous.[9]

Why the Republican opposition so hated Clinton as to pursue an impeachment predicated on this act is a fascinating question. For some reason, Clinton came to symbolize everything that the Republican right detested. Ann Althouse has pointed out that Clinton's capacity to "triangulate" (that is, co-opt) the Republican agenda may have increased the animosity of the Republican right toward him.[10] Rationally, one might think that the Republicans would be pleased to have a Democratic president pursuing a substantially Republican agenda, acting as a virtual Manchurian Candidate. But Clinton's acts of fellatio resulted in more than a shaming of the President. They brought forth from the New Testament Christian Right an Old Testamental wrath. In a parody of *A Man for All Seasons*, Clinton played word games just as he played with Monica—in both cases, denying consummation.

## The Liberal State, Culture, and Law

Shlomo Avineri, in *Hegel's Theory of the Modern State*,[11] contends that Hegel thought he had solved the problem of the state and human governance with his concept of liberalism. For Hegel, the state had to allow the functioning of capitalistic political economy, but at the same time humanize the structural problems that it necessarily caused. For Hegel a state that merely allowed capitalism to thrive could not be called a state within his ethical and political parameters. Hegel understood, following Adam Smith and the other economists of the Scottish Enlightenment, that capitalist political economy necessarily created an impoverished class. Despite that fact, Hegel thought it was possible to fashion a mode of governance that would soften the hard edges caused by capitalist political economy and allow the flourishing of individuals in community that he thought necessary for a mode of governance to be properly called a state. Hegel started his analysis based on the presumption that affective needs could be taken care of in the nuclear family, the building block of his state theory. Other free associations—including what became unions, political parties, and religious groups—could provide the necessary associations to humanize human society. The effective state had to allow the individual to grow and the community to thrive. In this sense Hegel was trying at once to resolve stoic philosophy and Platonic idealism.

Each of our authors analyzes what followed from these sexual escapades. But the Clinton event goes well beyond the sexual, and well beyond lying about sex. Viktor Frankl has noted that America is based on a paranoid's dream: life, liberty, and the pursuit of happiness.[12] There is a central paranoia at the heart of our liberal state. There is a constant fear, that is, that the Leviathan state will turn from its liberal core to something more malevolent. Can compassionate conservatism turn into fascism with a friendly face?

I take the vulnerability of the liberal state as a starting assumption. Roberto Unger makes that case in *Knowledge and Politics*[13] from the point of view of critical legal studies. Unger's critique from the "super liberal left" concerning liberalism was original and powerful. Significantly simplifying critical legal studies' contributions to contemporary legal thought, two points stand out: (1) law is just another moment of capitalist power, and (2) law—case law or statutory—is necessarily indeterminate and therefore manipulable by the interests of capitalist structural needs. But such critiques of the liberal state were in themselves hardly new. Max Weber, a defender of liberalism, had already articulated its internal contradictions, and despaired of "fixing" liberalism's antinomies. Carl Schmitt, an ardent critic of the liberal Weimar state and later an apologist for fascism, had identified such significant problems with liberalism that he argued that liberalism should be abandoned as the paradigmatic political form.[14] Whereas Weber instructed Schmitt, the liberal left now reflects on Schmitt's teachings. Liberal theorists are now attempting to provide a response adequate to his criticism, one that will supply a theoretical buttress supporting liberalism so it does not slide into a despotic form. The Clinton impeachment becomes our analytic object—our cockfight—for examining, in the American cultural context, the current status of the liberal state. The rifts within liberalism are, at least to some degree, manifest in the battle over Clinton's impeachment and removal.

As liberals, we expect more than the minimal experience that the embittered Oedipus reveals at Colonus. We expect a social space conducive to human flourishing and communal commitment. Particularly we seek to reconcile family values *and* individual freedom, the conditions for concrete human dignity, and the alleviation of class, race, and gender bias. These are the conditions we expect from the liberal state, even though modern globalization has placed the market beyond the sovereignty of the liberal state. Yet even Schmitt, who despised liberalism, feared its resiliency.

Before Habermas, the 1970s brought critical attention to the notion of a legitimacy crisis for liberal states. Schmitt (currently the topic of significant intellectual attention in the United States) argued that the liberal state was spiritually bereft and that it was necessarily in such unhappy balance as to be taken over by special interests outside its citizen base. The liberal state, Schmitt held, could not make decisions. Its impotence stemmed in part from the cacophony of voices that sought recognition on the one hand, and the reality of corporate capture of the state apparatus on the other. Schmitt's decisionism would collapse liberalism's indeterminacy into a dictatorship where all institutions, including the judiciary, became subordinated to the will of the leader.

Schmitt hated liberalism because, in his view, it could not stand for anything but private interests. The liberal state sapped the spirit of humanity as it inevitably became the captive of special interests. However, like early claims that capitalism is belated and moribund, announcing the death of liberalism is premature. The compatibility of fascism with capitalism must not be underrated. Can our "liberal" discourse become so poisoned as to undermine the toleration of even certain kinds of evil necessary to preserve liberalism from something worse? Most of us would prefer to believe that our liberalism, given contemporary historical contingencies, is less drastic than alternative forms of governance might be.

Cass Sunstein, employing fine-grained social science methodology, confronts the legitimacy crisis that seems structurally endemic to liberalism—including ours—from a perspective different from that of Weber, Schmitt, or Habermas. The impeachment concerns Sunstein beyond its implication for Clinton's status and deeply engages the question of how, in our political culture, the masses can become so disconnected from po-litical institutions as to threaten the continuing "liberal" hegemony. The power of the analysis is twofold: it asks a central question and does so in terms more consonant with our liberal way (at least for some who would find reading Schmitt or Habermas off-putting and Weber of only histori-cal relevance). Intellectual life in the U.S. academy has itself become dis-junctive and fragmented. Even people who may agree on the bottom line can fail to connect as a result of sectarian, methodological differences. Too often social scientists only read social scientists and critical theorists only read critical theorists.

Leon Trakman analyzes the Clinton impeachment in a comparative frame, contrasting it with the Trudeau sexual scandal that absorbed Cana-dian attention in the 1970s. Local analyses of analogous cases among the various liberal states provide some insight on how cultural variants shape different outcomes. This analysis also identifies the potential distinctions among real liberal states.

The United States is only one example of a liberal state. Canada, much of Europe, and Japan can be so characterized. So we have a bit of comparative analysis. Do other liberal states respond the same way in terms of the crisis of leadership of the "Clinton" type? We tend to tie the liberal state to a cap-italist political economy. The European cultures surrounding those liberal states differ significantly. The Trudeau experience is sufficiently like and un-like the Clinton event and sufficiently close to us to be instructive. I am told Europeans found the Clinton impeachment bewildering. Apparently the culture of European liberalism differs from that of the United States on the issues that characterize the Clinton impeachment. Do these liberal states have more cultural sophistication than we do? Have they achieved the de-gree of maturity that Eric Rothstein argues the American public may have attained—reflected by its ethical discriminations during the process—by largely rejecting the attack on Clinton as hypocrisy? Rothstein sees the cul-tural possibility that the American public can and did see through the sound bites and the circus, got beyond the aesthetics of sensation and titil-lation, and came to a mature judgment.

We need more comparative readings to understand the differences cul-ture makes for various capitalist states. These states help set boundaries or frames for distinguishing how culture interacts with legal and other state structures, which French philosopher Louis Althusser in the 1970s called state apparatus.[15] Boaventura de Sousa Santos, Professor of Law

and Sociology at the University of Coimbra, Portugal, to cite another example, has contributed to our thinking about culture and state in the un-
even development of the world's economies. His work makes clear that
culture may degrade in favor of the economic, but that Marxian determi-
nacy is no sure truth. Future work must take into account how cultures
define their respective good or "goods," as Santos points out.[16] The problem is even more severe in that even cultural homogeneity for most state
entities in the world has become fragmented or contested. Terms like culture and the liberal state are indeed abstract. All these terms must be
grounded in specific events. In this case the Clinton impeachment partic-
ularizes these terms for analysis. For many Americans, and for Europeans
in general, Clinton's victory vitiated the pollution. In theological terms,
Clinton's transgression was redeemed by the ugliness of his adversaries.

We must bear in mind that the capitalist state can be authoritarian and
closed to toleration, that the capitalist state can be and has been fascist.
So we must be aware of movement of the capitalist state away from its
precariously balanced center until we can devise ways to make the state
truly liberal through law, in the sense that the individual is given sufficient opportunity to flourish in family and community and still keep the
structurally dispossessed as a class in mind. The comparative view provides one important perspective. Canada is not the United States, as
Trakman points out. From the viewpoint of one who taught law in
Toronto in 1980, I believe that Canadian culture is more trusting of authority than is its American counterpart.

The abstract liberal state can only be grounded in a concrete historical
setting. The same can be said for the so-called republican state, the
rhetorical form called forth by communitarian discourse. The liberal
state emphasizes individual prerogative and personal choice; the republican points toward a common good beyond individual right. In each case,
for the authors represented in this volume, the target is the United States
and its position in the world economy. The essays here do not point to
any utopian possibility, with the exception of David Kennedy's wickedly
ironic defense of libertine politics. They reflect a certain discord, but they
also point to some open possibilities for discussion and for cultural and
institutional reform.

We are faced with a Rawlsian question: what does it take for all represented voices and those that have been repressed to agree to a procedural
set of constraints that will keep violence to a minimum and fairness to a
maximum in contemporary U.S. politics and culture? What of those who

find the impeachment itself a continuation of the banality and futility of liberal politics? Linda Oakley, an Associate Professor of Nursing, for example, points out that the Clinton impeachment certainly did not address the health crises in this country, despite initial efforts. For her, at the least the Clinton program stood for something socially necessary that must be addressed for the sake of the poor and others. Health politics, she knows, were not at the heart of the impeachment, but they are there programmatically, strategically, and ideologically. Impeachment politics were also health politics. Impeachment also diverted attention from other aspects of the legal agenda trapped in deadlock.

## Theology, Religion, and Culture

The discourse over the impeachment grew acrimonious and, apparently to the American public, vindictive, hypocritical, and illegitimate—at least for the majority. A sizable minority in this country of ours sees Clinton as the Antichrist. He lied, he seduced, he deceived, he fornicated, committed adultery, and did not have to covet every woman because he took what he wanted, and he had a healthy appetite. We and the public looked at three types of accusations: criminal sexuality, perjury and public lying, and political abuses of process. The Clinton camp manipulated legal and social processes. The anti-Clintonians were both public and private: public, expressed by Starr, and private, from a coterie of lawyers who hated Clinton to those with big money to support and manipulate the public record of Clinton's crimes and bad moral character. Corporate power and influence over the judgments and the agenda of governance were not played out on either side. Arizona Senator John McCain brought the soft money issue to the primary debates in his failing populist attempt to pry the Republican nomination from George W. Bush.

Since George W. Bush told the American public (at a debate with the array of Republican contenders against him) that Jesus was the philosopher who taught him more than any other,[17] Christ must be considered a player in current politics. Naming John Locke as the political philosopher that taught one candidate the most, did not measure up. And even Orrin Hatch was astounded. Jesus trumps Locke. (Locke would not have minded but might have pointed out that the City of God was still in the distant future.) Not to be outdone, Democratic presidential candidate and incumbent Vice President Al Gore has been quoted as saying that, when faced with a difficult decision he asks himself, "What would Jesus do?"[18] Joseph Lieberman, the Democratic vice presidential candidate, has been cautioned by the Anti-Defamation League for rhetorically overstepping the boundary between religion and state.[19] Lieberman said that because of his nomination, "I hope it will enable people, all people who are moved, to feel more free to talk about their faith and about their religion. And I hope that it will reinforce the belief that I feel as strongly as anything else, that there must be a place for faith in America's public life." He added, "We know that the Constitution wisely separates church from state, but remember: the Constitution guarantees freedom of religion, not freedom from religion."[20] The language of theology and institutional religion is very much alive in American politics and was played out in the impeachment game. But if theology is with us, what theology are we talking about?

Are we referring to the theology of love and forgiveness, or a theology of hate of difference? With respect to Clinton, so-called social issues (for example, abortion, homosexuality) seemed to occupy most of what may be viewed as theological space. Saint Paul, in his address to the Romans, certainly made it clear that homosexuality was sinful, but not more sinful or on any different level from a host of other sinful behaviors. His concern went beyond the sexual and involved love and care—a program beyond genital politics.[21] Too often our culture confounds the sexual as the whole of the holy. Capital accumulation is not of the Christian essence, but it is far less frequently decried as transgressive than homosexuality or abortion.

The very structure of the "appropriate" boundary between church and state was on the table during the Clinton debates. The Clinton situation intimated what was and will likely become a greater struggle in defining church-state interaction. For example, the future status of public education is up for debate in the school voucher controversy. A few votes on the United States Supreme Court can change social practice definitively for years. Besides vouchers, the place of God, and whose God, is also on the current political agenda. Creationism may have lost out for the moment as a curricular requirement in Kansas, but this battle is ongoing in our "liberal" contest. George W. Bush has signaled that he would like churches to dispense state welfare dollars. For the United States, such a reallocation of institutional power and obligation could prove revolutionary. Germany, I understand, has a variant on the inchoate idea. Germany does distribute welfare through established churches, and France also compensates established religion. However, although both are liberal states, their culture is markedly different from our own.

Clinton somehow became the personification of what certain segments of society detest, and others (in the center or left of center) certainly dislike, albeit for different reasons. Leadership frequently becomes the focus for dissatisfaction that otherwise cannot so easily be expressed. Presidents frequently take credit or blame for economic realities over which they have little control or even understanding. Oedipus Rex, the Usurper, marked the tragic fall of a self-deceived man who thought that reason could outdistance fate. Oedipus did not solve the riddle of humanity in answering the Sphinx, much less the riddle of his own history or identity. Pollution, miasma in Thebes, instigated Oedipus's investigations. A plague seized the state and the citizens turned to Oedipus to find and excise its cause. This was the assumed obligation of leadership. Something was transgressively wrong in the state of Thebes. Oedipus bought into this belief system. As long as the transgressive remained unpunished, the citizens thought, their plight would continue.

Leadership alone could address the problem. Oedipus, you will recall, anticipated the call of his people. He had already sent Creon to engage the Oracle. Tireseus was on call. Oedipus was a relentless investigator, well before Starr, and with as many resources at hand. He was Rex, after all, and he was going to get to the bottom of the problem and find the cause of the plague. Because there must be a cause. This is part of our received heritage. And, in fact, as Sophocles dramatizes, there was a very human cause for the pollution, and it seemingly centered on the primal act that the unsuspecting Oedipus took as his due after he had solved the Sphinx's conundrum. So much for rationality. So much for the integrity of deep investigation. Oedipus, of the hurt foot, carried the trauma with him and could in no way escape his fate. So cautions the conservative Sophocles.

But after Nietzsche, much less Foucault, many of us believe that we, like Oedipus, must look out for ourselves, individually and corporately. Any meaning is personal and social. If God exists, it is only as a trace. Pollution is but superstition. This is the secular view. But remnants at the level of the person—and discourse at the level of various groups—still hold to some view of "old-time" religion. Moreover, theology is returning even to the legal academy.[22]

The view that cultural pollution, at the spiritual level, can traumatize the body politic is embedded in our view of Athens and probably of Jerusalem as well. Where many of us scoff at the notion that AIDS is the punishment for sexual sin, I do not find it so clear that certain evil actions in the past—of Leviathan, bureaucracy-laden nation-states—do not pollute their present. Slavery still pollutes the United States culturally. Germany, the European Union notwithstanding, still suffers the taint of its fascist "experiment." How far do I want to push pollution as a metaphor? Is it an archaic heuristic visiting of the sins of the fathers onto the children of the third and further generations? Didn't the rewriting of the Ten Commandments in Deuteronomy create individual and not corporate or generational responsibility? The question is not rhetorical but rather historical and, in fact, ontological. Will the Clinton affair ramify through the future, auguring the future debilitation of "liberal democracy" such as most of us now enjoy?

Clinton, therefore, represents our Oedipus, a polluter of liberal trust on the one hand and a sinner on the other. This takes us to a level of rancor expressed with conviction and force in the essay by Richard Neuhaus, who asserts that Clinton is an alleged rapist among his other crimes. Clinton is and was an alleged rapist, adulterer, liar, and thief for many who decried his "triumph" in the Senate. Many feel deeply that there is and should be no toleration for his acts. History is cumulative and so a consideration of the Clinton "pollution" adds unease to other recent moments in American history (for example, the assassinations of King and the Kennedys), evoking cultural disgust. Neuhaus is not and was not alone in making Clinton symbolic of cultural decay. The House leadership, we are told, was taken behind the scenes and offered "proof" of Clinton's rape of a protesting woman before he assumed the presidency. This private viewing was persuasive, we are told, to many on the Republican side of the House. This is a strong conviction, one from a truly American pulpit, and is in line with a strain of continuous fundamentalist horror of certain, selective transgressive acts generally around issues of sexuality, but less generally around issues of political economy. (One should, however, credit the Catholic bishops' attack on capitalism as a notable exception to my general claim.)[23]

We must look to culture as an independent force if we are to make sense of the Clinton scandal and liberal institutions. Theology has always informed, if not dominated, our culture. Our "liberal," "secular" society has been recognized by the U.S. Supreme Court as a Judeo-Christian society. But theological implications for culture are not homogeneous in the United States, and presumably will become less so as more religions increase their membership and struggle for political voice. As Aviam

Soifer notes, it isn't clear whether a crucible is used to separate or to meld various elements. A Christian variant inspired some of the more virulent Clinton adversaries. Stephen Toulmin, however, reminds us that the history of Christianity itself until very recently would have opposed the attempt to degrade Clinton. How and why did certain aspects of Christian ideology and religious practice change so significantly—and in Toulmin's view, so wrongheadedly? What can be used to predict or impede such change (an open and important question for political theory)? But Christianity too, in practice provides other readings which help make the Clinton impeachment intelligible.

Lawrence Rosen grasps that our religiously informed culture provides the most profound vehicle for understanding the reasons for the outcome in the Clinton affair to date. Rosen reads our culture, in this case at least, as Baptist. Baptist theology, Rosen implicitly argues, differs from other competing theologies in the United States with respect to the outcome of the impeachment. Clinton is the man who has urges and faces constant temptations, who sins and seeks forgiveness. His acts were personal, Rosen argues and not, as were Nixon's, ever perceived to be abusive of state power by most of the culture. Clinton is most certainly sexual, probably self-deceived, but no Oedipus. But let us remember that Oedipus is the Usurper and not the legitimate King of Thebes. Clinton's legitimacy as president was questioned in the impeachment proceedings and will continue to provide a baseline for the future. Did his acts pollute the body politic as Oedipus polluted Thebes? The question of pollution is also central to these essays, as is the question of legitimation.

## Civil Religion and American Politics

As a scene of instruction, the Clinton impeachment does not reach the exemplary narratives of Oedipus, Abraham and the binding of Isaac, the travails of Job, or the passion of Jesus. But it is our cockfight and a worthy scene of instruction. This cockfight is central to America's civil religion. I learned in elementary school that the Johnson impeachment was unjustified, merely political. John Cooper reflects on that moral teaching and questions its truth. Cooper makes a case for identifying constitutionalism in U.S. history and culture as central to our secular religion. Impeachment is a limit case for our constitutionalism. For Cooper the historian, the Clinton situation brought the impeachment of Johnson—the first and previously the only impeachment in the history of the United States of a sitting president of the Republic—into focus again. Johnson should have been impeached and removed from office, Cooper argues. Cooper's contribution opens significant issues about the past and about current conditions of African American politics and identifications. In the limited space of his essay, Cooper suggests a broader argument for why Johnson should have been removed. Johnson's politics defeated the interests of the former slaves, ensuring a serfdom little better for many and perhaps worse for some than slavery itself. If this is true, the American people could have been educated on this fact and on Reconstructionist policy in general. Did any African American politician take the opportunity to educate the American people about the Reconstruction deal and sellout? This provides an interesting observation about the state of African American interests.

Instead African Americans mobilized and constituted a significant political and *moral* base for Clinton. Arguably, African American politicians were as rhetorically elegant as anyone in the entire Clinton affair. Why did they so identify with Clinton, the New Democrat, given the fact that his contributions to poor blacks (and the poor in general) were minimal? What prompted Toni Morrison to call Bill Clinton the first black President of the United States? Black comedian Chris Rock says it's because Clinton is always in trouble with the law, his friends are all going to jail, and his wife is a bitch. But I don't think that's what Morrison had in mind. My conjecture is that "the enemy of my enemy is my friend" goes some way to explaining African American identification with Clinton. Further, the African American leadership may have decided that remarking on anything but the impeachment process in hand could confuse the American people. Clinton did make an effort to appoint African Americans and women to high-visibility positions in government, but I do not have an adequate explanation otherwise for the seemingly overwhelming identification. Perhaps Lawrence Rosen's analysis of Baptist theology also ties in specifically to black identification with Clinton, the tempted sinner.

The meaning of impeachment also unfolds with the contribution from Mark Tushnet. Tushnet points out that the Clinton opposition chose to "legalize" the impeachment process. This was not constitutionally necessary nor, Tushnet argues, is this the best view of the meaning of impeachment. Tushnet complements Cooper's analysis.

Each of the last two centuries provided one case of presidential impeachment. Is this to be a normative standard like Washington's attempt to keep the presidency to two terms by custom and not by law? Or should we use impeachment more politically, like a parliamentary vote of no confidence? Tushnet makes a case for reconsidering the political as opposed to a more restrictive reading of what impeachment meant originally, and what it might, and should mean very differently, in the future. If Tushnet's analysis prevails, then the Clinton impeachment is truly significant—what has been called a watershed—in the governance of the United States into the new future. The Congress could, without moral obloquy, following Tushnet's direction, impeach the President for policy reasons alone. The impeachment process would, in these terms, move the United States toward a parliamentary form of government.

## The Limits of Law in American Liberal Culture

I think we have the potential—even in the face of postmodernism's ideology holding that theory can only be fragmentary, that reason is only open to momentary illuminations—to find the thread that could tie the public and private in liberal theory and contested practice together. My solution, however, is exhortatory. Weber's understanding of the gap between liberal theory and practice must be acknowledged.

So what is my theoretical insight that could hold the center together? I said at the end of the last section that liberalism cites the rule of law but actually depends on the use of discretion for legal execution. Tuerkheimer points to discretion in his grand jury analysis. Discretion is central to the understanding of how language is applied to the legal world beyond the grand jury. Legal theorists talk of linguistic indeterminacy, that is, language tied only to the object in the world based on the understanding of interpretative communities. "Keep off the grass," does not mean "do not use marijuana," but "do not step on the lawn."

Starr abused his discretion, though arguendo, he operated legally. Discretion in our legal polity must link with wisdom, and it must link with human care. At each level, the legal official charged with execution of the law must consider the common good over sectarian ideology before determining whether to arrest, charge, or deport, *inter alia*. Such judgment must conform, particularly in high-visibility cases, with concern for the individual and how others might read the context of that judgment.

If we live in a Judeo-Christian culture at odds with secular humanism, only *care* ties the strands of our ideologies together. But in fact, as I read

Judaism and Christianity and secular humanism, care is central to each. Love thy neighbor as a brother. Welcome the stranger. Love the sinner, if not the sin. Do unto others . . . Kant's categorical imperative attempts to utilize reason to universalize an ethic from personal experience. Bonhoeffer warns that we must go beyond our personal ethic to respond to the plight of the other. And Levinas, in *Nine Talmudic Readings*,[24] teaches that we owe a radical response to the other that is not grounded in any contractual obligation but in existence itself.

The problem is not that there is no thread that can tie Judaism, Christianity, and secular humanism together. Rather, we lack the wisdom and the care in the world to do so. The market relations that shape our culture dictate that it is foolish not to maximize profit. These market relations pour into the public terrain and expunge the various theologies that dictate more than arm's-length social relations.

But it is not only the theological strain that indicates pollution in contemporary life, exemplified nicely by the Clinton imbroglio. Clinton's defenders, perhaps not using the discourse of miasma, still advert to it with notions like sexual McCarthyism. Robin West articulately places *Kulturkampf* as central to her thinking in her essay. Did the Clinton contretemps continue a fall from grace for "our" American polity? In nontheological language, the language of critical political philosophy, has the impeachment affair added to a "legitimation crisis" that continues after the assassinations of the Kennedys and of King, *inter alia*? Is even the attenuated liberalism of Bill Clinton considered so dangerous by the radical right that status degradation, if not regicide, is in order? Are the raging discourses of postmodern liberalism so incompatible, and the general population so disconnected from those discourses, that the impeachment is symptomatic of something worse than lying about sex and presidential manipulation of media and staff in self-defense? Neuhaus is appalled, and I do not think his is merely rhetorical horror, but an honest conviction that must be addressed on its own terms.

A more measured prognosis, of course, is not lacking. According to the political scientists David Canon and Kenneth Mayer, at first blush at least, every prediction with respect to the impeachment turned out to be mistaken. Canon and Mayer do a fine job of demonstrating that all indices show that the impeachment remained remarkably impervious to prediction. What we do not have is a complete picture of any trade-offs that might have taken place. Why did the House leadership protect Clinton—a man that Minority Leader Dick Gephardt, for example, had reason to believe was selling out a good deal of the Democratic program in his triangulations? Were any deals made, or did the rancor of the Republican leadership itself allow the Democratic leaders to identify with Clinton? But matters in the body politic remain remarkably the same after the impeachment, Canon and Mayer point out. The question becomes whether there is a fault line that the Canon-Mayer analysis missed. If they are right, this may point to the capacity of our liberal culture to absorb what seems to be a crisis and turn it into meaninglessness.

Frank Tuerkheimer, in his description of federal grand jury practice, indicates that what Starr did with the grand jury, though perhaps not politically wise, was not out of line with grand jury practice. The Clinton impeachment process certainly brought the grand jury to public attention. But though the grand jury in Starr's hands looked sullied, it is not so clear that once back to low visibility, any reform of the grand jury as an institution is on the national agenda. Nor is it clear who might want reform or how reform would be effectuated. The problem with the liberal rule of law—and this is intrinsic to Tuerkheimer's paper—is that no rule is self-executing. When our institutions work, they work not because of legality itself but because of the refined judgment of those who must invoke and execute state process. The special prosecutor statute, whose use in Starr's hands so frightened so many of us, was itself constituted as a reform of the abuse of power. Those of us who study law in our liberal polity have long understood the problematics of discretion and its necessary place in the liberal polity. Starr acted "legally" but against the American grain. Our liberalism has within it the potential to turn against the values that many of us feel are central to the protection of individual liberty. Trust in procedural mechanisms is, it seems to me, misplaced. In unwise or malevolent hands, procedural reform may offer little protection today of the values that it originally was designed to address.

Due to the limitations of space, we have no essay addressing other changes in the operation of liberal state politics between the executive, judicial, and congressional branches. Tuerkheimer's analysis necessarily focused on the grand jury. It did not go to the relationship of the judiciary and the special prosecutor. Boa Santos is one commentator who has called attention to the politicization of the (American) judiciary.[25] The Clinton impeachment still presents an object for further analysis about how politics entered into the selection and continuation of Starr as Special Prosecutor. Clinton's appointments of federal jurists have been notoriously thwarted by Jesse Helms. Further, the degradation of the judiciary has become evident in recent years at the level of individual states. More money is being spent in more partisan ways for judicial jobs. If this process continues in this vein, public respect for the judiciary will evaporate to the point where judges will be seen as little but politicians.[26]

Clinton's appointments to the federal judiciary have been blocked in unseemly manner. The Fourth Circuit, whose jurisdiction includes a sizable African American population, is understaffed despite Clinton's attempts to appoint African American jurists to the circuit. The judiciary in the United States and within the various states is becoming more visibly politicized. The Clinton affair brought a further degree of scrutiny to the politics of judicial manipulation. Which federal judges arranged the appointment of Starr after the first special prosecutor had seemingly finished with Whitewater? Perhaps federal judges have always been less than neutral in their judgments, but the Clinton impeachment seems to me to have marked a visibility and a potentially dangerous tendency to increasingly politicize the judiciary, again at the cost of the legitimacy of the liberal state.

Elizabeth Rapaport describes the bind that feminist legal theorists confronted in the Clinton impeachment struggle. In our pluralist political and legal culture, many intellectuals ally themselves to agendas that reflect commitment to particular groupings. Most of these thinkers can easily make the case for why their advocacy for the particular is in the service of the common good. Jurisprudentially minded feminists confronted a theoretical conundrum in the battle over Clinton's survival. Enemies used their arguments on sexual harassment, for example, to disable Clinton. Gary Hart, on the one hand, and Robert Packwood, on the other, were both brought down by their respective sexual practices. Packwood was a legislative ally for women's issues on the moderate Republican side, a place that needed allies. Drucilla Cornell and Robin West make clear why they and most other feminists resolved to support Clinton, despite any personal or political distaste.

Feminist scholars have been particularly effective in demonstrating how drawing the public-private liberal line was and is a political decision, one that generally lowers the visibility of women's issues. West elaborates on Rapaport's analysis of the maturation of the realpolitik of feminist jurisprudence. Her analysis identifies the fault line and proceeds on each line. She argues for the need for a more fine-grained analysis of issues concerning feminism and power, and intimates a future direction for analysis. She also understands that the attack on Clinton constituted a

*Kulturkampf* designed to turn back the feminists' clock on reform. Feminists had to fight on two fronts, and they chose wisely, she argues.

Drawing on the Clinton case, Cornell and Jean Bethke Elshstain, each sensitive to feminist issues, provide different perspectives on how and where the fluid line between public and private might be and should be drawn. In this case, the dispute also centers around opposing "liberal" and Republican norms and ideals. The difference between the two positions opens a theoretical space that demands continued discussion. Did feminists, who for the most part have argued that the family with respect to wife abuse and with respect to the economy should be understood as public, somehow sell their principles short? But Cornell argues for discretion in relation to kinds of behavior that she associates with Clinton, whereas Elshtain fears a loss for feminists' concerns with workplace seduction and coercion. Each position is nuanced and demands separate attention and theoretical concern. Elshtain and Cornell identify a structural space in the liberal state that I would like to see developed beyond impeachment politics. Both theorists recognize the problem of the limits of legal manipulation. Cornell, the more "liberal" of the two, understands that often the law must rely on good faith in social relations; Elshtain, the more communitarian, fears that not using the law against Clinton in the impeachment matter will harm feminist gain and, in the long run, hurt the common good.

Sunstein, Elshtain, and David Novak desire that the United States become more a republic than a liberal state. In this volume and elsewhere, they have expressed a desire for a polity more dedicated to communal values, toward a common good, rather than one founded on liberal possessive individualism. Each points up a different constraint on communal life and legal arrangement reflected in the impeachment outcome. Sunstein analyzes the problem of continued state legitimacy in the event that too many become disaffected with core institutions of governance. Elshtain reflects on the shifting borders of the public and private divide in the present cultural mix, and fears a loss for women and the culture as an outcome, if Clinton's survival is interpreted as a win for his behaviors. Novak, from a conservative position, fears that the conservative desire to protect its communal values against resistance traumatizes the body politic. He revisits the law-morals question and argues that morality cannot and should not be forced on the recalcitrant by the state. But what of the voices that fear that the state approaches Sodom? What of these voices? They are, by no means, all fundamentalist. Some are themselves

liberal at the core, detesting perjury, sexual harassment, and abuse of political authority.

Liberalism necessarily has to draw a line between private and public,
which was severely contested in the impeachment process. Did Clinton
emerge as the betrayer of his ostensible feminist thrust? What is going on
when those who generally oppose legal reforms for women deploy the
very weapons against those who have pushed that feminist agenda, to the
extent to which it has been politically asserted? Elshtain, Cornell, Rapaport, and West specifically concern themselves with gender politics, how
the view from that perspective played out in the impeachment process,
and the theoretical and policy questions that have been left unresolved.

Cornell, Rapaport, and West, particularly, make clear that feminist jurisprudence has reached a level of resilience and political subtlety evoked by
the Clinton scandal. As all three make clear, feminists as pluralistic players
are not hard ideologues, not bound to a vapid set of rigid principles. Not
every feminist theorist agrees. Elshtain is one theorist who decries thwart-
ing principle and perhaps even the rule of law based on realpolitik.

In any case, Robert Gordon points toward a structural aspect to our
liberal polity that is consonant with Schmitt's insight. Gordon points out
that the left, through the last half of the twentieth century, has been
thwarted and frustrated in its attempt to express the moral outrage that
it felt about racism, poverty, and gender inequity, among other issues.
With the Clinton impeachment process, the right found itself similarly
thwarted. The liberal state, Gordon persuasively argues, did not allow the
effective expression of moral outrage, neither in the sixties and seventies
from the left nor in the *affaire* Clinton, from the right. The question for
Gordon and for us: How stable is our liberalism? Gordon points ironically to all that liberalism has promised at the level of ideology and the
significant and growing shortfall between promise and delivery.

## Language, Ethics, and Aesthetics

Sex, lies, power, and statecraft are four terms that run through the history
of political philosophy. Sex and lies are central themes in Kieslowski's
critically acclaimed *Decalogue*[27] and central to the Clinton impeachment.
Thou shalt not bear false witness. Thou shalt not commit adultery. Both
are part of the big ten from Sinai "with your mind in mind," as Firesign

Theater taught us in the 1960s. What is a lie that counts, and counts for what? Does lying about sex differ from other lying?

Lawrence Solan engages in a linguistic read of lying and the law as he "gleans" from his linguistic perspective the ambiguity of much social and private lying. He points out how much lying is built into the everyday practice of law. In fact, lying to the state as a mode of existence may be heroic and should be protected as much as possible. Kant would have told the truth even to the state official coming to arrest a friend. Would Kant have taken the same view if he had been writing during the Holocaust and the SS was coming for his friend, his child, father and mother? Minimally, Solan's analysis forces us to examine what might be called the taxonomy of lying, differentiating good lies from benign lies to corrupt lies.

The impeachment was as raw as a cockfight. The state intruded into the family of anyone who could make the case against Clinton. The family offered little protection or privilege when the state came calling—we found this out watching Starr operate. Remember that Tuerkheimer makes the persuasive case that Starr did what federal prosecutors generally do with grand juries. Should a mother lie to protect her daughter from a threat from the state? Our polity rests not so much on the rule of law but on the discretion that officials use when invoking legal process. No procedural mechanism in itself will safeguard the interests of liberty. Solan poses the question: Where does the line of everyday lying presume too much for the system to bear and potentially turn into too much corruption?

Anyone who has thought about the politics of the liberal state—and perhaps all states—understands that statecraft always involves a realpolitik fraught with lies. What is unresolved is not the question of lying but which lies are sufficient, in this case, to remove a president from office. American public opinion suggested that Clinton's lie did not reach such a threshold. But the problem of lying, public and private, remains open only to contextual solution. Lying itself remains a part of statecraft and personal defense. Only George Washington would so readily admit that he chopped down the cherry tree and only in the myth.

Lawrence Joseph, as only a poet who is also a legal scholar can, presents us with the Babel that overwhelmed the consuming public as we tuned into and out of the Clinton–Monica–Starr affair. Coming from the theological and legal left, Joseph makes the point in the Clinton affair that Schmitt predicted against Weimar on the far right. Liberalism—in this case media-motivated—presented a cacophony of voices, of virulence and outrage.

Language reached a level of hysteria separating from the event into a disconnected noise. Joseph forces us to confront the degradation of language in our culture. Crisis is everywhere and nowhere. This points beyond the fact that language is conventional, with only negotiated attachments to objects external to words. To be heard requires the hyperbolic, the fantastic, and the phantasmic. Reference is lost in an orgy of oral and written rage. The civil middle, the gray-on-gray of liberalism, is blotted out as pundits scream and the public tunes out. But the hysteria of linguistic usage in our liberal polity is matched by another tone, one evinced during the 2000 Republican convention, where the voice of the GOP was generally warm, calm, and inclusive. This use of mystifying language poses its own dangers—perhaps as dangerous as the rancor which at least calls attention to divisive fault lines in the national structure.

Andrew Weiner cites Shakespeare to point to the capacity of an earlier time to deal, at least theoretically, with an ethical complexity that liberal discourse seems to resist, despite its commitment to tolerance. Shakespeare, Weiner notes, took joy in the ontology of "is," whereas we feel defrauded by such legalistic wordplay. Weiner decries the lack of intelligent and critical debate that great Western texts should have taught as humanly open to institutionalization. The battle over the canon that has occupied academic politics in recent years brings into focus the fact that even the dead, white, male "great books" included wisdom that addressed the problem of difference. Of silencing, of injustice. This does not mean that academics should not have included more voices. Weiner points to the discouraging fact that we know more, even from the old classics, than we know how to put to liberal institutional use.

Eric Rothstein, a noted scholar of eighteenth-century literature, the Age of Reason, argues forcefully, with wit, play, and erudition that as a nation we have matured so as not to need a president who is ethically exemplary, just one who is competent. The American public, at least with respect to the Clinton case, rose above media mystification and resolutely held the line between personal relations and political concern. But Aviam Soifer shows that this gold standard itself can become parody. The maturity that Rothstein finds in the citizenry was certainly not based on the actions of the decisive players, but on the public response. *Boobus Americanus* was not so easily duped on the *sexual* question.

Soifer underscores the irony of a key moment in our constitutional crises, an aspect of what Cooper properly labeled our civil religion, played as if out of Gilbert and Sullivan. How could one understand the Chief Justice presiding over the impeachment proceedings wearing a costume sym-bolizing a judge who had corrupt intent toward his underage ward? Our process has reversed the alchemist formula. Soifer makes the case that our leadership and our media converted gold into lead. Who could make the case for the presiding U.S. Supreme Court Chief Justice enjoying himself, decked out in his Gilbert and Sullivan garb, chairing the Senate's response to the House's finding of impeachment? Rehnquist is a clever man and cer-tainly was letting those "in the know" know that he was aware of the banal-ity of this impeachment game. Rothstein's view is compatible with Soifer's. Rothstein hopes the maturity that the public showed will translate into ef-fective politics, ethics, and substance over scandal as mystifying entertain-ment. But when the leadership is so out of touch with polity, even a mature public may well become dangerously disaffected.

Clinton is not Oedipus and should not be held to that exalted and ulti-mately tragic standard. But what of principles beyond the utilitarian? If we do not need even our most august leaders, our president to be more than effective CEOs, should not transgressive behavior in itself invite, if not our wrath, our collective condemnation? Granted, the impeachment itself was condemnatory, but was it so insufficient that, as it turns out, we have reinforced public lying about private sexual sinning? Adultery is, after all, condemned by Christian and Jew and not generally held in re-pute even by its practitioners. But is it, in fact, a perquisite of high office for sufficiently power holding, engaging seducers, as Oakley suggests? Does the beat just go on, business as usual?

David Kennedy continues a tradition, last asserted in the late 1960s, that polymorphous perversity is a good and not a sin. In fact, in this cen-tury Kennedy's genealogy can be traced back to Wilhelm Reich and the notion that the individual eroticized body must be made free to have true political freedom. Herbert Marcuse and Norman O. Brown debated how best to do this. They agreed that (sexual) repression was but an expres-sion of a deeper repressive imperative on human and political expressive-ness.[28] To me, Kennedy evokes this debate. *Homo ludens* includes sexual play.[29] What to Neuhaus is symbolic of ethical decay, represents to Kennedy human maturity and the possibility of liberating human sexual-ity, still bound by shame, hypocrisy, and contempt for its loving and lib-erative potential. The battle is certainly joined with respect to Neuhaus, West, Rothstein, and Kennedy. Neuhaus would cabin us in moral stric-tures that repress any openness to human potential. Where Kennedy sees liberation in the libertine, Neuhaus sees licentiousness.

Is there any room for agreement between Neuhaus and West, who fears the reinstauration of his moral regime as state practice, Rothstein, who makes the case that we have outgrown such fetishized taboo, and Kennedy, who positively wants to welcome a new age? Oakley perceives male prerogative, where Kennedy regrets that Clinton did not have the gumption to say, "We did it and I enjoyed it." Given a chance, Monica, who stands forth heroically for Kennedy, could well have said, "Yes we did it. Yes it was a pleasure. More people should do it. Why not?" If no grounds for rapprochement on impeachment are available, does this mean that the cultural battle will be reengaged with as much rancor at the next available opportunity?

## *Penultimates*

The essays here are, necessarily, at best penultimate. They are also penultimate in the sense that the story continues to unfold and will likely alter as future events play out. The penultimate of my title also refers to the work of Dietrich Bonhoeffer for whom the term means, minimally, the moment before one encounters political and ethical abyss.[30] According to monotheism, it is a place where the mandate of the state should protect society and the individual from the nothingness that evil, according to monotheism, leads. If, as the young, idealist lawyer in Kieslowski's "Thou Shalt Not Kill" episode expresses it, the law should enhance, not diminish human thriving, individual and collective.[31] Do we have the will, and even if we do, can we enhance our institutions to yield results compatible with the convictions of the warring sides and form a republic and not just a marketplace as the American state continues to be transformed?

So I am looking for continuity and discontinuity in reading these essays. Agreement exists, often inchoate, but conflict and acrimony continue to exist. I do not believe that because people understand each other, they will be more kind to each other. The Greeks and the Trojans understood each other well indeed. They shared the same gods, festivals, rules of battle. That did not stop the Greeks from destroying Trojan society—the remnant with Aeneas, who to some represented the proto-Christian in Virgil's *Aeneid*, arrived ultimately to found Rome.

In fact, as I write this summary and critical commentary, the *New York Times Magazine* has published an essay quoting a former head of the CIA as stating, "God, the United States is a fascist state."[32] This is an extraordinary statement from a measured Ivy League-trained lawyer and deep insider. I mention this characterization because the people who are in dialogue here have thoughtful positions on the political nature of the state and its culture. These positions shape their epistemologies and ground their analyses and their personal sense about what happened. What implications might be drawn, and what practices are open to intellectuals whose disagreements are only more articulate renderings of more inchoate views in the culture at large? Intellectuals both reflect the world and try to influence it, frequently with minimal or ironic consequences.

So what might I say in "conclusion." Our liberal state is contentious. It may be fragile. It may be stronger than critical theorists anticipate. The liberal state absorbs and frustrates attempts to alter it, either progressively (on questions of race, poverty, and gender) or to turn the clock back and restore the Ozzie and Harriet 1950s retro American nuclear family. It may resist reactionary tendencies to restore some halcyon moment. It itself may fall prey to loss of power to international marketplace dictates, so that it may become only a site for market relations. It will remain the battleground that deepens any attempts to restore "morality" and to substitute a "transformative politics" for the uneasy status quo. Legal structures must and will continue to work with and against political and cultural constraints.

The best that intellectuals can do is to open up theoretical possibilities. But fashioning real policy reforms institutionally is always difficult, even in times of economic growth. Particularly when you have voices that resist those reforms. On the other hand, intellectuals can do more than specify the limits of the law and the political and cultural constraints on actualizing liberal ideology. The essays here, for example, embody sensitive writing about how women and other voices can express—or can be allowed to express—themselves without requiring a significant institutional shift. Also, intellectual contributions can be made to rethinking the relationships between theology, religion, and the state. Theology, as the thinking that provides the theoretical essence of religious practice, can open itself up to less doctrinaire and sectarian worldviews. Further, we can reconceptualize how impeachment itself can be recast to allow a flexibility for governance in our liberal polity. This would require new institutional understanding and might confound our contemporary sense of constitutionalism as a significant aspect of our civil religion. It might also make for a more parliamentary form of governance that we have long resisted by recasting impeachment as a policy device rather than a response to extreme abuse of office. We must also rethink the nature of personal and institutional lying. What is appropriate fiction, what is a lie, and what must be punished or endured to foster interpersonal civility and statecraft? We must remain aware that no analysis intrinsically captures reality, and that no analysis can define any moment as decisive for political advance. We have and continue to live with ambiguity and ambivalence. Reason, these essays demonstrate, even in postmodernity, is not futile, only fragmentary.

The Clinton impeachment and surrounding scandal may turn out to be only a historical footnote for scholars of the American presidency. Alternatively, it may reflect a continued disaffection and a deepening alienation from our basic liberal institutions. No methodology can answer the question of future consequence. Hegel's by now banal caveat, that the Owl of Minerva flies only at dusk, remains instructive. Liberalism has proven resilient in the United States. But the Weimar Republic, despite significant intellectual capital and a progressive ideology, turned quickly to the demonic (if we turn to a poetic metaphor) or fascist (if we turn to a structural analysis). Capitalism, the fascist experience teaches us, is compatible with forms other than liberal governance. My poet friend Bill Sherman reminds me that the novelist William Burroughs has defined the paranoid as somebody who is aware of all the facts. My friend and colleague Neil Komesar has always stressed that information is expensive and generally lacking.[33] These essays have examined only the surface of what this particular cockfight might suggest. Forces in the world outside our control will impinge upon liberal tolerance in the name of economic efficiency. We could end up being nostalgic for the old-fashioned liberalism that Phil Ochs lampooned when he sang "Love me, love me, I'm a liberal." On the other hand, the strands of decay and structural deficit in our liberal polity can be combated with intellect, goodwill, luck, and love.

## Postscript, January 1, 2001

The Clinton affair, such as it is to date, ended not with love but with an agreement among Robert Ray, the Special Prosecutor, Clinton, and the State Bar of Arkansas. The outcome? No prosecution, a five-year suspension of Clinton's law license, and a fine. Bush has assumed office and has started his attack on abortion rights, and promises to attempt the diversion of money to religious groups. And the beat goes on.

NOTES

1. I am grateful to Martha and Jonathan Kaplan and Pam Hollenhorst for significant help in editing this essay; with thanks to Jon Graubart and special gratitude to my friends and colleagues Alan Weisbard, Vincent Rinella, and Boaventura de Sousa Santos.

2. See, for example, Bertram Myron Gross, *Friendly Fascism: The New Face of Power in America* (New York: M. Evans, 1980). The terms "friendly fascism" or "fascism with a friendly (happy) face," have started to turn up in a variety of analyses. The question that deserves deeper analysis is whether the phenomena that are being pinpointed belong together, and whether any homogeneity amongst the phenomena points toward something about liberal governance generally, and more particularly, about contemporary liberal culture in the United States. See, for example, Andrea Peyser, "Buchanan Offers U.S. Fascism with a Happy Face," *New York Post*, October 27, 1999, 8; see also Courtland Milloy, "Gilmore Right on Real Issue of Freedom," *Washington Post*, May 3, 2000, B01 ("the strongest proponents of this move toward 'friendly fascism' appear to be Democrats . . .") [commenting on the use of video cameras for law enforcement on open streets].

3. Robert Paul Wolff has argued that liberalism demands at least some cognizable group before difference can be negotiated with any degree of political acceptance. See Robert Paul Wolff, Barrington Moore, Jr., and Herbert Marcuse, *A Critique of Pure Tolerance* (Boston: Beacon Press, 1965).

4. See Clifford Geertz, *The Interpretation of Cultures: Selected Essays* (New York: Basic Books, 1973).

5. See Clifford Geertz, "The World in Pieces: Culture and Politics at the End of the Century," in his book, *Available Light: Anthropological Reflections on Philosophical Topics* (Princeton: Princeton University Press, 2000).

6. Ron Fournier, "Clinton Returns to Arkansas for Execution of Brain-Damaged Cop Killer," *Associated Press*, January 24, 1992. (Page number unavailable online.)

7. See, for example, Ellen Goodman, "Wiping Off the Slate," *San Francisco Chronicle*, December 28, 1993, A17 (describing Lani Guinier as another hit-and-run victim of Washington politics who didn't become roadkill); Clarence Page, "Clinton's Message: Self-Help, Without Civil-Rights Rhetoric," *Chicago Tribune*, December 29, 1993, 15 ("He torpedoed controversial law professor Lani Guinier's nomination to avoid confronting Senate conservatives").

8. The Greeks gave us the notion of life as a game. What counted was coming in first. Who remembers who ran the second four-minute mile? Americans are still infected by this inherited Greek *agonistic* notion. We like to be number one. Alternatively, we like to see the underdog become number one.

9. See Robert Dallek, *Lone Star Rising: Lyndon Johnson and His Times, 1908–*

*1960* (New York: Oxford University Press, 1991), 189–91. See also Robert Dallek, *Flawed Giant: Lyndon Johnson and His Times, 1961–1973* (New York: Oxford University Press, 1998), 186–87.

10. See Ann Althouse, "Invoking Rashomon," *Wisconsin Law Review* (2000): 504.

11. See Shlomo Avineri, *Hegel's Theory of the Modern State* (London: Cambridge University Press, 1972).

12. See, e.g., Viktor E. Frankl, *Psychotherapy and Existentialism: Selected Papers on Logotherapy* (New York: Washington Square Press, 1967).

13. Roberto Mangabeira Unger, *Knowledge and Politics* (New York: Free Press, 1975).

14. See William E. Scheuerman, *Carl Schmitt: The End of Law* (Lanham, Md.: Rowman and Littlefield, 1999).

15. See Louis Althusser, *Essays on Ideology* (London: Verso, 1984). Althusser defined the state in terms of the institutions that allow the state to be reproduced, for example, the institutions of family and the media.

16. See Boaventura de Sousa Santos, *Toward a New Common Sense: Law, Science and Politics in the Paradigmatic Transition* (New York: Routledge, 1995).

17. Howard Fineman, "Praying to Win," *Newsweek*, August 21, 2000, 18.

18. Richard Perez-Pena, "Lieberman Issues Call on Role of Religion," *Wisconsin State Journal*, August 28, 2000, 2A.

19. Gustav Neibuhr, "Lieberman Is Asked to Stop Invoking Faith in Campaign," *New York Times National*, August 29, 2000, A17. See also Richard Perez-Pena, "Lieberman Defends His Call for Bigger Role for Religion," *New York Times National*, August 30, 2000, A17; Eleanor Brown, "Lieberman's Revival of the Religious Left," *New York Times National*, August 30, 2000, A27.

20. Perez-Pena, "Lieberman Issues Call," 2A.

21. The Boy Scouts of America prevailed before the U.S. Supreme Court in their quest to exclude homosexual scout leaders. Their worldview, a conservative Judeo-Christian condemnation of homosexuality, collides with the liberal demand not to discriminate against anyone based on religion, race, or sexual identifications. The continuing battle between the scouts and liberal demands for equal treatment reflect the continuing battle in liberal culture over genital politics and social legitimacy. See, for example, Kate Zernike, "Scouts' Successful Ban on Gays Is Followed by Loss in Support: Gifts Are Cut and Public Property Use Is Limited," *New York Times National*, August 29, 2000, A1.

22. Examples include production of journals such as *The Journal of Law and Religion* at Hamline University, and *Graven Images: Studies of Culture, Law and the Sacred* at the University of Wisconsin, as well as the availability of classes that merge the topics of law, theology, the family, and the state.

23. But see a significant Catholic intellectual strain in the United States that resists Pope Pius XI's 1931 encyclical critical of "soulless laissez-faire capitalism."

See Franklin Foer, "Spin Doctrine," *New Republic*, June 5, 2000 (page number not available online).

24. See Emmanuel Levinas, *Nine Talmudic Readings* (Bloomington: Indiana University Press, 1990).

25. Boaventura de Sousa Santos, "Law and Democracy: (Mis)trusting the Global Reform of Courts," in Jane Jenson and Boaventura de Sousa Santos, eds., *Globalizing Institutions: Case Studies in Regulation and Innovation* (Aldershot, Ashgate, 2000), 253–84.

26. See, for example, Michael Hawthorne, "Ohio Justices Clash with Gusto: No Holds Barred on State Court," *Cincinnati Enquirer*, August 22, 1999, A01.

27. Directed by Krzystof Kieslowski, *Decalogue* consists of ten short films made for Polish television in 1988. The films portray each of the ten commandments, while reflecting the pain, mystery, and humility of everyday events.

28. See Herbert Marcuse, *Eros and Civilization: A Philosophical Inquiry into Freud* (Boston: Beacon, 1974); Norman Oliver Brown, *Life against Death: The Psychoanalytical Meaning of History* (Middleton, Conn.: Wesleyan University Press, 1959).

29. See Johan Huizinga, *Homo Ludens: A Study of the Play Element in Culture* (New York: J. and J. Harper Editions, 1970).

30. See Dietrich Bonhoeffer, *Ethics* (New York: Simon and Schuster, 1995).

31. See Kieslowski, *Decalogue*.

32. Andrew Cockburn, "The Radicalization of James Woolsey," *New York Times Magazine*, July 23, 2000, 23 (quoting Woolsey at 29).

33. See Neil K. Komesar, *Imperfect Alternatives: Choosing Institutions in Law, Economics, and Public Policy* (Chicago: University of Chicago Press, 1994).

# Contributors

*David T. Canon* is Professor of Political Science at the University of Wisconsin-Madison. He received his Ph.D. from the University of Minnesota in 1987. He is author of *Race, Redistricting, and Representation* (University of Chicago Press, 1999), *The Dysfunctional Congress? The Individual Roots of an Institutional Dilemma* (with Kenneth Mayer; Westview Press, 1999), and *Actors, Athletes, and Astronauts: Political Amateurs in the U.S. Congress* (University of Chicago Press, 1990).

*John Milton Cooper, Jr.,* is the E. Gordon Fox Professor of American Institutions at the University of Wisconsin-Madison Department of History. He is author of *The Warrior and the Priest: Woodrow Wilson and Theodore Roosevelt* (Belknap Press, 1983) and has just completed *Breaking the Heart of the World: Woodrow Wilson and the Fight over the League of Nations* (forthcoming). He is a member of the Council on Foreign Relations and served in 1999 on the jury for the Pulitzer Prize in American History.

*Drucilla Cornell* is Professor of Law at Rutgers, the State University of New Jersey, S.I. Newhouse Center for Law and Justice. She is also Professor of Women's Studies at the State University of New Jersey, New Brunswick. She is the author of numerous books, including *At the Heart of Freedom: Feminism, Sex, and Equality* (Princeton University Press, 1998); *Beyond Accommodation: Ethical Feminism, Deconstruction, and the Law* (Rowman and Littlefield, 1999); and is editor of *Feminism and Pornography* (Oxford University Press, 2000).

*Jean Bethke Elshtain* is the Laura Spelman Rockefeller Professor of Social and Political Ethics at the University of Chicago. She is the author of numerous books, including *Public Man, Private Woman: Women in Social and Political Thought* (Princeton University Press, 1990); *Democracy on Trial* (Basic Books, 1995); and *Real Politics: At the Center of Everyday Life* (Johns Hopkins University Press, 1997).

*Robert W. Gordon* is Johnston Professor of Law and Professor of History at Yale University. A graduate of Harvard College and Law School, he has been a law teacher since 1972, at the SUNY-Buffalo, University of Wisconsin, and Stanford law schools, among others, before being appointed to the Yale faculty in 1995. He has written on the history of legal thought, legal education, and the legal profession, among other subjects; and is currently finishing a book on the history, present condition, and future prospects of the idea that lawyers are engaged in a public profession serving the public interest as well as private clients.

*Lawrence Joseph* is Professor of Law at St. John's University School of Law. He was educated at the University of Michigan, Cambridge University, and University of Michigan Law School. He is the author of four books. His book of prose, *Lawyerland*, was published by Farrar, Straus and Giroux in 1997. He is also the author of three books of poetry: *Before Our Eyes*, published by Farrar, Straus and Giroux in 1993; *Curriculum Vitae*, published in 1988 by University of Pittsburgh Press; and *Shouting at No One*, the recipient of the Agnes Lynch Starrett Poetry Prize, also published by the University of Pittsburgh Press in 1983. He has received two National Endowment for the Arts poetry fellowships, and a fellowship from the John Simon Guggenheim Memorial Foundation to write a book about Catholicism. He has also taught in the Council of the Humanities and Creative Writing Program at Princeton University.

*Leonard V. Kaplan* is Mortimer M. Jackson Professor of Law at the University of Wisconsin Law School. He was a cofounder and coeditor-in-chief of a journal, *Graven Images: Studies in Culture, Law and the Sacred*. He is a founder and codirector of the Law School's Project for Law and Humanities. He is president of International Academy of Law and Mental Health.

*David Kennedy* is the Henry Shattuck Professor of Law at Harvard Law School, and Director of the European Law Research Center. He teaches international law, international economic policy, European law, legal theory, contracts, and evidence. He has practiced with various international institutions, including the United Nations High Commissioner for Refugees and the Commission of the European Union, and with the private firm of Cleary, Gottlieb, Steen, and Hamilton in Brussels. He is the author of various articles on international law and legal theory, and founder of the New Approaches to International Law project.

*Kenneth R. Mayer* is Professor of Political Science at the University of Wisconsin-Madison. He is the author (with David Canon) of *The Dysfunctional Congress? The Individual Roots of an Institutional Dilemma* (Westview Press, 1999), and author of *With the Stroke of a Pen: Executive Orders and Presidential Power* (Princeton University Press, 2001).

*Beverly I. Moran* is Voss-Bascom Professor of Law at the University of Wisconsin Law School, and Director of the Wisconsin Center on Law and Africa. A graduate of Vassar College, the University of Pennsylvania Law School, and New York University Law School's LL.M. program in Taxation, she has taught and lectured on four continents, including Giessen University in Germany, the University of Dakar in Senegal, Peking University, People's University, and the East China Institute of Politics and Law in the People's Republic of China, the Addis Ababa University in Ethiopia, and the University of Asmara in Eritrea where she was a Fulbright scholar.

*Father Richard John Neuhaus* is President of the Institute on Religion and Public Life, based in New York City, and Editor-in-Chief of *First Things: A Journal of Religion and Public Life.*

*David Novak* holds the J. Richard and Dorothy Shiff Chair of Jewish Studies at the University of Toronto. He is also vice president of the Union for Traditional Judaism, and is the author of *Covenantal Rights: A Study in Jewish Political Theory* (Princeton University Press, 2000).

*Linda Denise Oakley* earned a Ph.D. from the University of Washington-Seattle. She was a Post-Doctoral Scholar at the University of California at San Francisco, and currently is Associate Professor at the University of Wisconsin School of Nursing. Linda teaches graduate and undergraduate courses on psychiatric mental health and conducts clinical research aimed at improving the way depressed adults cope with their illness.

*Elizabeth Rapaport* earned a J.D. at Harvard and a Ph.D. at Case Western Reserve. She is Professor of Law at the University of New Mexico School of Law, and was Visiting Professor at Duke University School of Law in Spring 2000. She writes principally about criminal law.

*Lawrence Rosen* is Professor and Chair of Anthropology at Princeton University, and Adjunct Professor of Law at Columbia Law School. Among his publications are *Bargaining for Reality: The Construction of Social*

*Relations in a Muslim Community* (University of Chicago Press, 1984); *The Anthropology of Justice: Law as Culture in Islamic Society* (Cambridge University Press, 1989); and *The Justice of Islam: Comparative Perspectives on Islamic Law and Society* (Oxford University Press, 2000).

*Eric Rothstein* is the Edgar W. Lacy Professor of English and a founding member of the Law and Humanities Project at the University of Wisconsin-Madison. His books are on English drama, fiction, and poetry from the Restoration through the eighteenth century. His recent articles on cultural historiography discuss diversity and change, "organicism," the methodology of Northrop Frye and of Michel Foucault, and considerations of interpretation and ethics in the principles of theodicy, in some discussions of Heidegger, and in Nabokov's *Lolita*.

*Aviam Soifer* is Professor of Law and former dean at Boston College Law School. He writes primarily about constitutional law and legal history and serves on the boards of a number of public interest organizations. His most recent publications include "The Disability Term: Dignity, Default, and Negative Capability," 47 *UCLA L. Rev.* 1279 (2000) and "The Fullness of Time" in Nancy Rosenblum, ed., *Obligations of Citizenship and Demands of Faith* (Princeton University Press, 2000). His book, *Law and the Company We Keep* (Harvard University Press, 1995) won the triennial Alpha Sigma Nu National Jesuit Book Prize in professional studies in 1998.

*Lawrence M. Solan* is Professor of Law at Brooklyn Law School. He holds a Ph.D. in linguistics from the University of Massachusetts, and a law degree from Harvard Law School, and is the author of *The Language of Judges* (University of Chicago Press, 1993).

*Cass R. Sunstein* is the Karl N. Llewellyn Distinguished Service Professor at the University of Chicago Law School and the Department of Political Science. He is the author of numerous books, including *Constitutional Law* (with Stone, Seidman, and Tushnet, 1986); *After the Rights Revolution: Receiving the Regulatory State* (Harvard University Press, 1990); *The Partial Constitution* (Harvard University Press, 1993); *Democracy and the Problem of Free Speech* (Free Press, 1993), *Free Markets and Social Justice* (1997); *One Case at a time: Judicial Minimalism on the Supreme Court* (1999); and *Legal Reasoning and Political Conflict* (1996). He is the editor of *Behavioral Law and Economics* (Cambridge University Press, 2000).

*Stephen Toulmin* is Henry R. Luce Professor at the Center for Multiethnic and Transnational Studies at the University of Southern California. Toulmin came to the United States in 1959; since then he has held distinguished professorships at numerous universities, including Columbia, Dartmouth, Michigan State, Northwestern, Stanford, and the University of Chicago. While at the University of California at Santa Cruz, he wrote *Human Understanding*, published by Princeton University Press in 1972. One year later, Toulmin and Alan Janik published *Wittgenstein's Vienna* (Simon and Schuster, 1973); next, Toulmin collaborated with Albert Jonsen on *The Abuse of Casuistry: A History of Moral Reasoning* (University of California Press, 1988). Toulmin has also collaborated with Richard Rieke and Allan Janik, coauthoring *An Introduction to Reasoning*, first published by Macmillan in 1979 and now in its second edition. Among his most recent work is *Cosmopolis: The Hidden Agenda of Modernity* (Free Press, 1990).

*Leon E. Trakman* holds commerce and law degrees from the University of Cape Town and a masters and doctorate degree in law from Harvard Law School. He is a barrister, solicitor, and Professor of Law at Dalhousie Law School. The author of five books and numerous articles, his most recent book, written with his research associate Sean Gatien, is on the philosophy of rights and entitled *Rights and Responsibilities* (University of Toronto Press, 1999). He wrote this book as the recipient of the Bora Laskin National Fellowship, Canada.

*Frank Tuerkheimer* is Robert L. Habush-Bascom Professor of Law at the University of Wisconsin Law School. He worked on the Watergate Prosecution staff where he was in charge of the investigation into illegal dairy industry contributions and was chief trial counsel in the case against former Secretary of the Treasury, John Connally.

*Mark V. Tushnet* is Carmack Waterhouse Professor of Constitutional Law at the Georgetown University Law Center, where he is presently Associate Dean for Research. He received his undergraduate degree magna cum laude from Harvard College in 1967. He received a J.D. and M.A. in history from Yale University in 1971. He clerked for Judge George Edwards and Justice Thurgood Marshall before beginning to teach at the University of Wisconsin Law School in 1973. In 1981 he moved to the Georgetown University Law Center. He has been a visiting professor at the University of Texas, University of Southern California, and

University of Chicago law schools. Professor Tushnet is the coauthor of four casebooks, including the most widely used casebook on constitutional law, *Constitutional Law* (with Stone, Seidman, and Sunstein). He has written nine books, including a two-volume work on the life of Thurgood Marshall, and edited three others. He has received fellowships from the Rockefeller Humanities Program, the Woodrow Wilson International Center for Scholars, and the John Simon Guggenheim Memorial Foundation, and has written numerous articles on constitutional law and legal history.

*Andrew D. Weiner* is Professor of English and affiliate Professor of Law at the University of Wisconsin-Madison. He is the author of *Sir Philip Sidney and the Poetics of Protestantism: A Study of Contexts* (University of Minnesota Press, 1978) and over twenty essays on Erasmus, Sir Thomas More, Sir Philip Sidney, Edmund Spenser, Giordano Bruno, William Shakespeare, and John Milton. He is also Co-Editor of the *Graven Images* monograph series and Co-Director of the Project for Law and Humanities at the UW Law School.

*Robin West* is Professor of Law at Georgetown University Law Center. She is the author of *Narrative, Authority, and Law* (University of Michigan Press, 1993); *Progressive Constitutionalism: Reconstructing the Fourteenth Amendment* (Duke University Press, 1994); and *Caring for Justice* (New York University Press, 1997).

# Index